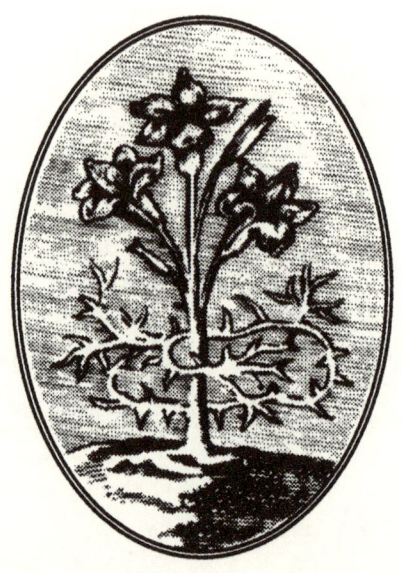

Sicut lilium inter spinas sic amica mea inter filias

On The Cover: We use the symbol of the "lily among the thorns" from Song of Solomon 2:2 to represent the Baptist History Series. The Latin, *Sicut lilium inter spinas sic amica mea inter filias*, translates, "As the lily among thorns, so is my love among the daughters."

HISTORY

OF THE

Baptist Denomination in Georgia

Vol. I

SAMUEL BOYKIN
1829-1899

HISTORY

OF THE

Baptist Denomination in Georgia

WITH

BIOGRAPHICAL COMPENDIUM AND PORTRAIT GALLERY
OF BAPTIST MINISTERS AND OTHER
GEORGIA BAPTISTS.

I WILL GIVE YOU PASTORS ACCORDING TO
MINE HEART, WHICH SHALL FEED YOU WITH
KNOWLEDGE AND UNDERSTANDING.
- *Jeremiah 3:15*

COMPILED FOR THE CHRISTIAN INDEX.

VOL. I

ATLANTA, GEORGIA:
JAS. P. HARRISON & CO., PRINTERS AND PUBLISHERS.
1881.

The Baptist Standard Bearer, Inc.
NUMBER ONE IRON OAKS DRIVE • PARIS, ARKANSAS 72855

Thou hast given a *standard* to them that fear thee;
that it may be displayed because of the truth.
-- *Psalm 60:4*

*Reprinted
by*

THE BAPTIST STANDARD BEARER, INC.
No. 1 Iron Oaks Drive
Paris, Arkansas 72855
(501) 963-3831

THE WALDENSIAN EMBLEM
lux lucet in tenebris
"The Light Shineth in the Darkness"

ISBN #1-57978-913-7

Note. This book, though anonymous, was actually written by Dr. Samuel Boykin, as is proved by what he wrote on the fly leaf of a copy, and signed, now in the vault of the Dargan-Carver Library. — H L Grice

TABLE OF CONTENTS.

CHAPTER I.

PRELIMINARY HISTORY, 1733-1770.—The Settlement of Georgia in 1733—The Result of a Colonization Scheme which Proved a Failure—Oglethorpe Returns to England in 1743—Georgia Became a Royal Province in 1752—John Reynolds the first Governor—Not till 1754 did the Province Begin to Prosper—A New System of Government—The First Legislature Met in January, 1755—The Second General Assembly met in 1758—Early Laws—Governor Ellis Recalled and Sir James Wright Appointed Governor in 1760—Indian Depredations—Prosperity Under Governor Wright's Administration—George III Proclaimed King in 1761—The Indian Treaty of 1763 gains Georgia Territorial Acquisition to the Mississippi—Its General Condition at that Time—Character and Ability of Governor Wright.

CHAPTER II.

THE FIRST BAPTISTS IN THE STATE, 1740-1772.—Whitefield's Orphan Asylum—Nicholas Bedgewood adopts Baptist Views and is Ordained—Early Georgia Baptists in the Neighborhood of Savannah—Benjamin Stirk Preaches Until 1770—Rev. Edmund Botsford Comes to Georgia in 1781—Some Account of Him—He Settles at Tuckaseeking—Daniel Marshall and Introduction of Baptist Principles into Northern Georgia—His Arrest for Preaching—Samuel Cartledge, the Constable—His Strange Conviction—Daniel Marshall's Trial—Some Account of Mr. Barnard, the Justice Who Tried Mr. Marshall—Kiokee Church—Act of Incorporation—Sketch of Rev. Daniel Marshall—His Death in 1784—His Last Words and Burial Place.

CHAPTER III.

THE REVOLUTIONARY PERIOD, 1772-1774—Labors of Edmund Botsford—Visits Kiokee—Preaches for Daniel Marshall—Loveless Savidge—His Conversion to the Baptist Faith—Botsford's Labors—"The Rum is Come"—He is Ordained—Botsford's Church Constituted in 1773—His Flight in 1779—Causes of the Revolution—"Liberty Boys"—Georgia Speaking Out—Condition of the State in 1772—A Provincial Congress Elected in 1775—In 1776 it was Resolved to Embark in the Cause of Freedom—Georgia in Active Rebellion—Georgia Subjugated in 1779, and the Royal Government Re-established in Savannah—Botsford and Silas Mercer Flee, but Daniel Marshall Stands Firm—His Trials and Labors—The Licensure System—Statistics From 1788 to 1794.

CHAPTER IV.

GROWTH AND ORGANIZATION, 1782-1799.—Peace—Savannah Again in Our Possession in July, 1783—Georgia's Desolate Condition—Baptist matters—Formation of the Georgia Association—Views of Sherwood, Benedict and Asplund—"Begun in 1784"—Two Sessions Annually for Half a Dozen Years—Extracts From Newton's Diary—Alexander Scott—Silas Mercer—Sanders Walker—Abraham Marshall—Evangelistic Labors at the Foundation of the Baptist Denomination in Georgia—James Matthews—Precarious Times—Formation of the Hephzibah Association in September, 1795—Formation of the Sarepta Association, in May, 1799.

CHAPTER V.

THE POWELTON CONFERENCES, 1800-1803.—The General Aspect of Affairs—The Condition Peaceable and Prosperous—But Zion Languishing—The First Step Upward—Henry Holcombe—Joseph Clay—C. O. Screven—Jesse Mercer—The Grand "Departure"—The Meeting of 1801—The Second Conference in 1802—The Report Adopted—Results—Incident in the Life of Mercer—Savannah Association Constituted in 1802—Its action in Regard to the Powelton Conference—The First General Committee—Action of the Committee—The Religious Condition in 1803—Origin of Baptist Interest in Savannah—A Church Organized in 1800—The Establishment of Colored Baptist Churches in Savannah—And a Brief Account of Them.

CHAPTER VI.

FIRST EFFORTS AT CO-OPERATION, 1803-1810.—The General Committee Organized for Work—First Circular Address—Remarks Concerning the General Committee—First Steps towards Establishing a School Among the Indians and a Baptist College—A Charter Refused by the Legislature—Jesse Mercer's Circular Address Defending the Committee—Mount Enon Adopted as a Site for the Proposed College—Incorporation Still Unattainable—The General Committee Merged into a Permanent Board of Trustees—Reasons Why the Charter was Refused—But the "Trustees of Mount Enon Academy" Incorporated—An Academy Established, which Flourished a Few Years Only.

CHAPTER VII.

THE FIRST FIVE ASSOCIATIONS, 1810-1813.—General Condition of Georgia in 1810—General Condition of the Denomination at the Same Time—Growth of the Georgia Association—Formation and Growth of the Hephzibah Association—Formation and Growth of the Sarepta Association—The Ocmulgee and Savannah Associations—Their Growth—Singular Formation of Black Creek Church—Statistics of 1813—A Revival—Laborious Times and Pious Men—Hostilities Against Great Britain Declared June 18th, 1812—Unanimity and Patriotism of Baptist Sentiment—Lumpkin and Rabun.

CHAPTER VIII.

MISSIONARY, 1813-1820.—1813 an Epoch—The Early Mission Spirit on the Seaboard—Influencing Characters—The Savannah River Association in 1813—Formation of the First Georgia Missionary Society—Missionary Enthusiasm—A Remarkable Circular—It is Read Before the Georgia Association by Jesse Mercer—Meeting Appointed at Powelton in 1815—A Strong Missionary Society Formed—The Georgia Association Takes Hold of the Missionary Work in Earnest—The Ocmulgee Association—Patriotic Circulars—The Mission Spirit in the Ocmulgee Association—"The Ocmulgee Mission Society" Formed in July, 1815—The Mission Spirit in the Sarepta Association—A Mission Society Formed in June, 1816—The Resolution of Dr. Sherwood in 1820—Spirit of the Hephzibah Association—It Favors the "General Committee"—Favors Itinerancy and Domestic Missions—The Hephzibah Baptist Society for Itinerant and Missionary Exertions, Formed in February, 1816—A Foreign Mission Society Formed in 1818—The Ebenezer Association Formed in March, 1814—The Tugalo and Piedmont Associations formed in 1817—State of Religion in the Second Decade of the Century.

CHAPTER IX.

INDIAN REFORM, 1818-1824.—Feeling in Regard to Indian Reformation in the Beginning of the Century—Extract from the Mission Board of the Georgia Association in 1818—Desire of the Indians—First Steps Taken by the Ocmulgee Association—"Plan" for "Indian Reform" Adopted—Interesting Letter from Doctor Staughton—General Government Appropriations—Appointment of Francis Flournoy—Some Account of Him—His Vindication and Death—Appointment of E. L. Compere—Establishment of a School and Mission at Withington Station—Action of the Ebenezer Association—Zeal and Liberality of the Ladies—Report of the Ocmulgee and Georgia Associations in 1824—General View.

CHAPTER X.

THE GENERAL ASSOCIATION, 1820-1823.—Action of the Sarepta Association in 1802—Considered Favorably by the Ocmulgee and Georgia Associations—Disregarded by the Ebenezer and Hephzibah—Considered unfavorably by itself—The General Meeting in Powelton in June, 1822—Notabilities Present—Sermon by Sherwood and Prayer by Mercer—The Constitution Presented by Brantly—Its Adoption—Extracts from the Circular Letter—Second Session of the General Association and its Action—Action of the Sarepta in 1823—The Sunbury Association Joins the General Association in 1823—The Ebenezer Declines to Unite with The General Association—Action of the Hephzibah—Brantly, Sherwood, Armstrong, Kilpatrick.

CHAPTER XI.

STATE OF RELIGION, 1822-1826.—The Sunbury Association, Slight Review—The Savannah Church, Some of its Pastors—State of Religion in the Sunbury Association, in the Third Decade of the Century—Augusta, a Baptist Church Constituted there in 1817—The Shoal Creek Convention—Efforts of the General Association—Uniformity of Discipline, Effort to Promote it Falls Through—

Want of Harmony—Address of General Association of 1825—Why Given—Position of the General Association in Regard to Education—The Association, Disappointed, Recommends the Formation of Auxiliary Societies in 1826—A Constitution Recommended—The Ebenezer Association—Mission Arguments of that Day—Prominent Men—Hephzibah Association—The Sarepta Association—Yellow River and Flint River Associations—Denominational Statistics in 1824.

CHAPTER XII.

EDUCATIONAL, 1825-1829.—' Indian Reform" Once More—Conclusion of that Mission—Cause of its Abandonment—Sketch of E. L. Compere—Contributions of the Georgia Baptists—Interest in Education—Few Educated Men—The State Convention and Education—Address of 1826—Columbian College—A Fund for Theological Education—Opponents of Education—Some of their Notions—Anecdotes Illustrative of Ignorance—" Go Preach My Gospel"—What Mercer Said About " Inspired Sermons"—Dr. A. Sherwood.

CHAPTER XIII.

MERCER INSTITUTE, 1829-1839.—The Penfield Legacy—Who Helped to Secure it—Sherwood's Resolution—$1,500 Raised—Instructions to the Executive Committee—Dr. Sherwood's Manual Labor School Near Eatonton—Mercer Institute Opened January, 1833—Plan of Mercer Institute—B. M. Sanders Placed at its Head—A Baptist College at Washington Proposed and Abandoned—Mercer University—Report of Trustees for 1838—Acts of Incorporation, of Convention and College—The First Board of Trustees—Their First Report, Showing the Organization of the College and its Financial Condition—Classes Organized in January, 1839—B. M. Sanders, the First President of Mercer University—His Farewell Address—The Blacks not Forgotten.

CHAPTER XIV.

ANTI-EFFORT SECESSION, 1817-1837—The Spirit of Opposition—Its Causes—First Manifestation in the Hephzibah—the Mission Spirit in that Association in 1817, 1818—Charles J. Jenkins—Sketch of his Life—The Association gives the Cold Shoulder to Missions and Education—Jordan Smith Leads off a Faction in 1828—Which forms the Canoochee Association—Resolution of the Piedmont Association in 1819—Isham Peacock—The Ebenezer Association, Session of 1816—Enters upon Indian Reform Mission in 1820—Abandons it in 1823—In 1836 Decides in Favor of Missions, etc.—A Division Occurs—Its Circular Letter of 1836—The Anti-Mission Spirit in the Ocmulgee—It Declares Non-Fellowship with those Favoring Benevolent Schemes—Troubles Begin—Formation of the Central Association—The Sarepta Joins the Convention—A Division of the Association Ensues—" Protest " and " Answer "—The Itcheconnah Divides—The Yellow River Follows Suit—The Flint River Keeps the Ball Rolling—While the Columbus and Western Feel the Doleful Effects of the Anti-Mission Spirit—Division is Consummated—The General Feeling of the Times, 1833-1837, Illustrated by Incidents.

CHAPTER XV.

RELIGIOUS HISTORY, 1826-1836.—The Great Revival of 1827—Accessions to the Different Associations—Reports for 1829—The Anti-Intemperate Society—Georgia Association of 1828 and 1829—The Sunbury Association—Religious Condition in 1830—Denominational Statistics—Religious Condition from 1830 to 1836—Described by Jesse Mercer—Dr. C. D. Mallary's Statement—What a Writer in THE INDEX Said—The Convention Still Presses Forward—Revival Incidents—The Convention Resolution of 1835—Campbell's Call for the Forsyth Meeting—Its Proceedings—Communications from Dr. Hillyer, Dr. Campbell and Rev. T. B. Slade—Peace Dawns Once More—The Meeting at Covington.

CHAPTER XVI.

GENERAL STATE OF THE DENOMINATION, 1840-1846—The Convention of 1840—THE CHRISTIAN INDEX removed to Georgia- Influence of the Paper—Mercer University in 1840—State of Religious Feeling—Report on State Missions for 1842 - Death of Jesse Mercer—Report on his Death, by C. D. Mallary—His Influence—Georgia Baptist Statistics—Report on State Missions for 1845—Report of Brethren Appointed to Attend the Organization of the Southern Baptist Convention—Account of the Organization of that Convention—Causes which Led to it—Georgians Present—Previous Course of the Abolitionists—Effect of the Division on Southern Contributions—Sketch of Dr. Johnson, its First President—Messengers to the Old Triennial Convention.

CHAPTER XVII.

DENOMINATIONAL HISTORY, 1845-1861.—Action of the State Convention in Regard to Separation—Effects of the Rupture on Southern Benevolence—Washington Association—Western Association—Rehoboth Association—Bethel and Columbus Associations—Coosa and Tallapoosa Associations—The United Baptists—State of Religion in 1850—The Hearn Manual Labor School—Noble Men of that Period and what they Did—The Cherokee Baptist Convention—Why Constituted—Its Formation and Progress—Cherokee Baptist College and Woodlawn College—Mission Among the Cherokees—David Foreman and E. L. Compere—*The Landmark Banner and Cherokee Baptist*—The North Georgia Missionary Association—The Ten Years Preceding the War—The Bible Board and Colporter Society—Exciting Questions—Associations in the Georgia Baptist Convention, and Cherokee Baptist Convention, before the War, and their Benevolent Contributions.

CHAPTER XVIII.

DENOMINATIONAL HISTORY, 1861-1881.—The Secession of the Southern States—Action of the Southern Baptist Convention, at Savannah—Of the Georgia Baptist Convention, at Athens—Of the Cherokee Baptist Convention at Calhoun—THE CHRISTIAN INDEX; Its History from 1833—The Property of Jesse Mercer until 1839—Of the Baptist State Convention until 1861—Of S. Boykin until 1865—Of J. J. Toon until 1873—Of J. P. Harrison & Co. to the Present Date—Evangelistic Labor in the Army—State of Religion After the Return of Peace—Colored Baptists; their Associations and Conventions—Atlanta Baptist Seminary; Drs. Robert and Shaver—Statistics of the Denomination in the State for 1881—Fifty Years Ago and Now.

CHAPTER XIX.

HISTORY OF MERCER UNIVERSITY, 1813-1881.—A Brief Retrospect—Origin of the Anti-Mission Baptists, Called " Old School Baptists "—Something of their Creed and Policy—The Regular Baptists Slightly Compared—Was the Tendency of the Convention Evil?—Mercer's Reply—Early Beneficiaries of the Convention—Mercer Institute, under Sander's Management—Manual Labor Suspended in the University in 1844—First Graduates of Mercer—Theological Department, Why Discontinued—Classical Department—Law School—How the War Affected Mercer—Removal of Mercer University—Future of the College—Presidents and Professors—The Several Administrations—Some of its Professors—Mercer the Rallying Point of the Denomination.

CHAPTER XX.

POSITION ON VARIOUS MATTERS, 1794-1881 —The Georgia Baptists and Patriotism—"Good Will to Man"—Marital Rights of Slaves—Temperance—The Baptists Never Likely to Form a Party—The Act of 1785 to Support Ministers out of the Public Treasury—Remonstrance of the Georgia Baptists—The Baptists and Religious Liberty—Mercer Writes that Section in the State Constitution—A Strong Baptist Protest—Education of Colored Ministers—Pulpit Affiliation in the Olden Time—No open Communion Among the Early Baptists of Georgia—Pulpit Courtesies Allowed to Pedobaptists, but their Official Acts not Recognized—The Constitution of the Richland Church—The Case of Mr. Hutchinson—Jesse Mercer on not Recognizing Pedobaptist Immersion—Extracts from Sherwood's Mannscripts.

PREFACE.

One hundred and fifty years ago, Georgia was not settled. And one hundred years ago, there were but few Baptists in the State. We had then not half a dozen churches here, and no District Associations at all. Now, counting Missionary and Anti-Missionary Baptists, we have eighty-five white Associations, 1,800 white churches and 120,000 white church members. In addition, there are, among the colored people, over thirty Associations, about 900 churches and 110,000 church members. The adherents of our faith, therefore, make a grand total of 230,000. The history of the rise and progress of a denomination containing such large numbers should be interesting and certainly is worthy of investigation. In truth, it appears but a simple matter of justice and propriety, that a connected historical account, even though brief, of the Baptists of Georgia should be compiled.

This attempt to present the main facts attending the origin and growth of Baptist sentiments in Georgia, is, necessarily, a compilation. It embodies, however, the results of an investigation of a large amount of materials collected from various sources. Among them we may mention complete files of the Georgia Baptist Convention and the Georgia Association; the volumes of THE CHRISTIAN INDEX since its removal to Georgia; and all the collections of the Georgia Baptist Historical Society, embracing the series of Minutes of District Associations in the State, preserved by successive clerks of the Convention; as also files of Association Minutes which friends have loaned us, and excerpts of the most important facts contained in them, which they have kindly written out for us. Beside these, the works of Benedict, Campbell, Mallary, Mercer and Marshall, have been of great service. The Analytical Repository, published at Savannah, by Dr. Holcombe, in the beginning of the century, has furnished valuable information. But the most weighty assistance, perhaps, has been rendered by the writings of Dr. Adiel Sherwood—especially the series of articles on "Jesse Mercer and his Times," prepared by him, twenty years ago, for THE CHRISTIAN INDEX much of which has never seen the light. We were so fortunate, also, as to secure the papers pertaining to Georgia Baptist History, collected by Dr. David Benedict, and deposited by him with the American Baptist Historical Society, Philadelphia; among which was the manuscript history of Georgia, by Dr. Sherwood, referred to by Dr. Benedict in the notes to his History of the Denomination.

These materials, and many more, have been employed to construct this brief History of Georgia Baptists, and for the purposes of the Biographical Compendium. All suitable facts have been used, wherever found, nor have we deemed it necessary always to quote our authority. It has been our great object to gather and connect together, as well as could be done in a limited space and within a short period, the main features, so far as they are ascertainable, of the history of our denomination in the State. We have aimed to present them in a compact and popular form—to make plain and clear statements; and therefore we have not sought after the embellishments of style, nor the mere graces of composition. We have striven especially to be accurate. Such facts only are given as we believe to be entirely raliable, and for which we have what commends itself to us as good authority; and we are confident that the reader may rely on the correctness of the record. If, occasionally, the same incident is mentioned more than once, this happens because different lines of research and narrative touch or cross each other, and it will be found that such dual notice, while it vindicates the truth of the statement, helps to fix the fact noticed in the mind.

To return thanks one by one to the brethren who have placed us under obligation by kindly assistance in this work, and to tell over their names from first to last, would be a sheer impossibility. But while we cannot thus mention all, there are some to whom special acknowledgment is due. We are indebted to Rev. J. H. Kilpatrick for files of the Georgia Baptist Convention and the Georgia Association; to Rev. W. L. Kilpatrick, for documents collected by him as Secretary of the Georgia Baptist Historical Society; to Rev. S. Boykin, for valuable services in the preparation of the History and many of the Biographical Sketches, and to Dr. Shaver, Rev. C. M. Irwin, and his wife, for diligent and faithful work on the Compendium. To these, and to all who have furnished us records or facts, we tender our most grateful thanks for their aid in placing on permanent record so many incidents fraught alike with interest and with profit. It is largely through their generous help that our fathers stand before the present generation on these pages, live over their lives among us, and incite us, in holy emulation, to live as they. We can say without affectation, and, we hope, without immodesty, that a desire to accomplish good animated us in the inception of this enterprise, and has sustained and guided us through all its stages. If the cause of Christ is promoted, and the readers of the volume now committed to the public are strengthened for more vigorous service to that cause, we shall feel, even in the absence of all other reward, that our "labor has not been in vain in the Lord."

THE INDEX PUBLISHING COMPANY.

Atlanta, Georgia, 1881.

HISTORY

OF THE

Baptist Denomination in Georgia

Vol. I

I.
PRELIMINARY HISTORY.
1733-1770.

I.

PRELIMINARY HISTORY.

THE SETTLEMENT OF GEORGIA IN 1733—THE RESULT OF A COLONIZATION SCHEME WHICH PROVED A FAILURE—OGLETHORPE RETURNS TO ENGLAND IN 1743—GEORGIA BECAME A ROYAL PROVINCE IN 1752—JOHN REYNOLDS THE FIRST GOVERNOR—NOT TILL 1754 DID THE PROVINCE BEGIN TO PROSPER—A NEW SYSTEM OF GOVERNMENT—THE FIRST LEGISLATURE MET IN JANUARY, 1755—THE SECOND GENERAL ASSEMBLY MET IN 1758—EARLY LAWS—GOVERNOR ELLIS RECALLED AND SIR JAMES WRIGHT APPOINTED GOVERNOR IN 1760—INDIAN DEPREDATIONS—PROSPERITY UNDER GOVERNOR WRIGHT'S ADMINISTRATION—GEORGE III PROCLAIMED KING IN 1761—THE INDIAN TREATY OF 1763 GAINS GEORGIA TERRITORIAL ACQUISITIONS TO THE MISSISSIPPI—ITS GENERAL CONDITION AT THAT TIME—CHARACTER AND ABILITIES OF GOVERNOR WRIGHT.

The history of the Baptist denomination in the State of Georgia, is almost coeval with the history of the State itself. Its early history, in truth, requires for its comprehension, a statement of some of the main events attending the original settlement of Georgia. For, in the ship Anne, which brought General Oglethorpe and his first colony to our shores, in January, 1733, there were Baptists, who were the ancestors of many living in Georgia to-day, belonging to our denomination.

The settlement of Georgia was the result of a benevolent endeavor, on the part of a large and most respectable association of English gentlemen, numbering among them some of the nobility, to provide an asylum for poor but respectable people, who had no means of supporting themselves in the mother country. They obtained a charter from George II, on the 9th of June, 1732, for a separate and distinct province between the Savannah and Altamaha rivers, to be named *Georgia*, in honor of the king who granted the charter. It was resolved by the trustees that none were to have the benefit of the transportation and subsequent subsistence charitably afforded, but those who were in decayed circumstances and, on that account, disabled from any profitable business in England. These persons were required to labor on the land allotted to them for three years, to the best of their skill and ability. One hundred and fourteen persons embarked at Deptford, four miles below London, and on the 17th of November, 1732, set sail from Gravesend. These were designated as "sober, industrious and moral persons," and James Edward Oglethorpe, Esquire, one of the trustees, consented to accompany them at his own expense, for the purpose of forming the settlement. He was clothed with power to exercise the functions of a governor over the new colony. Charleston harbor was reached January 13th, 1733, and Beaufort, January 20th. There the colonists remained until Oglethorpe had selected a site for his intended settlement. He chose the bluff upon which the city of Savannah now stands. His colonists arrived on the first of February, put up tents, and, occupying the interval in unloading, formally landed on the 12th of February, 1733.

In regard to this settlement of Georgia, two circumstances should be borne in mind. The first is, that it was originated by the people of South Carolina, that a barrier might be erected between themselves and the menacing Spanish authorities in Florida. The second is, that the colonization scheme proved a failure, and that Georgia was eventually settled by a totally different class of people, who emigrated, mostly, from the older States on the Atlantic border. Some very valuable emigrants from Germany and Scotland settled in the State.

It required but a short time for the trustees to discover that the poorer classes of people, which they sought to benefit, were useless as colonists. They then sought for a bold, hardy, industrious set of men who were accustomed to rural pursuits, and made proposals which were accepted by a number of Highlanders from Scotland, who settled on the Altamaha in January, 1736, and built a town now known as Darien. About the same time one hundred and seventy Germans arrived, and joined the seventy-eight Salzburgers, from Salzburg, Bavaria, who had settled at Ebenezer, thirty miles above Savannah, in March, 1733.

There were now, in the beginning of 1736, over six hundred white inhabitants in Georgia, of whom one-third were Germans. At the end of the eighth year over fifteen hundred colonists had been sent over, for whose benefit $560,000 had been expended; besides these, others had come at their own expense, but their number is not known. Ten years after Oglethorpe settled at Savannah there were twelve or fourteen towns scattered throughout the territory, from Darien to Augusta, which had been settled in 1735, and was now advancing in wealth and population.

Oglethorpe had, indeed, effected a wonderful change in the aspect of the entire country in ten years.

Indignant at calumnious misrepresentations made against him by a personal enemy, Lieutenant-colonel Cook, he embarked for England in September, 1743, and demanded an investigation by court-martial. After the most mature deliberation, the court adjudged the charges to be false, malicious and groundless. Oglethorpe's honorable acquittal was reported to the king, and Lieutenant-colonel Cook was dismissed from the service and declared incapable of serving his majesty in any military capacity whatever. General Oglethorpe never returned to America.

A change in the government of the province was established by the trustees. It was committed to the care of a president and four councillors, or assistants, who should act agreeably to instructions received from the trustees. But the colony did not prosper.

While this was due, partly, to war and the insecurity of life and property, it was mostly due to the system of government adopted by the trustees. Human ingenuity could hardly have devised a scheme better calculated to repress prosperity and hinder all material progress. Under that government, the province, during eighteen years, had not produced subsistence enough for its own consumption; and, for the first seventeen years of the colony's existence, one vessel-load, only, of Georgia produce was exported. It was not until after slavery was legally authorized, in 1749, and titles to land were made in fee simple, or "an absolute inheritance," in 1750, that the colony began to prosper. In 1752, the trustees, convinced that the province was not flourishing under their management, and wearied with the murmurs and complaints of the colonists, resigned their charter. The government reverted to the Crown, and Georgia became a royal province A proclamation, sent over in November, 1752, declared it to be the royal pleasure that the magistrates and officers in the colony of Georgia should continue in the exercise of their respective offices until some other provision should be made for the government of the province. The President and his assistants, therefore, continued to govern the country until the arrival of Captain John Reynolds, an officer in the navy, on the 29th of October, 1754, who had been appointed Governor by the King the preceding August. They acted under the control of the "Board of Trade and Plantations," appointed by the King for the superintendence of colonial affairs, at the head of which was the Earl of Halifax.

In the meantime these changes had produced beneficial results. After the charter was surrendered, the President and his assistants reported that settlers came daily from the other colonies in America, as well as from Germany and Great Britain. These consisted of a better class of emigrants.

Georgia now contained many citizens of great respectability, and colonists of a desirable character flocked into its borders. During 1754 a large colony of Puritans, originally from England, moved from South Carolina and settled at Midway, Liberty county. But the general condition of the country was wretched and by no means prosperous. Desolateness brooded over the land, and several years elapsed before Georgia began to prosper. "The town of Savannah," wrote Governor Reynolds to the Board of Trade, "is well situated, and contains about one hundred and fifty houses, all wooden ones, and mostly old. The biggest was used for the meeting of the President and assistants, and wherein I sat in council for a few days; but one end fell down whilst we were all there, and obliged us to remove to a kind of shed behind the court-house."

An entirely new system of government was now established. It was similar to that prevailing in the other colonies, and consisted of three branches—the Governor, his Advisory Council of ten, and the Commons, nineteen in number, elected by the people. The first Legislature met January 7th, 1755, at the call of the Governor.

Governor Reynolds was recalled August 5th, 1756, and Henry Ellis was appointed Lieutenant-Governor August 15th, 1756. During the administration of Reynolds lands were taken up, settlers flocked in, trade increased, and prosperity began to manifest itself; but he proved unequal to his position: his own council united with the lower house in preferring charges of mal-administration against him, and, after a trial in England, he was permitted to resign. His successor was a man of great prudence, discretion and firmness, and his administration was, on the whole, successful. By treaties with the Creek Indians, he mitigated some of the most serious evils and dangers of the Georgians; for, until after the Revolutionary war, the colonists were subject to the murderous ravages and depredations of the Creeks on the west and the Cherokees on the north. It should be remembered that for years the colony of Georgia embraced a territory only 150 miles long, and about thirty miles wide, except in the extreme southern portion. In 1750 the Creeks alone could bring three thousand five hundred warriors into the field, and the intrigues of the French made them exceedingly restive and dangerous neighbors; at the same time the military force of Georgia did not amount to five hundred. Notwithstanding the calamities of the times, the people generally were contented and tranquil; a visible spirit of industry and improvement manifested itself, and numbers flocked into Georgia from the northern colonies.

Thus stood matters during the administration of Governor Ellis, when the third session of the second General Assembly convened in Savannah, January 11th, 1758; and the event is recorded that mention may be made of a few of the laws passed at the time. One of these regulated trade with the Indians; another prohibited slaves from being taught handicrafts; another divided the province into parishes and established the Church of England worship. The following is the title of this last bill: "An Act for constituting the several Divisions and Districts of the Province into Parishes, and for establishing Religious Worship therein according to the Rites and Ceremonies of the Church of England; and also for empowering the Church Wardens and Vestrymen of the respective Parishes to assess Rates for the repair of churches, the relief of the poor, and other Parochial service." Savannah was in "Christ Church" Parish, and Augusta was in "St. Paul's" Parish. It has been claimed that this was a *nominal* transference to one of his Majesty's provinces of the statutes of the British realm; but we shall see that it conveyed a legal right which afterwards was sought to be enforced. It is well to contrast it with an extract from the original charter granted to the Trustees of the colony by George II: "And for the greater ease and encouragement of our loving subjects, and such others as shall come to inhabit in our said colony, we do, by these presents, for us, our heirs and successors, grant, establish and ordain, that forever hereafter there shall be a liberty of conscience allowed in the worship of God to all persons inhabiting, or who shall inhabit or be resident within our said province, and that all such persons, except Papists, shall have a free exercise of religion; so they be contented with the quiet and peaceable enjoyment of the same, not giving offence or scandal to the government." The exception of the Papists in this charter was for political rather than ecclesiastical reasons.

In the law just quoted, a salary of $125 per annum was allowed to each clergyman of the Church of England in Georgia. The passage of this law was rather singular, for there were Presbyterian, Lutheran and Moravian settlements in the State, besides that of the Salzburgers, all of whom had their own ministers. It may have been but a nominal recognition of the Church of England; but it was just such recognition as resulted in much persecution of the Baptists in Virginia and New England.

In 1759 the health of Governor Ellis gave way, and in November of that year he solicited a recall, which was granted, and Sir James Wright was appointed Lieutenant-Governor on the 13th of May, 1760, but did not arrive until the following October. Governor Ellis took his departure on the 2d of November, 1760, amidst the highest manifestations of regard, and deeply regretted by all; for his administration had been greatly beneficial to Georgia. This was indicated by the increase of settlers, their tranquillity and happiness in the more populous districts, and in the extension of trade: in 1760 the population of Georgia was 6,000 whites and 4,000 blacks, while commerce had more than doubled itself during the two and a half years since the departure of Reynolds. Still, it must be confessed that the province was in a languishing condition. The French and Indian wars on the north and west, the Spanish depredations on the southern borders, and the bad management of the British Indian agents, kept the frontiers in a constant state of alarm and disquietude. It has not been deemed necessary to enlarge upon the Indians and their affairs, in this short sketch; but they were a constant menace, and though they were restrained by the prudence and decision of Georgia's Governors, yet the people through long years, continually experienced harrassing alarms, and dreaded threatening invasions. Although their ravages and murderous expeditions were directed mostly against the more northern colonies, yet they made occasional inroads upon upper and lower Georgia, committing depredations and dealing death. During the first years of the colonial history, they were frequently excited to evil deeds by intriguing French emissaries; and after revolutionary hostilities began, when they were in friendly alliance with the royalists, they were more dreaded than ever. This will be readily understood when it is remembered that in 1774, when the population of Georgia was 17,000 whites and 15,000 blacks, with only 2,828 militia scattered from Augusta to St. Mary's, there were within the borders and along the frontiers of Georgia, 40,000 Creeks, Cherokees, Chickasaws and Choctaws, of whom 10,000 were warriors, any number of whom could be brought against the colony.

Governor James Wright was a South Carolinian by birth, of which colony he was Attorney-General for twenty-one years. He arrived in Georgia October 11th, 1760, and entered upon his gubernatorial duties early in November. He was an able man, educated in England, and every way well qualified for his position, and the State prospered under his administration: in six years its population increased from 10,000 to 18,000—10,000 whites and 8,000 blacks.

He enjoyed a privilege which has occurred but once in Georgia history. In February, 1761, intelligence of the death of George II., on October 25th, was received in Savannah, and on the 10th of February he proclaimed George III King in the most solemn manner, with the utmost civil and military pomp.

In November, 1763, Governor Wright, and the Governors of Virginia, North Carolina and South Carolina, and Captain John Stuart, Superintendent of Indian Affairs for the Southern District, held a Convention at Augusta, Georgia, with seven hundred Indians, including the chiefs of the Cherokees, Creeks, Chickasaws, Choctaws and Catawbas, at which a treaty was made which enlarged the boundaries of Georgia to the Mississippi. At that time the population of Georgia, though small, was substantial and industrious; its agricultural resources were rapidly increasing; its commerce required several thousand tons of shipping; its Indian trade was large and productive, and, rising in importance daily, it was fast becoming a noble, vigorous and flourishing State. The productions consisted mostly of indigo, rice, corn, peas and lumber, and its actual State boundaries, established by a treaty with the Cherokee and Creek Indians, at Augusta, January 1st, 1773, included in general terms the land east of the Ogeechee and Oconee rivers.

In closing this bird's-eye view of the early colonial history of Georgia, with which it was thought advisable to preface a history of our denomination, that the reader might have a clearer idea of the times during which Baptist principles gained a foothold in our State, it is deemed proper to insert the following from Stevens' History, in reference to the last royal Governor of the province:

"Each of the other Colonies had a charter upon which to base some right or claim to redress; but Georgia had none. When the Trustees' patent expired, in 1752, all its chartered privileges became extinct, and on its erection into a royal province, the commission of the Governor was its only constitution—living upon the will of the monarch, the mere creature of royal volition. At the head of the government was Sir James Wright, Bart., who during fourteen years had presided over it with ability and acceptance. When he arrived, in 1760, the colony was languishing under the accumulated mismanagement of the former Trustees, and the more recent Governors; but his zeal and efforts soon changed its aspect to health and vigor. He guided it into the avenues of wealth, sought out the means for its advancement; prudently secured the amity of the Indians, and, by his negotiations, added millions of acres to its territory. Diligent in his official duties, firm in his resolves, loyal in his opinions, courteous in his manners, and possessed of a vigorous and well-balanced mind, he was respected and loved by his people, and though he differed from the majority of them as to the cause of their distresses and the means of their removal, he never allowed himself to be betrayed into one act of violence, or into any course of outrage and revenge. The few years of his administration were the only happy ones Georgia had enjoyed, and to his energy and devotedness may be attributed its civil and commercial prosperity,"

In a letter to the Earl of Hillsborough, in 1766, when Revolutionary troubles first began to brew, Governor Wright calls Georgia the "most flourishing colony on the continent;" yet at that time it had no manufactures, a trifling quantity only of coarse homespun cloth, of wool and cotton mixed, was made, besides a few cotton and yarn socks, negro shoes and some articles by blacksmiths. Its productions were rice, indigo, corn, peas, and a small quantity of wheat and rye. Industrial enterprise was engaged in making tar, pitch, turpentine, shingles, staves, and sawing lumber, while attention was devoted to the raising of cattle, mules, horses and hogs. Most of the inhabitants were hardy farmers, possessed generally of negro slaves, and living in the eastern portion of the State. Manufactures were prohibited and commerce limited. Beginning with objections to the Stamp Act, which called into existence the "Liberty Boys," the province became more and more agitated from 1766 until the storm of revolution burst forth in 1775. Even then there were many respectable citizens in Georgia who inclined to royalty; but the majority sided with the State and aided in achieving independence.

It is not necessary, perhaps, to follow further the current of Georgia's political history. Our object has been simply to give a clear view of the condition of the State during the decade between the year 1760 and 1770, when Baptist principles were first gaining a firm foothold in Georgia. It has already been asserted that there are Baptists living in Georgia to-day whose ancestors came over from England in the same vessel with Oglethorpe, in 1732, and very shortly after. Among the former are the Baptist families of Campbell and Dunham, and among the latter that of Polhill.

II.
THE FIRST BAPTISTS IN THE STATE.
1740-1772.

II.

THE FIRST BAPTISTS IN THE STATE.

WHITEFIELD'S ORPHAN ASYLUM—NICHOLAS BEDGEWOOD ADOPTS BAPTIST VIEWS AND IS ORDAINED—EARLY GEORGIA BAPTISTS IN THE NEIGHBORHOOD OF SAVANNAH—BENJAMIN STIRK PREACHES UNTIL 1770—REV. EDMUND BOTSFORD COMES TO GEORGIA IN 1771—SOME ACCOUNT OF HIM— HE SETTLES AT TUCKASEEKING—DANIEL MARSHALL AND INTRODUCTION OF BAPTIST PRINCIPLES INTO NORTHERN GEORGIA—HIS ARREST FOR PREACHING—SAMUEL CARTLEDGE, THE CONSTABLE—HIS STRANGE CONVICTION—DANIEL MARSHALL'S TRIAL—SOME ACCOUNT OF MR. BARNARD, THE JUSTICE WHO TRIED MR. MARSHALL.—KIOKEE CHURCH—ACT OF INCORPORATION—SKETCH OF REV. DANIEL MARSHALL—HIS DEATH, IN 1784—HIS LAST WORDS AND BURIAL PLACE.

In this short chapter we shall discover the existence of Baptists in Georgia, on the seaboard, about the middle of last century. These soon became dispersed without forming a church; though, in the lower parishes of the State, Baptist families resided, scattered here and there through the country.

We shall next learn that it was about forty miles above Savannah that regular Gospel ministration first gathered Baptists in sufficient numbers to form a church; but, being without a regular ordained minister, they were simply constituted as a branch of the Euhaw Baptist church across the border, in South Carolina, and, as such, remained for several years. We shall then ascertain that the main influx of Baptists into our State, at first, was through Augusta as a door, and that they settled mostly in the counties west and north-west of that city. For a time the only ordained Baptist minister in the State resided twenty miles northwest of Augusta, where he was instrumental in constituting the first Baptist church formed in the State. In that section of the State our denomination first became numerous and strong, and has so continued there, to the present day.

In 1740, Mr. Whitefield began to build his orphan house, "Bethesda," nine miles below Savannah, in doing which he simply carried out a design proposed by John Wesley and General Oglethorpe. This enterprise was deemed necessary, as an effort of humanity. It was supposed that many poor emigrants would die in the new settlement, and leave children unprotected and penniless, for whom provision should thus be made. In 1741 the children, who had been boarded out at different places in the city, were admitted into the buildings, although they were not completed.

Ten years later, in 1751, Mr. Nicholas Bedgewood was Whitefield's agent at the Orphan House. He was an Englishman, twenty-one years of age, a classical scholar and an accomplished speaker. He embraced Baptist sentiments, and, in 1757, went to Charleston, South Carolina, where he united with the Charleston Baptist church, being baptized by Rev. Oliver Hart, the pastor.

Mr. Bedgewood manifested zeal and talents for usefulness, and was soon licensed to preach by the Charleston church. In 1759, two years after his baptism, he was ordained to the gospel ministry, and, as such, seems to have labored with success, for, in 1763, he baptized a number of the officers and inmates of the institution over which he presided. Among these were Benjamin Stirk and his wife, Thomas Dixon, a man named Dupree, and others. These appear to have united with some among the early settlers who were Baptists, and formed an arm of the Charleston Baptist church at the Orphan House. For we learn that Mr. Bedgewood administered the Lord's supper to the Baptists at the Orphan House. The following persons among the early settlers in Georgia, were Baptists: Wm. Calvert, Wm. Slack, Thomas Walker, and Nathaniel Polhill, all of whom were from England excepting Wm. Slack, who was from Ireland. In addition to these there were John Dunham and Sarah Clancy, husband and wife, who came over with Oglethorpe. A daughter of theirs was the mother of Rev. J. H. Campbell, still living, in Columbus, Georgia, an eminent Baptist minister.

Besides these there was William Dunham, whose grandson, Jacob H. Dunham, was a truly pious and evangelical Baptist minister in Liberty county, in the beginning of the present century. He and his wife were the first white persons ever baptized in Liberty county. Wm. Dunham settled on Newport river, where he died in 1756, leaving several daughters and three sons—James, Charles and John.

From Mr. Polhill are descended some of the most worthy Baptists of Georgia, among others, Rev. Thomas Polhill, the author of a book on baptism; Rev. Joseph Polhill, his son, a distinguished minister, of Burke county, who died in 1858; and Rev. John G. Polhill, now living, a minister of the fourth generation.

Thomas Dixon returned to England; Dupree died; Benjamin Stirk moved, in 1767, to Newington, eighteen miles above Savannah, after marrying Mr. Polhill's widow. And thus it happened that the Baptists at the Orphan House dispersed. The house itself was burned down, and ceased to exist as an institution. Indeed, its establishment in the place where it was built was a great error.

Mr. Bedgewood, himself, moved to South Carolina, where he married and became pastor of the Welch Neck church, on the Pedee river. Benedict, in his history, says: "Some of his posterity I have seen."

A number of Baptists have, however, always existed in the neighborhood of Savannah from its earliest settlement. In 1740, just seven years after the settlement of the colony, Rev. Mr. Lewis, of Margate, England, alleged, by way of reproach, that "there were descendants of the Moravian Anabaptists in the new plantation of Georgia." In 1772, several years prior to the war of independence, there were, in the lower parishes of Georgia, not less than forty Baptist families, among whom were fifty baptized church members, who had emigrated from England or removed to Georgia from more northern colonies.

Mention has been made of Benjamin Stirk, who was among the number of those who were baptized at the Orphan House, and who moved to Newington, eighteen miles north of Savannah, in 1767, after losing his first wife. A man of learning and natural ability, he developed into a Christian of great piety and zeal. He soon began to preach, and establish places of public worship not only in his own house and neighborhood, but at a settlement called Tuckaseeking, twenty miles north of Newington, where he discovered a few Baptists. As there was no Baptist church in Georgia, at that time, he connected himself with the Euhaw Baptist church, in South Carolina, of which church the brethren at Tuckaseeking were constituted into an arm, perhaps through Mr. Stirk's instrumentality. To them Rev. Mr. Stirk preached until 1770, when he finished his earthly course, thus ending the useful labor of a few years. The following year, 1771, the little band of Baptists at Tuckaseeking, hearing that Mr. Edmund Botsford, a licentiate of the Charleston Baptist church, was at Euhaw, South Carolina, sent him an invitation to come and preach to them. Accompanied by Rev. Francis Pelot, pastor of the Euhaw church, Mr. Botsford visited the Tuckaseeking brethren, and preached his first sermon to them on the 27th of June, 1771.

Born in England, in 1745, Mr. Botsford was early left an orphan. He sailed for the New World, and arrived at Charleston, January 28th, 1766. Converted under the ministry of Rev. Oliver Hart, he united with the Charleston Baptist church, and was baptized on the 13th of March, 1767. After a course of preparatory study, under the instruction of Mr. Hart, he was licensed to preach in February, 1771. In June he set out on a missionary tour, with horse and saddlebags, and travelled as far as Euhaw, where he remained preaching for Mr. Pelot until invited into Georgia. His services were highly acceptable to the Tuckaseeking brethren and, at their solicitation, he consented to remain and preach for them a year. But he did not confine his labors to Tuckaseeking, where he soon became very popular. He preached throughout all the surrounding regions, in both Georgia and South Carolina. There were a few Baptists at Ebenezer, a large settlement of German Lutherans, twenty-five miles above Savannah, and Botsford, visiting them, was invited to preach, providing permission to use a German meeting-house could be obtained from Mr. Robinson, the pastor. Mr. Robinson made no objection and referred the applicant to the deacon. The deacon replied, when permission was requested:

"No, no! Tese Paptists are a very pad people. Dey begin slow vurst: py and py all men follow dem. No! no! go to the minister! If he says *breach*, den I giff you de keys."

"The minister says he has no objection, and leaves it with you," was the answer of Mr. Botsford.

"Den take de keys! I will come and hear myself."

It was October 1st, 1771; and Mr. Botsford preached from Matt. ix: 13—"I will have mercy and not sacrifice; for I am not come to call the righteous, but sinners, to repentance." Afterwards the old deacon said: "Dat peen pad poy, put he breach Jesus Christ. He come again and welcome!"

"Py and py all men follow dem," was the honest German's prediction. Let us see how events warrant it. When uttered, not a Baptist church existed in Georgia; nor was there more than one ordained Baptist minister in the province. Scattered here and there might have been one or two hundred Baptists. Now, (1881) there are 1,630 ordained ministers, 2,755 churches, and 235,381 communicants. At that time there were probably 150 Baptist churches in all the original colonies. There are now (1881), in the United States, 16,600 ministers, 26,000 churches, and 2,200,000 church members. Verily, a little one has become a thousand!

We will now glance at the introduction of Baptist principles into Georgia, in the section of country a little northwest of Augusta, by Rev. Daniel Marshall. On the 1st of January, in the same year that Edmund Botsford visited Tuckaseeking, 1771, Daniel Marshall, an ordained Baptist minister, sixty-five years of age, moved from Horse Creek, South Carolina, fifteen miles north of Augusta, and settled with his whole family, on Kiokee Creek, about twenty miles northwest of Augusta. He had been residing for some time in South Carolina, where he had built up two churches, and, while dwelling at Horse Creek, had made frequent evangelistic tours into Georgia, preaching with remarkable zeal and fervor in houses and groves.

We will gaze upon him as he conducts religious service. The scene is in a sylvan grove, and Daniel Marshall is on his knees making the opening prayer. While he beseeches the Throne of Grace, a hand is laid on his shoulder, and he hears a voice say:

"You are my prisoner!"

Rising, the sedate, earnest-minded man of God, whose sober mien and silvery locks indicate the sixty-five years which have passed since his birth, finds himself confronted by an officer of the law. He is astonished at being arrested, under such circumstances, "for preaching in the Parish of St. Paul!" for, in so doing, he has violated the legislative enactment of 1758, which established religious worship in the colony "according to the rites and ceremonies of the Church of England." Rev. Abraham Marshall, in his sketch of his father, published in the *Analytical Repository*, 1802, says that the arrested preacher was made to give security for his appearance in Augusta on the following Monday, to answer for this violation of the law, adding: "Accordingly, he stood a trial, and after his meekness and patience were sufficiently exercised, he was ordered to come, as a preacher, no more into Georgia." The reply of Daniel Marshall was similar to that of the Apostles under similar circumstances, "Whether it be right to obey God or man, judge ye;" and, "consistently with this just and spirited replication, he pursued his luminous course."

We have Dr. J. H. Campbell's authority for it, that after Constable Cartledge, satisfied with the security given, has released his prisoner temporarily, to the surprise of all present, the indignation which swells the bosom of Mr. Marshall, finds vent though the lips of his wife. Mrs. Martha Marshall, who is sitting near, and has witnessed the whole scene. With the solemnity of the prophets of old, she denounces such proceedings and such a law, and, to sustain her position, quotes many passages from the Holy Scriptures with a force and pertinency which carry conviction to the hearts of many. The very constable himself, Mr. Samuel Cartledge, was so deeply convinced by the inspired words of exhortation which then fell from her lips, that his conversion was the result; and, in 1777, he was baptized by the very man whom he then held under arrest, and whom he led to trial on the following Monday. A North Carolinian by birth, he was at that time just twenty-one years of age. Converted and baptized in 1777, he was for some years a useful deacon of Mr. Marshall's church, at Kiokee, and assisted in the constitution of Fishing Creek church, in 1783, and of the Georgia Association in 1784.*

After the interruption caused by his arrest, Mr. Marshall proceeded with the exercises, and, we may well suppose, preached with more than usual boldness and faithfulness. Such a course was characteristic of the man. After his sermon, he baptized in the neighboring creek two individuals, relatives of the very gentleman who stood security for his appearance at court.

It is interesting to note that this magistrate, Colonel Barnard, was also afterwards converted, and he became a zealous Christian. Although (in deference to the wishes of his wife) he was never immersed, and lived and died in connection with the Church of England, yet he was strongly tinctured with Baptist sentiments, and would exhort sinners to flee from the wrath to come. He became a decided friend of Mr. Marshall and of the Baptists, and spoke of them very favorably to Sir James Wright, the Governor. Though somewhat eccentric in character, yet he was a good man, and died in a most triumphant manner.

Daniel Marshall, one of the founders of the Baptist denomination in Georgia, was born at Windsor, Connecticut, in 1706, of Presbyterian parents. He was a man of great natural ardor and holy zeal. Becoming convinced that it was his duty to assist in converting the heathen, he went, with his wife and three children, and preached for three years to the Mohawk Indians, near the head waters of the Susquehannah river, at a town called Onnaquaggy. War among the savage tribes compelled his removal, first to Connogogig in Pennsylvania, and then to Winchester, Virginia, where he became a convert to Baptist views, and was immersed at the age of forty-eight. His wife also submitted to the ordinance at the same time. He was soon licensed by the church with which he united, and, having removed to North Carolina, he built up a flourishing church, of which he was ordained pastor by his two brothers-in-law, Rev. Henry Ledbetter and Rev. Shubael Stearns. From North Carolina he removed to South Carolina, and from South Carolina to Georgia, in each State constituting new and flourishing churches. On the 1st of January, 1771, he settled in what is now Columbia county, Georgia, on Kiokee Creek. He was a man of pure life, unbounded faith, fervent spirit, holy zeal, indefatigable in religious labors, and possessed of the highest moral courage. Neither profoundly learned nor very eloquent, he possessed that fervency, earnestness and flaming ardor of zeal, united with a remarkable native strength of mind and knowledge of the Scriptures which fitted him for a pioneer preacher. From his headquarters in Kiokee he went forth in all directions, preaching the gospel with great power, and leading many to Jesus. By uniting those whom he had baptized in the neighborhood, and other Baptists who lived on both sides of the Savannah river, he formed and

---

*He commenced preaching in 1789, was ordained by Abraham Marshall and Sanders Walker, and for more than half a century was a zealous preacher of the faith he once persecuted. As late as 1843, at the age of 93, he travelled from his home in South Carolina on a visit to Georgia, and after preaching with his usual earnestness, in the very neighborhood where he had arrested Daniel Marshall, seventy-two years before, he was thrown from his horse as he was setting out for home, and so much injured that his death was the result.

organized the Kiokee church, in the spring of 1772; and this was the first Baptist church ever constituted within the bounds of Georgia.

The following is the act incorporating Kiokee church, and is extracted from "Watkins' Digest," page 409; also from the Digest of "Marbury and Crawford," page 143. Certain purely formal expressions are omitted:

"AN ACT *for incorporating the Anabaptist church on the Kioka, in the county of Richmond.*

"WHEREAS, a religious society has, for many years past, been established on the Kioka, in the county of Richmond, called and known by the name of 'The Anabaptist church on Kioka':

"*Be it enacted,* That Abraham Marshall, William Willingham, Edmund Cartledge, John Landers, James Simms, Joseph Ray and Lewis Gardener be, and they are hereby, declared to be a body corporate, by the name and style of 'The Trustees of the Anabaptist church on Kioka.'

"*And be it further enacted,* That the Trustees, (the same names are here given) of the said Anabaptist church, shall hold their office for the term of three years; and, on the third Saturday of November, in every third year, after the passing of this Act, the supporters of the Gospel in said church shall convene at the meeting-house of said church, and there, between the hours of ten and four, elect from among the supporters of the Gospel in said church seven discreet persons as Trustees," etc.

"SEABORN JONES, *Speaker.*
"NATHAN BROWNSON, *President Senate.*
"EDWARD TELFAIR, *Governor.*
"*December 23d, 1789.*"

Its meeting-house was built where now stands the town of Appling, the county-site of Columbia county. Of this church Marshall became the pastor, and so continued until November 2d, 1784, when he expired, in the seventy-eighth year of his age. The following, first published in the *Analytical Repository,* and taken down by his son, Rev. Abraham Marshall, in the presence of a few deeply afflicted friends and relations, were his last words: "Dear brethren and sisters, I am just gone. This night I shall probably expire; but I have nothing to fear. I have fought the good fight; I have finished my course; I have kept the faith, and henceforth there is laid up for me a crown of righteousness. God has shown me that he is my God, and that I am His son, and that an eternal weight of glory is mine." To the venerable partner, in all his cares, and faithful assistant in all his labors, who was sitting by his side bedewed with tears, he said, "Go on, my dear wife, to serve the Lord. Hold out to the end. Eternal glory is before us."

After a silence of some minutes, he called his son, Abraham, and said, "My breath is almost gone. I have been praying that I may go home to-night. I had great happiness in our worship this morning, particularly in singing, which will make a part of my exercise in a blessed eternity!" and, gently closing his eyes, he cheerfully gave up his soul to God. He attended public worship regularly, even through his lingering illness, until the last Sabbath but one before his dissolution, and even until the very morning preceding his happy change, he invariably performed his usual round of holy duties.

When he moved into the State, he was the only ordained Baptist minister within its bounds. There were very few Baptists in the State, and no organized church. He lived to preside at the organization of the Georgia Association, in October, 1784, when there were half a dozen churches in the State, many Baptists, and a good many Baptist preachers. His grave lies a few rods south of the Appling Court-house, on the side of the road to Augusta. "Memory watches the spot, but no 'false marble' utters untruths concerning this distinguished herald of salvation. He sleeps neither 'forgotten' nor 'unsung;' for every child in the neighborhood can lead you to Daniel Marshall's grave."—*Sherwood's Gazetteer of Georgia, 1837.*

After Mr. Marshall's death, Kiokee church, which he founded in 1772, was removed from Applington, the county site, four miles north, and a new brick house of worship was erected.

III.
THE REVOLUTIONARY PERIOD.
1772-1794.

THE REVOLUTIONARY PERIOD.

LABORS OF EDMUND BOTSFORD—VISITS KIOKEE—PREACHES FOR DANIEL MARSHALL--LOVELESS SAVIDGE--HIS CONVERSION TO THE BAPTIST FAITH. BOTSFORD'S LABORS—"THE RUM IS COME"—HE IS ORDAINED—BOTSFORD'S CHURCH CONSTITUTED IN 1773—HIS FLIGHT IN 1779—CAUSES OF THE REVOLUTION--"LIBERTY BOYS"—GEORGIA SPEAKING OUT—CONDITION OF THE STATE IN 1772—A PROVINCIAL CONGRESS ELECTED IN 1775—IN 1776 IT WAS RESOLVED TO EMBARK IN THE CAUSE OF FREEDOM—GEORGIA IN ACTIVE REBELLION—GEORGIA SUBJUGATED IN 1779, AND THE ROYAL GOVERNMENT RE-ESTABLISHED IN SAVANNAH—BOTSFORD AND SILAS MERCER FLEE, BUT DANIEL MARSHALL STANDS FIRM—HIS TRIALS AND LABORS—THE LICENSURE SYSTEM—STATISTICS FROM 1788 TO 1794.

We will now return to the history of Edmund Botsford. He has been laboring faithfully at Tuckaseeking, but has by no means confined his labors to that locality. In 1772 he enlarged the sphere of his labors, travelling up and down the Savannah river, and preaching incessantly in both South Carolina and Georgia. Through the blessing of the Spirit he made many converts, who were baptized either by Mr. Pelot or Mr. Marshall, for as yet Edmund Botsford was but a licentiate. In one of his preaching excursions he visited Augusta, and became the guest of Colonel Barnard, the justice before whom Daniel Marshall had been tried for preaching in the Parish of St. Paul. Colonel Barnard prevailed upon him to go and preach at Kiokee, promising to accompany him and introduce him to Daniel Marshall. Together they went to Kiokee meeting-house, and when they met Col. Barnard said:

"Mr. Marshall, I wish to introduce to you the Rev. Mr. Botsford, of your faith, a gentleman originally from England, but last from Charleston."

After the usual greetings, the following conversation, extracted from C. D. Mallary's Memoir of Botsford, ensued:

"Well, sir, are you to preach for us?" said Marshall.

"Yes, sir, by your leave; but I confess I am at a loss for a text," was Botsford's reply.

"Well, well! Look to the Lord for one."

The text that suggested itself to Mr. Botsford's mind was the following from Psalms 66:16: "Come and hear, all ye that fear God, and I will declare what he hath done for my soul." After service, Mr. Marshall said, "I can take thee by the hand and call thee brother, for somehow I never heard *convarsion* better explained in my life; but I would not have thee think thou preachest as well as Joe Reese and Philip Mulkey; however, I hope you will go home with me."

Mr. Botsford did so, and from that time a friendship, which was never dissolved, existed between the two.

That he might be more at liberty to engage in the evangelistic labors so dear to his soul, and so useful and needed at that time, Mr. Botsford terminated his engagement with the Tuckaseeking brethren near the close of 1772, and engaged exclusively in missionary work, travelling on horseback as far south as Ebenezer and as far north as Kiokee. His labors were blessed to the conversion of many, during the year 1772. It was during this year that Mr. Botsford, on his way to Kiokee church, where he had an appointment to preach, rode up to the house of a Mr. Loveless Savidge, ten miles northwest of Augusta, to make inquiries concerning the road. Mr. Savidge was a member of the Church of England, and, though a pious man, was tinctured with bigotry. To the faith and forms of the

English Establishment he was strongly attached. Having given the necessary directions respecting the road, Mr. Savidge said:

"I suppose you are the Baptist minister who is to preach to-day at Kiokee."

"Yes, sir. Will you go?" responded Mr. Botsford.

"No; I am not fond of the Baptists. They think nobody baptized but themselves."

"Have you been baptized?" asked the visitor.

"To be sure I have—according to the rubric."

"How do you know?" Mr. Botsford inquired.

"How do I know! Why, my parents told me I was. That is the way I know," answered Mr. Savidge.

"Then you do not know, only by the *information of others!*" and mounting his horse, Mr. Botsford rode on to Kiokee meeting-house, leaving Mr. Savidge to meditate on the words, *How do you know?* His mind constantly reverted to them, and they harassed him continually until, after an investigation of the subject, he became convinced that it was his duty to be immersed. Nor was it long before he was baptized by Mr. Marshall. He used to say, "Botsford's '*How do you know?*' first set me to thinking about baptism, and resulted in my conversion to the Baptist faith." He began to preach the very day he was baptized, became one of the many useful licentiates of the Kiokee church, was the first pastor of Abilene (then Red Creek) church, which he was probably instrumental in founding, in 1774, and of which he was pastor as late as 1790. He became a distinguished and useful minister, intimately connected with early Baptist history in the State, and died about 1815, when nearly ninety years of age.

To present some idea of Mr. Botsford's labors and the difficulties against which he had to contend, and to show the rude and uncultivated state of society at that time, we will give another incident which occurred in the same year he met Mr. Savidge and set him to thinking, 1772.

He was preaching at the court-house in Burke county. The congregation paid very decent attention at first; but, towards the close of his sermon, some one bawled out, "The rum is come!" and rushed out. Others followed, and the sermon was finished to a very small assembly. When Mr. Botsford went to mount his horse, he found many of those who had been his hearers intoxicated and fighting. One old gentleman, considerably the worse for liquor, came up, and taking hold of Mr. Botsford's bridle rein, extolled his sermon in profane dialect, swore that he should come and preach in his neighborhood, and invited him to drink. Declining the invitation to drink, Mr. Botsford accepted the appointment to preach, and rode away. His first sermon was blessed to the awakening of the old man's wife to an interest in her soul's welfare. One of his sons also became religious; others, to the number of fifteen, in the settlement, were hopefully converted; and the old man himself became sober and attentive to religion, though he never made a public profession.

The Baptist church in Charleston, hearing of the success that attended the ministry of Mr. Botsford, concluded to call him to ordination. Acccordingly he was ordained March 14th, 1773, Rev. Oliver Hart, of Charleston, and Rev. Francis Pelot, of Euhaw, assisting on the occasion.

During 1773 and 1774 Mr. Botsford's labors were abundant and successful, a large number being baptized by him. Says he, himself:

"In the month of August, 1773, I rode 650 miles, preached forty-two sermons, baptized twenty-one persons, and administered the Lord's supper twice. Indeed, I travelled so much this year that some used to call me the *flying preacher.*"

The following incident occurred on the 16th of July, in that year, at Stephen's Creek, South Carolina. Several candidates came forward for baptism; but one, a Mrs. Clecker, "did not know that her husband would permit her to be baptized."

"Is he present in the congregation?" asked Mr. Botsford.

"Yes, sir."

"Mr. Clecker, please come to the table!" exclaimed the preacher. Mr. Clecker came forward, and proved to be a little German. "I have reason to hope, Mr. Clecker," said Mr. Botsford," that your wife is a believer in Christ, and she desires to be baptized by immersion, but not without your consent. Have you any objection to make, sir?"

"No, no! Got forpit I should hinter my vife! She vas one goot vife."

Nevertheless, the little man was enraged at being thus summoned and publicly interrogated; and while the preparations were going on, he vented his wrath privately in swearing and abusing Mr. Botsford.

"Vat! ax me pefore all de peeble if he might tip my vife!" Of this, however, Mr. Botsford was ignorant. Coming up from the water, after the administration of baptism was all over, and passing through an orchard, he saw the little German, by himself, and leaning against a tree, apparently in trouble.

"Mr. Clecker, what is the matter?" asked Mr. Botsford. "O, sir, I shall go to de tivel, and my vife to hevin. I am a boor lost sinner. I can't be forgifen. I fear de ground will open and let me down to de hell, for I cursed and swore you vas good for notting. Lord, have mercy on me!" Afterwards he found peace in believing, and Mr. Botsford had the satisfaction of baptizing him in September, 1773. In November of that year, Mr. Botsford, assisted by Oliver Hart, of Charleston, and Francis Pelot, of Euhaw, South Carolina, constituted those who had received baptism into a church, about twenty-five miles below Augusta. Then styled the New Savannah church, it afterwards assumed the name of Botsford meeting house, but, after the Revolutionary war, the building was moved eight or ten miles to the place now known as Botsford's church, of the Hephzibah Association. It was the second Baptist church constituted in the State of Georgia. In the same year Mr. Botsford married Miss Susanna Nun, of Augusta, a native of Cork, Ireland, who had been baptized by Daniel Marshall, and, in May, 1774, the newly married couple settled on some land, purchased by Mr. Botsford, in Burke county; but, without allowing the charms or cares of domestic life to diminish his activity in his Master's cause. Mr. Botsford, from the tabernacle he had pitched on Brier Creek, started out into the surrounding regions, and preached the gospel with fervor and success. This continued until the spring of 1779, when, after baptizing 148 persons, rearing up one flourishing church, founding two others, and preparing the materials for others, Mr. Botsford hurried from the province, a fugitive, to escape the British and Tories; for Georgia had just been subjugated and the horrors of the Revolutionary war began to be seriously experienced by the settlers.

A glance at the political situation will now give the reader a clearer insight into the general condition of affairs. It is 1774. For many years England has been waging war with the French and Indians. Peace was concluded in 1763; but these wars, undertaken at the request and for the defence of the colonies, had cost the mother country $300,000,000, and on the 10th of March, 1764, the House of Commons declared it right and proper to tax America, as a relief in the endurance of this burden, added to the already large national debt. Soon after, the House of Commons voted that it was *expedient* to tax America, and enacted the celebrated "Stamp Act," on the 2d of March, 1765. This was resented strongly by the Americans, who not only refused to use the stamped paper, but destroyed it, and threatened the stamp officers with death. It was at this juncture, after November, 1765, whem the Stamp Act went into operation, that the patriotic society known as "Liberty Boys" was organized.

On he 18th of March, 1766, the Stamp Act was repealed, but on the 29th of June, 1767, an act was passed by Parliament imposing a duty on tea, glass, papers and painters' colors, which should be imported into the colonies. This was the culmination of disputes on the subject of taxation without representation, which had been raging between the colonies and Parliament for more than a quarter of a century. England contended for her right to raise a revenue. America contended that taxation without representation was unjust, and refused to submit to it. James Habersham, President of the Council, in Savannah, a loyalist, but a true patriot, declared that the money proposed to be raised by the Stamp Act was more than Georgians could bear, and would inevitably ruin them. Various causes of exasperation followed in quick succession—among other grievances, no petitionary appeals to Parliament being heeded. In the meantime immigrants are flocking into the country. Four additional parishes are laid off in 1765 between the Altamaha and St. Mary's rivers. In 1766 one hundred and seventy-one vessels were entered at the custom-house. Between the years 1763 and 1773, the exports of the province increased from thirty-five thousand

THE REVOLUTIONARY PERIOD.

to six hundred and eight thousand dollars, and the number of negroes in 1773 was 14,000.

The people now determined to speak out for themselves, and in February, 1770, the Georgia Legislature took into consideration the authority to impose taxes and collect duties for the purpose of raising a revenue, and to keep a standing army in time of peace, and to transport persons accused of treason to England for trial. The House of Assembly, after defining their rights, resolved "that the exercise of legislative power, in any colony by a council appointed during pleasure by the Crown, may prove dangerous and destructive to the freedom of American legislation—all and each of which the Commons of Georgia, in General Assembly met, do claim, demand and insist on, as their indubitable rights and liberties, which cannot legally be taken from them, altered or abridged by any power whatever, without their consent."

In 1772 the crisis approached. Committees were appointed in all the colonies to decide whether to submit to taxation by the British Parliament, or to make a firm stand in opposition. This is the time when Daniel Marshall and Edmund Botsford are making converts and establishing churches above and below Augusta. At that time so much of the territory of Georgia as was settled by white citizens was about one hundred and fifty miles from north to south, and about thirty miles from east to west, and but thinly populated. It presented a western frontier of two hundred and fifty miles, and had on the northwest the Cherokees, on the west the Creeks, on the South a refugee banditti in Florida, while Governor Wright controlled the King's ships on the coast. The population of the eastern district of the province was composed of whites and negro slaves—the latter most numerous, the former few in number. While a great majority of the inhabitants favored the cause of the colonists, yet, owing to the surrounding dangers, measures were adopted with cautious circumspection. The year 1774 passed without any decisive demonstrations, although the committees of safety were active and efficient. On the 18th of January a Provincial Congress met in Savannah and elected three delegates to the Continental Congress in Philadelphia, but they did not attend. The Provincial Congress met again July 4th, 1775, and elected five delegates to the Continental Congress. During its session a British schooner arrived at Tybee with 13,000 pounds of powder on board. This was captured by a vessel commissioned by the Provincial Congress of Georgia, and 5,000 pounds of the powder were sent to Washington, and enabled him to drive the British out of Boston. At the meeting of the Provincial Assembly, in January, 1776, the House resolved to embark in the cause of freedom—to resist and be free, and orders were given to arrest Governor Wright and his Council. This was done by Joseph Habersham alone, on the 28th of January, in the Governor's own house, where he was left a prisoner on parole; but he effected his escape on the night of February 11th. Georgia, in active rebellion, was now in the hands of the Provincial Congress, and remained so for three years. On the 29th of December, 1778, Savannah was captured by the British. Sunbury was captured on the 6th of January. The British hastened, conquering as they went, and, about the last of January, 1779, Augusta fell into their possession, and military posts were soon established by them over the most populous parts of Georgia.

On the 3d of March, General John Ash, with 1,700 men, was routed at Brier Creek, in Burke county, by Lieutenant Colonel Campbell, of the British army. On the 4th of March, 1779, the State being mostly reduced by the troops, the royal government was re-established in Savannah, and on the 13th of July, Governor Wright returned and entered again upon his gubernatorial duties. The province, almost defenceless, lay struggling ineffectually in the grasp of her conquerors. Dark days for religion followed. Marauding parties traversed the country ravaging, murdering and bearing off victims to the horrible prison ships at Savannah. Imprisonment, exile, confiscation, death and other dreadful calamities filled the land with mourning and suffering.

And how fares it with our Baptist brethren? In the spring of 1779, Edmund Botsford precipitately flies into South Carolina and thence into Virginia. Georgia is never again his home. Silas Mercer, father of Jesse Mercer, who had settled in Wilkes county in 1775, at the age of 30, and united with the church

THE REVOLUTIONARY PERIOD.

at Kiokee, fled to North Carolina. In 1777 Abraham Marshall also sought safety in flight, in company with Silas Mercer. But Daniel Marshall stood his ground and never deserted his post. Though rapine, violence and bloodshed filled the land with consternation, the perseverance and zeal of this brave soldier of the cross were not in the slightest degree abated. Assisted by a few licentiates who remained faithfully with him, he continued his Christian labors, and, even in those times which tried men's souls, the spirit of pure religion was progressive, and very many were converted to God. Still, but three churches were constituted anterior to the war, and but two that are known, during its progress. The former were, Kiokee, 1772; Botsford's, 1773; Red's Creek, 1774. The latter were Little Brier Creek, 1777; and Fishing Creek, 1782, according to Asplund's Register. There was another Baptist church the name of which is now unknown, situated on Buckhead Creek, in Burke county, of which Rev. Matthew Moore was pastor. During the war its members were scattered, and the church became virtually extinct. After the war Matthew Moore, who was a Loyalist, left the country. About 1787 the fragments of this unknown church were collected together, and by Rev. James Matthews and Rev. Benjamin Davis organized into Buckhead church. The baptizing place of Rev. Matthew Moore, in Buckhead Creek still goes by the name of "The Dipping Ford."

It is said that but few Baptists became Tories. Espousing the cause of liberty from high and holy motives, they had an eye not only to the temporal interests of the land, but to the rights of conscience, the prosperity of their churches and the general interests of the Redeemer's Kingdom. It was because they were such ardent friends of liberty that Botsford and Silas Mercer fled, through fear of the British; and it was because he was such a staunch patriot and faithful minister that Daniel Marshall clung to his home and to his ministerial duties. No dangers daunted him; no threats could intimidate him. Once, during the war, when a party of Tories demanded where his horses were concealed, he preserved an obdurate silence, regardless of the threats and impending death, and nothing but the disclosure made by his wife, unable longer to endure the torturing suspense and anxiety, preserved his life.

From the sketch of his life, written by his son, Abraham, the following is extracted: "No scenes, however, from the commencement to the termination of hostilities, were so gloomy and alarming as to deter my estimable father from discharging the duties of his station. Neither reproaches nor threatenings could excite in him the least appearance of timidity, or anything inconsistent with Christian and ministerial heroism. As a friend to the American cause, he was once made a prisoner and put under a strong guard. But, obtaining leave of the officers, he commenced and supported so heavy a charge of exhortation and prayer that, like Daniel of old, while his enemies stood amazed and confounded, he was safely and honorably delivered from this den of lions." From these incidents we not only learn the character of Mr. Marshall, but we discover also the trials and dangers amid which he and others of similar disposition maintained the Baptist cause in the early history of Georgia.

Mr. Daniel Marshall was twice married—the second time to Miss Martha Stearns, of Virginia, to whose unwearied and zealous co-operation the extraordinary success of his ministry is, in no small degree ascribable. A lady of good sense, singular piety and surprising elocution, she, in countless instances, melted a whole concourse into tears by her prayers and exhortations.

Bold and independent in his methods, superior to local attachments and undismayed by danger, Mr. Marshall was capable of the most difficult and arduous enterprises. He went from place to place, instructing, exhorting and praying for individuals, families and congregations, whether at a muster, a race, a public market, the open field, an army, or a house of worship—wherever he was able to command attention; and the fruits of his astonishing exertions abundantly showed that he was constrained by the love of Christ.

These statements regarding Mr. and Mrs. Marshall have been abbreviated from an editorial by Dr. Henry Holcombe, published in the *Analytical Repository*, in 1802. Eternity only can reveal the extent to which the Baptist denomination in Georgia is indebted to Daniel Marshall.

He inaugurated a system which largely accounts for the growth of the churches and the number of converts in that early day. This was the licensure of pious and zealous members by the church, and the active exertions to which they, as lieutenants, were incited. Many of these were specially designated "itinerants." Most of the best and most useful ordained ministers passed through these stages of preparation, and when their labors, united with those of regularly ordained ministers, made it advisable or necessary to organize a church in any particular locality, this was done, and the useful and zealous licentiate was ordained and placed in charge of the newly constituted church. This was the course through which Alexander Scott, Sanders Walker, Samuel Cartledge, Silas Mercer, Abraham Marshall, Loveless Savidge, Samuel Newton, Charles Bussey, James Simms, Michael Smalley, John Milner, William Davis, Jeremiah Reeves, Joseph Baker, Henry Hand, and many others, passed, all of whom became active, able and influential ministers; and it was thus that converts were made so numerously during and immediately succeeding the war, so that the statistical figures actually astonish us. By an examination of the records we discover that in 1772 there was one church; in 1773, two; in 1774, three; in 1777, four; in 1780, seven; in 1782, eight; in 1784, nine; in 1785, eleven; in 1786, fifteen; in 1787, twenty; in 1788, thirty-three; in 1789, thirty-five; in 1790, forty-two; in 1794, fifty-three, with nearly four thousand members.

The following short table will give a comparative view at three different periods:

YEAR.	CHURCHES.	MEMBERS	ORD. MINISTERS.	LICENTIATES.
1788	33	2,250	19	12
1790	42	3,211	33	39
1794	53	3,350	31	13

The figures in the first line are taken from the printed Minutes of the Georgia Association for 1788. Those of the second line are taken from Asplund's Register of 1790. And those of the third line are taken from the printed Minutes of the Georgia Association for the year 1794, when it convened at Powelton, October 19th, but the table of statistics is incomplete in regard to ministers, both ordained and licensed, and the number of these should be increased, for there were fifty-one ordained ministers in 1791. We feel very sure that there were some Baptist churches in Georgia in 1794 which were not connected with the Georgia Association—seven at least—Asplund's Register being our authority; so that it is, perhaps, proper to put the number of churches in the State, in 1794, at sixty, and the number of members at 4,500.

Another view will give a fair idea of the growth of the denomination: in 1772 there was one church; in 1773, two; in 1774, three; in 1777, four; in 1780, seven; in 1782, eight; in 1784, nine; in 1785, eleven; in 1786, fifteen; in 1787, twenty; in 1788, thirty-three; in 1790, forty-two; in 1794, sixty, with about four thousand five hundred members.

Our hasty summary of events has given us a few glimpses of civil affairs, deemed proper in order that the reader may bear in mind the condition of the country when Baptist principles first took root in our State, and the difficulties and dangers incurred by our Baptist fathers, in planting and nurturing those principles. From a feeble colony the province has passed through the evils of misgovernment and the calamities of war, to emerge a free State in the Federal Union. We have seen a few scattered Baptists begin to form themselves into churches in 1772 and 1773, and gradually increase in numbers, until, in 1794, the churches number sixty or more, with nearly five thousand church members. For ten years the churches have been formed into an Association, which has met regularly twice each year, most of the time, and which has consolidated, strengthened and established the denomination, giving staunchness to its formation and a correct scriptural character to its doctrines. These churches thus wonderfully increased in numbers and strength, by the active and self-sacrificing labors of our fathers, range up and down the Savannah river, in the eastern portion of the State, within the counties then known as Chatham, Effingham, Burke, Richmond, Franklin, Washington and Wilkes.

IV.
GROWTH AND ORGANIZATION.
1782-1799.

GROWTH AND ORGANIZATION.

PEACE—SAVANNAH AGAIN IN OUR POSSESSION IN JULY, 1783—GEORGIA'S DESOLATE CONDITION—BAPTIST MATTERS—FORMATION OF THE GEORGIA ASSOCIATION—VIEWS OF SHERWOOD, BENEDICT AND ASPLUND—"BEGUN IN 1784"—TWO SESSIONS ANNUALLY FOR HALF A DOZEN YEARS—EXTRACTS FROM NEWTON'S DIARY—ALEXANDER SCOTT—SILAS MERCER—SANDERS WALKER—ABRAHAM MARSHALL—EVANGELISTIC LABORS AT THE FOUNDATION OF THE BAPTIST DENOMINATION IN GEORGIA—JAMES MATTHEWS—PRECARIOUS TIMES—FORMATION OF THE HEPHZIBAH ASSOCIATION, IN SEPTEMBER, 1795—FORMATION OF THE SAREPTA ASSOCIATION, IN MAY, 1799.

It will be well now to pause and take a cursory view of the general situation of affairs, just at that joyful time when the dark clouds of war dispersed and the sun of peace rose and bathed the land in its bright and joyous beams. The defeat of Burgoyne, at Saratoga, and the capture of Cornwallis, at Yorktown, rendered the war unpopular in England, and it rapidly drew to a close.

Lord Cornwallis surrendered October 19th, 1781. As early as November 30th, 1782, provisional articles of peace were agreed upon, by American and British commissioners at Paris. A motion to suspend hostilities was made in the House of Commons on the 29th of February 1783. A change of ministry and policy occurred, and steps toward the establishment of peace succeeded. The withdrawal of the British forces from America then followed. On the 11th of July, 1783, the embarkation of British troops from Savannah began, and, on the same day, Colonel James Jackson, at the head of the colonial forces, marched in and took possession of the State metropolis, which had been in the hands of the enemy for three years, six months and thirteen days. It was not until September 3d, 1783, however, that definitive treaties between England, France and America, were finally ratified. Thus success crowned the American Revolution, and the glorious but terrible war for independence ended. In the eyes of all Europe the different colonies were free and sovereign States.

But what of Georgia? The fierce storm passed and left her in a desolated, ravaged, almost ruined condition. Negroes had been stolen and carried off, five thousand departing with the British troops from Savannah. Houses, plantations, produce and much other property had been wantonly destroyed by fire. Many widows mourned for the heads of as many families. At least one half of all the property of the State had been destroyed, and society was completely disorganized. Yet recuperation began and progressed, notwithstanding the Indian wars that ensued. Refugees began to return, among whom were Silas Mercer and Abraham Marshall. The former settled in Wilkes county, in 1783, after an absence of six years, spent with Abraham Marshall, mostly in North Carolina. The faithful preaching which had been done by Daniel Marshall and his efficient lieutenants, the licentiates of Kiokee church, began to manifest itself. The Baptists scattered throughout the country, by affinity gravitating towards each other, gradually united, formed churches, and soon began to take measures for the formation of an Association. The first preliminary meeting occurred at Kiokee church, in October, 1784, and five churches were represented: *Kiokee*, constituted in 1772; *Abilene* (then called *Red's Creek*, or Reed's Creek), constituted in 1774; *Fishing Creek*, constituted in 1782; *Greenwood* (then called Upton's Creek), constituted in 1784; and *Botsford* (then called Lower or Little Brier Creek), constituted in 1773. It is admitted that there is a little doubt to be attached to the statement that Botsford was one of the churches which united in forming the Georgia Association ; but Dr. Sherwood inclines to that opinion very decidedly.

There were two Brier Creek churches in Burke county, and two in Wilkes county. Those in Burke county existed prior to 1790, and are called by Asplund, "Head Brier Creek" and "Lower Brier Creek." This latter was constituted in 1773, and is now known as Botsford. Of this James Matthews was pastor in 1788. Those in Wilkes county were known as "Upper Brier Creek, or Brier Creek Iron Works," and "Head of Brier Creek," constituted in 1787. Of these two churches, Wm. Franklin was pastor of the former in 1788 and 1794, and of the latter Joseph Busson was pastor in 1790, and Isaac Bussey was pastor in 1794. The former may have been constituted in 1777, as stated by Mercer, on page 18 of his History of the Georgia Association. Head of Brier Creek church, of Burke county, is probably now Little Brier Creek, sometimes called Franklin's church, and was constituted by Wm. Franklin and Isaac Bussey, perhaps in 1777.

Dr. Adiel Sherwood, in his manuscript history of Georgia, called by Benedict, "Sherwood's Collection of Historical Papers," says : "We begin with the Georgia (Association). This was constituted in May, 1785, at the present location of Applington, Columbia county, then the site of the Kiokee church. Four or five churches united in the formation, and were, probably, Kiokee, Fishing Creek, Red's Creek (now Abilene), and perhaps Greenwood and Botsford. For several years there were two annual sessions one in May and one in October."

John Asplund, in his "Annual Register of the Baptist Denomination," published in July, 1791, says: "Georgia Association, Georgia—This Association began 1784. * * * * * They have two meetings yearly—the first on Saturday before the third Lord's day in May, and the second, the Saturday before the third Lord's day in October—and hold three days."

Asplund was in Georgia in 1790, and visited Abraham Marshall, from whom he obtained his information. Dr. David Benedict visited Georgia to gather materials for his history in 1810. He says, in a note to his "General History of the Baptist Denomination," in 1848 : "There is some difference of opinion between Mercer and Sherwood as to the date, (meaning 1784, and quoting from Mercers History of the Georgia Association), which I find thus given in my old work. I do not remember how this and some other facts were ascertained ; but am confident that they were communicated by Mr. Abraham Marshall, as I spent some time with him at his own house at Kiokee, in 1810, where his venerable father died. Mr. Asplund visited Mr. Marshall twenty years before, to whom he gave the same account as to date of this body, as appears by his Register for 1790."

Now let us see what Dr. Sherwood says, in his original manuscript history, which has been kindly placed in our possession by the American Baptist Historical Society, having been deposited with that Society by Dr. Benedict himself.*

"Rev. Jesse Mercer puts the date in 1784, in his History of the Georgia Association, and is guided by Asplund and Benedict. The first visited Abraham Marshall, to procure materials for his Register, about 1790 ; the last " |did so to gather| " materials for his History of the Baptists about 1811." |It was really in 1810.| "The reasons to be assigned are conclusive with the author that Mr. Marshall must have forgotten the date." |Dr. Sherwood now gives the following three reasons why he thinks the first session of the Georgia Association was held in May, 1785 :|

"1. In 1793 Mr. Marshall sends Dr. Rippon, of London, manuscript Minutes of the body for 1785-6-7-8 and 9.

"May 15th and 16th, 1785. This Association met at Kiokee, and consisted of only five churches."

"October 20th, 1787. Sixteen churches met at Greenwood. The increase was 600. 1,402 in all."

---

*NOTE.—These manuscripts were loaned to J. H. Campbell by Adiel Sherwood, and have been mostly preserved *verbatim* in his "Georgia Baptists," which fact should heighten our opinion of that very valuable work. Dr. Sherwood carries the history to 1835 or 1840.

"October, 1788, at Clark's Station—2,223 members.—*Rippon's Register.*"

"It would seem that if there had been a meeting prior to 1785, Mr. Mercer would also have given an account of it.

"2. On the 18th of May, 1785, Rev. Dr. Furman, then residing at Society Hill, South Carolina, writes Mr. Marshall, and this is an extract of his letter :

"'But I have not been able to learn whether any plan has been fallen upon, among you, for cultivating union and improvement among your churches.'

"'It appears to me desirable that all the churches in this State and Georgia should be united in Association.' He then invites Mr. Marshall to attend the Charleston Association next fall, and gives notice of the time and place of its session."

"If the Georgia Association had been formed in 1784, would Dr. Furman, who did not reside more than one hundred miles distant from Kiokee be ignorant of it up to May 1st, 1785?

In the Charleston Minutes for 1785 is this record:

"Rev. Silas Mercer and Peter Smith appeared as messengers from the Georgia Association, *lately formed*, and were cordially received."

"3. In December, 1837, the author had a conversation with the Rev. Samuel Cartledge, who was present at the formation of the Association, and the substance of his narration is as follows : He thought it was in the fall of the year, but remembers that a Remonstrance was agreed on, against an Act of the Legislature for the support of religion. An Act was passed at Savannah, February 21st, 1785, and is recorded in Manuscript Volume B., p. 284, in the Secretary of State's office, Milledgeville. Some of the features of the Act : "Thirty heads of families" might choose a minister "to explain and inculcate the duties of religion."

"Of the public tax paid into the treasury, four pence on every hundred pounds, valuation of property should be deducted and set apart for the support of religion. 'The mode of choosing the minister shall be by subscription of not less than thirty heads of families, which shall be certified by an assistant judge and two magistrates, on which the Governor shall give an order to the treasurer to pay out the money for the minister's support. All the different sects and denominations of the Christian religion shall have free and equal liberty and toleration in the exercise, etc.'"

"Among old papers in the Marshall family is a copy of a Remonstrance sent to the Legislature by the Association at its formation. It begins thus : 'To the honorable the Speaker and General Assembly of Georgia, the Remonstrance of the Baptist Association, met at Kiokee meeting-house, 16th May, 1785, showeth.'"

"This Remonstrance was carried to the next session of the Legislature by Silas Mercer and Peter Smith, and the act complained of was repealed.

"Mr. Cartledge remembers, too, that Alexander Scott was Moderator at this session, and that Mrs. Marshall, then a widow, grieved that her husband (as usual) was not in the chair; but Daniel Marshall died November 2d, 1784, and it is not likely that a session would have been held later in the season."

To all of this Dr. Benedict, in a foot note to the edition of his History, published in 1848, says justly: "Mr. Sherwood's arguments are plausible, and as there were no records to refer to, it would not be strange if Mr. Marshall was mistaken in a year. Again, as they [the Associations] met at first twice a year, and as old bodies, formed as this was, generally had preparatory meetings, and grew into an Association in an informal manner—*so it might have been in this case.* Under these circumstances it is not strange that there should be a discrepancy of a year in collecting materials so loosely thrown together."

Doubtless this passage conveys the real truth in the matter, and we may reasonably conclude, with Asplund, in his Register of 1790, that the Georgia Association "was begun" in October, 1784. by a preliminary or preparatory meeting, at which Daniel Marshall presided, and the Association was formed and named, but at which no regular business was transacted. On the 15th of the following May, the first regular meeting occurred, and Daniel Marshall having died meanwhile, Alexander Scott was elected Moderator.

As to Daniel Marshall, his son tells us that he attended public worship regularly until the last Sabbath but one before his dissolution on the second of November, 1784.

All this accords with Samuel Cartledge's recollection, that the Association was *formed* in the fall of the year, and yet, that its *first meeting* was after the passage of an Act of the Legislature against which the Association remonstrated; for the Act was passed in February, 1785, and the Remonstrance was adopted in May of that year. It should be remembered that a similar course was pursued by the Sarepta Association. The delegates from the eight churches dismissed by the Georgia met at Shoal Creek meeting-house, in Franklin county, in May, 1799, formed an Association and named it the Sarepta, and, in October of the same year, the Association held its first session, at Van's Creek meeting-house, Elbert county.

Dr. Sherwood expresses it as follows: "In May, 1799, the brethren met at Shoal Creek, Franklin, to confer about forming a new Association, having obtained letters of dismission of the Georgia, the preceding October. In the fall they met again, at Van's Creek, Elbert, and adopted the Constitution and Decorum of the Georgia, and sent messengers to the Georgia—Wm. Davis and G. Smith."

The Doctor himself appears to accept this conclusion as to the date, for he says, in the third edition of his "Gazetteer of Georgia," published at Washington city, in 1837: "Through the instrumentality of Mr. Marshall, and other ministers, the *Georgia Association* was constituted at Kiokee, at Columbia court-house, in 1784," making the number of churches five. In the interval between October, 1784, and May, 1785, it is not likely that Dr. Furman would hear of the preliminary meeting.

It should be borne in mind that until 1790 the Georgia Association met twice a year—in May and October. In May, 1785, it met at Kiokee, but where it met in October we now know not. In May, 1786, the body held its session at Fishing Creek, Wilkes county. It convened at Whatley's Mills (now Bethesda church), in May, 1787, and in October of the same year it assembled at Greenwood. It convened at Kiokee in May, 1788, and at Clark's Station in October. Long Creek entertained the convention in May, 1789, and Whatley's Mills in October. The session was at Botsford's (Brier Creek), in May, 1790, and at Abilene in October, 1790, when the Association adjourned to meet at Van's Creek, in October, 1791, abandoning semi-annual sessions.

A few extracts from the Diary of Rev. John Newton, the grandfather of Mr. John H. Newton, of Athens, and brother of sergeant Newton, of revolutionary notoriety, will show something of the spirit of the Association in that day. He was the pastor of Providence church, Jefferson county.

"*Saturday, May 19th, 1787.*—Started early (from Silas Mercer's), and got to the Association in good time. Brother Bussey preached—after him, brother Cook preached. Letters from the churches were read.

"*Sunday, May 20th, 1787.*—Sermons preached by Peter Smith, Jeremiah Walker and Abraham Marshall. Several others exhorted.

"*Monday, May 21st.*—The Association sat on business. Several ministers preached to the people in the woods; the power of God was present to heal. Brother Jeremiah Walker preached on baptism. Silas Mercer baptized brother Thomas. Lively times."

"*Tuesday, May 22d.*—After singing, praying and exhorting, we parted in peace and great love."

This meeting was held at Whatley's Mills (Bethesda).

"*Saturday, May 27th, 1788.*—I came to the Association (at Kiokee) and found many of the ministers here. Sanders Walker preached. Letters were given in from near twenty churches. Silas Mercer was chosen Moderator, and Jere Walker, clerk. All things done decently and in order.

"*Saturday, October 18th, 1788.*—We came to the meeting-house at Clark's Station. Vast multitudes gathered. Heard preaching. Read letters from the churches.

"*Sunday, October 19th.*—Heard several sermons.

"*Monday, October 20th.*—Went on business. Brother Hutchinson was received as a helper; several other ministers received as helpers. List of delegates called. *Query brought in:* What is Christian perfection? Answer God's children are perfectly justified before God, by the imputed righteousness of Christ, although they are imperfect in their sanctification."

"*Saturday, May 16th, 1789.*—Went to Association at Fowler's meeting-house (Long Creek). Brother Tinsley preached on "My grace is sufficient." Intermission. Large congregation.

"*Afternoon.*—Brother Cleveland preached. Brother Hutchinson gave an exhortation how God can love his people from eternity and yet condemn them in convictions. Election proved by one being struck under convictions and others left unconcerned as they were before."

"*Saturday, May 15th, 1790.*—Came down to the place of the Association, and found a large number of people.

"*Sunday, May 16th.*—Brother Matthews preached from 2d Corinthians, 6:20: 'Now then we are ambassadors for Christ.' Brother Holcombe's text, Psalm 126:3: 'The Lord hath done great things for us, whereof we are glad.' Brother Marshall's text: 'And this man shall be the peace when the Assyrian shall come into our land.' Brother Silas Mercer preached on brother Marshall's text.

"*Monday, May 17th, 1790.*—Letters from other Associations read. Appointed brethren Marshall, Mercer, Newton, Donald, Bussey and Sanders Walker, as a committee to prepare rules of Decorum, and present them at the next Association."

This, perhaps, refers to the articles of Faith and rules of Decorum adopted in 1791.

"*Monday, October 18th, 1790,*—Met early. Several ministers preached in the woods, at the stand. We sat on business and broke up before night, all in peace and love. Next Association to be on Saturday before third Sabbath in October, at Van's Creek."

Rev. John Newton came to Georgia from South Carolina, soon after the Revolution. Dr. B. Manly, Sr., in his history of the Charleston Baptist church, mentions him as a minister and a member of that church. He died soon after the session of the Georgia Association in 1790. The brother, John Cleveland, to whom he refers in the Diary, resided in South Carolina, but preached a great deal in Georgia.

In November of 1784, the spirit of the venerable Daniel Marshall took its flight to the realms of glory, but he had a worthy successor in his son Abraham, who fled to North Carolina with Silas Mercer, in 1777, and returned six years after. Among the other most noted ministers at that time was Alexander Scott, who must have been a very useful and efficient preacher, though deficient in education. He was Moderator of the Association in 1785. Afterwards he moved to South Carolina, becoming pastor of the Black Swamp church, and subsequently removed to Mississippi, of which State a son of his became governor. There was, also, Silas Mercer, who, about 1775, was baptized by Alexander Scott, uniting with the Kiokee church, by which he was licensed to preach. In fact, he began to preach immediately after his baptism, stepping from the water upon a log, whence he addressed the assembled multitude.

Born in North Carolina, February, 1745, he was raised an Episcopalian. After reaching manhood he experienced a saving change, but not until after he married and moved to Georgia did he became thoroughly convinced of the propriety of believer's baptism; then he was immersed. Before his death he was justly regarded as one of the most exemplary, useful and pious ministers of the Southern States. Yet he was not distinguished for literary attainments. He was, however, very zealous, and was instrumental in establishing several churches by his faithful labors. In him the lively Christian and able minister of the New Testament were happily united, and he should be classed among the fathers and founders of our ministers and churches.

Twenty-two Baptist churches in Wilkes county alone, were constituted and built up between the close of the war and the year 1790, mainly through the labors of Silas Mercer, assisted by Sanders Walker, John Millner, Sr., a licentiate and a powerful exhorter, Jeremiah Reeves, Sr., Matthew Talbot, William

Davis, Peter Smith, William Franklin and James Matthews. All of these, except, perhaps, John Millner, Sr., and Jeremiah Reeves, Sr., were pastors of churches in Wilkes county before 1790, and several of them were licentiates of Kiokee church. Among them Silas Mercer towered both as a preacher and a man of devotion, religious enterprise and indefatigable labors. He established an academy, which offspring of his benevolence, though presided over by James Armor, mouldered into non-existence soon after Silas Mercer's death, in 1796, for want of pecuniary support. The worthy founder of it, however, as such, and as a powerful preacher and advocate of the doctrines and ordinances of the Gospel, shall be embalmed in our memories and immortalized in our annals. Semple tells us that he seldom talked on any subject except religion; that in countenance and manners he had, considerably, the appearance of sternness; and that he was indefatigable in maintaining his opinions.

Sanders Walker, perhaps the first Baptist preacher ordained in Georgia, was one of the most useful ministers in that section of the State. Born in Virginia March 17th, 1740, he was, before conversion, of a turbulent and most unmanageable temper; but, after transforming grace did its work upon him, he was distinguished for the meekness and gravity of his deportment, and the *meek Sanders Walker* was the sobriquet applied to him. He began to preach in 1767, in South Carolina, but moved, first to North Carolina, and then, in 1772, to Georgia, where, as a licensed preacher, he united with the Kiokee church. His own ordination must have taken place anterior to May 20th, 1775, for on that day he and Daniel Marshall ordained Abraham Marshall. He labored mostly in Wilkes county, where he resided, and, in all likelihood, was mainly instrumental in the constitution of Fishing Creek church, in 1782 or '83, of which he was the pastor as late as 1790. In 1803 he was pastor of County Line church; and in 1805 he finished his course with joy, in the 65th year of his age.

Allusion has been made to Abraham Marshall, the son and successor of Daniel Marshall. It is a matter of great doubt if any of our religious sires who lived during and just subsequent to the Revolutionary war, are entitled to the exalted credit due to Abraham Marshall. Though an uneducated man, he acquired a surprising command of language. It is stated that he never enjoyed forty days of regular schooling in his life; for, born at Windsor, Connecticut, April 23d, 1748, he was a mere boy when his father moved with his family as a missionary to the Mohawk Indians, near the head of the Susquehanna river. He therefore had no opportunities for obaining an education, and used pleasantly to excuse his own want of cultivation by saying: "I was born a Yankee and raised a Mohawk." But he had religious training, real natural ability, eloquence, the most zealous earnestness, and genuine piety. He had decision of mind and strength of character, and his soul burned with love for sinners. For thirteen years in succession he went through the wilderness, in all directions, as an itinerant, preaching and spreading among the early settlers the good news of salvation by the Cross. His conversion took place about 1770, at the age of twenty-two, when his father lived in South Carolina. He united with the church, was baptized in the Savannah river, and immediately began to preach. In 1775 he was ordained at Kiokee church, but continued his itinerant labors with unabating zeal, even during his flight to North Carolina, until the death of his father, in 1784, when he assumed the pastorate of Kiokee church. Not even then did he discontinue altogether his itinerating labors, but during the whole course of his ministry, down to 1819, when his death occurred, he indulged in the work dear to his soul—itinerating; and his praise was emphatically in all the churches.

All through life his orderly deportment gave strong and conclusive testimony of his piety, and his unabating labors bore witness to his abounding zeal. In doctrine he was moderate and sound. In the church he was tender and submissive; in his family, soft and indulgent. He was a nursing father to young ministers and doubting Christians, and with solemn prayer and sweet words of encouragement ever comforted the sick and needy. For fifty years he preached faithfully, lived consistently and labored zealously; and when, at 4 o'clock, on the 15th of August, 1819, the summons, "Come up higher," was received, he

GROWTH AND ORGANIZATION.   33

said to the mourning and weeping friends and relatives at his bedside, "The time of my departure has come. I have fought a good fight; I have kept the faith; therefore there is laid up for me a crown of righteousness which my glorious Lord has prepared for me!" Then he gathered up his feet in his bed, like Jacob of old, and fell asleep in Jesus. Perhaps, more than any of our early Baptists, he was noted for his itinerant labors. The condition of the country required such labors, and he rendered them willingly and joyfully.

Thus it was that our Baptist fathers laid the foundation of our denomination in the State—by persevering, self-denying, self-sacrificing labors, almost disregardful of home-ties, certainly despising danger and fatigue, and unweariedly, incessantly, faithfully planting the cross in the dark places of the wilderness, with a zeal truly apostolic. Among them was James Matthews, Sr., whose history will bring into view again the old Botsford meeting-house, in Burke county. He was born in Virginia, October 15th, 1755, but raised in South Carolina, and experienced a hope through grace in his seventeenth year, when he was baptized, and united with the church on Little River. In 1782 he moved into Georgia and united with the Red's Creek (now Abilene) church, Columbia county, of which Loveless Savidge, the whilom sheriff who arrested Daniel Marshall, was pastor. Gaining the approbation of his brethren as a licentiate, he was called to ordination, and came under the imposition of hands by a presbytery composed of Loveless Savidge, D. Tinsley, Sanders Walker, and Abraham Marshall, in 1785. Filled with a fervid zeal in the Lord's service, and with an ardent love for the souls of men, he went forth as a missionary of the cross, and soon acquired general esteem. The first church which secured his services was on Brier Creek, in Burke county, and was the same founded by Edmund Botsford, in November, 1773. During the war it had dwindled away, and had nearly become extinct; but, under the ministry of James Matthews, it woke to new life and sprang into a vigorous existence, as the result of his labors. In less than one year seventy new converts were added to its membership by baptism. The good work spread out far and wide. Two other churches, Buckhead and Mobley's Pond, now Bethlehem, both in Burke county, were constituted, and the foundation was laid of a third, which was afterwards built up, now Rocky Creek, Burke county. For the benefit of his health, Mr. Matthews moved to Wilkes county, where he continued until his death, in 1828, preaching to various churches and baptizing many converts. He was a member of the first General Committee, in 1803, and so continued for a number of years.

All these, and many more devotedly pious, earnest-minded, laborious and self-sacrificing men, were the Baptist ministers who, previous to, during, and just subsequent to the Revolutionary war, by their extraordinary zeal and ability, laid the foundation of the Baptist denomination in Georgia. They were men who, regardless of pecuniary reward, and impelled by an ardent desire to warn others to flee from the wrath to come, preached wherever God gave them an opportunity to deliver the gospel message, whether in the rough settler's cabin, or in rude log meeting-houses, or beneath the spreading branches of the forest trees. The Holy Spirit's blessing accompanied their labors, hundreds were converted to God, and many Baptist churches were constituted in what was then a wilderness. In some respects it was worse than a wilderness, for the gospel was preached and churches were founded when men were compelled to carry guns to church and set sentries to watch during divine service, in order to protect themselves from predatory Indians. Even the plantations were cultivated in succession by armed squads of men, who posted sentinels to preserve themselves from surprise while so engaged. Frontier forts were built for the protection of the settlers, into which the women and children would be gathered while the men were banded together working the farms; and sometimes it happened that these forts would be attacked by the Indians during the absence of the men. Their repulse devolved upon the few brave and discreet men left for the purpose, assisted by the women, many of whom were good marksmen, and undaunted by danger. This state of affairs, owing to white encroachments on what the Creeks considered their lands, continued until the middle of the year 1796, when, after a formal treaty with Creek Indians near Muskogee, near the St. Mary's river, depredations which had prevailed on the frontier ceased; but the Federal power was requisite to enforce the State title to all the lands east of the Chattahoochee, which was effected after many years.

We have already seen how rapid was the increase of the denomination. At the session of the Georgia Association for 1794, which met at Powell's Creek meeting-house, near Powelton, on Saturday, the 19th of October, several churches moved, in their letters, for a division of the Association. There were, really, fifty-six churches in the Association, but four of them, with a total of 325 members, were South Carolina churches, which, about that time, obtained letters of dismissal, to join the Bethel Association, in that State.

The following was the action of the Georgia Association, in response to the letters requesting a division: "Agreed, that all the churches in the lower part of our union who see fit to form another meeting of this nature, have our consent; and that the one be called 'The Upper District Georgia Baptist Association,' and the other 'The Lower District Georgia Baptist Association.' The first meeting of the Lower District Association to be Saturday before the fourth Lord's day in September, at Buckhead Davis' meeting-house. The brethren, John Thomas, Jeptha Vining and Silas Mercer to attend as messengers. The meeting of the Upper District Association to be at the Kiokee new meeting-house, on Saturday before the third Lord's day in October, which Association is to hold the present constitution and records."

Silas Mercer was appointed to preach the Association sermon, and Saturday before the fith day in December was set apart as a day of fasting, humiliation and prayer.

The meeting appointed in September, 1795, took place; eighteen or twenty churches sent delegates, but, counting the South Carolina churches, twenty-two actually separated from the Georgia Association; but the name assumed by the new Association was *Hephzibah*, and delegates from its first session, in September, 1795, attended the meeting of the *Georgia*, in October of the same year, carrying their printed Minutes. See Mercer's History of the Georgia Baptist Association, page 34, which says that the Georgia Association contained thirty-two churches in 1795, of which two were newly constituted. In 1794 the Association contained fifty-six churches, of which four were in South Carolina. Twenty-two, then, must have withdrawn, among which was the colored church, at Savannah, which then contained 381 members, their pastor being Andrew Marshall. Eight other churches obtained letters of dismissal from the Georgia Association in 1798; and, in May, 1799, delegates sent by these churches met at Shoal Creek meeting-house, Franklin county, and formed a new Association, designated the Sarepta. This Association held its first session at Van's Creek meeting-house, Elbert county, in the same year. The next session was held in October, 1800, with Millstone church, Oglethorpe county, and letters from nine churches were read. Thomas Gilbert was elected Moderator, and William Davis, Clerk. Five other churches united with the Association, making nine in all, with a membership of 797.

Thus we have hastily traversed a period of more than half a century. We have discovered the introduction of Baptist sentiments into the State; have witnessed the foundation of the first Baptist churches; have watched the indefatigable and self-sacrificing labors of our pioneer Baptist fathers; have beheld the gradual influx of faithful laborers and the increase of Baptist churches; and now, at the close of the century, three flourishing Associations exist, while Baptists, by thousands, stretch from the Cherokee country on the north to the Atlantic on the south, occupying about one-third of the present territory of the State. We have seen the glorious sunshine of peace succeed the lurid gleams of war, and have beheld the desolation and destruction in the track of Bellona's car. We have obtained a partial view of old-time Baptist methods of procedure at our Associations; have learned by what labors and sacrifices our fathers laid the foundation of our denomination in Georgia; have had glimpses of the lives and characters of a few of the more prominent ones; have settled the foundation-period of the two first Associations formed in the State; and have reached the beginning of the new century, in which the Georgia Baptists, under new leaders and new methods and measures, enter upon a career of prosperity and usefulness, marred, nevertheless, by mistakes and dissensions superinduced by the infirmities incident to human nature.

V.
THE POWELTON CONFERENCES.
1800-1803.

V.

THE POWELTON CONFERENCES.

THE GENERAL ASPECT OF AFFAIRS—THE CONDITION PEACEABLE AND PROSPEROUS—BUT ZION LANGUISHING—THE FIRST STEP UPWARD—HENRY HOLCOMBE—JOSEPH CLAY—C. O. SCREVEN—JESSE MERCER—THE GRAND "DEPARTURE"—THE MEETING OF 1801—THE SECOND CONFERENCE IN 1802—THE REPORT ADOPTED—RESULTS—INCIDENT IN THE LIFE OF MERCER—SAVANNAH ASSOCIATION CONSTITUTED IN 1802—ITS ACTION IN REGARD TO THE POWELTON CONFERENCE—THE FIRST GENERAL COMMITTEE—ACTION OF THE COMMITTEE—THE RELIGIOUS CONDITION IN 1803—ORIGIN OF BAPTIST INTERESTS IN SAVANNAH—A CHURCH ORGANIZED IN 1800—THE ESTABLISHMENT OF COLORED BAPTIST CHURCHES IN SAVANNAH—AND A BRIEF ACCOUNT OF THEM.

We have now reached the beginning of a new century. New men are coming on the stage of action, and new measures begin to excite attention. Hitherto the period has been a formative one ; henceforth a period of growth and progress occurs. A class of ministers equally pious and zealous, and in some respects more cultivated, are stepping upon the scene.

A brief view of the denominational labors of the day, and of the general aspect of affairs, as well as of the political "situation," will enable us to advance more intelligently upon our historical journey.

Louisiana and Florida, ceded to France by Spain October 1st, 1800, have been purchased from France by the United States, for about $16,000,000. On the 20th of December, 1803, General Wilkinson, and a large body of emigrants, took formal possession of New Orleans. Georgia's claim to all the land between the Chattahoochee and Mississippi rivers, obtained by treaty with the Indians at Augusta, in November, 1763, had been sold to the United States, in 1802, for one and a quarter million dollars, the general government guaranteeing to Georgia a title from the Indians to all lands in the State east of the Chattahoochee, and especially of the lands lying between the Oconee and Ocmulgee rivers.

On the 16th day of May, 1795, Louisville, in Jefferson county, became the capital, and so continued until 1804. The State Constitution was revised in 1799, by a Convention of which Jesse Mercer had been elected a member, and in which he took a prominent part. The section on religious liberty was written by him.

By a treaty with the Indians, in 1796, the United States had put an end to Indian depredations in Georgia, and in 1800 the population of the State was double what it had been in 1790. In the beginning of the new century, she continued to extend her population by laying off and steadily but quietly settling new counties. Towns and villages sprang up in the wilderness. In 1803 the county of Baldwin was laid off, and a site for the town of Milledgeville was selected by commissioners appointed by the Legislature, with a view of making it the capital of the State, as soon as the proper buildings could be erected. These were completed in 1807, in which year Milledgeville became the seat of government. Thus, at the beginning of the century, the general domestic condition of Georgia was peaceable and prosperous.

While the dying century beheld the State and its material interests advancing prosperously, it witnessed a discouraging condition in the spiritual interests of the country, and of our denomination in the State. Several of our most able and active ministers were removed by death, and by their loss others were unnerved for designs of extensive usefulness. With few exceptions, the harps of surviving colleagues hung neglected on the willows. Learning drooped, religion appeared in mourning, and viperous infidelity, with elevated head, menaced Christianity with venomous fangs. These unpropitious circumstances exerted a chilling influence throughout all our churches. The interests of Zion languished and appeared "ready to die." This was the more humiliating to intelligent Baptists, as they enjoyed no means of securing an active and sympathetic co-operation, by the denomination, in any design intended to promote the interests of religion, learning or benevolence, and therefore they appeared insignificant or contemptible to opponents.

At this juncture a step was taken which resulted in that denominational sympathy and co-operation which summoned into action the best talent of our denomination in the State, and which, by uniting the energies and benevolent tendencies of the brotherhood, has called into being our Convention, with all its educational and benevolent enterprises, and has elevated our denomination to the proud position it now occupies. This step was the appointment by the Georgia Association, in October, 1800, of a meeting to be held at Powelton, May 1st, 1801, to confer as to the best means of reviving the religious interests of the churches. In the concoction of the scheme an intelligent observer cannot but discern the pious benevolence of Jesse Mercer, although it may be that Dr. Henry Holcombe, of Savannah, was connected with the movement in some way. He had been a resident of our State for one year only, but had already caused the constitution of a white Baptist church in Savannah, and it is not to be doubted that he longed to see the energies of our growing denomination aroused and combined ; and when events gradually matured, his powerful and cultivated mind made him a leader and organizer, a master-spirit among first-class men.

Dr. Henry Holcombe was an extraordinary man. Born in Virginia in 1762, he became a cavalry officer in the revolutionary war before he was of age ; and, converted at twenty-two, he preached his first sermon to his own command, while seated upon his horse. Raised a Presbyterian, he was led to adopt Baptist principles by investigating Scripture; and when convinced of the propriety of immersion, he rode twenty miles on horseback to propose himself as a candidate for immersion to a Baptist church. He was the means of the conversion of his own wife and her brother and mother, baptizing all of them, as well as his own father, who renounced Pedobaptist sentiments. He was a member of the South Carolina convention which approved the constitution of the United States ; and, while pastor of the Euhaw Baptist church, South Carolina, and residing at Beaufort, was called to Savannah. He was a man of commanding personal appearance, of unusual intellectual powers and of grand eloquence. Mainly self-taught he attained a high degree of culture, and though he resided in the State about twelve years only, he left his impress on it ineffaceably. The penitentiary system of Georgia was of his suggestion. He was the originator of the " Savannah Female Asylum." He published the first religious magazine in the South, a periodical called *The Analytical Repository ;* and with it he did much to arouse the dormant energies of Georgia Baptists and unite their efforts in great benevolent enterprises. The academy established at Mount Enon, in Richmond county, was a child of his brain, and as long as he remained in the State, it flourished. A strong advocate of missions and of education, he gave them the benefit of his powerful pen and eloquent voice, and as a member, and, for a time, as president of the " General Committee " and board of trustees for Mount Enon College, he wielded great influence and labored, with astonishing vigor and capacity, for the Baptist cause during the first decade of the century. Undoubtedly he stood *primus inter pares*.

Another noble mind developed by the exigencies of the time, and sent by God to help usher in the dawn of a brighter day for the Baptists of Georgia, was Hon. Joseph Clay, a man who stood pre-eminently distinguished for his talents, virtues and piety. He was the son of Colonel Joseph Clay of the revolutionary army, who, as a " Son of Liberty," was on the committee which drew

THE POWELTON CONFERENCES. 39

up the resolutions relating to the grievances of which the Colonies complained in 1774, and who was a member of the Council of Safety, in 1775, and a member of the Continental Congress from 1778 to 1780, besides filling many other important offices. Converted under the ministrations of Dr. Holcombe, Joseph Clay, Jr., renounced Episcopalianism and became a Baptist. At the time of his conversion he was District Judge of the United States for the District of Georgia, but nobly yielding to what he conceived to be the voice of duty, he exchanged the judiciary bench, in 1802, for a name and a place in our communion as a minister of the gospel. He was a leading member of the convention which formed the revised constitution of 1798, and the original draught was carefully prepared by him. Liberally educated, he was graduated at Princeton with the highest honors of his class. He was a most persuasive orator, a refined gentleman and an humble Christian. A native Georgian, he was born in Savannah, August 16th, 1764; was baptized and licensed to preach in 1802, and ordained in 1804, by Dr. Furman, Dr. Holcombe and Rev. Joseph B. Cook, pastors of the Charleston, Savannah and Beaufort Baptist churches. After that time he travelled and preached in different parts of the United States, in the employ of the General Committee, and, in September, 1806, was invited to succeed Dr. Stillman as pastor of the First Baptist church of Boston. He accepted, so far as to consent to spend one year with the church, and was installed August 3d, 1807. In November, 1808, agreeably to his engagement, he sailed for Savannah, expecting to return in the spring; but finding his health seriously declining, he obtained a dismissal from his pastoral charge in October, 1809, and did not return to Boston until December, 1810. On the 11th of January, 1811, he expired, after a long and tedious illness, in the 47th year of his age. The following in regard to him, from the pen of Dr. Henry Holcombe, was written at Savannah, in 1806, to Rev. Dr. Baldwin, of Boston:

"From early life he was distinguished by genius, docility and great amiableness of disposition and behavior. In morals, learning and politeness, he has always been distinguished among the most moral, learned and polite of his acquaintance. As a son, a brother, a husband, a parent, a master, a neighbor, a citizen and a friend, he is spoken of in this State in the most respectful terms. For acuteness of research, undeviating rectitude and manly eloquence, he has been much celebrated by his best informed acquaintance, in the capacities of a lawyer and a judge. As a gentleman of property, he is nobly distinguished for his liberality to the poor, and by the aid he gives to various benevolent institutions. And, as a Christian, and a minister of the blessed Jesus, whom he supremely loves, his praise is in all the Southern churches. Should you permit me to speak freely of Mr. Clay, after the pleasure and the honor of four or five years intimate acquaintance with him, I would say I believe him to be one of the greatest and best men I ever knew; but, in saying this, I would by no means be understood to intimate that I think myself able to form an accurate judgment of all the excellencies I believe him to possess."

Hon. John M. Berrien writes as follows of him: "His disposition was peculiarly amiable, and he was distinguished by a warm and active benevolence. These, combined with his social qualities, made him an object of universal affection and respect in the community in which he lived. If any one in that commuuity had been requested to point to a man of blameless conduct, *he* would have been designated."

Another man of polished mind and pious heart, who recruited the Baptist ranks in the first decade of the century, was Charles O. Screven, D.D., son of General James Screven, who was killed in Liberty during the revolutionary war. Born in 1774, he united, at twelve, with the Charleston Baptist church, of which his grandfather, Rev. Wm. Screven, was the founder and first pastor, in 1683. Rev. C. O. Screven was educated at Brown University, Rhode Island, where he graduated; and being licensed by the Charleston church, he visited Sunbury, Georgia, and began to preach in 1801, founding a Baptist church there. He was ordained by Dr. Furman, Mr. Clay and Mr. Botsford, in Savannah, on the 29th of May, 1804. Although a most cultivated Baptist minister and a polished Christian gentleman, he preached mostly to negroes, and was instrumental in turning many, both white and black, from darkness to light. He, too, aided in promoting the revival of religion which occurred in the first years of the century, and was the first president of Mount Enon Academy.

Major Thomas Polhill, who had served with reputation as a senator in the General Assembly, son of Nathaniel Polhill already alluded to among the early Baptists of Savannah, was, also, a distinguished member of that galaxy which shone so conspicuously at the time of which we write. He was born January 12th, 1760; was converted in 1789; and ordained by Dr. Holcombe and Rev. John Goldwire, on the 9th of December, 1805, renouncing his prospects of military and political fame, that he might devote himself to the duties of the sanctuary.

Prominent, also, among the workers, in the beginning of the century, were Abraham Marshall and Jesse Mercer. The latter, son of Silas Mercer, was born in North Carolina, December 16th, 1769, converted at fifteen and ordained in his twentieth year, by his father and Sanders Walker. Without doubt the most distinguished and influential Baptist minister ever reared in the State, his life and labors were so interwoven with the history of our denomination, that it is almost impossible to chronicle events of importance, for at least half a century, without connecting his name with them. No other man has exerted a greater or better influence upon the Baptist interests of Georgia. No one has labored more for their advancement or been more liberal in promoting them. Distinguished for meekness, piety, benevolence and wisdom, he was, also, a powerful preacher, though not a man of thorough education or high cultivation. His long-continued and indefatigable labors, his steadfast devotion to Baptist principles, his staunch piety and usefulness, and his great liberality, have embalmed his memory in the hearts and minds of Georgia Baptists. As we progress in our history his name and actions will be the subject of constant reference, obviating the necessity of a longer personal mention of him here.

We have now noted the most prominent actors among the historical characters of the Georgia Baptists, who moved in the drama enacted in the first decade of the nineteenth century, and put in train events which moulded the destinies of our denomination in the State. The names of others might be given, as John Harvey, John Robertson, Joseph Baker, Henry Hand, George Granberry, R. E. McGinty, John Ross, Edmund Talbot, Miller Bledsoe, George Franklin, William Franklin, Norvell Robertson and John Stanford.

These all lamented the languishing state of religion, and the want of co-operation, and earnestly desired to enter upon some course by which unity of action in spreading the gospel and carrying forward benevolent enterprises would be secured. Their minds were reaching out for some method of useful unison of effort.

It was just at this time, in the year 1800, and under these circumstances, that the Georgia Association, which met with the church at Sardis, Wilkes county, twelve miles northwest of Washington, in October, adopted the following resolutions, evidently the composition of Jesse Mercer:

· "That, as a spirit of itineracy has inflamed the minds of several ministers, who are desirous to enter into some resolutions suitable to carry into effect a design of travelling and preaching the gospel, a meeting be, and is hereby, appointed at Powel's Creek, on Friday before the first Sunday in May next, for that purpose.

"That the same day be observed as a day of fasting and solemn prayer to Almighty God for prosperity in the design, and for a dispensation of every new covenant mercy in Christ Jesus."

In his life of Jesse Mercer, page 153, Dr. C. D. Mallary says: "This proposition, which we shall soon see resulted in some important measures, originated with Mr. Mercer;" and Dr. Sherwood, in his manuscripts, from which frequent extracts will be made, writes as follows; "Mr. Mercer was connected with all the great religious movements of his age. The conferences at Powelton, 1801, 1802, 1803 were originated by him and Governor Rabun, and these ripened into the General Committee, a body from members of each Association then in the State, the object of which was to promote itinerant preaching and a school among the Creek Indians, then occupying the western part of the State—most of the lands on the west side of the Oconee."

This grand "departure" of our denomination was the first exhibition of a spirit and tendency which finally resulted in the constitution of the Georgia Baptist Convention twenty-two years later, and the establishment of Mercer University, and of all that harmony, unity of effort and co-operative benevolence which have given Georgia Baptists such a proud position in denominational annals. Attention is called to the latter of these resolutions. Those who delve into the early records of our denomination in Georgia will be struck by the frequency with which days of fasting, humiliation and prayer were appointed and observed by our fathers. Perhaps the zealous spirit and holy earnestness evolved by these devout observances, accompanied by divine blessing, were the real cause of the success of their ministry, and of the rapid growth of our denomination.

The meeting appointed was held at Powelton, May 1st, 1801, and several days were pleasantly and profitably spent in forming liberal and judicious designs for usefulness. Among those present were Jesse Mercer, John Robertson, Edmund Talbot, Adam Jones, John Harvey, Joseph Baker and Francis Ross. Other leading characters were present, among whom we may reckon Abraham Marshall and Henry Holcombe. The principal objects discussed were the formation of a missionary society to support two missionaries among the Creek Indians on the frontier, and itinerant preaching throughout the State. The results of the consultation were drawn up in the form of a letter addressed to the Georgia Association, calling the attention of the Association to the propriety and expediency of forming a missionary society in this State for the purpose of sending the gospel among the Indians on the frontiers.

Before adjourning, the ministering brethren generally were recommended to engage, as far as they possibly could, without unfaithfulness to existing obligations, in itinerant labors; and those present entered into an agreement to the same effect. An appointment for a similar meeting, at Powelton, was made for the year 1802.

The letter was received and cordially and unanimously approved by the Georgia Association at its session in October, 1801, and delegates were again appointed to the Powelton meeting for 1802, to devise and mature proper plans for carrying out the suggestions of the first meeting, and to revive and extend the influence of true religion.

This second conference met at Powelton on Thursday, the 29th of April, 1802, sixteen messengers from the different Associations being present on the first day, whose names are, Joseph Baker, Joel Willis, George Granberry, John Ross, Henry Hand, Edmund Talbot, Jesse Mercer, Francis Ross, John Robertson, John Harvey, Adam Jones, Benjamin Thompson, Miller Bledsoe, William Lord, William Maddox and Benjamin Maddox. The sermon was preached by Joseph Baker. John Harvey was unanimously elected Moderator, and Joseph Graybill, Clerk.

Reports from individual brethren, in regard to their different tours through the State, as itinerating preachers of the gospel, showed encouraging results, and it was

"*Resolved*, That it is the decided opinion of this Conference that the religious interests for which they are immediately concerned, begin already to assume an encouraging aspect, under the influence of the partial execution of their lately adopted measures."

And it was furthermore

"*Resolved*, That we feel ourselves bound to give itinerate preaching, for the ensuing year, all the aid and encouragement in our power."

On Saturday, May 1st, the committee met, and, after singing and prayer, the subject of union among Christians of different denominations was proposed for discussion by Jesse Mercer; and, "from the different impressive lights in which it was placed, appeared to excite a general and ardent desire to use every endeavor to hasten the time when the watchmen in Israel shall see eye to eye, and all the real disciples in Christ be one, as He and His divine Father are one." Then, on motion of Dr. Henry Holcombe, who had arrived from Savannah, a committee was appointed to concert a plan of promoting union and communion among all real Christians, to be respectfully submitted to the consideration of the Georgia Baptists that, should it be approved, they may concur in its adoption." Joseph Baker, Jesse Mercer and Henry Holcombe were nominated members of this committee, and on the third day, Saturday, they rendered a report.

They reported "that they are humbly of the opinion that the number and present situation of the Baptists of this State require a stricter and more intimate union among themselves. in order the most effectually to concentrate their powers for any particular purpose ; that they conceive this more eligible state of the churches might be effected by a choice of delegates to represent each church, annually, in the Association to which they respectively belong, vested with power to elect three members from each Association, to compose a General Committee of the Georgia Baptists, which should meet annually in some convenient and, as nearly as possible, central part of the State, with liberty to confer and correspond with individuals and societies of other denominations, for the laudable purpose of strengthening and contracting the bonds of a general union, on the pure principles of eternal truth, until all who breathe the spirit and bear the image of the meek and affectionate Jesus, shall enforce a strict discipline, and sit together at His table; and that the time and place for the first meeting of this committee, should it be eventually formed, shall be fixed on by the Association that shall meet last, conformably to existing appointments."

This report was agreed to and adopted unanimously; and then, after agreeing to meet again on the Friday before the first Lord's day in May, 1803, further to mature their designs of usefulness, and particularly to form, if possible. a Missionary Society, the Conference adjourned, with many demonstrations of brotherly love.

A result of this, as of the previous meeting, was a vast amount of itinerating labor. Our ministers traversed the whole State, two and two, preaching with unwonted power and earnestness, and carried out fully, in spirit and in reality, the resolution adopted concerning "itinerate preaching." An incident in the life of Jesse Mercer during that year. 1802, will not only illustrate the spirit which animated our ministers, but will demonstrate the nature of their labors, and show the results of their zeal and earnestness. Mr. Mercer had, for a fortnight, been on a preaching tour, and had spent most of the time in a revival. On his return he attended the regular meeting at his church at Whatley's Mill, now called Bethesda church. Aware that the church was in a languid state, his sermon was on the deceitfulness of the heart in crying, *Peace, peace, when there is no peace.*

He became deeply affected at the end of his discourse, and addressed his congregation as follows: "Dear brethren and friends, I have been, for a great part of the last two weeks, addressing a people that I believe are truly awakened to a sense of their lost, helpless and ruined state, and are crying out in their agony, *What shall we do to be saved?* Among them my tongue seemed to be loosed, and I could point them with great freedom to the way of salvation through a crucified Saviour. On my way hither I felt the deepest concern in contrasting your lifeless condition with theirs. I even bedewed the pommel of my saddle with tears," and here lifting up his hands he exclaimed, "O, my congregation, I fear you are *too good* to be saved!" And he burst into an irrepressible flood of tears. Descending from the pulpit and recovering himself a little, he poured forth a most solemn and impassioned exhortation, during which many came forward and asked for prayer in their behalf. From that sermon and occasion one of the most interesting revivals which has ever blessed that favored church commenced, and forty-nine were added to the church by baptism before the expiration of the year. During the same year thirty-eight were added to Phillips' Mill church, by baptism, as the result of a pleasant revival. Of this church, also, Mr. Mercer was pastor. Sardis church, likewise under the charge of Mr. Mercer, reported to the Georgia Association, in October, 1802, the addition by baptism of thirty-three new members; and Powelton church, of which he was pastor, reported to the Association twenty-nine added by baptism. Nearly all the churches in the Georgia Association reported considerable gains that year—for instance, Salem, Oglethorpe county, 26; Freeman's Creek, Clarke county, 56;

Lower Beaverdam, Greene county, 28; Rocky Spring, Lincoln county, 31; Big Creek, Oglethorpe county, 88; County Line, Wilkes county, 23; the colored church in Augusta, 220. The conclusion is, that there must have been a considerable revival resulting, we may justly presume, from the itinerary labors advised by the Powelton meetings; for 732 were reported as the whole number baptized in the Georgia Association.

The churches of the Sarepta Association reported, in 1801, 388 converts baptized; in 1802, 1,050 baptized. Evidently religion had greatly revived, owing to the blessing of God on the faithful dissemination of evangelical doctrines, in accordance with the measures adopted in the first Powelton Conference.

The proceedings of the second Powelton meeting were approved by the Georgia Association of 1802, and Abraham Marshall, Sanders Walker and Jesse Mercer were appointed to attend the third meeting, in May, 1803, as three regular delegates from the Association, to aid in consummating the plan proposed by the meeting of May, 1802.

The Savannah Association, which met at Savannah in January, 1803, appointed Henry Holcombe, Aaron Tison and Thomas Polhill, delegates to this first Baptist Convention of Georgia. That Association had been constituted at Savannah on the 3d of April 1802, by representatives from the Newington church (white), the Savannah (white) church and the First (colored) church of Savannah. Its action with reference to the Powelton meeting of 1802 may be learned from the following, which is a report rendered by Alexander Scott, chairman of a special committee, which was unanimously adopted: "If to aim at the most important end subordinate to the glory of God, namely, 'the complete union of His people;' if to aim at this end, on the most pure and liberal principles—'the principles of eternal truth;' in fine, if to aim at an excellent end, on excellent principles, by excellent means, be *laudable*, the plan your committee have strictly investigated—the plan recommended to your serious attention by the ministers, in conference, last May, at Powelton—is laudable in a very high degree, and claims your warmest patronage."

This report, which appears in the Minutes of the Savannah Association for 1803, was unanimously adopted, and preceded the election of the brethren just mentioned, to represent the body in the General Committee of that year, James Sweat being appointed to fill the place of either, in case of failure on their part to attend.

On the 29th of April, 1803, therefore, the third yearly Baptist conference was held at Powelton, Hancock county. Twenty-four ordained Baptist ministers were present, besides a large number of the brethren and of citizens. Henry Holcombe was elected Moderator and Jesse Mercer, Clerk.

At the opening of the session it was found that the following Baptist ministers were present: Francis Ross, John Ross, Miller Bledsoe, Henry Cunningham (colored), from Savannah, Charles Goss, Stephen Gafford, William Green, Henry Holcombe, John Harvey, James Heflin, William Lord, William Lovell, Abraham Marshall, Benjamin Mattox, James Matthews, Jesse Mercer, Robert McGinty, William Mattox, Benjamin Thornton, Edmund Talbot, Joel Willis and Sanders Walker. Two others appeared afterwards; for in his Circular Letter in the Minutes of the meeting of the committee for 1806, Dr. Henry Holcombe says: "There were present twenty-four of our ordained ministers, with incalculable numbers of their brethren and fellow citizens. Thus had a little one, the almost immediate offspring of our pious fathers, according to the prophecy, become a thousand; and a handful of corn sown by them with tears, on the top of a mountain, waved in a golden and copious harvest."

That was a proud day for the Baptists present. Glorious old Powelton, the nursery of Georgia Baptist enterprise, beheld a grand concourse that day, when the Baptists of Georgia were first united in heart and endeavor; and yet a greater and more glorious day, still, dawned upon the famous village, when on the 27th of April, 1822, the Georgia Baptist Convention was formed there. That Convention, however, was but the immediate successor, on more acceptable principles, of the General Committee, created on this April 30th, 1803—just nineteen years previous.

At that time there seems to have been a general revival of religion in both England and America, and the missionary spirit was considerably heightened. God was doing glorious things everywhere. It was natural, therefore, for the day to be consumed in hearing accounts of the progress of religion, and of the prosperity of the churches, and of the doors open for missionary effort ; and in discussing the plan to unite the Baptists of Georgia more closely, and to promote union among all Christians. On the next morning, April 30th, 1803, a committee of twelve, with the title of *The General Committee of Georgia Baptists*, was chosen. In the afternoon of the same day, this committee held its first meeting, the conference having dissolved in the morning. The following named members of the committee took their seats, and elected Abraham Marshall chairman, and Henry Holcombe, secretary : *Francis Ross, John Ross, Miller Bledsoe, William Green, Henry Holcombe, Abraham Marshall, James Matthews, Jesse Mercer, Robert McGinty, Edmund Talbot and Sanders Walker.*

The first action was the adoption of the following :

"*Resolved*, That the encouragement of itinerant preaching, the religious instruction of our savage neighbors, and the increase of union among all real Christians, which were the leading objects of the late conference, shall be zealously prosecuted by this committee."

As the result of the discussions of May 1st, it was resolved that the committee be rendered permanent by annual delegations from the Georgia Associations, or otherwise; that it not only encourage itinerant preaching, but, individually, practice it, as far as was consistent with indispensable duties; and that, whenever circumstances will justify the attempt, an English school be established among the Creek Indians, as the *germ of a mission*. The following day a Circular Address to the Baptist Associations, and to all gospel ministers of any other denominations in the State, was adopted, and the time and place of the next meeting were appointed, viz: Fourth of May, 1804, at Kiokee.

This " conference " might be called the first regularly appointed Baptist Convention ever held in Georgia. Delegates were appointed to it by two of the four Baptist Associations in the State, though there were ministers there from all four of the Associations. The Hephzibah and Sarepta failed to appoint delegates. It established a method of co-operation which never received the hearty endorsement of Georgia Baptists, and which expired after about seven years of existence; yet it did considerable good during its brief career. One cannot but regard its establishment as providential, for it set in operation agencies that awoke the denomination in Georgia from a lethargic state, and aroused a general revival spirit. We have, already seen how that spirit was evidenced in 1802, by the figures exhibited. Other figures show that the itinerant system inaugurated by these devout and self-abnegating fathers, was attended by the divine blessing, and wrought wonders.

The number reported as baptized, in the year 1803, in the *Savannah* Association, was 378; in the *Sarepta*, 375; and in the *Georgia*, 689. The records of the Hephzibah Association, for that period, being lost, its additions are not known.

To the Minutes of the Georgia Association, for 1803, which appear not to have been printed until 1804, Jesse Mercer, the Clerk, appended the following :

" Doubtless there is a glorious revival of the religion of Jesus. The wicked of every description, have been despoiled of their boasted coat of mail ; even deists, who stood in the front of the battle, have had their right arm broken, their hope disappointed, and their prognostications metamorphosed into falsehood. As the fruit of this work there have been added to the churches of the Georgia Association, more than 1,400 ; to those of the Sarepta, more than 1,000, a year ago, and we doubt not but that number has greatly increased by this time. [Actually 375 had been added to the Sarepta during 1803; while, for the years 1801, 1802 and 1803, there were added to the churches of the Sarepta Association 1,813, by baptism.] To those of Bethel (a South Carolina Association), more than 2,000. There is and continues a great work in some of the churches of the Hephzibah and Savannah (Associations), and is kindling in others. More than a hundred have been added to one church in the Charleston

Association. We are authorized to say that, in six Associations in Kentucky, there are at least 10,000 young converts. To all which we add that other accounts from different and distant parts, verbally received, state that the Lord is doing excellent things in the earth."

Perhaps this is the proper place to introduce a few short sketches of some of the prominent actors on the stage of our denominational history at that time, of whom the reader may naturally be curious to obtain some information.

Rev. John Harvey was a very distinguished and useful minister in his day, and was President of the Powelton Conference in 1802, being at that time a member of the Powelton church. He seems to have been greatly respected and to have occupied a very prominent position, and to have been extensively useful. Rev. John Robertson was a man of very high character, of liberal disposition and a devout Christian. He began to preach in Wilkes county, but moved to Putnam and became a member of the Tirzah church. He was Moderator of the Shoal Creek Convention and of the Ocmulgee Association, and occupied other prominent positions, among them the first vice-presidency of the Ocmulgee Mission Society. In his fidelity the brethren had the utmost confidence. Lazarus Battle was a pious and distinguished layman, treasurer of the Mission Board of the Ocmulgee Association, a member of the Executive Committee, a man of uncommon wisdom in council as well as energy in action, both as a Christian and a citizen.

In the year 1824 the Ocmulgee Association adopted the following report concerning the death of Rev. John Harvey, Rev. John Robertson and Lazarus Battle:

"In the death of these three distinguished persons, society has sustained no common loss—a loss irreparable to the church, to the settlements in which they lived, and through the whole circle of their acquaintance; deeply felt by their families and friends, and by the community in general. To speak of all their virtues, (were we capable,) would far transcend the limits of this work and our present design. Suffice it to say, their upright lives bore testimony to the truth of the religion they professed, and they left satisfactory evidences that they are the happy sharers of the blessed fruit thereof. Brother Harvey spent a long life in the faithful ministry of the word of life. The same may be said of brother Robertson, who was late Moderator of this Association. And brother Battle was not only a useful member of society as a faithful Christian, but eminently so as a citizen. He was treasurer to the Mission Board, and his public spirit was indefatigable."

Rev. Robert McGinty was a man of high standing and good influence; polite and easy in his manners; pious in character; strongly missionary in spirit; an excellent Moderator and a sound, sensible preacher. He was one of those who helped to form the General Committee, at Powelton, in 1803, and was a member of the Committee. He was Moderator of the Ocmulgee Association, President of the Ocmulgee Missionary Society, and for years the Moderator of the Flint River Association. Raised in Wilkes county, he was baptized at the same time and place with Jesse Mercer, in 1787, and was ordained prior to 1799.

Rev. Edmund Talbot was highly respected and a man of great piety and usefulness. In all the records he is spoken of most respectfully, as a man of high character and undeviating rectitude. Born in Virginia, March 28th, 1767, he came to Georgia from South Carolina at twenty, and was baptized by Sanders Walker at twenty-two. He was son-in-law of Rev. John Harvey, President of the second Powelton Conference, and, while greatly fond of itinerant labors, he was a most excellent and successful pastor. He, too, was a member of the first General Committee, and aided in the attempt to establish a Georgia Baptist college at Mount Enon. He was a Moderator of the Ocmulgee Association, and a vice-president (and acting president) of the Ocmulgee Missionary Society. His influence was always on the side of missions and education, and opposed to what was erroneous and hypocritical; not learned, but plain and straightforward. In person he was tall and slender, and he lived to see our State Convention a quarter of a century old.

Rev. Joseph Baker, who assisted in the Powelton Conference of 1802, was from the Hephzibah Association, and was from North Carolina, having settled in Washington county in 1794. where he was called to ordination and served the Bethlehem church. He afterwards moved to Baldwin county, and was pastor of Fishing Creek church until his death in 1820. Few men of his day were as highly esteemed as he was, and very few so useful.

Rev. Miller Bledsoe, who assisted at the Powelton Conference of 1802, was a Virginian, born October 7th, 1761, and had been a valiant revolutionary soldier. Converted in 1788, he soon began to preach, and was ordained in 1792. He emigrated to Georgia in 1793, and settled in Oglethorpe county, where he preached and labored faithfully as the contemporary and co-laborer of Silas Mercer. He was a good and useful man, and lived to be nearly eighty years of age.

Rev. George Franklin, another Virginian, was a very prominent and useful man in Georgia at the period of which we write. He was for fifteen years Moderator of the Hephzibah Association, and was a valued member of the General Committee. He represented Washington county in the Legislature of the State, and was a member of the State Convention which revised the Constitution in 1788. He was born in Virginia about 1744, but moved to Carolina, where he married Miss Vashti Mercer, an aunt of Jesse Mercer, and a half sister of Silas Mercer, and moved with the Mercer family to Georgia in 1774. He was ordained at Little Brier Creek church, in 1789, by his father, Rev. Wm. Franklin, Rev. Silas Mercer and Rev. John Newton, Silas Mercer preaching the ordination sermon. He doubtless assisted in organizing the Hephzibah Association, in the Minutes of which Association, for the year 1816, may be found this entry: "In consequence of the death of our venerable and beloved brother, George Franklin, whose loss the Association is sensibly affected with, and by reason of which the Association is disappointed in the Circular Letter to have been prepared by him for the present session—after a short deliberation agreed, on motion, that a committee be appointed to prepare one, previous to the adjournment of the Association, and that the following brethren be that committee, viz: F. Boykin, C. J. Jenkins, N. Robertson." George Franklin was a good man, and a good preacher, and was, beyond doubt, one of the most pious, useful and talented ministers in Georgia. The records show that both he and his father, Rev. William Franklin, ranked as such in their day. The latter died suddenly in the streets of Louisville, some suspicion being excited at the time that he was murdered.

The Circular Letter alluded to above, was written by Francis Boykin, and the subject was, "What are the probable causes of the present languishing state of religion?" It is a plain, straight-forward, Scriptural document, adducing three causes for spiritual declension: 1. Neglect of the public services of religion. 2. Covetousness. 3. Neglect of the discipline in the churches required by God's word. This Francis Boykin, the grandfather of S. Boykin and T. C. Boykin, now living, was born in Virginia, and was of Welsh descent, being descended from Edward Boykin, who settled in Isle of Wight county, Virginia, in 1685. His father, William Boykin, emigrated from Southampton county, Virginia, to South Carolina, in 1755 or '56 and settled at Kershaw. He was a captain of cavalry in the Revolution, and participated in the battle of Fort Moultrie, and in most of the State during the Revolutionary war, and rose to be a Major in a regiment of infantry. He was a man of fine personal appearance, and was said to be, when in uniform, one of the handsomest men in the army. His wife was Catharine Whitaker. He moved to Georgia in 1800, settled in what is now Baldwin county, died in 1821, and his remains rest on the plantation of S. E. Whitaker, Esq., ten miles from Milledgeville. He was a prominent member of the Hephzibah and Ocmulgee Associations, and was occasionally appointed a delegate to the Georgia Association and to write circular letters. A son of his, James Boykin, was among the founders of the Columbus church, of which he was for years a beloved deacon, and was also among the few who donated an amount larger than $1,000 to Mercer University.

Let us now glance at the formal establishment of a Baptist interest in Savannah. In the year 1794 there were eight or ten Baptists, only, in the city. They determined, however, to erect a house of worship, the prime movers and chief agents being Jonathan Clark, George Mosse, Thomas Polhill and David Adams. There seems to have been some kind of church formation as early as 1795, for in that year the city conveyed to the church a lot, the petition for which was drawn by Robert Bolton, in behalf of the church. With one or two exceptions, the Baptists were poor in purse, and it was only by the generous contributions of friends in South Carolina, and of persons of different denominations in the city, that they were enabled to erect, in 1795, a house of worship, on Franklin Square, fifty by sixty feet in size. This was done under the superintendence of Ebenezer Hills, John Millen, Thomas Polhill, John Hamilton, Thomas Harrison, and John H. Roberds, trustees. Having no Baptist minister, and the house being in an unfinished state, it was, in 1796, leased to the Presbyterians, who had just lost their church edifice by fire. They furnished the building with pews and a pulpit and occupied it for three years. In 1799, while the house was still under lease to the Presbyterians, Rev. Henry Holcombe, of Beaufort, South Carolina, who was pastor of the Euhaw church, received and accepted a call from the pewholders of in the building, consisting of persons of different denominations, to preach and act as pastor to the congregation, with a salary of two thousand dollars. He entered upon his labors in 1799, preaching to large and respectable congregations, with unwonted power and eloquence. Under his ministrations, the interests of religion among the different denominations increased; for, beside the Episcopal building, this was the only house of worship in the city, and religion was in a languishing state. If any sort of church organization had existed, it seems to have expired, for early in the year 1800, twelve Baptists entered into a written agreement to apply for letters of dismissal from other churches and constitute themselves into a church at Savannah. Their names were Henry Holcombe and his wife, Frances Holcombe, George Mosse, Phebe Mosse, Joseph Hawthorn, Mary Hawthorn, Elias Robert, Mary Robert, Rachel Hamilton, Esther McKinzie, Elizabeth Stanley, and Martha Stephens. Of these, two came from each of the following churches: Charleston, South Carolina, Black Swamp, South Carolina, Sandy Hill, South Carolina, while six were furnished by the Euhaw church, also in South Carolina. On the 17th of April the house of worship was dedicated; on the 11th of September the first baptism occurred, Dr. Holcombe baptizing the venerable Mrs. Mary Jones, relict of Lieutenant-Governor Jones, in the Savannah river; on the 26th of November, 1800, the church was fully constituted, with a membership of fourteen, two, Mrs. Mary Jones and Mrs. Eunice Hogg, having been received into fellowship. Rev. John Goldwire, pastor of the Newington church, Georgia, preached on the occasion; and Rev. Alexander Scott, pastor of Black Swamp church, South Carolina, made the prayer, and delivered a solemn and pathetic charge and exhortation. The duties and privileges of the day closed with the administration of the Lord's supper, which was repeated on the third Sunday in April, 1801, to twenty communicants. In the same year a charter of incorporation, executed by John McPherson Berrien, and signed by Governor Josiah Tatnall, was granted. On the 25th of January, 1802, the church presented a written call to Dr. Henry Holcombe, who replied, accepting, on the 24th of March. In the summer the Presbyterians withdrew to their new and spacious house of worship, and the Baptists occupied their own building, the membership increasing to sixty-seven by the end of the year, and to seventy-seven at the beginning of 1804.

Thus we see that the first church was established in the city of Savannah, mainly through the instrumentality of Henry Holcombe, in the year 1800, a dozen only composing the nucleus of the church.

This appears to be a suitable place in which to introduce an account of the establishment of colored Baptist churches in the city of Savannah.

About two years before the Revolutionary war a colored man, and a slave, by the name of George Leile, was converted in Burke county, by the preaching of Rev. Matthew Moore, a Baptist minister. Baptized by Mr. Moore, George Leile was licensed to preach by the church of which Moore was pastor, and his labors were attended with success among the people of his own color. About the beginning of the Revolutionary war George Leile, who had been liberated by his master, Mr. Henry Sharp, went to Savannah and began to preach at Bramton and Yamacraw, near the city, and also on the surrounding plantations. At the close of the war, when the British evacuated Savannah, George Leile, who was, also, sometimes called George Sharp, accompanied them to Kingston, Jamaica, where he soon raised up a large church. Before leaving for Jamaica he baptized Andrew and his wife Hannah, and Hagar, slaves of Jonathan Bryan, and Kate, who belonged to Mrs. Eunice Hogg. Nine months afterwards Andrew, commonly called Andrew Bryan, began to preach at Yamacraw, and many converts were the result. Although persecuted by wicked and cruel white people, who thus sought to interrupt their worship and put a stop to their religious meetings under a pretence that they were plotting mischief and insurrection, they were sustained by Chief Justices Henry Osburne, James Habersham and David Montague, Esquires, after an examination. Permission to worship in the day was given them. A barn, for a house of worship, was granted them at Bramton, by Jonathan Bryan, the master of Andrew and his brother Samson. A number of respectable and influential people befriended them, and, by *well-doing* they at length disarmed and silenced their bitterest persecutors. Andrew learned to read, and for two years preached to great numbers without interruption, in his master's barn, although neither licensed nor ordained; and converts began to increase. Their condition, as being destitute of any one qualified to administer the ordinances, became known at a distance, and they were visited by Rev. Thomas Burton, an aged Baptist minister, who baptized eighteen converts. In 1788, Rev. Abraham Marshall, of Kiokee church, visited them, in company with Jesse Peter, a young colored minister of Augusta, baptized forty-five more, and on the 20th of January organized them into a church, and ordained Andrew Bryan to the ministry, as their pastor. Thus was Andrew Bryan fully authorized to preach and administer the ordinances, and his church, at length, properly organized. Permission was granted them to build a large house of worship, in the suburbs of Savannah.

Their humble virtues and orderly lives gained for them public esteem, and banished all fears and suspicions in regard to their conduct and motives. The number of church members, at first eighty, increased rapidly, and several gifted men arose among them. In the course of time it became advisable to organize two other churches with members from the mother church, and on the 26th of December, 1802, the *Second* colored Baptist church, of Savannah, was constituted with two hundred members. A third, called the *Ogeechee* colored Baptist church, was constituted on the 2d of January, 1803, with two hundred and fifty members. Two new colored ministers were also ordained: Henry Cunningham, on the 1st of January, 1803, and Henry Francis on the 23d of May, 1802—the former to become pastor of the Second church, and the latter of the Ogeechee. Notwithstanding this diminution of numbers, the First church still contained four hundred members.

In April, 1802, the First colored church united with the white church of Savannah, and the Newington church, twenty miles north of Savannah, in the formation of the Savannah Association; and in January, 1803, we find all three of these colored churches and the two white churches enrolled as constituent members of the Association. The membership of the Savannah white church was sixty-seven; that of Newington church was seventeen; while the combined membership of the three colored churches was eight hundred and fifty.

Andrew Bryan died on the 12th of October, 1812.

In 1812 this Association adopted the following: "The Association is sensibly affected by the death of the *Rev. Andrew Bryan*, a man of color, and pastor of the First colored church in Savannah. This son of Africa, after suffering inexpressible persecutions in the cause of his divine Master, was at length permitted to discharge the duties of the ministry among his colored friends in peace and quiet, hundreds of whom, through his instrumentality, were brought to a knowledge of the truth as it is in Jesus. He closed his extensively useful and amazingly luminous course, in the lively exercise of faith, and in the joyful hope of a happy immortality."

About ninety years of age when he died, his remains were interred with peculiar marks of respect. During his funeral services, remarks were made in honor of his memory at the meeting-house, by Dr. Kollock, Presbyterian and Dr. Wm. B. Johnson, Baptist, and at the grave by Rev. Thomas T. Williams.

Such was the end of the man who, an ignorant slave, was imprisoned and inhumanly whipped for preaching the gospel, just after the Revolutionary war, and who, while suffering the lash, said to his persecutors, holding up his hands in emphasis, "I rejoice not only to be whipped, but would freely suffer death for the cause of Christ."

He left an estate valued at $3,000. His nephew, Andrew Marshall, a slave, was his successor, and carried forward his work with great power and prosperity until his death, in 1856, when he was worthily succeeded by William J. Campbell, who died, after a long life of consecration and usefulness, on the 16th of October, 1880, greatly lamented and esteemed, especially by the white people. Perhaps it may have struck the reader as an irregularity on the part of Abraham Marshall to ordain a minister and constitute a church by himself. Speaking on the subject to Doctor Benedict, the historian, he said, "There I was alone, and no other minister was within call. A church, which has become large and flourishing, was suffering for the want of organization and administrators. All things were ripe. It was something I found necessary to be done, and I did it, and all worked well." In the year 1790 the First colored church of Savannah, still doubtful as to its own organization, sent a letter to the Georgia Association asking an expression of opinion on the matter. The Association replied that it was an extraordinary case, and therefore warranted extraordinary means; and decided that, under the circumstances, the action of Rev. Abraham Marshall was proper. The eminently beneficial results which followed prove that such was indeed the case.

In this chapter we have witnessed the beginning of a new era in the denomination in Georgia. We may call it the era of co-operation. The languishing state of our Zion called for some special effort on the part of good men, and the result was the Powelton Conference of 1801, which was followed by very beneficial results. A general system of itinerating was inaugurated, which prevailed for many years in our Associations, ministers going out, two and two, and preaching the gospel in destitute neighborhoods, and to churches too poor to sustain a regular pastor. The Powelton Conferences brought into public view the best, most able and cultivated men of our denomination, and put them in active co-operation, in pursuance of plans for the promotion of personal religion and education, and for reforming and evangelizing the Indians in Alabama. It was very evident to discerning minds that the condition and prospects of the denomination in our State, lethargic and without unity of either aim or effort, was in the highest degree discouraging. Although there were three or four Associations, they possessed no common object of attainment, nor did any one of them have any special grand object in view. The old leaders were passing off the stage of action, leaving the churches in a state of semi-paralysis; while the new leaders and prominent men lived far apart, and many of them were barely acquainted with each other. The Baptists of Georgia were like an army with comparatively efficient captains, but lacking in organization and generalship. Religion was at a low ebb, and education was in a still lower state; nor was there any immediate prospect of the denomination being elevated, educationally. Yet, without it, how could we hope ever to become respectable in the eyes of the world, and maintain our denominational position creditably? This was the problem to be solved; and it called forth the prayers of the devout and the cogitations of the serious. Mutual consultation and deliberation, as well as unity of aim and effort, became not only proper but necessary; and the Powelton Conferences were the result of a general understanding. We are yet to see what eventuated.

A view of some of the more prominent men of that day has been given to exhibit their general animus and capabilities.

The reader will be surprised at the interest manifested in religion by the Baptist colored people of Savannah and Augusta, exceeding as it did the interest among the whites. In both of those cities, from an early date, large Baptist churches of the colored people have existed.

VI.
FIRST EFFORTS AT CO-OPERATION.
1803-1810.

VI.

FIRST EFFORTS AT CO-OPERATION.

THE GENERAL COMMITTEE ORGANIZED FOR WORK—FIRST CIRCULAR ADDRESS—REMARKS CONCERNING THE GENERAL COMMITTEE—FIRST STEPS TOWARD ESTABLISHING A SCHOOL AMONG THE INDIANS AND A BAPTIST COLLEGE—A CHARTER REFUSED BY THE LEGISLATURE—JESSE MERCER'S CIRCULAR ADDRESS DEFENDING THE COMMITTEE—MOUNT ENON ADOPTED AS A SITE FOR THE PROPOSED COLLEGE—INCORPORATION STILL UNATTAINABLE—THE GENERAL COMMITTEE MERGED INTO A PERMANENT BOARD OF TRUSTEES—REASONS WHY THE CHARTER WAS REFUSED—BUT THE "TRUSTEES OF MOUNT ENON ACADEMY" INCORPORATED—AN ACADEMY ESTABLISHED, WHICH FLOURISHED A FEW YEARS ONLY.

We will now resume our consideration of more general affairs, and direct our attention to the formation and first proceedings of the General Committee. Its organization and first meeting occurred at Powelton, Hancock county, on the 30th of April, 1803. In the morning the committee of twelve was elected by the Convention, which was then styled "Conference," after which "the 'Conference' was dissolved," and never again assembled. In the afternoon, at three o'clock, the committee assembled and organized by the election of Abraham Marshall as chairman, and Henry Holcombe as secretary, and adopted the resolutions given in the last chapter. The sessions of the committee continued during the days of May the first and second, and it adjourned to meet at Kiokee on Saturday before the first Sunday in May, 1804, after adopting the following Circular Address, evidently from the pen of Dr. Henry Holcombe:

"*The General Committee of Georgia Baptists, held at Powelton, the first of May, 1803, to the Baptist Associations, and all Gospel ministers, not of their order, within this State, wish the "unity of the Spirit in the bond of peace:*

"RESPECTED FRIENDS—We have the satisfaction to inform you that one of the distinguishing traits of our present meeting has been unprecedented harmony. An appearance of coolness and misunderstanding, which had palsied our measures, has vanished before the light of candid investigation. The sense of our churches, on the subject of a general union among themselves, has been carefully collected from a number of their ministers, deacons and other intelligent characters; and we have seriously considered what general line of conduct is proper to be pursued by us towards good men who are not in our connection. The *results* we have the honor to lay before you, in hope of your approbation and concurrence.

" In the first place, therefore, we take the liberty to address ourselves to the Associations:

"*Beloved in the Lord:* We are happy to learn that the failure, by two of your number, in choosing delegates to form a General Committee, agreeably to the plan recommended by our second Conference, must be ascribed to the want of that complete information relative to the necessity and object of the measure, which we hasten to communicate. In doing this, it is necessary to remind you that a little more than three years ago our common interests as Christians were languishing and seemed almost ready to expire. There were, indeed, individuals who bore an honest testimony to the truth, and a few well-disciplined churches; but in a general view, you will readily recollect, our situation was discouraging in the extreme. Several of our most able and active ministers had just been removed from time; others, as to any designs of extensive usefulness, were unnerved by the consequential shock; learning drooped, religion appeared in mourning and was daily menaced by crested infidelity. All this was published in *Gath;* and to add to our humiliation, possessing no means of co-operating in any design, we were unnoticed or viewed with contempt by the common enemy.

"Many solitary individuals, unknown to each other, lamented this situation of affairs; but who could step forward, not only at the risk of a mortifying disappointment, but of *censure,* to propose any measure for the general good? All being equal, this was no one's duty in *particular*, and yet, it must be acknowledged, it was the duty of every one who possessed the requisite abilities. Under these circumstances, a meeting of ministers, and other active friends of religion, was proposed and happily effected at Powelton, on the 1st of May, 1801, to confer on the best means of reviving the interests of the churches. At this memorable Conference, zeal rekindled and formed the pious determination of propagating the gospel by itinerant preaching, not merely throughout the State, but, if possible, among the neighboring savages.

"A twelve-month afterward, agreeable to appointment, a second Conference at the same place, by concerting a plan of *general union*, evinced the utility of the first, and led to the third, which, as you have seen, has terminated in this Committee, as a *bond of union, centre of intelligence, and advisory council* to the Baptists of this State. The *necessity* that existed for such an issue of our deliberations, it is humbly presumed, will be obvious to every intelligent and impartial person; and the leading object of this Committee is to advance your general interests by drawing your lights to a focus and giving unity, consistency and, consequently, energy and effect to your exertions in the cause of God. With a steady view to an object so desirable and important, we trust that converted individuals, unconnected with any religious society, and of our denominational sentiments, will join themselves to our churches; that the churches will punctually support their representatives in the Associations; and that these venerable bodies will appear, *by three delegates from each, at the time and place appointed for the meeting of this Committee.* In that case, the seats which we have the honor to fill, as the Committee of the late Conference, we shall most cheerfully resign to your delegates; but so essential to the Baptist interests in this State do we deem the General Committee, that, should there be a deficiency in your representation, we are bound, as appears by our Minutes, to supply it by the method which may appear most eligible. But we have no doubt of your forming the Committee by your own delegates, except it should be prevented by an interposition of divine providence.

"Such are at once the simplicity and magnitude of the object in contemplation, that we think it unnecessary to add a syllable more—especially as the utility of our late arrangements *tending to it* is so honorably attested by the addition of thousands to your enlightened bodies.

"We proceed, most respectfully, to solicit the attention of all gospel ministers, *not of our order*, in this State.

"REVEREND BRETHREN—We are assured by revelation, and have the happiness to *feel*, that all who love our Lord Jesus Christ in sincerity, make but one family. If of this description, our Father, our elder Brother, and the Spirit that is given us, are the same; and the same our hopes, our fears, our desires, our aversions, our sorrows and our pleasures. Whenever we act like aliens towards each other, it is because we are disguised by our imperfections, or misrepresented by our adversaries.

"Impressed with these sentiments, we shall be happy to see you all, or any of you, at our next meeting, that we may enjoy the opportunity, in our public capacity, of evincing to you and to the world our sincere disposition and earnest desire to cultivate and maintain friendship and fellowship, not only with you, but with all the true followers of Jesus Christ, of your respective denominations.

FIRST EFFORTS AT CO-OPERATION.

"You have repeatedly done us the honor publicly to invite us to your sacramental tables, and, though, in our view, there were serious objections* to our acceptance of your liberal, and, we doubt not, affectionate invitations, we prayed that all the disciples of our common Lord might be one, even as He and the Father are one. To this prayer we are cordially willing to add, in conjunction with you, our best endeavors to remove every obstacle to our communion at that board which, we trust, will be succeeded by an infinitely richer banquet in our Father's house.

"With the greatest respect and affection, we invite you, Reverend Brethren, to an investigation, in order to a scriptural adjustment of the comparatively small points in which we differ, and remain your, the Associations', and the public's unworthy servants in the gospel.

ABRAHAM MARSHALL, *Chairman.*
HENRY HOLCOMBE, *Secretary.*"

It will be recollected that the three objects set before themselves for accomplishment by the General Committee were: 1. The encouragement of itinerant preaching; 2. A mission among the Indians; 3. The increase of union among all real Christians.

This last object, in a Baptist organization was, doubtless, a mistake. It cast a cloud over this entire movement, and, although the General Committee scheme lasted perhaps seven years, and did some good, it was never cordially adopted by the denomination, and was dissolved about the year 1810. Jesse Mercer was compelled to defend the committee, and to answer the objections and fears entertained by many that it was intended to prepare the way for open communion; and we find in the Minutes of the Georgia Association for 1805 this significant entry: "The Minutes and Circular Address of the General Committee were read, and, as many serious apprehensions were entertained by many well-disposed persons, that *evil* might result from the continuance of the committee, the subject was again discussed; and, after a fair, deliberate investigation, was carried in favor."

It will be seen, however, that the *union* plank of the platform is dropped; that mission enterprise is allowed to languish; and that the establishment of a college, which could not be incorporated, became the sole engrossing subject of consideration and object of effort. It does not surprise us, therefore, to discover that the denomination gives the cold shoulder to the General Committee, becomes indifferent to an election of delegates, and allows it gradually to go out of existence. The plan itself was not adapted to the genius of our denomination; nor were the objects proposed those most likely to rally the support and enthusiasm of our churches. They never expect to capture Pedobaptist denominations by a *coup d'etat.*

The second meeting of the General Committee took place at Kiokee, on the 4th of May, 1804, and was composed of the following brethren: Sanders Walker, Abraham Marshall, James Matthews, Jesse Mercer, George Granberry, John Ross, Miller Bledsoe, Henry Holcombe, Joseph Clay, Edmund Talbot, Thomas Rhodes, —— Moreton.

Sanders Walker was chosen President, and Jesse Mercer, Secretary. Two Episcopal and two Methodist ministers were present, and were invited to seats; but "the committee perceived with regret that no official attention had been paid to their circular address on *Christian Union.*" They resolved, notwithstanding, "to continue their sincere endeavors to promote it, by all means consistent with the rights of conscience and a plain declaration of the whole revealed counsel of God." We find no further action taken on this subject, however, nor any direct allusion to it, in the subject proceedings of the committee; their attention becoming almost wholly engrossed in the foundation of Mt. Enon College, the inception of which was due almost entirely to Dr. Holcombe.

At the second session Rev. Joseph Clay, of Savannah, was appointed to com-

---

*For instance: No general consultation, by our denominations respectively, had been held on the propriety or impropriety of a mixed communion; nor did any discipline exist among us to prevent members excommunicated by *one* from being received by *another* denomination, to meet, in a new connection, their aggrieved brethren at the Lord's table.

municate with Colonel Hawkins, United States agent among the Creek Indians, for information regarding the best method of establishing an English school in the Creek Nation. It was also unanimously resolved to take immediate measures for establishing a literary institution to be denominated, *The Baptist College of Georgia,*, and a committee of five was appointed to apply to the Legislature for a charter for the incorporation of the General Committee under the title of "The Trustees of the Baptist College of Georgia," and to determine upon a proper location for the college. Their names were Abraham Marshall, George Granberry, Henry Holcombe, Joseph Clay and ——— Moreton. The Circular Letter is an able document, entirely devoted to the "Importance of Education," and prepared. not by Jesse Mercer, as Mallary says, but by ——— Moreton, of the Sarepta Association. The session of the General Committee for 1805, took place at Bark Camp, in Burke county, in May. The following named delegates appeared: From the Hephzibah Association—George Franklin, ——— Ross and V. A. Tharpe; from the Georgia Association—Abraham Marshall, Jesse Mercer and W. D. Lane; from the Savannah Association—Henry Holcombe, Thomas Polhill and Joseph Clay. The Sarepta Association being unrepresented, the committee, agreeably to one of its rules, supplied the deficiency by the appointment of Edmund Talbot, Joel Willis and ——— Scarborough. Henry Holcombe was elected chairman, and Joseph Clay, secretary.

Abraham Marshall, as chairman of the committee appointed to petition the Legislature for a charter of incorporation for a Baptist college, reported to this session of the General Committee, that they had petitioned the Legislature for incorporation, but without success; that there is reason to believe "that this failure is owing entirely to causes which may be removed by proper explanations." Nevertheless, it was "*resolved unanimously*, that the committee would persevere in their efforts to establish a college or seminary of learning for the education of youth of every denomination, though they should never obtain the slightest legislative aid. Hoping, however, that the denial of their reasonable and rightful request of a charter of incorporation has been owing to causes which are removable, and knowing that there are advantages in the possession of such an Act, which the Legislature has been accustomed to grant, we trust that their liberality will not permit them, after the opportunity of mature deliberation, to withhold from us so just a privilege, and for a purpose so universally beneficial."

Brethren Abraham Marshall, Jesse Mercer, Joseph Clay, D. W. Lane and Thomas Polhill, were then appointed a committee to receive subscriptions, select a site and obtain a charter for the college, or seminary, and Joseph Clay was appointed treasurer.

Joseph Clay read a letter from Colonel Hawkins, United States agent among the Creek Indians, in which he expressed approbation of the desire of the committee to establish a school for the instruction of the Indians in the Creek Nation, and affirming his determination to aid them should they realize their design; "intimating his intention to give his opinion, after a convention of the chiefs, of the proper *time when* and *place where*, the school should be established." Of course the committee deemed it best to defer further action, relative to this subject, till their next meeting.

In regard to itinerant preaching, several members of the committee having expressed their sense of the benefits which have accrued and would result from it, "and of the propriety of some of their body being successively engaged in this service, as they might feel themselves disposed and at liberty, the brethren Mercer and Clay proposed, themselves, to make a tour through the greater part of the State, in the ensuing fall." Their proposition was approved.

After agreeing to meet at Clark's Station, in Wilkes county, on Saturday before the third Sunday in May, 1806, the committee adjourned.

The Circular Address issued by the General Committee at this meeting, in 1805, was written by Jesse Mercer, and is erroneously referred to on page 16 of Campbell's "Georgia Baptists," as being a circular of the "Georgia Association."*

* NOTE.—In the original manuscripts of Dr. Sherwood, the words, "of the Georgia Association," do not appear, and were inserted, perhaps, to afford what was deemed necessary information.

It was intended to exculpate the committee from blame, in the eyes of the denomination, on points which the attentive reader will admit gave some ground for apprehension in the minds of the membership at large. As the document affords the best defence ever offered, it is given entire, as a matter of historical interest, not that it is supposed for a moment, that the staunch Baptists who composed that committee ever actually contemplated open communion. The first proposition to discuss "union and communion," in 1802, was undoubtedly a mistake; and the appointment of a committee to "concert a plan of promoting union and communion among all real Christians," in an *organization* in which it was proposed to secure the general co-operation of the Georgia Baptists, was another, and greater, mistake.

The Circular is here given :

"The General Committee of Georgia Baptists, in session at Bark Camp, in Burke county, to the Baptist Associations in this State severally, present sentiments of respect—greeting :

"DEAR BRETHREN—Since our earliest existence, in our present capacity, we have been reproached of ill design. And, it being believed that the things which we held up to the public attention as the objects of our pursuit were not the only ones which we had in view, multiform and irrational have been the conjectures of the credulous. To attend to the evil surmisings of ignorance and ill will, would be as unnecessary as impossible; suffice it to notice a few which may be rather termed the *fears* than the *opinions* of the more thinking part of those who have indulged these vagaries of imagination.

"It has been feared that we were about to form a *precipitate* communion with other religious denominations, which (it is doubted) would be in itself improper, and in its consequences mischievous to all true religion. Though to commune at the Lord's table with all the truly gracious is desirable in the extreme ; and though it is the duty of all ministers to exert themselves to lead all the followers of the meek and lowly Jesus in *the unity* of the Spirit and *the bonds of peace*, yet it should seem that this duty must be discharged with a truly pious and inflexible regard to the purity, sufficiency and unity of the gospel. That no unrighteous compact be formed, *directly* or *indirectly*, with unbelievers, or the Sons of Belial, that violence be practiced on no ordinance or doctrine of God's holy Word, and, that proper measures should be adopted and pursued till all the churches of the saints be freed from all those superstitious innovations, human traditions and vile hypocrisies which have been so long the disgrace of their solemn Assemblies, and still are the baneful sources of that unhappy difference which now wards off the desired communion. *This done*, and communion will instantly follow in beautiful, sweet and desirable succession; but *this not done*, and we are obliged to think that it would be undesirable and destructive.

"But it has been insinuated that we were aiming to establish our religion by law. This suggestion, though made by some possessing marks of respectability, we are constrained to view the most unreasonable, foreign and absurd. He who takes but a superficial view of this subject, will readily see that to seek such an establishment is to declare, in direct terms, the weakness and insufficiency of the religion so to be established ; or (in other words) that its supports are incompetent, and inferior to that coercion extended in such establishment. Consequently, such a measure adopted by the Baptists would set them in direct opposition to their openly avowed, most sacred and distinguishing principles of faith ; and also cast the most undeserved contempt upon that temper and disposition of mind which so long without variation or abatement, distinguished them as the zealous advocates of Civil and Religious Liberty. When things are placed in this light, it is evident that, except we could dishonor ourselves, *despose* the church, *subvert* religion and *desert* the divine will, we cannot have any clandestine views in contemplation.

"Lastly : It has been thought we are adopting measures to establish in our church—in particular—a learned ministry. It should, and we hope, will be acknowledged, that learning is indispensable in *some*, and may be useful in *every* degree ; and therefore not an evil in itself considered. But a slight attention to this subject will show that the evils deplored are the wretched offspring of the abuse and not the possession of literary abilities; and that these abilities owe their origin to certain circumstances which have operated therewith. When licentious and unbridled passions accompany learning in the ministry, and devotion is united with gross ignorance in the people, it may be suspected that intrigues of philosophy, and vain deceit, innovation and perversion, with a view to filthy lucre, will generally obtain.

"Many of the Popish clergy viewed ignorance in their people so favorable to their lucrative establishments that they taught that it was the *mother of devotion;* at which an enlightened mind would start with abhorrence, and pronounce it the *nurse of superstition,* and every abomination. It therefore follows, that if these circumstances could be detached, learning would immediately shine forth in its native lustre and intrinsic worth, tending to the better state of society in general. To that part of this work which belongs to the divine agency, we make no pretensions; but so far as learning will tend to the removal of ignorance, prejudice and presumption, so far it is ours, and should be attended to with promptitude and perseverance. *This is our design*, to accomplish which we have adopted certain measures, which we are pursuing ourselves and recommending to others.

"The proposed college is not, therefore, designed for the education of our children *with a view to the ministry*, nor is this seat of learning one in which young men already in the ministry *shall*, but *may be* further taught in some proper degree. But it is to be viewed as a civil institution to be religiously guarded and conducted for the better education of the rising generation, and to promote the general and common interests of morality and religion.

"To do good, as we have opportunity, is a sacred injunction. That this good should be done in relation to the following as well as the present generation, is equally certain. That we have it in our power to do good, in no way, to greater advantage than by establishing some lasting source of knowledge and moral virtue, is a certain truth. To hand down to the next generation a number of young men both moral and sensible, must not fail to awaken the warmest desires and provoke the best endeavors of all well-disposed parents. Herein, then, we erect an altar on which, not only ourselves, but all others, may offer the sacrifice of well-doing with which (saith the Word) God is well pleased. To this, dear brethren, we exhort you, not as having dominion over you, but that you may have fruit, which may abound to your account. By perusing our Minutes you will see the nature and spirit of our proceedings, and be able to judge of our designs more fully. We pray the divine blessing to rest upon you in your family, church and associational connections, and subscribe ourselves yours in bonds of the dearest relation.

"H. HOLCOMBE, *Chairman.*
"JOSEPH CLAY, *Secretary.*"

The regular Annual Meeting of the General Committee for 1806 was held at Clark's Station, May 17th, 18th and 19th, and the Minutes present us with a knowledge of the virtual demise of the committee, and its assumption of a state of existence tantamount to that of a permanent *Board of Trustees* for Mt. Enon College.

The special committee appointed for the purpose had determined to adopt Mt. Enon as a site for the college, and this determination was ratified in the meeting at Clark's Mills. The holder of Mt. Enon, Dr. Henry Holcombe, offered it, embracing 202 acres, to the committee without reservation, agreeing himself to give $100 for two acres for a building lot, and exhibiting papers which showed that $2,500 were engaged by worthy persons for lots, in case his donation was accepted. Committees were appointed to procure titles to the Mount, in behalf of the committee, to survey and lay it out in lots, and to prepare a constitution and by-laws for the body, as trustees of the college, to be presented at the next session.

Jesse Mercer, chairman of the second committee, appointed to solicit a charter, reported that appearances of success as to obtaining a charter were so unfavorable that nothing had been attempted.

FIRST EFFORTS AT CO-OPERATION.

The following extract from the Minutes explains the cause of some of the opposition to granting a charter to the college: "On being informed that a number of respectable characters had objected to the institution in view, from its being styled *The Baptist College of Georgia*, as seeming to savor of party spirit, the committee, superior to *party consideration*, unattached to *names*, and desirous of removing occasion of offence, when, as in this instance, it may be *innocently* done, resolved unanimously to call it *Mount Enon College*. The committee also determined, as soon as possible, to appoint two agents—one to preach on the western frontier of the State and visit the Creek Nation with reference to the establishment of a school as the germ of a mission there; and the other to make a preaching tour throughout the United States to solicit funds to aid in establishing Mount Enon College."

Then, in order the more effectually to execute their designs, they formed a *permanent body* of brethren Benjamin Brooks, Joseph Clay, Lewis C. Davis, Stephen Gafford, Henry Holcombe, Abraham Marshall, James Matthews, Jesse Mercer, Benjamin Moseley, Thomas Polhill, Thomas Rhodes, and Charles O. Screven. The nature of the change thus effected in the body is explained thus in the Circular Letter adopted, and apparently the indication is that the Associations were indifferent, if not actually suspicious of, or hostile to, the committee: "Instead of receiving a delegation from our associate bodies, in addition to our appointment by your Conference, we resume our original standing, as exclusively your committee, to fill up vacancies which may happen among us, by our own suffrages. We shall have nothing to do with our Associations, *as such*, in future; but, as a bond of union, a centre of intelligence, and an advisory council to the Baptists of this State, *as Baptists*, shall encourage itinerant preaching, the instruction of savages, and the increase of civility, affection and fellowship among all real Christians.

"The change, of which this is the nature, has been made, *partly* because the Associations were not unanimous in sending delegates to our body, and *partly* because, as trustees of the college, which, as subordinate and subservient to the grand objects of our appointment, we have resolved to establish, the more permanency we possess, individually as well as collectively, the weightier will be our responsibility, and, of course, the more shall we be entitled to confidence."

The reader may be curious in reference to the reasons why a charter was not granted to the proposed college. The main reason was, apprehension of a successful rival to the State educational institution—Franklin College—which went into operation in 1801. Another, and strong reason, was, that as it was proposed to call the new institution a *Baptist college*, it would, of course, teach Baptist doctrines only, and rear up and educate such numbers of Baptists that other interests would be imperilled. It was supposed, for instance, that if the Baptists became directors of a college, their numbers and influence would become dangerous to the liberties of the State; and it was even insinuated in the public prints of the day that the Baptists were the leading denomination in Georgia, and that if they obtained a charter for a college, with a celebrated writer at their head, the treasury would be in an alarming condition, and eventually everything would be under Baptist direction. (*Vide* White's Statistics.)

Hoping to disarm prejudice in one way, the committee concluded to abandon the name *Baptist College* and substitute *Mt. Enon College*, as it was definitely settled to accept Dr. Holcombe's donation of two hundred acres of land, and adopt that locality for the site of the college. Accordingly, in December, 1806, an adjourned meeting was held at Mt. Enon, and a constitution was adopted, in order to carry into effect the design of their appointment, the first article of which was, "This body shall be known and distinguished by the name and style of the *General Committee of Georgia Baptists, and Trustees of Mt. Enon College*."

The meeting convened on the 6th, and continued to the 9th of December, 1806. The members of the committee present were sufficient to form a quorum, namely: Jesse Mercer, H. Holcombe, Lewis C. Davis, James Matthews, A. Marshall, Charles O. Screven, Thomas Rhodes, and Benjamin Brooks. The absent members were Benjamin Moseley, Stephen Gafford, Joseph Clay, and Thomas Polhill.

Jesse Mercer was made Chairman, and H. Holcombe, Secretary. After the adoption of the constitution, Henry Holcombe was elected President of the Board of Trustees; Jesse Mercer, Vice-President; Thomas Polhill, Secretary, and B. S. Screven, Treasurer. Rev. Charles O. Screven was elected President of Mount Enon College. Drs. Holcombe and Screven were appointed to contract for building a boarding and school-house, and Rev. Joseph Clay was chosen to collect funds for the erection of a college edifice. The Circular Letter and its Appendix, of that year, written by Dr. Holcombe, are exceedingly able and intensely interesting articles, and deserve a permanent place in history.

It is, perhaps, not necessary to quote the Constitution in full; but the 11th article, which is given, shows how the "Christian Union" project had been discarded:

"That this committee shall give all the aid in their power to itinerant preaching and missionary efforts; and use their best endeavors to collect funds, and form arrangements to establish and endow a grammar school and college on this Mount."

It seems that the Legislature could not be prevailed upon to grant a charter for a Baptist college, but, in 1807, it did graciously incorporate "the trustees of Mt. Enon Academy," and, consequently, at their meeting in August, 1807, it was resolved, "to open a grammar school" on the 1st of September following, under the direction of Dr. Charles O. Screven, until a "proper character" could be procured to place at the head of the institution.

The school was, indeed, opened in 1807, and, under the temporary care of Dr. Screven, and flourished for five or six years; but, on the departure of Dr. Holcombe for Philadelphia, in December, 1811, it began to decline and soon ceased to exist. He had been the Ajax upon whose broad and able shoulders the school rested, and his power and force of character sustained it.

This was the first earnest effort made by Georgia Baptists to establish a college. Their failure was due to inability to secure a charter of incorporation, to an unfortunate selection of a location for it, and to the want of funds—in plain terms, *debt*.

Its cessation of existence was accompanied, perhaps preceded, by the expiration of the General Committee; for we have Dr. Sherwood's authority for asserting that it was formally dissolved about 1810. But we have seen that it virtually changed itself into a Board of Trustees, and in 1807 it appears solely in that character, nothing else but the college seeming to claim its attention.

These facts have been dwelt on for the reasons that they are, strictly speaking, a part of the history of our denomination in the State, and because they exhibit the first general effort at co-operation among the Baptists of Georgia, and, also, because they manifest the interest taken by our fathers in the cause of education.

This was not, however, the first school established in Georgia under Baptist auspices; for Silas Mercer had opened an academy and employed a teacher at his residence, called Salem, nine miles south of Washington, in 1793. At the death of Silas Mercer in 1796, Mr. Armor, who had been employed, gave up the rectorship of Salem Academy, and Jesse Mercer, assisted by a brother, took charge of it himself for a while.

There were, in the beginning of the century, six incorporated academies in the State. They were at Savannah, Augusta, Sunbury, Louisville, and one in each of the counties of Burke and Wilkes. In 1802, Mrs. Allen opened a school for females at Athens, and in 1805, Madam Dugas opened a boarding school at Washington, which flourished for a number of years. Meson Academy, Lexington, was commenced in 1804 or 1805. In 1811 the Mount Zion Academy was put in operation, and, soon after another at Powelton. All these various circumstances combined produced the extinction of the Mount Enon Academy, for which solicitude was manifested by so many eminent Baptists.

The following is the description of it as it appeared in 1805:

"Mount Enon rises in the high region of pine land which separates the Ogeechee from the Savannah river, and the low from the back country. The range is good; the land tolerably productive with manure; the air very salubrious; and the water equal to any below the mountains. The principal springs

FIRST EFFORTS AT CO-OPERATION.   61

issue from the rocks on its north and west sides, and produce, the one ten and a half, the other five and a half gallons in a minute. In the immediate vicinity of this place are Richmond Baths, and general saw, grist and bolting mills, and, at the distance of ten to twenty miles, a landing at New Savannah for large boats, Cowles' Iron Works, Waynesborough and the city of Augusta. It is by computation two miles in circumference and two hundred feet high."

The *Boarding House* and lot were held by trustees until 1833, when they were sold for fifty dollars, to Dr. B. B. Miller, and the house was moved to Hephzibah, where it is now the residence of Mrs. Dr. Miller.

The history of Mount Enon Academy will be closed by a humorous saying of Ben. J. Tharpe, in regard to Mount Enon, in the days when he went to school at Powelton. He had ridden over to gratify his curiosity, and after his return from Mount Enon he soberly enunciated his theory concerning the place, to a friend. Said he: "It appears to me as if, after making the world, the Lord had a big bag full of sand left, and, not knowing what else to do with it, he emptied it all out at Mount Enon."

The present chapter affords a singular phase of our denominational history. Apparently it presents to our view a series of mistakes; but we shall find the Baptists of Georgia making a good many mistakes. The experiences gained by the General Committee, and by those who established Mount Enon Academy, proved of great value afterwards, in the organization of our State Convention and in the establishment of Mercer Institute. The great lesson, learned at Mount Enon and practiced at Penfield, was not to incur indebtedness.

We should remember that, in the matter of organization and co-operation, everything was new and untried, and that almost insuperable difficulties hedged in every Christian enterprise. To select objects upon which all could concentrate was, indeed, difficult; and to induce that concentration was still more difficult. In this case it was impossible, and we may add, without its being a matter of surprise, Mount Enon was not the proper place for a college, and union among Christians of different denominations, was not the proper endeavor of a Baptist convention.

Hinting, only, that it was too early, probably, to seek the establishment of an institution of high grade, we will add that there were elements in the denomination, as will be seen hereafter, which militated against the successful accomplishment of the objects sought to be attained by the General Committee. But we must let the future speak for itself. One thing was surely learned by the experience acquired, and that was, the necessity of combination, and of some instrumentality by which the energies and liberality of the Baptists could be elicited, combined and directed,

VII.
THE FIRST FIVE ASSOCIATIONS.
1810-1813.

VII.

THE FIRST FIVE ASSOCIATIONS.

GENERAL CONDITION OF GEORGIA IN 1810—GENERAL CONDITION OF THE DENOMINATION AT THE SAME TIME—GROWTH OF THE GEORGIA ASSOCIATION—FORMATION AND GROWTH OF THE HEPHZIBAH ASSOCIATION—FORMATION AND GROWTH OF THE SAREPTA ASSOCIATION—THE OCMULGEE AND SAVANNAH ASSOCIATIONS—THEIR GROWTH—SINGULAR FORMATION OF BLACK CREEK CHURCH—STATISTICS OF 1813—A REVIVAL—LABORIOUS TIMES AND PIOUS MEN—HOSTILITIES AGAINST GREAT BRITAIN DECLARED, JUNE 18TH, 1812—UNANIMITY AND PATRIOTISM OF BAPTIST SENTIMENT—LUMPKIN AND RABUN.

And, now, let us gather up the threads of our history, and advance to the establishment of the Georgia Baptist Convention.

The population of the State had advanced from 162,000 in 1800, to 252.432 in 1810, of whom 145 414 were slaves. Under the governorship of Josiah Tatnall. John Milledge, Jared Irwin and David B. Mitchell, the Commonwealth enjoyed a high state of prosperity. Its exports increased, in ten years, from $1,755,939 to $2,568,866. The Legislature and Executive department moved from Louisville to Milledgeville in 1807. Although Georgia had claimed all the territory of the State for more than a quarter of a century, yet it was not until 1802 that the land between the Oconee and Ocmulgee rivers was actually acquired from the Indians, and it was only by different treaties in 1814, 1817, 1819, 1821 and 1825. that the Indian titles to all the land east of the Chattahoochee were extinguished; in fact, finally required the force of arms on the part of the United States government to gain possession of all lands east of the Chattahoochee, and effect the extinguishment of Indian titles. This had been guaranteed by the general government when, in 1802, it purchased Georgia's claim to all the land between the Chattahoochee and Mississippi rivers.

It was these Creek Indians living in the western part of Georgia, and in Alabama, in whom our Baptist fathers interested themselves so earnestly. in the beginning of this century, and who were not finally removed west of the Mississippi until 1836. And it is the descendants of these same Indians for whose spiritual benefit we are still laboring and bestowing our substance in the Indian Territory.

The General Committee, though desirous to do so, never engaged in any benevolent work among the Indians; this was undertaken, however, as we shall see, by the Associations themselves, about 1820. Let us glance again at the condition of the Associations first formed in Georgia, so as to impress their formation and early growth upon our minds, and obtain a bird's eye view of the denomination in the State, during the first decade of the century.

The Georgia Association was formed in 1784, by the union of five churches. In 1788 there were twenty-seven Georgia churches in connection with this Association, which contained 2,270 members. In 1790 there were forty-two Baptist churches in Georgia, whose membership was 3,211; and in the following year, 1791, there were forty-seven churches, whose total membership was 3,557, there being thirty-two ordained ministers and forty-five licentiates. In the year 1794, fifty-two Georgia churches, with one whose application was refused, are reported in the Minutes of the Georgia Association. For fourteen of these churches

(5)

the members of preceding years are given. Allowing a fair estimate for increase, and counting one church rejected because of some variance with the Kiokee church, and the total is fifty-three churches, and 3,650 members. All these facts and figures are taken from printed records.

The Association met, in 1794, at Powell's Creek—now Powelton—and it was agreed to divide the Association, those desiring it being permitted by formal resolution to form another Association, towards the south, in the following September. Delegates from eighteen churches met at Buckhead Davis' meeting-house, on Saturday before the fourth Lord's day, and formed the Hephzibah Association, which, in 1803, included twenty-two churches, with 1,132 members; in 1804, twenty-three churches and 1,492 members—a gain of 373; in 1805, twenty-eight churches and 1,765 members; in 1808, delegates from forty-one churches reported a membership of 1,400, allowing twenty-four for the Bethany church, Washington county, whose numbers are not reported; in 1811, there were thirty-two churches and 1,785 members; in 1812, thirty-six churches and 1,865 members; in 1813, thirty churches and 2,022 members.

In October, 1798, eight churches were dismissed from the Georgia Association to form a new Association, in the northern part of the State. After a preliminary meeting, in May, 1799, at Shoal Creek church, where they met and formed an Association which was named The Sarepta, in the fall of the same year—October—they held their first session at Van's Creek church, Elbert county, when the Constitution and Decorum of the Georgia Association were adopted. Nowadays we should call this the second meeting.

There were, in this Association, in 1801, seventeen churches and 1,256 members; in 1802, there were twenty-five churches and 2,527 members; in 1803, there were thirty-three churches and 2,693 members; in 1804, thirty-five churches and 2,760 members; in 1808, forty churches and 2,375 members; 1810, forty churches and 2,220 members; and in 1811, forty churches containing 2,050 members.

Again, the Georgia, in 1810, dismissed twenty of its fifty-two churches, to form the Ocmulgee Association. In November of that year the Ocmulgee Association was formed at Rooty Creek meeting-house, eight miles east of Eatonton, by the union of twenty-four churches, four of which came, probably, from the Hephzibah Association. During the session four other churches were admitted. There were thirty-four churches represented in 1811, which had a membership of 1,877. The following year, 1812, thirty-three churches, with a membership of 2,667, were represented, showing a gain of 801 in one year. Correspondents were received in that year from the Georgia, Sarepta and Hephzibah Associations.

The fifth Association in the State was the Savannah, which was formed on the 5th of April, 1802, by the union of three churches—the Savannah church, the Newington church, and the colored church of Savannah. The membership of all these churches was about eight hundred, the very large preponderance being with the colored church in Savannah. The delegates from the three churches were as follows: Rev. Henry Holcombe and Elias Robert, from the Savannah (white) church; Rev. John Goldwire and Thomas Polhill from the Newington church, and Rev. Andrew Bryant, Evan Great and H. Cunningham from the Savannah (colored) church. The delegates met on Saturday, April 3d, and constituted the Association on Monday, the 5th, adopting for its creed the English Confession of Faith of 1688, and the summary of church discipline of the Charleston Association. It was resolved to divide the colored church as soon as practicable, and to ordain colored ministers regularly to take charge of these churches; and it was also agreed that, when engaged in business, the members call each other "brethren."

In consequence, the Second colored church was constituted December 26th, 1802, and the Ogechee colored church was constituted on the 2d of January, 1803. Henry Cunningham was ordained on the 1st of January, 1803, to take charge of the Second colored church; and Henry Francis, who had been ordained on the 23d of May, 1802, assumed the pastorate of the Ogechee colored church. These two latter churches were considered members of the Associa-

THE FIRST FIVE ASSOCIATIONS. 67

tion, and sent letters and delegates to the session which met at Savannah, January 15th, 1803, without making application for admittance. The membership of the five churches, in January, 1803, was: Savannah, sixty-seven ; Newington, sixteen ; Savannah, First colored, four hundred ; Savannah, Second colored, two hundred ; Ogechee, colored, two hundred and fifty. Seven other churches applied for admission, and were received : Black Swamp, ninety members, Alexander Scott, pastor ; Coosawhatchie, sixty members, Aaron Tison, pastor ; Pipe Creek, thirty-five members ; Bethesda, twenty-eight members, James Sweat, pastor ; Three Runs, thirty—all five in South Carolina—Black Creek, seventy-seven members, Isham Peacock, pastor ; Lott's Creek, forty-five members, Henry Cook, pastor. Total membership, 1,298. These two last named churches were in Georgia, about thirty miles southwest of Savannah.

Mr. Peacock was called to ordination by the Lott's Creek church, of which he was a licentiate, and was a very useful and zealous, but not learned, young preacher. His ordination took place at Black Creek, the presbytery being Dr. Holcombe, Rev. John Goldwire and Rev. Henry Cook, in the morning of August 15th, 1802. The same presbytery constituted the Black Creek church, on the afternoon of the same day, with thirteen members, all of whom had in the meanwhile been baptized by Mr. Peacock, after his ordination. The new church then presented him a call to become its pastor, which he accepted. To add still further to these remarkable facts, the thirteen members were all converts under the preaching of Mr. Peacock, and had been all received for baptism by experience only the day previous.

These facts are taken from the Association Minutes, and from Dr. Holcombe's *Analytical Repository*, and from Dr. Benedict's History, and may be relied on as correct.

The five Georgia churches in 1803, increased to eight in 1804, and to at least nine in 1805, when the Sunbury church joined. In 1806 the name of the Association was changed to Savannah River, because its churches were on both sides of that river, most of them being in South Carolina. The growth of the Georgia churches of this Association was as follows : 800 members in 1802 ; 1,055 members in 1803 ; 1,418 members in 1804, and 4,300 members in 1813, the great majority of whom were colored members.

In the city of Augusta, also, there was a large and flourishing church of colored people, which contained, in 1813, 588 members. This church, the name of which is Springfield, was formed in 1791, and connected itself with the Georgia Association as early, at least, as the beginning of this century. In 1803 it had 500 members, and in 1814 it had 600 members. It established, fourteen miles below Augusta, an arm, or branch, called Ebenezer, which, for more than half a century, has been a large and flourishing church. Jacob Walker, the most prominent pastor of the Springfield church, occupied a position in Augusta fully equal to that held by Andrew Marshall in Savannah. At his death the whole city of Augusta manifested the greatest respect and sorrow, as for one of its most eminent citizens.

The following estimate, the figures of which have all been taken from printed Minutes, gives a fair view of the statistics of our denomination in Georgia, in the year 1813 :

Georgia Association,	35 churches,	3,428 members.
Hephzibah Association,	36 churches,	2,037 members
Sarepta Association,	44 churches,	3,140 members.
Ocmulgee Association,	39 churches,	2,850 members.
Savannah River Association,	10 churches,	4,300 members.
Total,	164 churches,	15,755 members.

About this period a great work of grace occurred in Georgia. During the year 1812, 1,265 converts were baptized in the Sarepta Association, 1,492 in the Savannah Association, and in the Georgia, 362 baptisms were reported at its session for 1813. Churches were being constituted continually in all parts of the State. For several years in succession the different Associations had been appointing days for fasting, humiliation and prayer, and sometimes two such days of humiliation for imploring mercy and blessing were appointed for the same year. At its session in 1811 the Georgia Association adopted the following: "In concurrence with the Hephzibah Association—

"*Resolved*, That Friday before the fourth Lord's day in December next, be observed as a day of fasting and prayer to God that He would graciously pour out His Spirit more abundantly on church and people, and that he would spread the wing of His providence over our nation and avert impending calamities."

In 1811 the Sarepta appointed the following 4th of July as a day of fasting and prayer for the outpouring of blessings; and, at its session in 1812, the 1st of June was appointed as a day of fasting and prayer to Almighty God to avert the calamity of war.

The Ocmulgee, in September, 1812: "*Resolved*, That the first day of January next be observed by this Association as a day of fasting and prayer."

The spirit of itineracy was the prevailing spirit among the churches and Associations, as is evidenced by the following, adopted by the Georgia Association, at its session of 1811: "Itineracy has the decided patronage of this Association, and it is strongly recommended that the ministers of this body encourage it by prompt exertions."

The ministers universally engaged themselves devotedly in itinerant labors, and constituted churches all over the eastern half of Georgia; churches as far apart as Freeman's Creek, in Clarke county, Richland Creek, in Twiggs county, and Trail Branch, in Pulaski county, belonged to the Ocmulgee Association; and a general spirit of earnestness, piety and zeal prevailed. The missionary spirit was strong and pervading, and for several years we find no traces of an anti-missionary spirit. The men whom we have special occasion to admire, for their piety, zeal and devotion during those years, were Abraham Marshall, of Applington, second to none in zeal and ministerial usefulness, and now near the end of his laborious pilgrimage; Jesse Mercer, full of zeal, earnestness and activity, and already assuming that position of leader in every good work and word which he occupied so long; Robert McGinty, Edmund Talbot, James Matthews, William Davis, M. Reeves, Joel Willis, Elijah Moseley, F. Flournoy, Joseph Baker, V. A. Tharp. Henry Hand, Norvell Robertson, George and William Franklin, John Stanford, Littleton Meeks, Francis Calloway, David Montgomery, Dozier Thornton, Miller Bledsoe, C. O. Screven, William Rabun, Wilson Lumpkin, Lazarus Battle, Charles J. Jenkins, Thomas Byne, and many others, all of whom earnestly preached the Word, all over the State, seeking to bring sinners into the fold of Jesus, and strengthen saints in the principles of our faith. The five last mentioned, however, were not ministers, but distinguished laymen.

The period which we are regarding was that just preceding and during the war of 1812—when, on account of the English claiming and exercising the right to search American ships for deserters, thus frequently impressing our citizens into the British service, and also on account of the capture, by British cruisers, of American vessels, under the plea that they were a lawful prize, because bearing French products—our government felt compelled to declare hostilities against Great Britain, on the 18th of June, 1812,

It will be interesting to the reader to learn the position taken by our denomination with reference to that war. The very prospect of such a war had exercised a baneful influence upon the prospects of the country, and had called forth the appointment of days for fasting and prayer, which we have already seen. The effects of the war upon Georgia commerce will be apparent when it is stated that the exports of the State for the years 1812 and 1813 diminished about one and a half million of dollars.

Among the Baptists the unanimity of sentiment discerned in the appointment of days for fasting and prayer, was shown also by the adoption of patriotic resolutions in their associational meetings. The Sarepta Association, at its session held at Big Creek church, Clarke county, in October, 1813, adopted the following:

"On motion, *Resolved*, That whereas the Georgia Association has seen proper to set forth a declaration of their pleasedness with, and determination to support, the government of their country, in its present administration, and to admonish the churches, in their connection, to unity and perseverance in the present war and its prosecution; we do concur therewith, and order that the same be published in the Minutes as from us to the churches in union with us."

This reference is to the action of the Georgia Association at Fishing Creek, Wilkes county, in its session, a few days previously, in the same month. The article was drawn up by a committee, consisting of Jesse Mercer, Wilson Lumpkin, William Rabun, and J. N. Brown, and, after being read several times, was adopted without dissent. It stands thus:

"That however unusual it may be for us, as a religious body, to intermeddle with the political concerns of our country, yet, at this *momentous* crisis, when our vital interests are jeopardized, to remain silent would indicate a *criminal* indifference. We, therefore, in this public and solemn manner, take the liberty of saying that we have long viewed with emotions of indignation and horror the many lawless aggressions committed on the persons, rights and property of the people of these United States by the corrupt, arbitrary and despotic government of Great Britain and its emissaries. And, as it has been found necessary to resist such wanton and cruel outrages by opposing force to force:

"*Resolved, unanimously,* That it is the opinion of this Association, that the WAR so waged against Britain is JUST, NECESSARY and INDISPENSABLE; and, as we consider everything dear to us and to our country involved in its issue, we solemnly pledge ourselves to the government of our choice, that we will, by all means within our power, aid in its prosecution, until it shall be brought to an honorable termination. And we also exhort and admonish, particularly the churches belonging to our connection, and brethren and friends in general, to take into consideration the command of our Lord by His apostle, ' to be subject to the powers ordained of God over us,' and to be jointly united in the common cause of Liberty and Independence—to be examples to all within their reach, by a peaceable and quiet endurance of the privations and afflictions of the present war; by a promptness to defend their violated rights when called on to personal service, and by a cheerfulness in meeting the accumulated, though indispensable, expenses thereof—in all things showing themselves the real friends of Liberty and Religion, by bringing all their energies to bear on the measures of the government, thereby the more speedily (*under God*) to bring about a happy termination of these calamities, by the restoration of an honorable and lasting peace. And, for that purpose, we further exhort them to let their united supplications ascend to the Lord of Hosts that he would graciously preside over the councils of our nation, be our sun and shield, and cover our armies and navies in the day of battle."

Two of the members of this committee, in after life, reached the exalted station of governor—William Rabun and Wilson Lumpkin. The latter was one of the noblest men our State ever produced. Although born in Virginia, in 1783, he was brought to Georgia, in 1784, and may, therefore, be called a Georgian. He became a Baptist in early manhood, and remained faithful to his religious principles until his death, on the night of December 28th, 1870—a period of seventy years. Though an active politician, he took a lively interest in religious and church matters. From the State Legislature he passed to the House of Representatives in Congress, and thence to the gubernatorial chair, and, afterwards, to the United States Senate; in all of which positions he did honor to his State and credit to his denomination. On retiring from public life, in 1841, he took up his residence in Athens, Georgia, where he spent the remainder of his days, honored and respected as became a man of his exalted worth and character.

The former, Governor Rabun, was a North Carolinian, born in April, 1771. When a young man, he moved to Georgia with his father and settled in Powelton, Hancock county, by which he was sent to the Legislature. He was, for many years President of the Senate, and as such became Governor, March 4th, 1817, on the death of Governor D. B. Mitchell. In November, 1817, he was regularly elected to the gubernatorial office, for two years, but died before the expiration of his term of office, in October, 1819. He was truly a religious man, a strong Baptist and an active and zealous church-member. Even while Governor of the State, he was the clerk and chorister of his church, at Powelton, and represented it in the Georgia Association. By request of the Legislature, at his death, Jesse Mercer preached a sermon before that august body, a few extracts from which will present the reader with a just estimate of his character, by one who knew not how to flatter nor how to prevaricate :

"Your late excellent Governor was the pleasant and lovely companion of my youth ; my constant friend and endeared Christian brother in advancing years ; and, till death, my unremitted fellow-laborer and able support in all the efforts of benevolence and philanthropy in which I had the honor and happiness to be engaged, calculated either to amend or meliorate the condition of man. * * *

"It was his felicity to have many friends, few enemies, rare equals and no superiors. He is gone, and has left an awful chasm behind him. A widow bereft of a tender and kind husband ; children of an affectionate and loving father ; servants of a humane and indulgent master ; neighbors of a constant friend and pleasant companion ; the Baptist church of her bright ornament, member and scribe ; two mission societies of their secretary ; the Georgia Association of her clerk ; and the State of a firm politician and her honored chief. O, what an awful death was Governor Rabun's ! *The beauty of Georgia is fallen !*"

As an evidence of Governor Rabun's spirit and independence of character, we give an extract from a letter of his to General Jackson, written June 1st, 1818. It was in reply to a letter from General Jackson, in which the action of the Georgia State troops, in attacking the Indian town of Chehaw, was very severely censured. The General's letter contained this passage : "Such base cowardice and murderous conduct as this transaction affords, has no parallel in history, and shall meet its merited punishment. You, sir, as Governor of a State within my military division, have no right to give a military order while I am in the field." In his reply, after referring to a communication from General Glascock, on which General Jackson based his censure, Governor Rabun says : "Had you, sir, or General Glascock, been in possession of the facts that produced this affair, it is to be presumed, at least, that you would not have indulged in a strain so indecorous and unbecoming. I had, on the 21st of March last, stated the situation of our bleeding frontier to you, and requested you, in respectful terms, to detail a part of your overwhelming force for our protection, or that you would furnish supplies and I would order out more troops, to which you never yet deigned a reply. You state, in a very haughty tone, that I, a Governor of a State under your military division, have no right to give a military order while you are in the field. Wretched and contemptible, indeed, must be our situation if this be the fact. When the liberties of the people of Georgia shall have been prostrated at the feet of a military despotism, *then, and not till then*, will your imperious doctrine be tamely submitted to. You may rest *assured* that if the savages continue their depredations on our unprotected frontier, I shall think and act for myself in that respect."

The joint-committee of the Legislature which was appointed to consider the death of Governor Rabun, referred to him, in their report, as an ornament of society, an undeviating and zealous patriot, and an unwavering friend of humanity. Says the report : "Nature had endowed him with a strong and vigorous mind, and a firmness of character which never forsook him. Love of order and love of his country were conspicuous in his every action, and justice he regarded not only as a civil but as a religious duty. His public life flowed naturally from these principles. Ever obedient and attentive to the admonitions of his conscience, his public acts were marked with an integrity which did honor to his station. His private virtues were of the highest order." The following resolution, recommended by this joint-committee, was unanimously agreed to by the Legislature :

"*Resolved*, That the Executive and Judicial officers of this State, together with the members of this Legislature, do wear crape on the left arm for sixty days ; and that the members of both branches do attend at the Baptist church, on Wednesday, the 24th instant, at twelve o'clock, for the purpose of hearing a funeral sermon, to be delivered by the Rev. Jesse Mercer, on this mournful occasion."

The General Committee, as well as the Board of Trustees for Mount Enon Academy, has ceased to exist. Although there are five Associations, there is no bond of general union, and the churches have no common object of interest. Clay is dead; Holcombe has moved to Philadelphia; and C. O. Screven has retired to Liberty county, where he is laboring faithfully. Dr. Wm. B. Johnson is pastor of the Savannah church, and the elder Brantly, who had for several years been the rector of the Augusta Academy, in 1811, accepted the charge of the Beaufort, South Carolina Baptist church. Jesse Mercer is efficiently supplying several churches. Rev. Abraham Marshall is still pastor of Kiokee church and Moderator of the Georgia Association. George Franklin, Edward Talbot and Charles Culpepper are exercising a good influence, as pastors, in the Hephzibah Association. The prevailing spirit in the churches is that of itinerary, but one Association only having, thus far, developed any plan approaching a systematic missionary effort, and that was the Savannah River, which has a mission committee and sustains her own State missionaries.

It was just at this time, 1812, that Adoniram Judson and Luther Rice were both converted to Baptist principles on their passage to India, although they sailed in different ships. The following year, 1813, Mr. Rice returned to America, laid their case before the Baptist world, and, immediately a missionary enthusiasm was excited which resulted in the formation of the old Baptist Triennial Convention, in 1814, and of many missionary societies. Luther Rice soon came South, and was partly instrumental in originating the great missionary movement in Georgia.

Baptist churches are springing up rapidly in the State, where the whites dwell; but the territory of the whites extends no further west than the Altamaha and Ocmulgee rivers. Pulaski, Twiggs, Jones and Jasper counties are on the western frontier, and Franklin is the most northerly county. Our churches generally lie between the Ocmulgee and Savannah rivers, very few existing on the seaboard. In truth, about one-third only of the State has been surveyed and laid out into counties, the rest being inhabited by Creek and Cherokee Indians, who gave a great deal of trouble, and resisted the encroachments of the whites so violently that the military power of the general government had to be invoked.

But a spirit of gloom broods over the State on account of the war with Great Britain. Our denomination, however, patriotically concedes the justice of our cause; while the Associations all appoint, annually, days of fasting and prayer, for the effusion of the Spirit and the removal of war's calamities.

VIII.
MISSIONARY.
1813-1820.

VIII.

MISSIONARY.

1813 AN EPOCH—THE ARLY MISSION SPIRIT ON THE SEABOARD—INFLUENCING CHARACTERS—THE SAVANNAH RIVER ASSOCIATION IN 1813—FORMATION OF THE FIRST GEORGIA MISSIONARY SOCIETY—MISSIONARY ENTHUSIASM—A REMARKABLE CIRCULAR—IT ISPREAD BEFORE THE GEORGIA ASSOCIATION BY JESSE MERCER—MEETING APPOINTED AT POWELTON IN 1815—A STRONG MISSIONARY SOCIETY FORMED—THE GEORGIA ASSOCIATION TAKES HOLD OF THE MISSIONARY WORK IN EARNEST—THE OCMULGEE ASSOCIATION—PATRIOTIC CIRCULARS—THE MISSION SPIRIT IN THE OCMULGEE ASSOCIATION—"THE OCMULGEE MISSION SOCIETY" FORMED IN JULY, 1815—THE MISSION SPIRIT IN THE SAREPTA ASSOCIATION—A MISSION SOCIETY FORMED IN JUNE, 1816—THE RESOLUTION OF DR. SHERWOOD IN 1820—SPIRIT OF THE HEPHZIBAH ASSOCIATION—IT FAVORS THE "GENERAL COMMITTEE"—FAVORS ITINERACY AND DOMESTIC MISSIONS—THE HEPHZIBAH BAPTIST SOCIETY FOR ITINERANT AND MISSIONARY EXERTIONS, FORMED IN FEBRUARY, 1816—A FOREIGN MISSION SOCIETY FORMED IN 1818—THE EBENEZER ASSOCIATION FORMED IN MARCH, 1814—THE TUGALO AND PIEDMONT ASSOCIATIONS FORMED IN 1817—STATE OF RELIGION IN THE SECOND DECADE OF THE CENTURY.

An epoch is made of the year 1813, because in that year an impetus was given to the mission cause in Georgia, which worked a great revolution among the Baptists in the State, and finally resulted in the formation of our State Baptist Convention, and the establishment of Mercer University.

Those who study the musty records of our denomination in Georgia, will find frequent references to communications from the General Baptist Mission Committee in Philadelphia. Let it be put on record that this Committee did much to foster the mission spirit in Georgia. Let it be put on record, also, that Luther Rice materially assisted in arousing and promoting a missionary spirit in our State, by visiting various localities in the State, forming mission societies, and maintaining with them a regular correspondence. But, while there was a strong missionary spirit inherited, as we might say, from that noble man, Daniel Marshall, who left his home in Connecticut to labor among the Mohawk Indians, yet, for want of co-operation, it had never been developed.

The first effort at denominational co-operation was, as we have seen, a failure. Allusion is made to the "General Committee" formed at Powelton in 1804; and the reasons of its failure have been partly traced. Had it engaged more actively in missionary effort, and made no attempt at promoting Christian union among different denominations, it might have merged into a general convention such as we now have, and which is much more adapted to the genius of our denomination. We shall now take up and trace out the different threads of influence that led to and resulted in the formation of our State Baptist Convention, which, at its origin, was merely a missionary society.

In the beginning of this century, the southern part of our State was fortunate in having two educated and cultivated ministers, who promoted the cause of missions largely. These were C. O. Screven and Henry Holcombe. The latter exerted a powerful influence by his bi-monthly *Analytical Repository*, published in 1801 and 1802, in which he advocated missions and gave missionary news.

To those may be added the courtly and cultivated William T. Brantly, Sr., who resided in Beaufort, South Carolina, and was for eight years one of the ruling spirits of the Savannah Association, which embraced about three times as many churches in South Carolina as it did in Georgia, on which account its name was changed to the Savannah River Association in 1806. The elder Brantly was a man cultivated in the highest degree and eminently of a missionary spirit. Two other master minds in the Savannah River Association were Dr. William B. Johnson, the successor of Dr. Holcombe, as pastor of the Savannah church, and Alexander Scott, both of whom were powerful advocates of missions and of the mission cause. For years Scott was the Moderator of the body, and Thomas Polhill was clerk. He, too, was a strong advocate of missions, and a man of intelligence and education, who, in 1812, issued a very respectable work on Baptism, containing two hundred pages, in reply to "A vindication of the rights of infants to the ordinance of baptism," by Rev. James Russell. He was for a time an active member of the General Committee of the Georgia Baptists, and labored zealously for both missions and education for ten years, having been ordained in November, 1805, and dying in December, 1814.

The influence of thes lofty characters, added to a missionary enthusiasm excited by the conversion of Adoniram Judson and Luther Rice to Baptist principles, awakened a strong missionary sentiment in the Savannah River Association. As early as 1812 there was money sent up by the churches of this Association, for the support of itinerant and missionary efforts, and at the meeting held with the Sunbury church, in that year, a committee was appointed to receive and appropriate it. They employed Rev. Thomas Trowel as an itinerant missionary. A committee was also appointed, of which Rev. William B. Johnson, D. D., was chairman, to prepare and report, at the meeting for 1813, "a plan for the more permanent and effectual prosecution of itinerant and missionary efforts contemplated by the body." Dr. William B. Johnson was also appointed to prepare the Circular Letter for 1813, on this subject: ": THE IMPORTANCE AND ADVANTAGES OF ITINERANT AND MISSIONARY EFFORTS."

The Association met at Union church, Barnwell district, South Carolina, on the 27th of November, 1813, and the Circular Address prepared by William B. Johnson, was adopted and published in the Minutes of that year. It is a tract of remarkable ability, occupying nine closely printed, large pamphlet pages. We find also in the Minutes of this noteworthy session, that a special committee was appointed to consider all communications addressed to the body, and report upon them. In its report, the committee expressed their cordial approbation of the great design then forming in America for sending the gospel to the heathen, and also of those measures the Baptists of the United States were then pursuing for the accomplishment of this object. Information concerning these designs and measures had been communicated in letters from the Philadelphia and Charleston Associations, and in a Circular Address from the representatives of the Boston, Salem and Haverill Societies for Foreign Missions.

Connected with their recommendation, the committee stated that in the communications referred to honorable mention was made of the ability and and persevering zeal of brethren Rice and Judson, missionaries to the East, whose secession from their former religious connection, and union with the Baptist denomination, had originated the great design now contemplated in America, and the measures taken for its accomplishment. Luther Rice, being present, was requested to address the body and state any matters relative to this subject which he deemed worthy of attention. He arose and stated that he had lately returned from Calcutta to America, and that he had visited different Associations and places in the United States for the purpose of encouraging American Baptists to support foreign missions. He said he had met with uniform success, and it was his fixed determination, as he knew it to be that of his colleague, Mr. Judson, then in the East, to prosecute the foreign mission work which engaged their attention as soon as suitable provision should be made for its support and furtherance.

The Association appointed a day for fasting, humiliation and prayer for the removal of the awful scourge of war, and for an outpouring of the Spirit upon the churches and the world in general. It resolved, also, "That this Association do concur with the recommendation of the committee in relation to the design now forming in America, and the measures pursued for its accomplishment.

"*Resolved, also,* That the churches be exhorted to use their best endeavors towards the support of foreign missions."

Dr. William B. Johnson, from the committee appointed the previous year to prepare and report a plan for the more permanent and effectual prosecution of itinerant and missionary efforts contemplated by the Association, reported a Constitution, which was adopted, for the organization of a General Committee, to be formed out of the churches of the Association, in which the direction and management of this important matter should be vested. This committee, called the "General Committee of the Savannah River Association for the encouragement of itinerant and missionary efforts," composed of thirteen delegates from various churches, organized by the election of the following officers: William B. Johnson, President; Thomas F. Williams, Secretary; H. W. Williams, Treasurer; Drs. C. O. Screven and William T. Brantly, Assistants. It was located in Savannah.

This was the first Georgia associational organization for missionary purposes. There had been sent up by the churches $230.26½, and the amount on hand, from the preceding year, was $106.80. The committee at once employed two itinerant preachers, licentiates, for one year, Rev. Thomas Trowel and Rev. Allen Sweat, at $80 each. They also agreed to assist Rev. Charles Felder, pastor of the Springtown church, and Rev. Jacob Dunham, a licensed preacher in the Sunbury church, to the amount of $50 each, and to give each $10 worth of books.

This Association concluded to divide in 1817. The South Carolina churches retained the name and records. The Georgia churches formed a new Association at Sunbury, Georgia, and held its first session at Sunbury in November, 1818. In 1819 the missionary plan of the Savannah River Association was put into operation in the Sunbury Association, by the annual appointment of a standing committee of seven, which, for a great many years, employed associational missionaries, whose labors redounded to the glory of God and to the salvation of many souls. These missionaries were regularly appointed and paid by the Standing Committee from funds sent up for the purpose by the churches. Let it not be supposed, however, that because mention is thus made of the missionary work in the Sunbury and Savannah River, that none was performed by the other Associations of a similar nature. On the contrary, we see repeated mention of itinerant labor, in the minutes of all our early Associations, and it is approved and encouraged. For instance, the Hephzibah Minutes of 1813 and 1816 say: "A number of churches in our connection expressing in their letters a desire for the continuance of itinerant preaching, the ministers and preachers agreed to continue it in the usual mode," etc. In 1814 the Ocmulgee passed a resolution that its ministers go forth, two and two, in this work; and the Georgia had encouraged it from its organization; but these were voluntary and unpaid laborers, although we read of occasional appropriations of money for itinerant preaching.

The enthusiasm in regard to foreign missions aroused at the meeting in 1813, which we have just been considering, was productive of remarkable and lasting effects, proving that meeting to be but one link in a most wonderful chain of providential events, by which the Almighty set the Baptists of America to work in behalf of foreign missions. Immediately after the adjournment of the Association, a Baptist Foreign Mission Society was formed in Savannah, whose officers were identical with those of the General Committee of the Savannah River Association, except that William T. Brantly was formally made the corresponding secretary. On the 17th of December, 1813, this Society adopted a constitution and a circular letter, which were sent to the Baptist churches and Associations of the State, and resulted, in the year 1815, in the formation of missionary societies in the Georgia and Ocmulgee Associations, and led to the formation of similar societies, in February, 1816, in the Hephzibah Association, and in June, 1816, in the Sarepta. The missionary spirit was now strongly developed. But the necessity for co-operation soon became evident. First, the Ocmulgee, Ebenezer and Georgia Associations resolved to co-operate in an Indian mission, in 1821. Then the necessity of a more extensive union was perceived, and in

1822 the "General Association" was formed, which, in 1827, changed its name to "The Baptist Convention for the State of Georgia."

But it will be necessary, and will prove interesting, to trace out the different steps which led to these results. Let us, therefore, revert to the "Savannah Baptist Society for Foreign Missions" as our starting point. First, let us glance at its constitution. It reads thus:

"Believing it to be the duty of Christians, as circumstances in Divine Providence shall enable them, to adopt measures for effectuating that grand command of Christ, 'Go ye into all the world and preach the gospel to every creature,' and particularly encouraged to this duty by present indications of a providential and propitious nature, we, whose names are subjoined, do for this purpose, cordially associate ourselves as a society, and agree to be governed by the following constitution:

"1. This society shall be known as " *The Savannah Baptist Society for Foreign Missions.*"

"2. The avowed and determined object of this society is to aid in sending forth and supporting missionaries for the purpose of translating the Scriptures, preaching the gospel and gathering churches in heathen and idolatrous parts of the world.

"3. The immediate management of its concerns shall be vested in a Board of Directors, consisting of a president, vice-president, recording secretary, corresponding secretary, treasurer, auditor and seven trustees, to be elected by ballot at the first, and at each annual meeting of the society, by a majority of the members present. A majority of the Board shall constitute a quorum to do business. Also, the Board shall appoint as many assistants as they may deem necessary for carrying into effect the object of the society, each of whom shall be furnished with a copy of this constitution, for the especial purpose of obtaining subscriptions and donations, and of collecting and transmitting the same to the treasurer of the society, annually, at or before the time of the annual meeting."

4. Prescribes the time and place of the annual meeting.
5. Prescribes the powers and duties of the president.
6. Gives the duties of the recording secretary.
7. Gives the duties of the corresponding secretary.
8. Gives the duties of the treasurer.
9. Prescribes how money shall be paid out.

"10. This society shall consist of all such persons as subscribe and pay into the treasury annually, any sum which they, individually, may think proper; *Provided*, that such annual subscription shall not be less than two dollars. Delegates from such auxiliary Baptist societies as contribute to the funds of this society, shall be considered as members. Any person may withdraw his name at pleasure.

"11. It shall be the duty of the directors, as they may deem it expedient, to solicit contributions from such persons as may not choose to become members, to obtain subscribers to the society, as opportunity may offer; to receive subscriptions and donations for the benefit of the society, and to pay the same over to the treasurer, and in all respects to advance, as far as practicable, the interest of the institution.

"12. The Board of Directors shall, without delay, appoint a delegate or delegates, to meet delegates from other similar societies, for the purpose of forming a "GENERAL COMMITTEE," or of devising and adopting some other practicable method to elicit, combine and direct the energies of the whole Baptist denomination of the whole United States in one sacred effort to diffuse amongst idolatrous nations the glorious light of the gospel of salvation.

"13. All donations to this society, specifically donated for the *translation* of the Scriptures, shall be appropriated to that particular object."

14. Indicates how the constitution may be altered.

"REV. WILLIAM B. JOHNSON, *President.*"

"REV. CHARLES O. SCREVEN, *Vice-President.*"

"Rev. William T. Brantly, *Cor. Sec'y*,   Henry W. Williams, *Treasurer*,
Thomas F. Williams, *Recording Sec'y*.   William E. Barnes, *Auditor*.

TRUSTEES:

"Rev. James Sweat,   Charles J. Jenkins,   Rev. George D. Sweet,
Thomas Fuller,   John Shick,   John Stillwell,
                     Elias Robert."

This constitution reads as though it may possibly have been modelled after a stereotyped form, circulated by Luther Rice, or the General Committee for Foreign Missions in Philadelphia; but the CIRCULAR ADDRESS issued by the society, and which exercised a marked influence on our denomination in Georgia, is evidently original, and deserves a place among the permanent records of the Georgia Baptists. It is headed:

"THE SAVANNAH BAPTIST SOCIETY FOR FOREIGN MISSIONS,

" *To the Inhabitants of Georgia, and the adjacent parts of South Carolina:*

" FRIENDS AND BRETHREN—As the great family of man are connected together by the same fraternal bond, it is the high duty and interest of all its members to use the best means in their power for the benefit of the whole. Of all those means which have been employed for this great end, none have been found so effectual as the preaching of the everlasting gospel. The obligations to contribute to its extension, therefore, must be proportionably binding.

" The gospel of Christ exhibiting the most important truths and furnishing the most exalted motives for action, accurately delineating the path to pure, unalloyed happiness, and deriving its authority from Jehovah himself, produces, in its diffusion, results in relation to the benefit of man, which human sages, lawgivers and kings have for ages labored in vain to effect. Alienated from his God by sin, deprived of the favor of his Creator by apostacy, man wanders in the earth a wretched object, a forsaken rebel, a child of hell. No ray of light, no gleam of hope issues from his dark abode to point out the way to restoration, happiness and glory. No human efforts can relieve his hopeless condition. But in the gospel of Christ the sun of righteousness is seen rising with healing under his wings. His divine rays, wherever they penetrate, scatter the mists which overwhelm man with despair. These discover to him the way of deliverance and joy, and lead to the portals of bliss. On a great part of the earth, these rays have fallen with the happiest effect, illuminating the extensive regions, turning their inhabitants from darkness to light, and preparing them for immortal felicity. But a far greater part of the earth remains unvisited by these beams, and consequently continues in darkness, and sees no light. But this part waits their appearance, and shall not wait in vain. The time approaches when those who have long sat in the region and shadow of death, shall have light to spring up unto them. The sun of righteousness shall diffuse among them the beams of light, and the whole earth shall be full of his glory.

" Late events in divine providence prove, with convincing testimony, that this time fast approaches. Wars and rumors of wars, the overturning of nations, the rapidly increasing destruction of the Man of Sin, and the growing spread of divine truth—events predicted by the prophets, and represented by them as prelusive to the general diffusion of the gospel—clearly show that the universal triumph of Christ, the King of Zion, is not far distant. What deserves particular notice in this view, is the missionary spirit which, within a few years past, has been kindled with enthusiastic ardor in Europe, at the altar of divine love. Under its influence great things have been attempted and performed in idolatrous nations.

" America, catching the same hallowed spirit, has been animated to similar exertions. Besides many societies formed for missionary efforts in this country, one, to the immortal honor of our Congregational and Presbyterian brethren, has been organized by them, of considerable extent and importance. Under their patronage, missionaries have been sent out for the purpose of effecting establishments in the East, for the diffusion of the gospel among the heathen tribes. That our brethren of these denominations should not be *alone*, in this great work, God, in the arrangements of infinite wisdom, has been pleased to bring some of their missionaries over to the Baptist persuasion. These, still desirous of pursuing their generous, disinterested career for the benefit of the heathen, now present themselves to the American Baptists for support. And shall they present themselves in vain? Friends and brethren, can the finger of divine Providence, so evidently marking out the path for us, be mistaken? Can the Lord's will, so clearly made known in this dispensation, be misinterpreted? Surely not! It cannot be! If then, it be the high duty and interest of the great family of man to promote each other's happiness, and the benefit of the whole, and that it is cannot be denied; and if the diffusion of the gospel of Christ be the most effectual means of securing these objects—a truth that must be admitted; then is it undoubtedly our duty and our interest to embrace the present auspicious moment, and engage with joyful haste and determined energy in the great work of evangelizing the poor heathen.

"Since the secession of our dear brethren, Rice, Judson and lady, the individuals alluded to above, several missionary societies have been formed by the Baptists in America. These societies have for their object the establishment and support of foreign missions; and it is contemplated that delegates from them all will convene in some central situation in the United States, for the purpose of organizing an efficient and practicable plan, on which the energies of the whole Baptist denomination, throughout America, may be elicited, combined and directed, in one sacred effort for sending the word of life to idolatrous lands. What a sublime spectacle will the convention present! A numerous body of the Lord's people, embracing in their connection from 100,000 to 200,000 souls, all rising in obedience to their Lord, and meeting, by delegation, in one august assembly, solemnly to engage in one sacred effort for effectuating the great command: 'Go ye into all the world, and preach the gospel to every creature!'

"What spectacle can more solemnly interest the benevolent heart! What can be more acceptable to our heavenly Father! We invite you, dear friends and brethren—we affectionately and cordially invite you—to embrace the privilege of uniting in so glorious a cause, so divine a work. God has put great honor upon us in giving us so favorable an opportunity of coming up 'to the help of the Lord against the mighty.' In doing so, he has conferred on us a distinguished privilege. Shall we be insensible of the honor? Shall we disregard the privilege? God forbid! Living in a country whose generous soil yields, with moderate industry, more than a sufficiency of the comforts of life, and professing, in great numbers, to be redeemed from our iniquities, our obligations to exert ourselves for the benefit of our race and the glory of God, are great indeed. O, let us feel, impressively feel, the force of these obligations and act correspondently with them! And we trust, in our attempt to act in this manner, no sectarian views, no individual prejudices, no party considerations, will have leave to operate any unfriendly influence upon a design conceived in disinterested benevolence, and having for its object the good of man and the honor of his Creator.

"Connected with this address to you, friends and brethren, is the constitution on which our society is organized. According to this, you may either become members with us, or donors, or both. In either character we will cheerfully receive your aid; and, in both, we hope to have the pleasure of ranking great numbers of you.

"Wishing you grace, mercy and peace, we remain affectionately, your servants in the gospel, for Christ's sake.

"WILLIAM B. JOHNSON, *President.*
"WILLIAM T. BRANTLY, *Corresponding Secretary.*

"*Savannah, 17th December, 1813.*"

It was this noble document, in all likelihood, the production of William T. Brantly, Sr., and the attendant constitution, which, according to a suggestion in the letter from the Whatley's Mill church (now Bethesda), Jesse Mercer presented and read to the Georgia Association, at its session, in 1814, and then moved for the approbation of the Association, which was given most willingly and unanimously. On account of "its evident importance," it was thought proper to recommend the subject to the consideration of the churches, and Friday before the first Sabbath in May, 1815, was appointed as a day on which all who were individually disposed, of the Georgia and of other Associations, might meet at Powelton, Hancock county, to form a society and digest a plan to aid in the glorious effort to evangelize the poor heathen in idolatrous lands. The meeting took place at Powelton, on the 5th of May, 1815, and a strong missionary society was formed, called "The Powelton Baptist Society for Foreign Missions," of which Jesse Mercer was made President, and Wm. Rabun, Secretary. Wm. Rabun was, at that time, President of the State Senate. In its first year the society raised $483.34, of which Rev. John Robertson gave $12.31½, as Dr. Adiel Sherwood informs us.

At its next session, in October, 1815, at Long Creek, Warren county, as might be expected, the Georgia Association was all alive to the subject of missions. It received from "The Baptist Board of Foreign Missions, for the United States," through its agent, Luther Rice, the report of the board, accompanied by letters desiring the aid of the body, "to spread the gospel of Christ among the heathen in idolatrous lands." The Association unanimously agreed to co-operate in the grand design; and, the more effectually to do so, resolved itself into a body for missionary purposes. Jesse Mercer, Benjamin Thompson, Joseph Roberts, William Rabun and James N. Brown, were appointed a committee to digest rules for its regulation, and to address a circular to the churches of the Association upon the subject, and to correspond with the Foreign Mission Board. The following year, at its sesssion with the church at Baird's meeting-house, the committee submitted a report which begins as follows, and which was adopted:

"The Georgia Association, impressed with a sense of duty, and anxious to participate in the missionary operations now going forward, does, for that purpose, make, ordain and establish the following Constitution."

By this constitution, seven trustees were to be chosen annually, to be denominated "The Mission Board of the Georgia Association," which should be a component member of "The General Missionary Convention of the Baptist Denomination in the United States of America for Foreign Mission." It was also to be an organ for the churches of the Association for domestic missionary operations, and act according to instructions and the means in hand. It was empowered to appoint an agent to excite a missionary interest among the churches and to collect funds, and to appoint one of their own body to represent them in the Triennial Convention, in 1817. It was instructed to maintain a correspondence with the Board of Foreign Missions, and to report annually to the Association. The first Board appointed consisted of Jesse Mercer, William Rabun, Thomas Rhodes, James Matthews, William Davis, Malachi Reeves, and Joseph Roberts. This board continued in existence eleven years, being discontinued in 1827, when the Association resolved to send its missionary funds through the State Convention.

Concerning the Mission Board of the Georgia Association, Dr. C. D. Mallary says, in his Life of Jesse Mercer, that it "prosecuted its business with much success for many years; assisted in the establishment of a mission among the Creeks; received and disbursed considerable sums of money; kept up a correspondence with the General Board, and presented to the Association, from year to year, spirited and animating reports of their proceedings and of the general condition of the cause of missions. Mr. Mercer was uniformly appointed as a member of this Board, was generally its President, and invariably one of its most liberal and efficient supporters."

We find the following in the Minutes of the Georgia Association for 1817: "Our Mission Board made a satisfactory report relative to the disposition of the funds committed to their direction at our last session; whereupon they were dissolved, and the following brethren appointed for the ensuing year, to-wit: Mercer, Matthews, Davis, Rhodes, Reeves, Roberts and Rabun." William Rabun, who was also Clerk of the body, was at that time Governor of Georgia. He died in October, 1819, at his plantation, near Powelton, Georgia.

We now turn our attention for a few moments to the original Ocmulgee Association. Its early history excites admiration. Its originators were pious, godly men, full of zeal and religious earnestness, and they were ardent in their endeavors to promote piety, to maintain correct church order, to spread the gospel within State bounds, and to advance the cause of foreign missions. Indeed, this was the spirit which animated all our early Baptist fathers in the State, to an eminent degree, but they were without those facilities for fostering all these causes which we now possess, and therefore their efforts were less concentrated, and not so intelligently directed.

Constituted November 10th, at Rooty Creek, Putnam county, by James Matthews, John Robertson, Robert McGinty, Benjamin and Edmund Shackelford, a committee appointed by the Georgia Association, Joseph Baker was elected Moderator, and William Williams, Clerk. Twenty-eight churches sent delegates to its second meeting, in 1811, and six others were received, and its Circular Letter, written by Edmund Talbot, breathes an earnest spirit of pious zeal for true Christian fellowship. From many devout exhortations, this only is extracted: "Ye are the light of the world; cherish, guard, exercise and extend your fellowship with unwearied solicitude. The salvation of men depends wholly on the success of the Christian cause; it is the cause of God. It constantly and rapidly gains ground, flourishes, triumphs. Its effects *will* reach, *must* reach, the remotest nations and the latest posterity."

Its session of 1812, September 5th–8th, at Shoal Creek, Randolph county, was a notable meeting. On Sabbath Jesse Mercer, John Ross, and the eloquent Thomas Rhodes, preached "to numerous and more than politely attentive audiences, wherein saints were comforted, convicted souls trembled, and arrows were made fast in the hearts of the King's enemies." The Tirzah church made its report exculpating Rev. Francis Flournoy, and a most stirring Circular Letter, written by Rev. Elijah Moseley, was read and adopted. As a part of the history of the times, and as exhibiting the spirit of our Baptist fathers with reference to the war of 1812, it is presented in full to the reader.

After an apology for writing a Circular on a subject so diverse from those ordinarily selected, and with a graceful allusion to the blessings of peace, the horrors of war, and the necessity of the conflict forced upon the country, the writer proceeds:

"Your progenitors, brethren, from the commencement of the *Christian era*, during the darkest as well as the most luminous ages of antiquity, and in all modern times, have been the asserters of civil and religious liberty; and, very generally, the most conspicuous sufferers for it. Do you, then, whose fathers have suffered so much for you—who have been so highly favored with its enjoyment—now deem it worth defending? Is it a precious gift of God?—a blessing? If so, can you, without impiety and a species of sacrilege—the acting in contempt of *Deity*—relinquish the right of self-government and, by that means, bring upon your souls an accumulation of guilt, of varied stains, indeed, but of deepest dye?

"Were you a sect of yesterday, grown out of and arisen from the squabblings of parties for power, wealth and influence in any corrupt and corrupting national establishment, the case would, indeed, be different. But the contrary being true, and living in this country, so highly favored of the Lord, where each denomination enjoys fully every religious right, equal protection, and as much liberty as is believed to be consistent with human happiness, an indifference to, or supineness in defence of, these blessings, would evince a state of mind most depraved, and indicate the absence of every truly virtuous and religious principle.

"It has been said that 'our constitution and form of government are unsuited and incompetent to sustain the shock of war.' Let us disprove this aspersion, by the prompt support we give them in the present conflict; and demonstrate that the government has our confidence and esteem, and that we will sustain it with united hearts and hands.

"This, brethren, is not a war of passion and of mad ambition on our part. Deeply do we sympathize with many of the virtuous subjects of the government our country is contending against. We lament, with genuine sorrow of soul, the individual miseries that it will probably occasion; the useful and valuable lives that will be sacrificed; the many amiable and worthy characters that, probably, in consequence thereof will go, with lacerated hearts, to the grave.

"These reflections affect us deeply. But in the eye of Eternal Justice we stand acquitted of this evil; it devolves on the head of the aggressor—the iniquitous and corrupt government opposed to our rights.

"Let us not imitate our enemies in savage ferocity. The exercise of the virtues of charity, humanity and generosity, as practiced by you, may, and, we trust, will, in some degree alleviate the miseries of war. To the practice of them we exhort you, *in the name of Jesus*. If war excites or discovers great vices, it may, also, be a season of practicing great virtues—the virtues that adorn and ennoble our nature. The brave and virtuous sons of freedom should ever be humane; to them it is an ornament of glory. The character of an honest, virtuous American is an honorable one; but the being inflated with a spirit of national vanity is ridiculous. We should guard against 'imbibing any portion of that spirit which cost the angels their seat.'

"The necessity of union among the citizens of our country, cannot be too frequently inculcated. An honest difference of opinion may, and, probably, does exist among men of virtue and talents, too, who are the real friends of their country, with respect to the war. The right of private judgment should be respected and ever held sacred. No consistent republican, or true friend of his country wishes to impair it; for the right of exercising our own understanding is the foundation-principle—the basis—upon which our government rests. Leave the abuse of liberty and of the freedom of speech and of the press, to the correction of the laws. No doubt the legal remedy will be applied; but, remember that, whenever this right is interdicted, *freedom expires!* Incendiaries, masked pretenders to republicanism and patriotism, will endeavor to excite an intolerant spirit—a spirit of party and caballing; will labor to effect the proscription of all who do not think as they affect to think! Divisions, of the most mischievous and pernicious consequences, are thus, not unfrequently, effected. Enemies of this description are capable of doing you more essential injury than all the British navy! Ships lost can be replaced; cities demolished can be rebuilt; but *union* lost is seldom regained; and *freedom* once flown is gone FOREVER!

"A spirit of moderation and forbearance will tend greatly to conciliate. 'Let your moderation be known to all men' is an apostolic injunction. Subjects the discussion of which would be proper enough at other seasons, should be avoided in times of peril and difficulty if the least degree of irritation may be the result; and every conciliatory measure, in the adjustment of our comparatively small matters of difference, should be pursued.

"We exhort you to the strict execution of gospel discipline in the churches; but, in the exercise of it, guard with watchful care against the mingling of unholy tempers and passions in your own minds. By lenient faithfulness in brethren, many sorrows may be prevented to many precious souls.

"The exhortation of our beloved Chief Magistrate, in his proclamation recommending a day of humiliation and prayer for averting national calamities and for a speedy return of the blessings and benign influence of peace, should be frequently revolved in our minds. Surely only the profane, and those inimical to our happy and free government—the wretched advocates of rapine and bloodshed—could be regardless of, or inattentive to, that call!

"But a greater than James Madison calls upon us to 'watch and pray.' Jesus Christ, our Saviour, our Redeemer, our God, calls us! He calls us by His Word, Spirit and Providence, to 'pray without ceasing.' This duty, always necessary and pleasant to a lively faith, with peculiar propriety is more solemnly incumbent at a period like the present, when our young men are going forth to battle in defence of all that the heart of man holds dear—our violated rights, our civil and religious liberties, our wives and our little ones, the rich inheritance bequeathed to us by our fathers. They go forth to fight in defence of the tombs of our fathers, of the country which was the theatre of their glory, and to preserve their graves from the unhallowed tread of the enemies of *Freedom!* The Lord Jehovah is our strength and shield: to him let us look with humble confidence and dependence. His omnipotent arm, so often made bare for the defence of his people, will support us through the perilous conflict. If we forsake him not, he will never leave us a prey. By their rapacity, intolerance and injustice, our enemies appear to be making God their enemy also. May we never imitate their madness! but may we, by putting away every evil practice and every evil thing from among ourselves, seek humbly his continual dwelling and blessed presence among us. Then, indeed, would united republican America become 'a praise in the earth.' Perhaps the reputation of republicanism for all time to come, and the fate of unborn millions, is depending on the union and exertions of this generation. The Empire of Freedom, of Reason, of Religion, and of Laws, is again, under God, to be sustained in America by a few hands— by the true, consistent republicans who are the friends of liberty and law. May we escape the execrations of posterity, by handing down to them, unimpaired, the rich inheritance of Freedom we now possess! If history proves any one truth clearly, it is this: That no nation, without public and private virtue, ever retained its freedom long. Religion, virtue, the practice of justice and mercy, and the love of truth, are essential to the very existence of a republican government, producing happiness to the governing and governed alike. Americans only are republican! May they, by their piety, and by the practice of all the lovely train of social virtues, prove themselves a grateful people for the blessings they enjoy, and not altogether unworthy of them!"

These eloquent extracts, expressing such noble and elevated sentiments, will serve as a fair exponent of the spirit and general disposition of the Baptists of that day, and have, therefore, been deemed worthy of historical embalming.

The session for 1813 sent forth a similar letter by the hand of Francis Flournoy, breathing pious and patriotic sentiments, in strong and nervous language, which reads like the blast of a bugle.

The letter for 1814, however, breathes a different spirit. It discusses fully the ministerial work, after speaking of their strong obligations to be thankful, even amid the gloomy prospects of religion which had so universally prevailed. Strong ground in regard to itinerancy was taken, and it was

"*Resolved*, That the *ministers* of this Association, or as many of them as can, shall join, two and two together, and perform an itinerant tour of *preaching* of at least two weeks, and report to the next Association."

The following was also adopted, on motion of Francis Flournoy:

"*Resolved*, That the 18th day of June, (being the day on which war between America and England was declared,) be observed by this Association as a day of fasting and prayer—not that we mourn because war was declared, but we mourn on account of the causes which forced our government to such a dreadful alternative, and because no other remedy could be found to heal our wounded and expiring rights but the blood of our enemies. And also that the 24th day of August (being the day on which the *metropolis* of our country was captured), be observed in the same solemn manner; and that we invite our brethren and friends in general, and our sister Associations in this State in particular, to join us in the dedication of these days; and that they be observed annually, the former till peace be restored, and the latter till the capital of our country be rebuilt."

The Circular Letter for 1815, written by Peter F. Flournoy, begins: "With grief we read in almost all your letters lamentable tidings of barrenness and declension in religion; yet, seeing that most of you are praying, according to the instructions of Christ to his disciples, 'Thy kingdom come,' we are encouraged to hope that God will ere long send a plentiful rain to refresh His heritage from its weariness." And yet, in that year, the reports from the itinerant preaching, recommended the previous year, were favorable, and it was

"*Resolved*, Therefore, to pursue it more extensively."

The membership, in 1815, was 2,666 in forty-one churches, against 2,886 in 1814; and yet the missionary influence exerted by the Foreign Mission Board in Philadelphia, and extended by Luther Rice, and which went out, especially from the Savannah Missionary Society, in 1814, was felt in this Association, and resulted in the organization of the "Ocmulgee Missionary Society," in July, 1815. This proved to be a strong and influential society, which succeeded in arousing a genuine missionary influence in the churches of the Association, and obtained from them in contributions a very respectable amount of money for missionary purposes. Its sixth annual session was held at Tirzah church, Putnam county, in 1821, when Edmund Talbot preached an appropriate sermon, from Isaiah xxxii: 8, "But the liberal deviseth liberal things, and by liberal things shall he stand." Robert McGinty was elected President, and Benjamin Milnor, Edmund Talbot, and John Robertson, Vice-Presidents, while Abner Davis was made Secretary, William Walker, Treasurer, and William Williams, Auditor Besides these officers there were seven trustees. In addition to the balance in the Treasurer's hands, the contributions from various churches, swelled the total amount in the treasury to $445.80, of which $150 was appropriated to the General Mission Board of Philadelphia. At that session Edmund Talbot acted as President. The Circular Address sent forth with the published Minutes is an admirable missionary tract, elegant in style, and is a very strong document in favor of foreign missions. Evidently written by a man well acquainted with the foreign mission news and statistics of the day, it presents them in a strong light, and with great skill and eloquence. Apparently it is from the pen of Edmund Talbot.

One is not surprised to find the Circular Letter of the Association for 1816, written by Wilson Whatley, on the "Sin of Coveteousness;" nor to find December 24th set apart as a day of thanksgiving for blessings both *national* and *individual*, the war being over.

Friday before the first Sabbath in January was also set apart "as a day of humiliation, fasting and prayer to God, that He would graciously look on Zion in her low estate, and pour out on her a gracious and plentiful shower to refresh His heritage." A similar resolution was adopted in 1817, "for the revival of true religion." "Brother Culpepper" was received as a messenger from the Hephzibah Missionary Society, and a strong and Scriptural Circular Letter, by Lazarus Battle, on the "Baneful effects of Drunkenness," was read and adopted.

The missionary spirit of the Association was now thoroughly aroused, and it soon became engaged vigorously in mission work, contributing to the Indian and foreign missions.

Let us turn our attention, now, to the Sarepta Association. At its session in October, 1815, after there had been presented an "Address" of Rev. Luther Rice, agent of the Baptist General Board of Foreign Missions, and also the annual report of the Board itself, soliciting co-operation "in the great and good work of missionary labor," the Sarepta Association recommended that the brethren meet on Friday before the first Sabbath in June, 1816, at Moriah meeting-house, Madison county. for the purpose of adopting measures in aid of missions, and to form themselves into a missionary society, if they think proper. Jesse Mercer attended this meeting, for he says, in a letter to Dr. Benedict, dated June 13th, 1816: "The mission spirit increases in our State; but, I fear, is to be checked by some unfavorable reports from Philadelphia, among the members of the Board, etc. I should be glad to hear something about it, so as to be able to set it in a right light before the people in this State, who are easily discouraged in money matters, as you know the Baptists to be. The very sound of it drives every good feeling from many of their hearts. I lately attended the formation of a mission society in the bounds of the Sarepta Association, and the greatest difficulty seemed to be how their money was to be applied, and whether it would be judiciously appropriated, etc. If you should know anything worth transmitting, I would thank you for it."

This letter was ominous of the sad and calamitous anti-mission troubles of the denomination in the State, which began in 1819.

Thus, we see that the Sarepta Association took its first decided stand in favor of missions in 1815, and in the following year, 1816, a missionary society was formed, about the first of June. In 1817, the Association resolved, "That we cordially receive the thanks of the Board of Foreign Missions, and present ours to them, for their attention and information furnished us in their annual reports and letters," but no contributions for missions appear to have been sent up by the churches.

Again, in 1818, the Sarepta Association expresses gratitude to the General Board for Foreign Missions, for its circular, and acknowledges the reception of a memorial from the Kentucky Missionary Society, inviting co-operation in the establishment of an Indian mission, to which the Clerk, Charles J. Jenkins, was directed to respond by letter. The succeeding year, 1819, witnessed further developments. An interesting letter was received from the Baptist Board of Foreign Missions, containing a request "that the Association give its views relative to a plan for the establishment of a seminary for the education of young men called to the ministry."

Charles J. Jenkins, the Clerk, was formally appointed Corresponding Secretary for the Association, in its communications with the Foreign Board, and he was instructed to answer that the Association was not prepared to offer any plan in reference to the establishment of a theological seminary. The same request was made of all the Baptist Associations by the Foreign Board. It seems that, at its previous meeting, the General or Triennial Convention, had made a constitutional provision for the erection of a classical and theological seminary, "for the purpose of aiding pious young men who, in the judgment of the churches of which they are members, and of the Board, possess gifts and graces suitable to the gospel ministry." Under this provision the Mission Board of the Triennial Convention, drew up a plan for such an institution, which was found so objectionable that further operations were suspended until the next session of the Convention, The result, however, was the establishment of Columbian College, at Washington city, in which the Baptists of Georgia manifested much interest, and for which they contributed large sums. This was no new idea in Georgia. As far back as August 9th, 1814, Dr. William B. Johnson, of Savannah, wrote to Rev. Luther Rice, in Boston: "There is another subject which has occupied much of my thoughts, since my return, to the furtherance of which I am willing to bend my exertions. It is the establishment of a central theological seminary. I think more is to be done in this business northwardly than southwardly; and, though I have no pretensions to great talents, learning, influence, or property, yet I am willing to employ what I have received from the Lord, in these respects, for the promotion of His glory in this, or in any other way."

The Missionary Society of the Sarepta Association seems to have accomplished good, and exerted beneficial influences; the missionary spirit increased, and money for missions began to flow into the associational treasury. At the session of 1820, held at Van's Creek, October 21-24, it was

"*Resolved*, That the clerk of the Association for the future be considered as treasurer of the same, believing that we have churches and individuals in our bounds whose hearts pity the miseries of the heathen, and who desire to contribute something to relieve them. Information is, therefore, given that the treasurer of the Association will gratefully receive the least mite, either for foreign or domestic missions, and it shall be devoted to the object specified by the donor."

It was at this session of 1820 that Rev. Adiel Sherwood, then pastor of Bethlehem church, near Lexington, drew up the following resolution, which he offered, although it was read by the clerk, Charles J. Jenkins, father of Hon. Charles J. Jenkins, afterwards Governor of Georgia:

"*Resolved*, That we suggest for our own consideration, and, respectfully, that of sister Associations in this State, the propriety of organizing a general meeting of correspondence."

After much discussion the resolution was passed.

Dr. Sherwood was then a young man and a new comer in Georgia, but one who had thoroughly identified himself with the Baptist denomination in the State. Having been licensed by the Brushy Creek church, of the Sarepta Association, he afterwards, in 1819, put in his letter with the Bethlehem church, near Athens, and became its pastor. He was ordained in 1820, at Bethesda church, Greene county, during a meeting of the Executive Committee, or rather, "Mission Board" of the Georgia Association, Jesse Mercer, James Armstrong and Malachi Reeves participating.

At its session in 1821, held at Salem, Oglethorpe county, the Sarepta Association adopted the following: " We view with pleasure the exertions of our missionary brethren in various parts of the earth, and especially of the Sarepta Missionary Society."

It is apparent that the Sarepta has exhibited, in a greater and greater degree, the mission spirit, and for five years it has been, through a missionary society, collecting and disbursing funds for mission purposes in a commendable degree, and it has, by its action of 1820, become the originator of our Georgia Baptist Convention, although it does not seem to have taken an active part in the mission connected with Indian reform.

We will now glance at the spirit that animated the Hephzibah Association, from its formation to that period in our denominational history which we have reached—the time when our State Convention was formed.

The Association, as we learn from the Minutes of the Georgia Association for 1794, was constituted in September, 1795, by the union of various churches in the southern part of the latter Association. Being the second Association formed, there was no other body with which the dismissed churches could connect themselves, and therefore no letters of dismission were given. Permission was granted, in October, 1794, to such churches as might desire to form a new Association, to do so; and a committee was appointed to constitute these churches into an Association in September, 1795. Eighteen churches seem to have united in its formation at Buckhead; but the body grew rapidly after a few years, and thirteen years after its formation contained forty-one churches, with a membership of 1,400.

It cordially approved of the Powelton Conferences, sent delegates to those meetings, and when the "General Committee" was formed its delegates appeared regularly and took their seats, and acted with it until 1807. At that time George Franklin, Edmund Talbot, Francis Flournoy and Thomas Johnson represented this Association on the General Committee Board of Trustees for Mount Enon Academy. Previously, Robert McGinty, Francis Ross, John Ross, Edmund Talbot, Joel Willis, Sanders Walker, A. Tharp, Henry Hand, and others, had acted as representatives. In fact, this Association was thoroughly in unison with that whole movement.

Nothing special marked the history of the Association in the first decade of its life, to make it materially differ from those we have been considering. In its Minutes for 1813 we learn that a number of the churches having in their letters expressed a desire for the continuance of itinerant preaching, "the ministers and preachers agreed *to continue it in the usual mode,*" and they united in couples as follows: Franklin and Robertson, Hand and Stanford, Bateman and McGinty, Bush and Shirey, Hillman and Huff, Granade and Perryman, Brinson and Merchant, Pool and Mott, Armstrong and Martin, Pearce and Hawthorn, Smith and Robertson, Franklin and Cutts, Culpepper and Ross, Steeley and Vickers, Manning and Whittle.

The first Saturday in December was "recommended as a day of solemn humiliation, fasting and prayer, to implore the divine mercy and blessing on our government, land and nation; and to beseech the Almighty to remove from us those calamities with which we are afflicted; and that it may please Him to pour out a plenteous effusion of His Spirit and grace upon all the churches of His saints."

This was in reference to the war then pending with Great Britain.

The influence of the Foreign Mission Board and of the Savannah Mission Society in this Association is very palpable. The circular and constitution sent forth by the latter led to the appointment in 1815 of a meeting at Bark Camp the following February, for the purpose of organizing a missionary society. A missionary for Montgomery and contiguous counties was appointed, and the Association determined to engage more earnestly in the domestic mission work. On February 15th, 1816, a number of very respectable members of the Association met at Bark Camp and organized a missionary society after the model of the Foreign Mission Society of Savannah. The preamble and constitution are nearly identical; but the "avowed and determined object" of the "Hephzibah Baptist Society, for itinerant and missionary exertions," was "the encouragement and support of itinerant and missionary efforts."

A list of the officers elected is given: *President*, Rev. Charles Culpepper; *Vice-President*, Rev. John Ross; *Recording Secretary*, Haywood Alford; *Corresponding Secretary*, Littleton Spivey; *Treasurer*, Thomas Byne; *Trustees:* George Porthress, James Jackson, John Cock, Isaac Brinson, Elisha Perryman, James Stephens, Eleazer Lewis.

This Society entered upon a vigorous existence. We find its delegates received and welcomed by the Georgia Association for many years. The Ebenezer and Hephzibah Associations also gracefully recognize its existence and welcome its delegates. In the Minutes of the Hephzibah Association for 1816 the following entry occurs: "A letter from the Hephzibah Baptist Society, for itinerant and missionary exertions, together with their Constitution and Minutes of their respective meetings, were received and read, and, in conformity with the request of that Society, through certain delegates appointed for that purpose, soliciting the approbation and advice of this Association, on motion, agreed to return the following answer:

"We received your friendly communication, soliciting our advice and concurrence in what we think to be your laudable designs. All we can say at present is, dear brethren, go on in the prosecution of your designs in that way you think may be most conclusive to the glory of God and the prosperity of Zion; and that the God of Israel grant you success in the same, is our hearty prayer."

The Association itself supported a missionary within its own bounds in 1816 at a cost of one hundred dollars, and yet the destitution could not be met sufficiently. The ministering brethren of the Association itself were earnestly requested to visit the pastorless churches, and preach to them as often as their engagements would admit. It cannot be denied that there seems to have been a remissness or unwillingness on the part of the churches, properly to sustain their pastors; for the Association earnestly recommended the churches which were without pastors, to be "attentive to the important and necessary duty of making provision, according to their ability, for a proper and regular support of pastors," and, also, properly to remunerate those ministers who should visit them as supplies.

The churches, in their letters, express a desire for the continuance of itinerant preaching, which was heartily assented to, and the brethren again paired off, two and two, with an understanding that they would thus engage in voluntary missionary work; but the conviction creeps into the reflecting mind that this custom really worked ill among the churches, as it appears to have disinclined them to sustain regular pastors, and, perhaps, assisted in producing that anti-mission spirit, which prevailed so painfully for many years. Still, in 1816, the Association with emotions of gratitude to God and thankfulness to the Board, listened to the pleasing information relative to the prosperous condition of Foreign Missions contained in letters from Dr. Staughton, Secretary, and from Rev. Luther Rice, Agent of the Board of Foreign Missions, in Philadelphia.

When, in 1817, a formal vote was taken whether the Association should contribute to the funds of the Baptist Board of Foreign Missions, it was decided in the negative; but a resolution was adopted that all those friendly to Foreign Missions were recommended to meet in January, 1818, at the Bethel Meeting House, near Louisville, Jefferson county, for the purpose of forming a Foreign Mission Society, distinct from the Association. A Foreign Mission Society was formed, and yet, with a domestic Mission Society at Bark Camp, and a Foreign Mission Society at Louisville, the Association itself became anti-missionary in sentiment.

The sixth Association formed in the State was the Ebenezer. It was constituted in March, 1814, at Cool Springs meeting-house, in Wilkinson county, from churches dismissed from the Hephzibah and Ocmulgee Associations—six from the latter and eight from the former. The Hephzibah appointed brethren C. Culpepper, George Franklin, N. Robertson and J. Shirey; and the Ocmulgee appointed Joseph Baker, V. A. Tharpe, D. Wood, H. Hooten, and Edmund Talbot, presbyteries to meet at Cool Spring meeting-house, Wilkinson county, on Saturday beforethe first Sabbath in March, and constitute the churches lying in the forks of the Oconee and Ocmulgee rivers into an Association. This was done, and the first regular session was held the following August.

In the first years of its formation, the Ebenezer Association corresponded with the General Baptist Mission Committee, in Philadelphia, and took an interest in "Indian Reform" among the Creeks.

Two new Associations were formed in 1817—the Tugalo and the Piedmont, The former was constituted chiefly from churches dismissed from the Sarepta Association, but some of its churches were in South Carolina. It was composed at first of the following churches: Tugalo, Beaverdam, Poplar Spring, Lower Nail's Creek, Double Branches, Line, Hunter's Creek, Leatherwood, Eastanallee Chaujie, and Liberty. In 1821 it contained nineteen churches, of which thirteen lay in Georgia, with a membership of 776. There were twenty-one churches in 1822; but nothing was done in reference to co-operation with the General Association.

The Piedmont was also formed in 1817, and was really an anti-mission Association from its organization. The churches represented in its second session, in 1818, at Wesley's Creek meeting-house, were Jones Creek, Liberty county; Wesley's Creek, McIntosh county; Sarepta, Tatnall county; Black Creek, Tatnall county; Purchase, on Satillo river. With a total membership of 121, there had been nine baptisms during the year.

At its session in 1819 this Association voted to have nothing to do with missions. The Association then contained five churches and 294 members, and, of course, formed no connection with the General Association. One of its most prominent members was Isham Peacock, to whose ordination reference has been made, and who developed into a whisky-drinking, anti-missionary preacher, and lived to a great age.

There were now eight Associations in the State—the Georgia, the Hephzibah, the Sarepta, the Sunbury, the Ocmulgee, the Ebenezer, the Tugalo and the Piedmont—but, although some interest was manifested in missions, yet the general state of vital religion was by no means gratifying. We find in all the Associations days appointed for fasting, humiliation and prayer that God would revive the churches and graciously visit afflicted Zion with His Spirit. This unpropitious state of affairs was due partly, perhaps, mostly to the war with Great Britain, accompanied as it was by warfare with the Indians, whom the English stirred up to hostilities from Canada to Florida. When peace was established, in 1815, war with the Indians ceased in Georgia and Alabama, but broke out again in 1817, and continued for two years, until the strong arm of General Jackson quenched hostility in blood at Horse Shoe Bend, in Alabama, bringing peace, and by treaty acquiring for the State a title to the land in her borders. These wars cast over the religious spirit of the day a pall of gloom and discouragement that lasted for years. An idea of the moral condition of the period may be obtained by the following extract from the Minutes of the Georgia Association for 1815, which met that year at Long Creek, Warren county:

"Received a letter from the committee of the Hopewell Presbytery, requesting the appointment of some of this body to meet in a general association of the different denominations, to be assembled at Athens, Tuesday before the Commencement, in 1816, to combine their efforts to promote *morality* and *virtue*, as well as religion."

Abraham Marshall and Ed. Shackelford were appointed for the purpose, but we have no report of the proposed meeting. In the Minutes of 1816 we do, however, find this entry: "Recommended to the churches to appoint and observe among themselves days of humiliation and prayer to Almighty God, as regards the low state of religion and abounding iniquity."

In the same year the Hephzibah Association agreed to observe "a day of humiliation, fasting and prayer" that God would "bless our country, revive religion, and pour out a plentiful effusion of His Holy Spirit upon all the churches of His saints." In the following year, 1817, the Ebenezer Association "agreed to observe Saturday before the fourth Sabbath in July next as a day of fasting and solemn prayer to Almighty God to revive His gracious work among us, and make us more active in the ways of religion."

The second decade of the century was, then, a period in which demoralization prevailed and religion languished; nor was it until the latter half of the third decade that God manifested His spiritual power with wonderful effect.

The years of this chapter embrace that period in Georgia Baptist history when the attention of the denomination was first generally directed to foreign missions. The impetus given to this grand cause by the conversion to Baptist principles of Luther Rice and Adoniram Judson and his first wife, was sensibly felt in Georgia, and the interest it excited was strong and abiding. Mission societies were soon formed in all the Associations, and did efficient service in the mission cause. The Savannah River Association, which, in Georgia, became the Sunbury in 1817, supported missionaries within its own bounds; the Associations in middle Georgia took hold of the Creek mission vigorously, while the Sarepta Mission Society sustained a mission among the Cherokee Indians in North Georgia. Several of the Associations remitted respectable amounts to the Baptist Board for Foreign Missions, in Philadelphia, and at different times some of our prominent brethren attended the sessions of the Triennial Convention. In this chapter, however, we have but the beginning of these events. So far there has been but little opposition to missions. That disposition was aroused after the Anti-missionary Baptists of the more Northern States had held a convention, in 1815, incited by the missionary enthusiasm of the day, and had enunciated their principles; and we shall find that, after this period, a strong anti-missionary sentiment becomes developed in Georgia. But the more pious, intelligent and best educated ministers and church members, beyond doubt, were in favor of the mission cause.

IX.
INDIAN REFORM.
1818-1824.

IX.

INDIAN REFORM.

FEELING IN REGARD TO INDIAN REFORMATION IN THE BEGINNING OF THE CENTURY—EXTRACT FROM THE MISSION BOARD OF THE GEORGIA ASSOCIATION IN 1818—DESIRE OF THE INDIANS—FIRST STEPS TAKEN BY THE OCMULGEE ASSOCIATION—"PLAN" FOR "INDIAN REFORM" ADOPTED—INTERESTING LETTER FROM DR. STAUGHTON—GENERAL GOVERNMENT APPROPRIATIONS—APPOINTMENT OF FRANCIS FLOURNOY—SOME ACCOUNT OF HIM—HIS VINDICATION AND DEATH—APPOINTMENT OF E. L. COMPERE—ESTABLISHMENT OF A SCHOOL AND MISSION AT WITHINGTON STATION—ACTION OF THE EBENEZER ASSOCIATION—ZEAL AND LIBERALITY OF LADIES—REPORT OF THE OCMULGEE AND GEORGIA ASSOCIATIONS IN 1824—GENERAL VIEW.

There was an earnest desire among Southern Baptists, in the times of which we write, to civilize and improve their Indian neighbors. Repeatedly the Associations of Georgia received communications from the Baptists of Kentucky, soliciting co-operation in this work. Those of Mississippi also expressed a similar desire. The United States Congress, with a just appreciation of the matter, in 1819, appropriated ten thousand dollars annually for this purpose, subject to the direction of the President, Mr. Monroe. In Mr. Monroe's opinion it was best, in order to render this beneficence as extensively beneficial as possible, that this sum should be applied in co-operation with the exertions of benevolent associations. With the Georgia Baptists the idea of Indian improvement and evangelization had been a favorite one ever since the beginning of the century, Under the direction of the general committee, Judge Clay had corresponded with Major Benjamin Hawkins, United States Indian agent, who resided on the Indian frontier, with reference to the establishment of an English school among the Indians ; but the period was not a propitious one for the enterprise, and the project, as a matter of Christian enterprise, remained in abeyance for nearly a score of years, without by any means fading from the minds and hearts of Georgia Baptists. The report of the Mission Board of the Georgia Association for 1818 has these words ;

"The evangelizing of our own Indians is *alone* the *broad work* of ages. We invite the Association to inspect the moral state of the heathens in our own country ; and we ask, that if they had been taught to *cheat, steal, lie and swear*, by men called Christians, does it not prove they can be, and that it is a shame they have not been, a long time ago, taught the fear of God, the *sin* and *Saviour* of man, and, also, to pray !" The minutes of the Georgia Association for the same year, 1818, contain these words : "Received a communication from the Secretary of the Kentucky Mission Society, inviting our co-operation in the establishment of a school in that State for the education of the youth of both sexes, belonging to such of the neighboring *Indian tribes* as may be disposed to avail themselves of the opportunity."

In that same year, the chiefs of the Creek Nation made it known that there was a prevailing desire among the Indians for instruction ; and some of the chiefs expressed the opinion that, if schools were but established, their benefits would be so apparent that the Indians themselves would support them.

All these facts combined to urge immediate entrance upon a work for which Providence seemed so manifestly to be opening the way, especially as the proposition of the President secured the one great and desirable object, that those to whom the instruction of the Indians was confided should be moral and religious persons. This gave to "Indian Reform" the character of a true mission. Pertinently, therefore, did the Mission Board of the Georgia Association ask, in its report for 1819, "Thus the door is flung wide open before us, and invites our entrance. Shall we now engage or not? The question we respectfully submit to the decision and instruction of the Association."

The Ocmulgee Association had already determined to engage in the work of "Indian Reform," among the Creeks, and, in 1819, had deputed Rev. Francis Flournoy to act as its agent in a visit to that Nation, and obtain a site for a school, while a committee was appointed to draught a plan of operations. It was composed of Elijah Mosely, Abner Davis, Edmund Talbot and Pitt Milner.

At the session of the Ocmulgee Association for September, 1820, held at Bethesda, Jasper county, this committee presented its report, which was designated A PLAN OF SCHOOL TO BE THE GERM OF A RELIGIOUS ESTABLISHMENT AMONG THE CREEK INDIANS.

Its different items were:

1st. The Institution shall be situate in that section of the Nation which lies between the Euchee creek and the Tallapoosy river, to be fixed on by the superintendent.

2nd. It shall be considered under the patronage of the Baptist Board of Missions in the United States, and directed by the joint counsel of the Ocmulgee, Georgia, Ebenezer, and such other Associations as may hereafter co-operate with them, or such trustees as they may appoint for that purpose, according to the regulations prescribed by the general government for Indian improvement.

3rd. No person shall be employed in the institution who is not of decent and respectable character, whose example shall not be worthy of imitation, and whose religious sentiments are not strictly in unison with the Particular Baptists.

4th. The immediate superintendence of the Institution shall be committed to a regular and exemplary minister of the Baptist order, who also shall be considered as a missionary to the Nation.

5th. The superintendent, teachers and families engaged in the Institution, shall, from the commencement, adopt such course of conduct as shall be best suited, in their view, to impress on the Indians an engaging sense of civilized life, moral propriety and religious obligation, by leading their view toward God as Creator and final Judge of all, and toward Jesus Christ, as the only possible Saviour of sinful men.

6th. Young Indians of both sexes shall be received into the Institution (as soon as the necessary means are had) to be educated in reading, writing and arithmetick, and the civil arts, etc., at the expense of the founders, (except where the Indians shall choose to bear a part or the whole of the charge, in which case they shall have their wish freely.)

7th. The superintendent shall make a regular annual report to the constituents of the progress and prospects of the Institution, and suggest such things, from time to time, as he shall think necessary.

This "plan," called in Georgia Baptist history the "Plan for Indian Reform," was adopted by the Association, and the appointment of Francis Flournoy by the General Board as the Superintendent of the Institution, was cordially concurred in by the body. Rev. B. Milner, Abner Davis, Benjamin Wilson, William Williams and Wilson Lumpkin were appointed a Committee of Five, to be called Trustees, to act for the Association in the establishment of a mission among the Creek Indians, but as they never succeeded in holding a meeting during the year, for want of a quorum, their appointment was revoked in 1821, and three Trustees, William Williams, Abner Davis and John Milner, were elected to hold their appointments during good behavior. The churches were recommended, in 1820, to take up an annual collection for the support of the school among the Creek Indians, to be transmitted to the Association in 1821, when Lazarus Battle was appointed Treasurer to hold the mission funds. The following year, 1822, a "Mission Board" of seven members was formally elected to assume control of the mission affairs of the Association, the Ocmulgee Mission Society was incorporated with the Association itself, and the body was fairly embarked in the missionary work.

In May, 1820, Dr. William Staughton, Corresponding Secretary of the Board of Managers of the Baptist General Convention of the United States, (the old Triennial Convention,) addressed a long and most interesting communication to the Georgia Association, in behalf of the Board. It contains a general view of the Baptist missionary operations of that period, both foreign and domestic; but such extracts only as pertain to Georgia Baptist history will be given here. It says:

"The managers have resumed their mission among the Cherokees with renewed ardor. Missionary measures were for some time suspended in that quarter, from the uncertainty whether these Indians would continue to occupy the land of their progenitors, or retire westward. Liberal appropriations have been made to enable brother H. Posey, assisted by Mr. Dawson, a well qualified teacher, to effect a permanent and, with the blessing of the Redeemer, a prosperous establishment in that benighted region.

"In the Georgia and Ocmulgee Associations, the generous wish is maturing into holy effort to instruct and evangelize the Indians of the Creek Nation. The Board rejoices in their purposes of Christian benevolence, and will be happy in the co-operation of their counsels and exertions. They have appointed the Rev. Francis Flournoy, a brother in whom the Managers place great confidence, as possessing excellent qualifications, to commence the good work in such way as his own judgment and the advice of his brethren shall conclude most expedient."

The letter alludes to various other missionary stations among the Indians in the West and Southwest, showing that more than sixty years ago Indian missions were in great favor with our denomination, as they have been ever since. The following extract is interesting:

"They [the Board of Managers] consider it due to the impartiality and benevolence of the general government, to state that it has always contributed liberally to the Western Stations, with a view particularly to Indian reform, and has promised to augment such assistance in proportion as the extent of the efforts of the Board shall widen."

We thus behold the United States government, by special appropriations, sustaining largely our General Convention in efforts to "reform" the Indians—which word included the two ideas of *instruction* and *evangelization;* and we see the Convention, through its Board of Managers, taking the initiative in establishing a mission for "Indian Reform" among the Creek Indians in Alabama, in co-operation with our Georgia Associations. The following extract from the report of the Mission Board of the Georgia Association, for 1820, which was adopted, gives a clear and concise view of the state of affairs with reference to that mission in 1820:

"With regard to a school among the Creek Indians, we were of opinion, as the Ocmulgee Association had set forward a design of the same nature, that it would be proper to form a co-operation with them in the effort. And we are happy to inform you that a pleasing concert has been readily formed in this important object. But previously the Baptist Board of Missions for the United States had anticipated it as a work of no distant period, and only wanted a proper person to begin, to enter actively into the design. On the suggestion of brother Rice, concurred in by brethren Mosely and Mercer, biother Francis Flournoy was appointed to the superintendence of the contemplated establishment, and to be missionary to the Nation; and we are gratified that this appointment has been concurred in by the Ocmulgee Association; and we hope soon to receive his acceptance of this appointment, and see him enter on the duties of his station."

Francis Flournoy was born in Chesterfield county, Virginia, and was a man of decided ability and education. He seems to have occupied quite a prominent and even influential position in the Ocmulgee Association, of which he was

Clerk from 1815 to 1821, and was appointed to preach in 1817, in case of failure on the part of R. E. McGinty. He was for a number of years pastor of the Tirzah church, in Putnam county. About 1811 he was impeached as a State Commissioner and tried, and was laid under censure by the Legislature. In 1811 R. E. McGinty moved, in the Ocmulgee Association, that the church at Tirzah, of which F. Flournoy was a member, "be advised to call able help from the different churches, to examine the records of the trial of brother Flournoy, and sum up all or any of the testimony that was had before the High Court of Impeachment, and more fully and manifestly declare his case, as they may find it." The Tirzah church observed the above, and in, 1812, the following report was adopted, which completely exonerated Francis Flournoy from all blame:

"*The Baptist Church of Christ at Tirzah, to the Ocmulgee Association:*

GREETING—In obedience to your recommendation, we have called to our assistance a number of the best informed helps that we could obtain, for the purpose of re-examining the evidence exhibited before the High Court of Impeachment of this State against brother Francis Flournoy, who, having met and taken up the case, after giving it a calm, fair and dispassionate investigation, were unanimously of opinion that no just cause of condemnation can, with any propriety, be attached to brother Flournoy.

It is, therefore, with pleasure that we declare to you, and all others whom it may concern, that, nowithstanding the many oppressions under which brother Flournoy has labored, he is still held by us as an orderly Christian and faithful minister of the gospel of Christ. JESSE MERCER, *Moderator.*
WILLIAM RABUN, *Clerk.*
Tirzah, 4th of July, 1812.

In 1819 Mr. Flournoy was sent as an agent of the Ocmulgee Association to the Creek Nation, to inquire and consult in regard to the propriety and feasibility of establishing an English school in the Nation as the germ of a mission. While there he was regularly appointed Superintendent of Indian Improvement in the Creek Nation, which appointment was cordially concurred in by the Ocmulgee Association.

He was murdered at night, in his fifty-sixth year, while encamped near Monticello, in Jasper county. The murderer was a runaway negro, who hoped to obtain money by the crime, and who was arrested and executed.

At its session of 1819 a committee was appointed by the Ebenezer Association to co-operate with that of the Ocmulgee Association in establishing a Reform Mission among the Creek Indians; and, in 1820, the Association formally concurred in the "Plan for Indian Reform" adopted by the Ocmulgee, appointed trustees, and requested its ministers to explain the entire matter to their churches, and propose to them methods for raising money, in support of the mission. Considerable enthusiasm and great unanimity were exhibited by the Association in sustenance of this "laudable pursuit," during the years 1821 and 1822; and at its session in the latter year it was

"*Resolved*, That brother Compere, Missionary for Indian Reform, be invited to take a tour of preaching through our bounds, and solicit contributions for that purpose."

In anticipation of immediate joint action, the Georgia, Ocmulgee and Ebenezer Associations had formed a Board of Managers, through the respective trustees appointed to take charge of this Indian Reform Mission. Nothing was done, however, previous to the session of 1821, as Francis Flournoy declined the appointment as Superintendent, on account of his private embarrassments, and because no official action could be taken at any time by the Board of Managers, for want of a quorum. Toward the close of 1822, however, Rev. Lee Compere, of South Carolina, was appointed Superintendent, and he accepted the appointment. He was considered "well fitted for the work," as a man "possessing piety and talents," and as one whose "praise is most in those churches and among the brethren with whom he has most frequently been."

Appropriations were made and Mr. Compere proceeded to his field of labor;

but it was found that the Methodist Conference of Georgia and South Carolina had, through their agent, Mr. Capers, concluded a treaty with the Creek Indians, which threw obstacles in Mr. Compere's way, and retarded his operations. The Georgia Associations received assurances that the Board of Foreign Missions, in Philadelphia, would take the Creek Mission under its patronage and support, in connection with the co-operating Associations. The Mississippi Domestic and Foreign Mission Society appropriated one hundred dollars to the same mission; while it was ascertained that the full proportion of the appropriation from the United States could be relied on with certainty.

At length, in 1823, the cheering acknowledgement of successful accomplishment was made to the Georgia Association, by its able Mission Board: "It affords us real gratification to inform you that the institution so long held in anxious anticipation among the Creek Indians, is now in successful and promising operation, under the superintendence and management of brother Compere and his devoted associates. Many formidable obstacles, like the mountain which obstructed the building of the temple of the Lord, have subsided and become a plain. Between thirty and forty children have already been submitted to the entire care and direction of the missionaries; and the prospect is good for as many as can be supported on the same terms.

The heavy expenditures and incidental expenses attendant on making the establishment thus far, have been sustained by the very liberal patronage of the General Board, and various other collections and resources, which the report of the Board of Trustees for the united Associations will show, and to which report we refer you for particulars. We regret, deeply regret, that the Ebenezer Association has declined further co-operation in this institution, without giving us notice, or assigning a solitary reason."

The following is the action of the Ebenezer in this matter, at Stone Creek, Twiggs county, in 1823: "Took under consideration the Indian Reform—whether to continue or discontinue; and it was discontinued." V. A. Tharpe was Moderator, and John McKenzie, Clerk.

As not being out of place, another extract is here given from the report made to the Georgia Association, in 1823, a part of which has just been quoted:

"The moneys designated in our funds, $369, for the Creek mission, and the sum requisite to meet the expenses of our messenger, Adiel Sherwood, to the Convention, last spring, at the city of Washington, have been appropriated for those purposes. To sustain our membership in the Convention and to re-imburse, in some measure, the amount afforded by the General Board, to aid in the commencement of our Creek Mission, we have also appropriated the sum of $600. The money placed in our hands for the theological institution (Columbian College), has, also, been forwarded. We are impressed with the propriety of not suffering the Foreign Mission Funds to be the least impaired by our Creek Mission; but, that, ultimately, we in the South should sustain the institution in the Creek Nation, and reimburse entirely, if not replenish the funds of the General Board.

"Dear brethren, we recommend that you lay it to heart and devise plans the most promising to procure the support, at least, for this infant establishment, of so much promise. We acknowledge with thankfulness to God, the pious deeds of several benevolent females in the church at Shiloh, in making and forwarding sundry garments for the children at the Creek school, and hope that many Rhodas in other churches will emulate their benevolence, in furnishing *cloth*, rather than garments, as the cloth can be made up better at the Station."

"Withington Station," where this Indian Reform Mission and School were, was situated about thirty miles south of the locality now occupied by the city of Montgomery, Alabama, and was in the very midst of the Creek Nation.

But how has the matter been progressing in the Ocmulgee Association? Let the report of the Mission Board of that Association, for the year 1824, afford the answer. It should be remembered that, in 1822, the Association incorporated in its own organization the operations of the flourishing Ocmulgee Mission Society, appointing as its successor an Associational Mission Board, which was elected annually.

"The Mission Board of the Ocmulgee Association to their constituents, send Christian salutation :

"BELOVED BRETHREN—The second year is now closed since we first became charged with your funds, and the management of your missionary concerns. In discharging the duties of the trust confided to us, our steady aim and constant endeavors have been to give such direction to the means put into our hands as might best promote the interest and coming of the kingdom of our blessed Redeemer. The transactions of the first year of our appointment are already before you. It now becomes our duty to place before you the state and progress of those concerns subsequent to our last report. Permit us to observe that the Withington Station continues in a prosperous condition, and promises well to become a light, indeed, to the poor, benighted Creeks. There are now forty-two pupils in the school, who are daily progressing in the arts of civilized life and in the acquisition of useful knowledge. The progress already made by some of these pupils, in writing, has surpassed our expectations, specimens of which have been furnished us by the Superintendent, which we cannot forbear exhibiting herewith to your view. The Superintendent's books and accounts have also been submitted to the examination of the Executive Committee, and are found correct. You have to lament, with us, the afflicting dispensation that has recently taken away one of the members of your Board, who was also its treasurer. The pious and useful endeavors, and the enlightened counsel of our late brother, Lazarus Battle, are no more to be had and enjoyed by his brethren on earth. But he has rested from his labors, *and his works do follow him !"*

In 1823 the Ocmulgee Association appropriated $250 to the Withington Station, and in 1824 the Georgia Association appropriated $350 to the same purpose ; in each Association mission matters were for the several succeeding years managed by mission boards or committees of seven, which were animated by a good missionary spirit, and did good work, too. The report of the Mission Board of the Georgia Association for 1824, says, in regard to the school at Withington Station :

"We are happy to say the school is still in a flourishing and prosperous condition. The Superintendent, brother Compere, attended the late session of the Ocmulgee Association, and presented to the Executive Committee of the United Board his books and accounts, which were found correct; and specimens of writing, and a letter from one of the boys in the school to the patrons of the institution, expressive of gratitude for, and praying a continuance of, those benefits which the benighted condition of their parents forbids them to afford ; all of which were not only satisfactory, but highly pleasing. The prospect is truly encouraging, and inspires zeal in the prosecution.

"The President of the United States has taken a lively interest in the support of our institution, and has given it a good proportion among others. The General Board also continue to extend their fostering care towards it ; but their funds are quite exhausted. And in this regard we regret to say that the contributions from the churches are *diminished* where they should have abounded. Many of the churches still remain inactive. Will they never be *provoked* to emulation ? Will they be content always to lie still at home, while their brethren go to war in the good cause of benevolence and charity ? But to the praise and honor of some of our beloved sisters and friends be it said, that they are producing a remedy for this deficiency. We have been presented by brother J. H. Walker with a subscription from a benevolent female society in the church and congregation at Greenwood, of about five hundred yards of cloth for the clothing of the children at the Withington Station, which will be ready for transportation in a few weeks. The grateful acknowledgments of the Board are hereby voted them for their kind and charitable labors of love towards the children of the roving tribe."

This much of the report is given, as it presents a fair idea of the estimation in which this mission was held at that time by many Georgia Baptists.

The reader has now some idea of the "Indian Reform" Mission in which the Baptists of Georgia engaged with great enthusiasm for a few years. The "plan" upon which it was conducted, as adopted by the Ocmulgee and Georgia Asso-

INDIAN REFORM.

ciations has been given already, and those two were the main Associations which co-operated in sustaining the mission, though others assisted incidentally.

This was the second general enterprise in which the Baptists of Georgia united their efforts, the first being the objects whose attainment was sought by the "General Committee," consisting mainly of itinerant labors and the establishment of a Baptist college.

It is pleasant to record that a much more cheering, hopeful and prosperous condition has begun to prevail in the denomination. It begins to act with some unity of purpose. While Abraham Marshall has passed away, his son, Jabez Pleiades, has risen up to supply his place, and other strong and useful men have become identified with us. The elder Brantly has charge of the Augusta church; James Armstrong, Adiel Sherwood, J. H. T. Kilpatrick, Henry J. Ripley, have migrated to the State, while James Shannon has been converted from Presbyterianism.

A better tone begins to exist in the churches, and an unwonted activity and interest in denominational matters has been excited. The General Association has been formed; two more Associations, Yellow River and Flint, are organized, and the number of Baptists in the State is about eighteen thousand.

The State has now a population of about 400,930, of whom, in round numbers, 225,048 are white, and 175,882 are colored slaves; but emigrants are pouring in daily, and the tide is flowing rapidly towards the Chattahoochee. The Creeks were overcome by General Jackson in 1819, and the lands between the Altamaha and the Chattahoochee were acquired. By treaties in 1817, '18 and '19 the land in the territory now embraced by the counties of Newton, DeKalb, Gwinnet, Walton, Hall and Habersham were acquired. In 1821, the State, by treaty, obtained from the Creek Indians a title to the lands lying between the Flint and Ocmulgee Rivers, including the counties of Monroe, Bibb, Crawford, Dooly, Houston, Upson, Fayette, Pike and Henry. By a treaty at the Indian Springs, in 1825, the lands between the Flint and Chattahoochee rivers were acquired, embracing the counties of Coweta, Campbell, Carroll, Troup, Talbot, Muscogee, Harris, etc. While Georgia claimed the entire state, by right of eminent domain, yet the Indians held a title to these lands, as individuals, and they resided in Western Georgia and Eastern Alabama, an object of interest and concern to the Christian and philanthropist, and an object of care and benevolence on the part of our general government, which, from that time to the present, has never ceased to approprite funds and apply measures for their amelioration and instruction.

As yet there are no large towns, but few villages, and but few village churches, while all the churches lie in the eastern half of the state. The denomination is, however, rapidly spreading westward and southward with the tide of emigration.

X.
THE GENERAL ASSOCIATION.
1820-1823.

X.

THE GENERAL ASSOCIATION.

ACTION OF THE SAREPTA ASSOCIATION IN 1820—CONSIDERED FAVORABLY BY THE OCMULGEE AND GEORGIA ASSOCIATIONS—DISREGARDED BY THE EBENEZER AND HEPHZIBAH—CONSIDERED UNFAVORABLY BY ITSELF—THE GENERAL MEETING AT POWELTON IN JUNE, 1822—NOTABILITIES PRESENT—SERMON BY SHERWOOD AND PRAYER BY MERCER—THE CONSTITUTION PRESENTED BY BRANTLY—ITS ADOPTION—EXTRACTS FROM THE CIRCULAR LETTER—SECOND SESSION OF THE GENERAL ASSOCIATION AND ITS ACTION—ACTION OF THE SAREPTA IN 1823—THE SUNBURY ASSOCIATION JOINS THE GENERAL ASSOCIATION IN 1823—THE EBENEZER DECLINES TO UNITE WITH THE GENERAL ASSOCIATION—ACTION OF THE HEPHZIBAH—BRANTLY, SHERWOOD, ARMSTRONG, KILPATRICK.

It has been seen that the resolution which led to the organization of the Georgia Baptist Convention, was adopted by the Sarepta Association in October, 1820, at Van's Creek.

The first Association to meet, afterwards, was the Ocmulgee, which met at Bethel, Jones county, September 1st, 1821, and on the following Tuesday it adopted a resolution declaring: "That this Association do heartily concur with the Sarepta in the resolution for the organization of a general meeting of correspondence;" and Rev. Robert McGinty, John M. Gray and Cyrus White, were appointed delegates to represent the Ocmulgee Association.

On Monday, October 15th, the Georgia Association, during its session of 1821, at Clark's Station meeting-house, Wilkes county, by resolution, "Agreed that this Association concur in the suggestion and recommendation of the Sarepta and Ocmulgee Associations, in the formation of a general meeting, ' to be composed of messengers from all the Associations in this State, or as many of them as shall come into the measure;' that this meeting commence at Powelton, on Thursday before the fifth Sabbath in June, 1822; that we send up five members of our body to that meeting, viz: Jesse Mercer, William T. Brantly, Winder Hilman, James Armstrong and Jabez P. Marshall."

In the *Georgia* that year the Sarepta Association was represented by Adiel Sherwood, and the *Ocmulgee* by Jeremiah Reeves and Joel Colley, who doubtless reported the action of their Associations. It is fairly presumable, therefore, that a general understanding existed in regard to the meeting at Powelton, in June, for the formation of a General Association.

In the Sunbury Association the resolution of the Sarepta was received in 1821, but was postponed until the next session, " for the further consideration of the churches;" and, at the meeting of 1822 its decision was again postponed for a year—that is, until 1823.

The Ebenezer and Hephzibah Associations disregarded the invitation to unite in forming a General Association; but, what is more remarkable, the Sarepta Association, after having, in 1820, adopted the resolution, "that we suggest for our own consideration, and, respectfully, that of sister Associations in the State, the propriety of organizing a general meeting of correspondence," when it came to consider the matter in accordance with its own resolution, in 1821, passed the following: "We do not conceive that there is a necessity for such a meeting."

The truth is, the resolution, as originally drawn up by Adiel Sherwood, was as follows: "*Resolved*, that we suggest, respectfully, to the consideration of sister Associations in the State, the propriety of organizing a general meeting of correspondence." This was amended so as to read, "*for our own consideration*, and, respectfully, that of sister Associations," etc.

As a matter of course that subject was brought in for consideration by the committee of arrangements for 1821, and the action stated above was taken. J. H. Campbell asserts that this resolution was drawn up by Isham Goss. Nevertheless, we find that for several years, Mr. Goss represented the Sarepta Association in the General Association as a messenger.

Isham Goss was the son of Benjamin Goss, and was born in Virginia before his father moved to Georgia. He had three brothers—John, Jesse Hamilton and Horatio J.—all of whom were Baptist preachers. The two former removed to Virginia, where they died in the faith, after lives of usefulness. Isham embraced a hope at the age of nine, and became a preacher at Beaver Dam Church, through the instrumentality of that useful man, William Davis. In his early ministerial career he was greatly beloved by his churches—Beaver Dam, Trail Branch, Cloud's Creek and others—and he exerted a great influence in the Association. Repeatedly he was its Clerk and Moderator, and he was also President of the Sarepta Missionary Society. About 1820 or 1821 he became subject to a severe headache, brought on by a partial separation of the bones of the skull, from which he could find no relief, except from stimulants. This resulted in a partial derangement, from which he never fully recovered. He confessed to a nephew in 1839, the year he died, that he had engaged more than became a minister in worldly pursuits, in hopes of acquiring wealth, which, with a too great addiction to stimulants to assuage his extreme pain in the head, resulted injuriously to him morally, spiritually and physically. He was excluded from church fellowship, but, having moved into the bounds of the Yellow River Association, was restored to the church and ministry. He, however, never recovered his usefulnesss.

It can be said of him that he never drank when well, and that Dozier Thornton and Jesse Mercer were friends and frequent visitors at his house. We have reasons to doubt his being the author of the anti-Convention Resolution of 1821.

Thursday, the 27th of June, 1822, arrived. It was the day appointed by the Georgia Association for the assembling of delegates, from the different Associations in the State, to form one General Association.

The meeting took place at Powelton, and there was a large assemblage present. But two Associations, however, were represented: *Georgia*, by Jesse Mercer, Wm. T. Brantly, Winder Hilman, James Armstrong and Jabez P. Marshall; and the *Ocmulgee*, by Cyrus White. Robert McGinty and J. M. Gray failed to attend. Adiel Sherwood was there—the man on whose motion the Convention assembled, and yet he was entitled to no seat, because his Association, the Sarepta, had, on reconsideration, declared against the necessity of such a meeting, and, of course, sent no delegates.

The Convention met in the house of worship of the Powelton Baptist Church, and organized by the election of Rev. Jesse Mercer as President, and Rev. Jabez P. Marshall as Secretary. Jesse Mercer was, at that time, fifty-four years of age. Rev. Wm. T. Brantly, then thirty-four years old, was chosen Assistant Secretary.

It was then resolved that all members from distant churches and Associations, lay members as well as ministers, together with the members of the church with which the Convention was held, be invited to take part in the deliberations. Among those who accepted seats were Rev. Adiel Sherwood, Rev. Humphrey Posey, Rev. Lee Compere, and Rev. Elisha Perryman.

A free interchange of sentiment on the part of those present resulted in the appointment of Jesse Mercer, William T. Brantly, Cyrus White and James Armstrong as a Committee to draft a Constitution, to be reported the ensuing day. Before adjournment on Thusday, Rev. A. Sherwood was appointed to preach at the opening of the session next morning; Rev. H. Posey was appointed to preach at its close,

On Friday the Convention met at 10 o'clock, and Rev. A. Sherwood preached a written discourse from the words, "Prepare ye the way of the Lord," Luke iii: 4, in which he very forcibly demonstrated the need of such an organization as was designed by the Convention proposed to be formed, and he portrayed strongly the evils of sectional feelings and jealousies arising from a want of union, and he depicted clearly the advantages of united action. He was then pastor of a church in the Sarepta Association, but he had travelled extensively through the State, and for several years, had been a State missionary in the employ of the Savannah Missionary Society. He was at that time thirty-one years of age, and full of fire and zeal, a man of excellent education and abilities, and very tall and commanding in appearance. His sermon, bristling with facts and information, presented the strongest reasons why the Baptists of Georgia should unite in some method of co-operation.

At the conclusion of the sermon, Jesse Mercer, President of the body, led in prayer. During his prayer he alluded to the divisions and petty jealousies which had contributed to block up "the way of the Lord," and, making a hearty confession for himself and others, in respect to these, and alluding to the searching manner in which the scattered and disjointed condition of the denomination had been described in the sermon, he most touchingly exclaimed, "Hast thou found us out, O, our enemy!" He then made a feeling exhortation approving of a Convention, weeping while he spoke, and melting the entire assembly to tears. His prayer and moving exhortation greatly aided in the adoption of the Constitution. Indeed, it was a matter of doubt which contributed most to effect the purposes of the Convention, the prayer of Mercer or the sermon of Sherwood.

Rev. William T. Brantly then read the Constitution which had been prepared, article by article, presenting the grounds why each article should be adopted, and repeatedly, during his address, referring in the most commendatory manner to the sermon which had just been delivered, appealing to its facts and arguments as reasons for the adoption of the Constitution. He did not conclude his address until the morning of the next day, Saturday, 29th of June, when, after mature deliberation and a full discussion, the Constitution was adopted.

The following is a copy of the Constitution then adopted:

"WHEREAS, it is highly expedient that a more close and extensive *union* among the churches of the Baptist denomination in the State of Georgia should exist, and that a more perfect consent and harmony and good understanding cannot be established without stated meetings of delegates from the several Associations, to confer together on subjects of general interest and plans of public utility; and to devise and recommend schemes for the revival of experimental and practical religion; for the promotion of uniformity in sentiment, practice and discipline; for the extension of the gospel by missions and missionaries, by Bibles and tracts, and for the fulfilment of that scriptural injunction, "provoke one another to love and to good works;" and since it hath seemed good to the Georgia and Ocmulgee Associations to make the first attempt to accomplish these important objects in the State of Georgia, and delegates being appointed from these bodies to meet in convention at such time and place as might be agreed upon, and these delegates, namely: Jesse Mercer, William T. Brantly, Winder Hilman, J. P. Marshall and James Armstrong, on the part of the Georgia, and Robert McGinty, J. M. Gray and Cyrus White, on the part of the Ocmulgee, having been appointed to convene at Powelton, June 27th, 1822, did accordingly assemble and adopted the following plan of operation:

" 1. This body is constituted upon those principles of Christian faith generally acknowledged and received in the Baptist denomination.

" 2. The constituents of this body are the Baptist Associations in the State of Georgia, or as many of them as may think proper to accede to the terms of this convention.

" 3. It shall be known and distinguished by the name of 'The General Baptist Association of the State of Georgia,' and shall form the organ of general communication for the denomination throughout the State.

" 4. Each Association may send not less than three and not more than five delegates to represent them in this body, and all delegates shall hold their appointments until others are elected to succeed them.

"5. The officers of this union shall be a Moderator, and clerk and assistant clerk, who shall be appointed by ballot at each annual meeting, and shall form a committee of the body during the recess of the meeting; but this committee may be increased as occasion may require.

"6. The Moderator shall perform the same duties that devolve on Moderators in the several Associations, and in addition to this, shall be authorized to call meetings of the committee in the interval of annual meetings should it be deemed expedient.

"7. The clerk, who shall likewise be treasurer, shall enter in a book all the transactions of this body. The assistant clerk shall take charge of all distant communications to or from this body, and shall write all the letters which it may require.

"8. Questions of difficulty may be referred from any of the Associations to the deliberation and advice of this body.

"9. Acts and proceedings of this body shall be submitted, from time to time, to its constituents for inspection, and no decision shall be further binding upon any Association than the decisions of the Associations are upon the churches which compose them.

"10. The following are the specific objects of this body: 1. To unite the influence and pious intelligence of Georgia Baptists, and thereby to facilitate their union and co-operation. 2. To form and encourage plans for the revival of experimental and practical religion in the State and elsewhere. 3. To promote uniformity of sentiment and discipline. 4. To aid in giving effect to the useful plans of the Association. 5. To afford an opportunity to those who may conscientiously think it their duty to form a fund for the education of pious young men who may be called by the Spirit and their churches to the Christian ministry. 6. To correspond with bodies of other religious denominations on topics of general interest to the Redeemer's Kingdom, and to promote pious and useful education in the Baptist denomination.

"11. It shall have power to form rules, make arrangements and appoint committees for the accomplishment of any or all the above objects, provided none of these rules and arrangements shall be inconsistent with the Scriptures and the known principles of the Association.

"12. Two-thirds of the whole number of delegates shall form a quorum, and a majority shall decide a question.

"13. The above Constitution shall be liable to amendment or alteration by two-thirds of the delegates present, provided the change may have been proposed by a member of the General Association at the preceding meeting.

JESSE MERCER, *Moderator*.

J. P. MARSHALL, *Clerk*."

It will be perceived that the foregoing differs materially from the Constitution of the Convention at present. Various changes were, indeed, made from time to time; but the most material alteration was made in 1845, by a select committee, which, in a report, presented the Constitution as it now exists, and which was unanimously adopted at Macon in 1846.

Thus was formed that body which, in 1827, changed its name to "THE BAPTIST CONVENTION FOR THE STATE OF GEORGIA," and which more, perhaps, than any other one cause, has harmonized and combined the efforts of the Baptists of Georgia, and effected those beneficial results which have made Georgia one of the leading and most benevolent Baptist States in the South.

The same committee which prepared the Constitution presented a Circular Address, which was received and adopted, and extracts from which are given here to show the views and arguments of those fathers who formed our State Convention, and established those measures of denominational progress, elevation and co-operation which the wisdom of three score years has sanctioned and approved. The graceful periods are evidently from the polished pen of the elder Brantly:

"All the reasons which may be applied to the support of Associations, separate and local, will evince the utility of one more general and comprehensive. If it has been found profitable to bring together the piety and wisdom of a given compass; and if the united intelligence and zeal of that limited space have been found to possess a happy result, would it not seem desirable to increase the effect by enlarging the extent of the field and strengthening the means of operation? If delegates from churches, combining their counsels and efforts, have not been without works that speak for them, and vindicate their claims to respect and consideration, might we not presume that delegates from Associations, forming an annual meeting from each section of the State, would bring together a mass of information, of matured observation, of solicitude for Zion's prosperity, and of the true spirit of love, which would flow back with augmented energy to the several points from which it emanated?

"Viewing the known principles of independence upon which all Baptist churches are constituted, it is worse than idle to raise any alarms about the power and authority of a General Association. The idea of a spiritual judicatory does not exist in the Baptist denomination,

"Nay, such an idea cannot exist until the whole present system shall have been subverted, and a new one substituted in its place. Now, a General Association does not go one step out of the old track; it grows naturally and spontaneously out of those elements of order already established and organized. It claims to be a member of the same family, the elder branches of which are so widely diffused and so well known. As the offspring of these, it will, of course, fall in with the designs and aid the operation of the parent bodies.

"Why, then, will you cast an eye of suspicion upon the artless, humble plan, which your wisdom ought to foster and prayers to respect? Why awaken apprehensions against a well-meant and hopeful scheme, which promises a new era in the history of our churches; and which, by the blessing of God, will confer a unity of design and strength of action highly conducive to the interest of the common cause, upon all our existing arrangements?"

The Address then goes on to mention the purposes, or objects proposed by the General Association:

"The revival of religion is one of the important objects which this new Association will hold in anxious contemplation. To those who regard a low estate of religion as an affliction to the church, under which she is to repose with quietude and indolent submission, our remarks cannot be applied; but to those who regard such a state as an affliction, under which she is to feel the movings of active repentance, and to perform works suitable to the awful tokens of God, our observation must have a reasonable reference. For who will say, under any view of our religious condition, that it is not time to seek the Lord, nor yet to break up our fallow-ground? It is a humbling truth that the general rule with churches, throughout the State, is to have the gospel preached only once a month; those who have it oftener are not numerous exceptions to the rule. Hence three Lord's days in every month pass away with scarce a prayer to consecrate their hours, or a holy song to hallow the wasting season. Whilst the ways of Zion, unbeaten by the foot of the early pilgrim, lie mourning in desertion and neglect, and are almost lost to the eye of the unfrequent traveller, the sacred abode itself presents a moving desolation—a building which seems almost to invite the approach of the enemy; a few withered faces and tottering forms; some heartless exercises performed with impatience and closed with haste; a little worldly conversation and a few inquiries about prices current, and the scene is concluded until the next stated time. Brethren, if we draw a picture which has no reality, come forward and disprove our representation. Refute our assertions by facts, and show us, if you have it to show, the reverse of the picture. But if you cannot show the reverse, then meet us in solemn, prayerful deliberation upon the best methods for producing a change in this dismal history of events.

"The want of exact uniformity in discipline is a source of frequent disturbances in our churches. It has often happened that cases have been disposed of in one church, whilst another church could not acquiesce in the decision of its sister institution, and long contentions have ensued upon this diversity of disciplinary measures. Meanwhile, Christian fellowship has been suspended, rivalship and jealousy have prevailed, and angry disputes among brethren have existed, to the no small detriment of the sacred cause. At the same time it has been easy for imposing characters to shelter themselves from deserved censure, by relying on the peculiar modes of an individual society, and disclaiming the principles of other bodies. To obviate such a state of things is one design of our general union. It is true that the influence even of this meeting might not produce an immediate change in this evil; but it might adopt expedients to counteract it and gradually to produce a sameness in the usages of all the churches.

"Nor is it too much to hope that this General Association may be the instrument of calling forth more laborers into the Lord's harvest. The present small number of devoted laborers is rapidly becoming still more reduced. Within the last few years the interest of the Georgia Baptists has lost by deaths, removals, and otherwise, a large portion of its most distinguished and zealous ministers. The names of Baker, Marshall, Sweet, Winn, Williams, Franklin and Boyd, Bateman and Willis, though embalmed in the dearest recollections of the churches and brethren who knew and appreciated their worth, live in our memory only to tell of the dismal vacuity which their removal from earthly scenes has caused.

"Such losses impel the emotions of Zion beyond the first transports of grief, and extend the sorrowful affection until the force of a mighty reaction rolls back the current of woe in a full tide of penitence, prayer and holy action. To spend our time in unavailing regret is not the right way to improve an afflictive bereavement. To sit down in forbidden repose until the rust of inaction consumes our energies, is not the way to repair a breach. It is the Lord's work to qualify men with talents and grace for the holy employment of the ministry; but it is our work to pray for the sending forth of such; to watch the bruised reed that waves before the blast and to prop it with seasonable succors; to fan the half-suffocated spark of the smoking flax; and to run eagerly with those who have their faces set as if they would go up to Jerusalem, to strengthen them in the way. But, to speak without a figure, it is most evident that our churches have only themselves to blame for the fewness of their ministers. And if the fault is chargeable upon them, and not upon God, is it not time for them to be roused to a sense of their deficiency, and begin to do that which they have left undone? Let pious young men receive the aids of learning; let their dormant faculties be drawn out by the light of science; let the burden of poverty be taken from the shoulders of those who already labor in word and doctrine; let churches see that their ministers are freed from the oppressions of worldly care, and have their time devoted to the study of the Scriptures and the care of souls; let concerts for prayer be punctually attended and devoutly observed; let the slumbering energies of discipline be roused into wholesome action; and let all hearts beat in unison with the holy promises of final success, and with the coming glories of the Saviour's happy reign.

"Our meeting has been numerously attended, and the ministration of the word obtained a cordial and attentive reception. The parting scene on Sabbath was truly affecting. The flowing eyes and speaking faces seemed to say, 'Behold, how good and how pleasant it is, for brethren to dwell together in unity!'

"JESSE MERCER, *Moderator.*

"J. P. MARSHALL, *Clerk.*"

The General Association, before adjourning, appointed brethren to present its transactions to the Ocmulgee and Georgia Associations, and requested certain others to represent it in the Ebenezer, Sarepta and Tugalo Associations, the object with reference to the three last named being to secure them as constituents; but, when the second meeting of the Association occurred, at Powelton, on Thursday, June 26th, 1823, the Ocmulgee and Georgia were, again, the only two Associations represented.

In response to the appeal of the General Association, the Ocmulgee Association replied, partially, as follows, by letter, at her session in September, 1822:

"The transactions of your first convention have been presented to our body, by our much esteemed brother, Jesse Mercer, and have been taken into consideration. We have now to state that your specified objects meet our unanimous approbation. * * * We cannot close this poor token of love without expressing our hope that the General Baptist Association of Georgia will prove a lasting blessing to the cause of the Redeemer's kingdom. * * * We further request your next convention to be within our bounds.

"R. McGinty, *Moderator*.
"James Anthony, *Clerk*."

The Sarepta Association, although not prepared to become a constituent member of the General Association, nevertheless appointed Joseph Davis to prepare a friendly letter of correspondence, to be handed in at the next meeting of the body, by I. Goss, M. Bledsoe, R. Thornton, I. David and James Sanders, who were appointed correspondent messengers. It may be well to state here, that, although the Sarepta did not become a constituent member of the State Convention until 1836, it was not from a spirit of opposition so much as from a desire to preserve harmony and fellowship among her churches and church-members.

The *Ocmulgee* was represented by Cyrus White, John Milner, J. M. Gray and W. Williams, while the *Georgia* sent as delegates Jesse Mercer, James Armstrong, William T. Brantly and Jabez P. Marshall, Jesse Mercer was again elected Moderator, J. P. Marshall Clerk, and William T. Brantly, Assistant Clerk.

It is not at all necessary to collate a history of the mere business details of the General Association. It will be sufficient to put on record such general action of the body as manifested the aims, endeavors and sentiments of the founders of our State Convention, in regard to the condition of the denomination at large.

A. Sherwood, I. Goss, and I. David were received as corresponding messengers of the Sarepta Association, and admitted as constituent members; and all the ministering and lay brethren present were invited to assist in a free communication of sentiment, but not granted the privilege of voting. A. Sherwood, William T. Brantly and James Armstrong, were appointed a committee to arrange and bring forward business for the Association. The succeeding day, Friday, they submitted a report which embraced the following objects:

1. That correspondence be extended to every Association in the State, and to other religious bodies, as far as practicable, by address and messengers, which was adopted.

2. " That a plan be formed to promote uniformity of church discipline."

A. Sherwood, James Armstrong, William Williams and William T. Brantly were appointed to digest a plan and report the next day,

3. " That a more strict attention be paid to the practical duties of religion."

To meet this proposition; " It was agreed that this body earnestly and respectfully recommend to the churches in their union throughout the State, that they be punctual and regular in assembling at their places of worship; that they conscientiously regard the Sabbath, especially as a day of public worship, and, whether they have a preacher or not, read the Bible and other good books; explain the Scriptures; establish Sunday-schools; introduce and maintain social prayer meetings; preserve church discipline; encourage promising gifts; enforce Christian government in their families; educate and catechize their children; instruct their servants; and, especially, that ministers take the lead in these important objects."

4. " That the delegation from each Association present a succinct account of the state of religion within their boundaries." This was adopted.

5. That agents for the Association be appointed. This was referred to brethren Brantly, Sherwood and Goss, as a committee, and their report, made the following day, stated that " they had considered the subject so far as the time allotted them would permit, and recommend that several agents in various sections of the State be requested to use their exertions to promote the interest of this body; to travel and to preach to the churches; to enlist the feelings of ministers and other influential members in our behalf; to encourage family religion and the establishment of Sabbath-schools; to make particular inquiries among the brethren as to the expediency of establishing a Classical and Literary

Seminary, to be under the patronage of the Baptists in South Carolina and Georgia; to receive such donations as may be offered in aid of our general purposes."

The Committee on Uniformity of Discipline also reported on Saturday, 28th, as follows:

"That, in their opinion, the matter is one of too great magnitude to be fully discussed within the space of one meeting, and that it is a point on which much inquiry should be made throughout the denomination. They therefore recommend that a correspondence be opened with such State Conventions as may have been already formed, and also with distinguished individuals touching this subject, and that the information so obtained be laid before the next meeting of this body."

This was adopted, and Jesse Mercer and William T. Brantly were appointed to carry the design of the report into effect. Taking into consideration the part Rev. I. Goss took in the Sarepta Association against the General Association, it is singular that for several years he represented that Association, and was appointed to preach the Introductory sermon, at Eatonton, in 1826, which he did. It seems that they were received as messengers or correspondents, merely, from the Sarepta Association, and not as representatives from constituent bodies. To secure the co-operation of the non-acquiescing Associations in the State, messengers were appointed, in 1823, to represent the General Association and urge a formal connection with that body. Roberts was appointed to attend the Hephzibah Association, A. Sherwood to attend the Sunbury, J. M. Gray the Piedmont, I. Goss and J. Mercer the Tugalo, J. Armstrong and M. Reeves the Sarepta, J. Milner and William Davis the Ebenezer; and, in addition to this, a special appeal was made to each Association in the Circular Address, which is given as a part of the history of the times:

ADDRESS FOR 1823.

The General Association of Baptists in the State of Georgia to their brethren throughout the State and elsewhere, with Christian salutation:

BRETHREN—We had looked forward with much pleasure to our present meeting, animated by the confidence that the Associations which were not represented in our body at its formation, would at least send up their delegates to this meeting to obtain information satisfactory to themselves as to the character and objects of this Convention. In this confidence we have not been wholly disappointed. Respectable brethren from the Sarepta and Ebenezer Associations were in attendance, and, we trust, may be appealed to for our justification from any suspicion of improper designs in forming a more extensive union.

Should there be any good reasons against the united efforts of the Baptists, we should be happy to know them. Should it be so that, although union exists in the State for the purposes of legislation, yet the union of Baptists would have a mischievous operation; should it be true that, although the frame of society among us is composed of many remote and separate members, which coalesce, yet the coalition of Associations would have a ruinous tendency; should it be true that, although men of the world may unite upon any extensive scale for the accomplishment of secular designs, yet Christians, even of one State, may not come together without being the instruments of evil; should it be true that men without religion are trustworthy, but lose their credit and honesty so soon as they become followers of Christ; and should it be true that those who have been active in forming the General Association of Georgia are men of such suspicious virtue that a conspiracy against Christian liberty and morals is to be apprehended, then reject their offers, expose their treachery, warn good men against their insidious impositions, and guard yourself against their demands. But, is any one prepared to confirm such charges against the General Association? It has set up no claims to obedience and submission from its members; it has enacted no laws to bind the conscience or restrict the liberty of any man; it has arrogated to itself no ecclesiastical jurisdiction of any limits; no papal threats, no episcopal canons, no spiritual decrees have been issued from its tribunal. What, then, is the harm which this union threatens? What is the evil which is likely to grow out of it? We presume that the mischiefs apprehended are some of the following: This union threatens to disturb the slumbers of those Christians who are more fond of a calm and quiet life than of the pains and sacrifices of a godly conversation. It intends to exhibit the alarming spectacle of a body of believers holding forth the Word of life, living up to the requirements of their station, awake upon their several posts of duty and attentive to the events of Providence; sending out Bibles, supporting missionaries at home and abroad; maintaining personal, experimental and practical religion in their churches, in their families and in their own hearts. All this is immensely obnoxious to the resentment of an opposite spirit. It makes religion too much a business; requires too many sacrifices; is quite too active and industrious; requires too much praying, too much preaching, too much money, and, in a word, makes too much noise about the interests of another world. If these are the worst faults of the General Association, we should hope it might obtain the indulgence of those who have solemnly admitted the obligation which the word of God imposes upon all its friends, to consecrate their lives to the sacred cause, to be zealous in extending the knowledge of salvation to others, as they are grateful for its saving benefits to themselves; to manifest, in some degree, the same spirit which actuated the early Christians, who were all for Christ and Heaven.

Brethren of the Hephzibah Association: We invite you to join with us in the common cause. Our proposition for a union of this sort you have once rejected; but we humbly trust you will be induced to reconsider the measure. We love you in the Lord with a genuine Christian affection, and ardently desire that you might see as we see in this highly important concern. We have laid no snare for you, but offer you the same privileges and powers which are common to the Associations composing this body. We cannot believe that you would reject a useful plan, knowing it to be so; and we cannot feel contented that you should remain without the knowledge of that which you certainly would approve were you aware of its worth and importance. At least make trial by sending up delegates, and if you are then discontented with us, you shall have our cordial approbation for withdrawing.

Brethren of the Sarepta Association: We were happy to see your messengers at our late meeting. You have evinced a disposition to make yourselves acquainted with the character and objects of our body, and in this you have acted rightly. We approve the caution and circumspection with which you proceed in this business, and feel anxious that we should be thoroughly known before we receive the official testimony of your respect and concurrence. When you have examined with care, and have then united with us, your approbation will be worth something, as it will have resulted from an enlightened and honest conviction. We would not have you dragged with precipitation into a new scheme, as such haste would neither be useful to the scheme itself nor creditable to you. But we would hope, at the same time, that you have already discussed this subject long enough, and that you are now prepared to accede to the terms of our new and interesting union. Let us hope, brethren, that we shall have the happiness to welcome your delegates to the bosom of our next meeting, and that you will from that time form a component part of this union.

Brethren of the Sunbury Association: We had hoped that your just discernment would have appreciated the merits of the proposition, which was submitted at your last meeting, to unite with us in forming one general body from all the Associations. Still, we cannot think that you declined the measure from any motives unfriendly to the common interests of the Saviour's kingdom. You have only to observe the characteristics of the times in which we live, to perceive that these are the days of co-operation in everything which beautifies the followers of the Saviour. Should we fail to collect the strength of our denomination, to embody the separate parts in one great whole; should we overlook the obvious advantages of united exertion, we should be justly reproached by the zeal of other Christians, and should be wofully indifferent to the great things which God has wrought for us. Let us indulge the hope that we shall enjoy the company of your delegates at our next meeting.

Brethren of the Ebenezer and Tugalo Associations: The plan of a General Association has already had a second trial, and is found, upon experiment, to possess all the advantages which were anticipated. It has brought together, in friendly acquaintance and harmonious deliberation, brethren who, otherwise, would not have been known to each other; it has drawn close the ties of Christian affection; it has created good-will and amicable understanding upon several subjects of general utility, and has paved the way for further attainments in these important particulars. Our desire is that you may be partakers with us of the benefit. We rely upon your Christian candor to bestow upon this subject the attention which it merits, and we believe that you will not be inclined to reject it without a trial. Come, then, and examine for yourselves. Allow us to know you better, to love you more, to have your society as we march on towards the prize of the incorruptible inheritance.

Brethren of the Georgia and Ocmulgee Associations: We are happy to say to you that you have done well in devising a more extensive union. As your delegates we have enjoyed the refreshing comfort of another interview. We seemed to act under the impulse of one spirit, and to have in view but one object. All our discussions were friendly, courteous and affectionate.

A large concourse attended the preaching on the occasion, and we have reason to believe that much good was done. Much remains to be done on the plan of our united exertions, and your delegates cherish the confidence that you will not weary in well doing.

JESSE MERCER, *Moderator*.

J. P. MARSHALL, *Clerk*.

This extract manifests the earnestness with which the originators of our State Baptist Convention sought to carry out their purposes, as well as the lofty ends they had in view, and successive years have but demonstrated the wisdom of their pious endeavors.

The Sunbury Association convened in 1823, at Power's church, Effingham county, and when, on Saturday, November 8th, the question of forming a connection with the "General Baptist Association for the State of Georgia" was resumed, after some deliberation, it was

"*Resolved*, That this body adopt the proper measures to become a constituent member of the Association;"

And H. J. Ripley, H. Milton, W. Connor and Samuel S. Law were appointed delegates to its next session.

Adiel Sherwood and J. H. Walker, from the *Georgia*, and J. H. T. Kilpatrick, from the *Hephzibah*, appeared as messengers that year, and may have influenced the body in its action.

In 1822 the subject of uniting with the General Association was brought up in the Ebenezer Association, at Mount Horeb, and its decision was referred to the meeting of the following year, 1823. When the session for that year occurred, at Stone Creek, the Association "took under consideration the reference of last year, relative to the General Association, which was *thrown under the table*."

In 1822, Dr. Brantly presented the subject of union with the General Association, in the Hephzibah Association; but the connection was rejected by the body, very decidedly.

The third session of the Convention met at Eatonton in April, 1824. Three Associations were now constituent bodies—the Georgia, the Ocmulgee, and the Sunbury, all of which sent delegates, the Sarepta being represented by corresponding messengers.

The General Association again sent forth a letter of correspondence, extracts from which will enable us to comprehend some of the notions then entertained by our leading brethren regarding the objects of the Association:

" Several of the objects which have engaged our attention possess a high importance in the views of distant and highly respectable brethren who have favored us with their correspondence.

"The inquiries which were made according to the resolution of last year, on the subject of some standard confession of faith, church discipline and catechism, and other forms of church transactions, so far as those inquiries were extended,

have led to the belief that the time is not remote when this matter will be generally agitated among the brethren of our large and growing denomination throughout the United States. There is but one voice from all—that something should be done in this way, and that speedily. The only difference of sentiment which may be apprehended is upon the best method of accomplishing the design. . . .
. . It has, therefore, been deemed expedient to continue the correspondence of last year, touching this design, and to request respectfully and affectionately from you the full and explicit declaration of your views, to be laid before our next annual meeting.

"We trust, brethren, that there is among you a growing solicitude for the spiritual welfare and religious instruction of the rising generation. When the hearts of parents are turned to the children; when the moral and religious claims of the young begin to be vindicated from neglect and abuse; when a general movement of holy anxiety begins to prevail towards those who are to form the rudiments of future society, we may look forward to happy and cheering seasons of "refreshing from the presence of the Lord." Be not weary in well doing! Prepare the minds of your offspring, by early cultivation, for a favorable reception of the truth as it is in Jesus. Let them be taught to respect religion with all its institutions, to honor the pious persuasion of their parents, to regard this world as "but the bud of being"—the dawn of eternal day—and to prepare for the everlasting duration, where their character and portion must be forever fixed and unchangeable.

"Cultivate the spirit of prayer with augmented care and assiduity. * * * Strive to promote the spirit of brotherly love and union, and endeavor to put to silence the ignorance of foolish men, rather by holy living than by spirited controversy; more by the silent eloquence of a godly conversation than by the noisy contentions of unproductive words. Let the love of Christ dwell richly within you, and earnestly cultivate that heavenly plant which, in its early bud, is happiness, and, in its full bloom, is Heaven. Let its sacred sweets be shed around like the bruised myrtle, and, by its soft attractions, let your spirits be drawn forth to whatsoever things are lovely and of good report.

"Continue, brethren, to send up your delegates to the General Association. This is the medium of Christian acquaintance, of extended co-operation, and of harmonious understanding. It is here the hearts of your ministers are cemented in love and encouraged to persevere in duty amid trials and conflicts. Here is the scene of unity and peace, of order and friendship.

JESSE MERCER, *Moderator.*

ADIEL SHERWOOD, *Clerk.*

The session of the General Baptist Association for 1823, it will be remembered, appointed several agents to visit various sections of the State, and use their best exertions to promote the interests of the Association, encourage family religion, establish Sunday-schools and make particular inquiries among the brethren and churches, so as to ascertain the general opinion in regard to the expediency of establishing a classical and literary seminary. In reporting, at the session of 1824, held in Eatonton, April 22d, 23d and 24th, some of them stated that they found many persons favorable to weekly church services, and to the establishment of Sunday-schools, several of which had been already commenced and were prosperous ; but the plan for a seminary of learning met with the cold rebuke of many influential members of the Baptist churches. Still it was affirmed that there were many members and friends who earnestly desired such a seminary, and would aid in its establishment when the public mind was more enlightened and when more efficient support could be anticipated. With reference to the state of religion in the different Associations connected with the body, the following statements were made : In many churches of the Ocmulgee Association there appeared to be an absence of zeal in the promotion of practical religion and the spread of the gospel; but, in others, there was a warm engagedness in the Redeemer's cause. In the families of the brethren the standard of religion had been erected; Sabbath schools had been established and were prospering; weekly and concert prayer-meetings were constantly maintained and promptly attended; and to these churches, which were chiefly in the counties of Henry, Newton and the upper parts of Jasper, there had been considerable additions. In truth the prospects within the Ocmulgee were more flattering than they had been a year previous, except with respect to the support of missions. There appeared to be little ground for hope that the support of the mission cause would be warmer or more liberal than it had been previously.

A more favorable report was received from the Sunbury Association, which contained in that year, 1824, eighteen churches, ten ministers and 5,257 members. Several of its churches had enjoyed the reviving influences of the Holy Spirit, and had been favored with unusual accessions to their numbers. For the most part, its churches were harmonious and well affected towards the spread of the gospel, and in it a general improvement in the denomination manifested itself. Special mention was made of the Missionary Committee, in that Association, whose duty it was to attempt supplying destitute churches and neighborhoods in the bounds of the Sunbury with the preaching of the gospel.

It was stated that to almost all the churches of the Georgia Association, there had been additions by baptism during the year. Especially was this the case at County Line church, in Oglethorpe county, and at Bethel church, in Wilkes county. Many churches, however, had been so refreshed as to "thank God and take courage," and in some the precious revival influences were still visible. The whole number baptized in the Association had been 293. It contained thirty-seven churches, twenty ministers and 2,986 members. The members of a few churches assembled at their meeting-houses punctually for worship, *every Sabbath*; and Sunday-schools were established and in a prosperous condition.

The Clerk, Adiel Sherwood, appends these remarks to the general proceedings of the General Association for 1824: "All the deliberations during the session, were conducted in entire harmony and in much brotherly love. No unhallowed spirit was discoverable; but so apparent in the conduct of the brethren were those kindly feelings of the Christian, that every one appreciated the sentiment of the Psalmist, 'How good and how pleasant it is for brethren to dwell together in unity!' The preaching of the word was attended with the manifest approbation of our Lord. The congregations were frequently bathed in tears, and there is ground to hope that much good has been done."

This was, indeed, a notable meeting and was attended by some eminent men. From the *Georgia* Association, there were Jesse Mercer, W. T. Brantly, James Armstrong, Malachi Reeves and Adiel Sherwood; from the *Ocmulgee*, Jonathan Nichols, Edmund Talbot, B. Milner, J. Colley and ——— Robinson; from the *Sunbury*, H. J. Riply, the commentator; from the *Sarepta*, Miller Bledsoe, Isham Goss, Henry David and James Saunders. Basil Manly, Sr., then a young man, was present, as a representative from the South Carolina State Convention. Many others were there who were invited to seats, among whom were Thomas Cooper, Elisha Battle, William Flournoy, William Williams, J. Robertson, B. Haygood, J. Gray, Wilson Connor, Cyrus White, James Brooks, and many others.

Brethren F. M. Gray, Cyrus White, Wilson Connor and Adiel Sherwood were appointed agents of the Association, to travel for three months throughout the the State, preach, take up collections and form auxiliary societies, wherever practicable, and look to the body, at its succeeding session, for compensation; and the churches were earnestly recommended to form Baptist Tract Societies, auxiliary to the parent society recently established at Washington City.

It was at this meeting that Adiel Sherwood and Basil Manly were appointed to preach on Sabbath morning. There was a very large assembly present and Jesse Mercer, then in his fifty-fifth year, sat in the pulpit with them. Adiel Sherwood was to preach first, then in his thirty-third year, an ordained minister of four years only, and full of zeal and fire, and pastor of the Greenesboro church. B. Manly was even younger, low in stature, but with a pleasing voice and a most pathetic delivery.

Sherwood, who was to preach first arose, calmly surveyed the immense congregation for some moments, and, instead of beginning his discourse, observed in his own quaint way, " Where shall we obtain bread to feed so great a multitude? As for myself, I am penniless and unprovided; but there is a lad here who has five barley loaves and two little fishes." He then turned and laid his hand upon the head of Basil Manly, who was leaning forward, his face resting upon his hands. " And this," Sherwood proceeded, " with the presence and blessing of Jesus shall constitute a feast for all." To quote Dr. Manly's own words concerning the circumstance, " This well nigh upset me. But it drove me to prayer. The Lord loosed my own mind and unlocked the fountain of tears, so that it was computed that through a great part of the discourse, there was an average of at least five hundred persons continually bathed in tears. In all this *Bochim* there was nothing so affecting to me as the sympathetic streams I saw coursing down the furrowed cheeks of Father Mercer, when I turned round in the pupit." After the sermon the ministers descended from the pulpit, mourners were invited forward, hundreds threw themselves on their knees and Jesse Mercer led in a most affecting and tear-compelling prayer.

As various new characters have entered upon the stage of action, it will be interesting to the general reader to give some information relative to them. One of the most distinguished men of the denomination, the venerable Abraham Marshall, has gone to his reward, universally mourned by his brethren. He departed this life on the 15th of August, 1819, in the seventy-second year of his age. The excellent William Rabun, Governor of Georgia, has been laid in the tomb, also, a whole State making great lamentation over his demise. But Jabez Pleiades Marshall has risen up to succeed his father, as pastor of Kiokee church, and is taking a noble stand among the best and most useful Baptists of the day. Thorough-going as a missionary Baptist, he entered heart and soul into all the benevolent plans of the day, and was frequently called upon, by his brethren to act for them in responsible positions. As a preacher he was clear, zealous and touching, never entering the pulpit without careful preparation, and preaching strongly the doctrines reckoned strictly orthodox among Baptists. Frail in body and constitution, and yet zealous and indefatigable in his exertions, he wore out the delicate machine in which his persevering spirit worked, and passed away at an early age, in 1832. For seven years he was either Secretary, or Assistant Secretary, of the State Baptist Convention.

Another controlling and influential character, who has entered with vigor on the stage of action among the Baptists of Georgia, is William T. Brantly, a courtly, courteous, highly cultivated and thoroughly educated minister and scholar. He became rector of the Richmond Academy, in Augusta, in 1819, and was instrumental in founding the first Baptist church of that city, and also in erecting a handsome 'Baptist house of worship which cost $20,000. He was an eloquent preacher, of commanding presence and courtly address, who exerted a great and beneficial influence in the State during his six years' residence in Augusta. He was a man who strongly advocated, on all suitable occasions, the cause of education, missions, Sunday-schools and temperance. He was a polished writer, a distinguished educator, and a very successful pastor. It is highly probable that he was the author of the circular issued by the Foreign Missionary Society of Savannah, in 1813, the effect of which was so potent for good among the Baptists of Georgia. He assisted greatly in the establishment of the Georgia Baptist Convention, and his hand, in all likelihood drafted its Constitution, for he was chairman of the committee appointed to prepare it, and he was its chief advocate and exponent.

Another individual whose influence for good was widely felt and long exercised in Georgia, was Adiel Sherwood. Born at Fort Edwards, New York, October 3d, 1791, he arrived in Savannah at seventeen years of age, in the year 1808, and immediately identified himself with the Baptists of the State, entering at once heartily into all their benevolent and evangelical plans, and laboring with a zeal, earnestness and intelligence that made him one of the master-builders of our denomination in the State. Splendidly educated, intensely earnest, devout and energetic, he stamped himself upon our denominational history in the State ineffaceably. The originator of our Convention, he was also the prime mover in the establishment of Mercer Institute, the Manual Labor School which merged into Mercer University, in which he was, for a time, Theological Professor. For ten years he was Secretary of the State Convention, and for many years was one of the most successful pastors and preachers in the State. From 1818 to 1865 he was more or less identified with the Baptist history of Georgia.

James Armstrong, a native of New York also, who emigrated to Savannah and there united with the Baptists, in 1810, afterwards settling in Wilkes county, where he was ordained, in 1814, was another useful man, who has begun to take a most active part in Baptist matters. For more than twenty years he was a useful and influential minister, and, as a member of the Mission Board of the Georgia Baptist Convention, and as a participant in every benevolent effort, was active, earnest, practical, sensible, exceedingly useful, and greatly beloved. At his death, in 1835, he was Treasurer of the State Convention.

Rev. J. H. T. Kilpatrick has also entered the State and taken up his residence in Burke county. Born in North Carolina, in 1793, highly educated, and with a spirit burning with zeal for missions, temperance, education and Sunday-schools, he was worthy to take a stand beside Mercer, Brantly, Sherwood, Screven, Talbot, McGinty, Marshall, Davis, Reeves, Thornton, and the others, then the strong pillars who were holding up the Baptist cause in Georgia. For years he struggled against the anti-mission and anti-temperance spirit in the Hephzibah Association, and, in the course of time, became the universally recognized defender of Baptist faith and practice in his section, one of the oldest, wealthiest and most influential sections in the State.

XI.
STATE OF RELIGION.
1822-1826.

XI.

STATE OF RELIGION.

THE SUNBURY ASSOCIATION, SLIGHT REVIEW—THE SAVANNAH CHURCH, SOME OF ITS PASTORS—STATE OF RELIGION IN THE SUNBURY ASSOCIATION, IN THE THIRD DECADE OF THE CENTURY—AUGUSTA, A BAPTIST CHURCH CONSTITUTED THERE IN 1817—THE SHOAL CREEK CONVENTION—EFFORTS OF THE GENERAL ASSOCIATION—UNIFORMITY OF DISCIPLINE, EFFORT TO PROMOTE IT FALLS THROUGH—WANT OF HARMONY—ADDRESS OF GENERAL ASSOCIATION OF 1825—WHY GIVEN—POSITION OF THE GENERAL ASSOCIATION IN REGARD TO EDUCATION—THE ASSOCIATION, DISAPPOINTED, RECOMMENDS THE FORMATION OF AUXILIARY SOCIETIES IN 1826—A CONSTITUTION RECOMMENDED—THE EBENEZER ASSOCIATION—MISSION ARGUMENTS OF THAT DAY—PROMINENT MEN—HEPHZIBAH ASSOCIATION—THE SAREPTA ASSOCIATION—YELLOW RIVER AND FLINT RIVER ASSOCIATIONS—DENOMINATIONAL STATISTICS IN 1824.

To the bird's-eye glance at the state of religion in the Associations in 1823 and 1824, furnished by the Minutes of the General Association for the latter year, it will be instructive, as well as interesting, to add what can be gathered from other sources, so as to present as correct a view of the denomination as possible.

And, first, we will revert to the seaboard, and make a few historical statements. It will be remembered that the *Savannah* Association, formed in 1802, changed its name to *Savannah River* in 1806, and, at its session held in Newington, twenty miles above Savannah, in 1817, divided, the Georgia churches forming themselves into *The Sunbury Association*, in 1818. The number of churches was twelve, containing a membership of 3,541, most of whom were colored.

With a regular mission committee, whose duty it was to receive and disburse mission funds, employ missionaries and make an annual report, this Association, from first to last, was unalterable and firm in its attachment to the mission cause and in engagement in missionary labor. Its reports and circular letters give no uncertain sound, but are ever bugle-blasts, calling with seraphic zeal upon the churches, fully to perform their share of duty in evangelizing the world, and inciting them especially to maintain, year after year, effective mission labor among the numerous colored people along the Georgia coast. With reference to this condition of affairs, it is only proper to bestow due credit for its existence upon Henry Holcombe, Alexander Scott, Thomas Polhill, James Sweat, William B. Johnson, C. O. Screven, William T. Brantly, Thomas F. Williams, Andrew Marshall, Andrew Bryan, Henry Cunningham, Jacob H. Dunham, Thomas S. Winn, Evans Great, Matthew Albritton, Thomas Meredith, and Deacon Josiah Penfield, whose eloquent pen and Isaiah-like spirit thrilled the Association with utterances similar to those of the prophets of old.

The white church of Savannah, it will be remembered, was constituted in 1800, and Dr. H. Holcombe was its first pastor. He remained in the pastorate until 1811, when he was succeeded by Dr. Wm. B. Johnson, who served the church until 1815, when its membership was about one hundred.

In 1815 Dr. Johnson moved to South Carolina, and Benjamin Screven became pastor of the church, and so continued until 1819. James Sweat succeeded Benjamin Screven, and was pastor three years, when he resigned, and Thomas Meredith took charge, serving during 1823 and 1824, the church containing in 1823 seventy-one members. In 1825, when Henry O. Wyer took charge of it, this church contained sixty-three members only; but the membership nearly trebled itself during his pastorate of nine years.

Rev. Henry O. Wyer was an extraordinary preacher, and deserves more than a passing notice in this historical sketch. He was born in Massachusetts in 1802, and came to Georgia in 1824. In 1825 he was ordained by Rev. William T. Brantly and Rev. James Shannon, and was installed pastor of the Savannah church. He died of pneumonia, in Alexandria, Virginia, May 8th, 1857, at the age of fifty-five.

To exhibit the state of religion in the Sunbury Association, we make a few extracts from its annual Minutes. In the "Corresponding Letter" of the Sunbury Association for 1822, we find this gratifying statement: "It is a source of gratitude to us, as well as delight, to be able to state that the circumstances under which we are this season assembled, are peculiarly interesting. The people throughout the whole of this section of country seem to have experienced a general religious excitement. The congregations which have assembled for the purpose of worshipping God with us are unusually large, attentive and tender. Many, particularly of the young people, seem to be laboring under the most pungent conviction; while others are enabled to 'rejoice in hope of the glory of God.' The season is truly animating and refreshing to the pious heart; and we entertain a hope, apparently well grounded, that the time of refreshing from the presence of the Lord has come, and that this excitement may prove to be the commencement of a general and powerful revival of true godliness."

And again: "It affords us pleasure here to state that the labors of our domestic missionaries have been acknowledged and blessed. As an evidence of this, the people among whom they have been laboring have presented us with most urgent solicitations that they may still be allowed to share the benefit of their services. We are pleased to see the manner in which missionary effort prospers wherever it is made."

The Corresponding Letter for 1823 says: "Several of our churches have been blessed, during the last year, with the reviving influences of the Holy Spirit, and have beheld many, both old and young, bow to the sceptre of Immanuel. In other of our churches present appearances excite the hope of similar favors. The desire for the universal spread of the gospel is also becoming more general." In that year the Sunbury decided to unite with the General Association, and its first messengers were sent in 1824. H. J. Ripley alone attended.

The Minutes and Letter for 1824 speak of the successful labors of two Associational missionaries and of the formation of one missionary society. On some of the churches God had been graciously pleased to pour out the influence of His Spirit. Harmony and brotherly love presided at the Association; but it was a matter of grief "to be obliged to state that there are still some among us opposed to the cause of missions." But the brethren were exhorted not to exercise unkindly feelings towards them, but to pray for them, "that the veil which darkens their understandings may be removed." C. O. Screven was Moderator, and H. J. Ripley, Clerk. The session of the Sunbury for 1825 was interesting. Some eminent and useful men belonged to the body at that time; among them was the eloquent, zealous and pious Henry O. Wyer, of the First church of Savannah; Dr. C. O. Screven, pastor at Sunbury; H. J. Ripley, pastor at Newport; James Shannon (a very learned man, converted from Presbyterianism by the thesis, "Did John's baptism belong to the *old* or *new* Dispensation?"); S. S. Law, of Sunbury; Andrew Marshall, pastor of First colored church of Savannah, and others. In its report, the Committee on Domestic Missions asserts its increasing conviction of the deserts of their Domestic Mission, adding: "Since it was established many souls have been converted; several churches which had, for some time, been gradually declining, have been revived and strengthened, and one church has been constituted through the labors of their itinerant brethren."

STATE OF RELIGION.

The Corresponding Letter for 1825 says: "The state of the churches constituting this Association, in some instances, gives us pain. There is too much indifference to spiritual things among us, and some of our churches are evidently in a declining state; yet, the Lord has blessed us, and caused His power to be made manifest among us. His preached Word has been made effectual in the conversion of sinners, and we indulge a hope that His children have been revived, and their faith more firmly established upon the Rock of Ages. We have enjoyed much Christian affection and harmony since we have come together, and hope that we feel as a band of brothers, engaged in promoting the glory of our Father's Kingdom."

In that year S. S. Law was Moderator, and H. J. Ripley was Clerk. The number of churches was 17; ordained ministers, 12; licensed preachers, 1; members, 5,165; baptisms during the year, 228.

Let us now turn our vision to the City of Augusta. Remarkable to say, sixty years after its foundation, no Baptist church existed in that city, although there were large Baptist churches in existence throughout the region around. In May, 1817, the first Baptist church was constituted, with eighteen members in the city, Abraham Marshall preaching on the occasion. During 1818 and a part of 1819 he acted as pastor of this church, but in the latter year, the trustees of Richmond Academy, for the second time, secured the services of Dr. Wm. T. Brantly, as rector of the Academy, and he, by permission of the trustees, preached to the Baptists gratuitously in the chapel. In the following year, 1820, he was elected pastor of the church, which then contained twenty-four members, and he served it most usefully until his removal to Philadelphia, as Dr. Henry Holcombe's successor, in 1826, when the membership of the church was seventy-four. Within two years after entering upon his charge of this church, Mr. Brantly had the pleasure of preaching the dedication sermon of a handsome church-building which cost $20,000, the result of his own personal labors, and in which he preached to large congregations.

During his pastorate at Augusta, Dr. Brantly wielded a weighty, and judicious influence in Georgia, ever raising his eloquent voice and using his polished pen in favor of those noble and grand causes which have tended to elevate and enlarge our denomination. For four years he served as Assistant Secretary in the General Association, and when he left the State in 1826, the General Association

"*Resolved*, That as our beloved brother, the Rev, William T. Brantly, who has much endeared himself to us by his Christian deportment and faithful discharge of ministerial duties, is about to remove his residence from this State, we furnish him with a letter expressive of our affectionate regard and religious fellowship."

From Augusta we will turn our gaze to the centre of the State, bearing in mind that the state of religion in the churches was such as to bring grief to every devout mind. Divisions of sentiment existed. Religion in the family was neglected. Practical godliness was illustrated by comparatively few professors. The ordinary duties of religion were not sufficiently attended to. Church discipline was not duly regarded; and the support of pastors was by many not considered obligatory. On all these subjects the General Association requested its agents to preach, when on their travels; and the consequence was, as we learn from Sherwood's manuscript notes, on the 30th of May, 1823, messengers, who were chiefly laymen, sent by thirteen different churches, met in convention at Shoal Creek, in Jasper county, to take into consideration the necessity—1. Of a revival of practical religion; 2. Family and church discipline; and 3. The duties of Christians as church-members, in support of the ministry. The only two ordained ministers present were John Robertson, who was made Moderator, and Cyrus White, who was elected Clerk. Certain originators of the scheme, namely Shackelford, McDowell, McLendon, Smith and Hambrick, being present, were invited to take seats.

On the third item several texts were quoted showing the duty of members to support the ministry. Resolutions in favor of these three articles were adopted by the Shoal Creek Convention, and a Circular Address was issued which maintained that the support of the ministry, church expenses, etc., are a charge on the church, "and bind every member in proportion to what he hath."

These articles were adopted by laymen chiefly; and, among the members of the Convention were William Walker, William Flournoy, Thomas Cooper and Wilson Lumpkin, all of whom were rich men, as were most of those who attended. Dr. Sherwood says, in his own quaint way: "If *they* would not flinch, certainly the *poor* ought not."

The General Association adopted these measures for its own, in June of that year, and vigorously urged them; but some of the Associations differed and were offended, as though the General Association was guilty of interference or presumption. The Ocmulgee, itself, at its session in November of that year, 1823, rejected the "third item," which afterwards became a subject much discussed, and a cause of bitter persecution—especially of Mr. Cyrus White.

To his note recording these circumstances, Dr. Adiel Sherwood appends this remark: "When we are offended with plain directions to duty, it is good evidence that we dislike it." From which we may infer that many were disinclined properly to sustain the gospel *at home;* yet, in that very Association $318 were sent up for missions that year, $445 the year previous, and $280 the succeeding year.

It is to be feared that the custom of gratuitous itinerant work performed by all the ministers during the summer, in the different Associations at that day, was, in some respects, at least, prejudicial to the cultivation of a spirit of liberality among church-members; for at the very session in which the Ocmulgee condemned "*item third*," sixteen ministers agreed to spend, each, some weeks in itinerant labor among the settlements in the new counties.

Another endeavor on the part of the General Association was to originate some scheme or plan for the promotion of "a uniformity of church discipline." Jesse Mercer and William T. Brantly were appointed a special committee, in 1823, to correspond with the Associations, Conventions and distinguished individuals of the denomination, regarding the subject, and lay the information obtained before the body. As the views of the denomination were not supposed to be fully understood, the session of 1824 continued the committee, requesting it to gather further information, and report at the next session. In 1825 the committee reported, judiciously, that the matter rest for the present; "but," to quote from the Minutes for that year, "members of the Hephzibah, Sarepta and Tugalo Associations being present, stated the earnest solicitude of their respective bodies, that some measures should be taken to carry into execution the subject above mentioned.

"*Whereupon it was resolved*, That those several bodies and all the Associations in the State, be affectionately invited to send delegates for that special purpose, to our next session."

The next session was held at Augusta, but, as will be readily surmised, nothing further was done in the matter. It appears singular, however, for such a request to be made as representing the "solicitude" of bodies not in connection with the General Association.

In his Manuscript History of Georgia, Adiel Sherwood, who was the clerk of the General Association of the State, at that time, presents, in his private memoranda, some of the obstacles in the way of the measure proposed, which appeared, of course, to infringe upon the sovereignty of the churches. He says: "What is approved by one church is condemned by another in the same vicinity. For instance, some think that the testimony of respectable worldlings may be adduced *pro* or *con.* in regard to a member's conduct; others admit of that from the church only. Some maintain that public offences require private dealing, and quote Matthew chap. xviii; others more correctly (?) confine Matthew's directions to offences against your own person. Some approve of washing the saints' feet as an ordinance; others reject the perpetual obligation altogether; while some perform the ceremony at times, but not as an ordinance."

To say no more on the subject, this terse presentation of its difficulties manifests the injudiciousness of any attempt at promoting or enforcing a strict uniformity of discipline among independent and sovereign churches.

These difficulties, showing the actual impossibility of introducing perfect uniformity of discipline, caused the measure to be dropped entirely, but it cannot be doubted that the more intelligent members of our denomination, in that day, experienced the evils resulting from the laxness of discipline, and foresaw the numerous troubles which afterwards resulted from loose and divergent views of church discipline and desired to avert them.

To show something of the want of harmony, and divergence of views in regard to discipline, and the general state of unchristian feeling that existed at that period, it may be noted that in 1825, the Hephzibah Association *rejected a petition* to send messengers to the General Association and correspond with it, and to seek to bring about a *uniformity of discipline*. The next year, 1826, it appointed brethren Cummings, Huff, Granade, Gray and Brinson, a committee, to visit Bethesda church and rectify some disorder; "and if order cannot be effected, then the committee to be clothed with authority *to expel all the disorderly part of the church*, and give letters of dismission to those that are in order, to join some church that is in order, provided the church will act in conjunction with the committee." In regard to this, Dr. Sherwood, writes, "This is the earliest record of Associational usurpation."

At its session in 1825 at Rocky Creek church, on the 13th of September, the Ebenezer

Resolved, "That we set apart Friday and Saturday, before the fourth Sabbath in January next, as days of fasting and solemn prayer to God, that He would pour out his blessings on the churches in general, *that brotherly love may abound more and more*, and that His common blessings may be generally poured out on our land."

The General Association wisely sought to unite the efforts of the denomination in promoting harmony, good order, godliness and zeal in the advancement of missions, education, temperance, and the establishment of Sunday-Schools and Bible societies.

In its address to the Associations, in 1825, it solemnly urged them to co-operate in attaining these ends, soliciting "a fair hearing" for its cause. Evidently the production of Jesse Mercer, it concludes thus:

"If you have objections to our plan, we say, as we have always said, meet us, and we will endeavor so to shape the Constitution of our Association as to remove every objectionable feature. We do not wish, nor expect, to have a system partial or exceptionable; but it has been our aim to act upon a plan in which all the Associations might harmonize.

"Do you object to us that we are advocates for *missionary exertions?* Then, brethren, your controversy is not with us, but with the apostles of our Lord, and with the Saviour Himself, who by his own command gave the first missionary impulse, under the force of which a grand system of missions has been ever since in successful operation. To our common Master, then, we refer you, and by his judgment you and we must stand or fall.

"Do you object to us that we *connect money and religion*, in conducting our plans of usefulness? Then your objection lies no more against us than against the inspired advocates of the Christian faith, who appealed to the beneficence of the churches for equalizing pecuniary burdens, and for diffusing the glad tidings of the gospel.

Do you object to us that our plan contemplates the *education* of indigent young men, called of God and their churches to preach the gospel? We meet this objection with the assurance that we never thought the cause of God needed either the learning or the ignorance of any man to help it on; but we have always considered that every minister of the gospel should be apt to teach, which he could not be unless he had previously learned something; and that God had made it incumbent on us to seek the best preparation for His work. If you who decry and undervalue education will come forward and exhibit to us specimens of your own preaching, according to the form of sound words, with as cogent reasonings, with as pure a style, and with as uncorrupt doctrines, as we find in the New Testament, then we will allow you the full weight of a consistent judgment in this matter. Or, if you will send forward any one of your own number, who has been himself favored with the advantages of education, and he shall say that learning and intellectual improvement are needless or hurtful appendages to the ministerial character, then we will confess that we have formed a hasty judgment on the subject, and that it will be well for us to revise our decision.

"Do you object to us that we are *seeking some peculiar pre-eminence*, and aiming to climb the heights which ambition descries from a distance? But here, brethren, we could with equal speciousness retort the imputation, were we not restrained by brotherly love and forbearance. For, whether do we, who unite in one body where no distinction or pre-eminence can exist, or they who stand off with the reproachful insinuation, 'I am holier than thou!' more justly incur the suspicion of sinister aims?

"But we will not believe that you are so far gone in the spirit of captiousness and cavilling, and we therefore reiterate our most affectionate invitation to you, and add our earnest prayer that you may stand, perfect and complete, in all the will of God, rooted and grounded in the faith, and at all times prepared to give to every one that asketh a reason of the hope that is in you, with meekness and fear.   JESSE MERCER, *Moderator.*
ADIEL SHERWOOD, *Clerk.*"

This extract is given for three purposes—to show something of the aims and objects of the General Association; to exhibit the earnestness with which the Association brethren sought to secure the co-operation of others; and to manifest the spirit which animated the leaders in the General Association. One of the prime objects of the General Association was to advocate the cause of missions, and in the very session of the body which sent forth the above address, Jesse Mercer preached a missionary sermon, on Sabbath morning, after which a missionary collection was taken up that amounted to $218! At the present day such a collection would hardly be surpassed.

The General Association from its origin, took also a bold and outspoken position in regard to education, both theological and classical. In 1826, its executive committee was instructed to "prepare a plan to provide a fund for purposes of theological education," and, in their report the following year, "they recommend that each member of this body, and the several ministering brethren in our bounds, be requested to use their exertions to advance this object by removing prejudices and showing the value of education to a pious ministry. There are in the State, *more than twenty thousand members.* Is there one of these who would be *deprived of the privilege* of giving fifty cents for so desirable an object?"

The Association in 1826, resolved also, that it felt "a deep and lively interest in the design of the Convention of South Carolina, to establish a Seminary of Learning in the neighborhood of Edgefield Court-House, and that we do cordially concur with said Convention in carrying its design into effect, and that we will to the best of our means, contribute to its advancement." Brethren Brantly and Mercer, were even appointed to meet the South Carolina committee at Edgefield S. C., and confer with it.

So far but three Associations have formally connected themselves with the General Association—the Georgia, Ocmulgee and Sunbury. The Sarepta, however, acknowledges and approves of its existence by sending corresponding messengers. This was the case, for a time or two, also, with the Yellow River Association, which was formed in 1824. The other Associations held aloof; but the Hephzibah and Ebenezer obtained a *quasi* representation through the delegates sent by the missionary societies within the bounds of those Associations. There is no denying that there was a decided opposition to the General Association, arising mainly from an apprehension that the Association might seek to exercise too much power over the Associations and churches, and attempt to diminish or curtail their freedom of action. Perhaps reason for opposition was also found in its attempt to promote uniformity of discipline,* as there certainly

---

*The reader should be informed that desire for a uniformity of discipline was no new thing in Georgia among our churches. As far back as 1808, steps to that end had been taken in the Hephzibah Association; for, in the Hephzibah Minutes of 1809, we find this entry: "Agreeably to a resolution of last year, brother Hand presented the Philadelphia Confession of Faith and Summary

was, in its strenuous endeavors to advance the cause of missions, education and temperance.

Grieved and disappointed that so few Associations coincided with its views and operations, after the lapse of four years, the General Association, in 1826, resolved, unanimously, "That, as several of the Associations in this State have not encouraged the designs of the General Association and, as it seems now doubtful when or whether they will concur, therefore the second Article of our Constitution is so amended that Auxiliary Societies may be admitted as component parts of this body on exhibiting their Constitutional Rules for our approbation :

"*Provided*, That, in all cases, when the Associations, in which the societies shall be located, may manifest a wish to join our body, the said Auxiliaries shall be blended with the Associations in which they are located." In accordance with this action, afterwards, for years, the Hephzibah, Sarepta, Yellow River, Flint River, Pike County Auxiliary Societies, and many others sent delegates to the State Convention. They constituted what we now simply denominate Mission Societies. The form of Constitution for these Auxiliaries, prescribed by the session of 1826, was as follows :

"It will be seen, by reference to the twelfth Article of these Minutes, that Auxiliary Societies are entitled to send delegates to this body, and enjoy all its privileges. A form of Constitution for such is here submitted, with the earnest wish that they may be formed in many neighborhoods. Why could not each church resolve itself into an Auxiliary?

"Article 1. The subscribers, cordially approving of the object and Constitution of the General Association of the Baptists of Georgia, do agree to form a society, to be called the Auxiliary Society of ——, whose sole object shall be to co-operate with the General Association in encouraging missions, and *especially* the education of pious young men of our denomination preparing for the ministry.

"2. All persons paying one dollar or upwards annually, shall be members of this society.

"3. The business of this society shall be conducted by a Board of Directors, composed of a chairman, a clerk, a treasurer and two other members, who shall hold their offices one year, or till others are chosen.

"4. The duties of these officers shall be the same as those of similar officers in other well-regulated societies.

"5. The funds of this society, shall be transmitted annually to the treasury of the parent institution.

"6. No persons shall be messengers to the parent society, but such as are decidedly friendly to its interests and of good moral character.

"7. The Board of Directors shall meet when the interests of the society require it, and may call a meeting of the members annually or oftener.

"8. This society may receive donations from other than regular members.

"9. All moneys paid into the general treasury, shall be appropriated at discretion, but, when the object designed to be assisted shall be designated by the donors, to such objects it shall be sacredly applied.

"10. This Constitution may be altered at any regular meeting of the society, two-thirds of the members present concurring therein."

In accordance with this constitution, many "Auxiliaries" were formed the names of some of which are recorded here, in addition to those already given : *McDonough, LaGrange, Jasper County, Butts and Monroe, Putnam and Baldwin, Sharon, Rocky Creek, Chattahoochee, Morgan County, Gwinnett County, Tugaloo Society, Muscogee, Troup, Athens, County Line, (Talbot County,) Walton County, Gainesville, Monticello, Columbus, Twiggs County, Mercer Institute, Newton County, Mountain Creek, (Harris County,) Island Fork, (Gwinnett County,) Meriwether County, Macon, Thomaston, Piney Grove, (Richmond County,) and Coweta and Heard Counties.*

of Discipline. The Association, wishing to proceed with caution in a matter of such importance, thought proper to recommend a convention of delegates from the several Associations with whom we correspond, to meet at Powelton, in Hancock county, on Saturday before the first Sunday in May next, to review and (if need be) revise the same. Brethren Franklin, Talbot, Boykin and Robertson are appointed to represent this Association in that Convention." Through a lack of proper authoritative records, we are unable to ascertain what was the result of this action, but we opine that nothing **was done of any material influence.**

Almost alone with the aid of these Auxiliaries the noble old Georgia Association for at least ten years carried on the business of the Convention, promoting its interests and maintaining in our State among Baptists, an interest in every good word and work. But it should be clearly understood, that the best men of the denomination in the State, were all the while actively co-operating with one another in the Convention, as the body is now called; for, in pursuance of a resolution offered in 1827, the name "General Association" was formally changed in 1828, to that of "*The Baptist Convention of the State of Georgia.*"

For a few moments, now, we will consider the Ebenezer Association. Formed of fourteen churches, in 1814, with a membership of 675, its increase was as follows: in 1816, twenty churches, 681 members, twenty-six baptisms; in 1818, twenty-one churches, 876 members, thirty-two baptisms; in 1820, twenty-five churches, 1,065 members, fifty-six baptisms; in 1821, twenty-six churches, 1,085 members, thirty-eight baptisms; in 1822, twenty-six churches, 1,019 members, forty-four baptisms; in 1823, twenty-eight churches, 1,048 members, sixty-seven baptisms; in 1824, twenty-nine churches, 969 members, forty-eight baptisms; in 1825, thirty churches, 1,070 members, and ninety-one baptisms; in 1827, thirty churches, 1,074 members, one hundred and twenty-nine baptisms; and in 1828, there were thirty-two churches, 1,198 members, and during the year two hundred baptisms. In the the year following, 1829, there was an increase of four churches, the members increase to 1,431, and there were two hundred and seventy baptisms. In 1829, thirty-four churches had 1,502 members, there having been four hundred and ten baptisms. The Corresponding Letter of that year speaks with gratitude of a very general outpouring of the Spirit in the bounds of the Association, and affirms that the churches were united in love and fellowship, showing the effects of the great revival of 1827.

In its early years it corresponded with the General Baptist Board of Foreign Missions, at Philadelphia, and approved of the establishment of a theological institution. It appears that the Board of Foreign Missions, with a view to the establishment of what, in the end, proved to be Columbian University, requested the opinions of our Georgia Baptist Associations concerning the measure. The reply given by the Ebenezer Association, in 1819, was:

"The Board of Foreign Missions having requested the sentiments of the churches and Associations, respecting the establishment of an institution for the education of young men called by the churches to the ministry, and who have not funds of their own to aid them in obtaining a suitable education; the opinion of this Association is that an institution of that kind, upon proper principles, is laudable, but not being satisfactorily informed as to the plan spoken of, hope the same will be had in consideration until next Association."

The next year, 1820, the Association adopted the following:

"We are of opinion that such an institution appears laudable, but as we are unable to foresee any special benefit arising from it to the churches generally, we can, therefore, only say, we are willing that our brethren who are in favor of such a plan should pursue that object; and if, at any future period, we get more fully convinced of its utility, we shall the more cheerfully come into the measure."

In the same year the Ebenezer concurred with the Ocmulgee Association in the plan for Indian Reform, appointed trustees to act in concert with those of the other Associations, and urged its ministers to explain the plan and raise funds to carry the laudable scheme into effect. This co-operation was continued the next year, and a Circular Letter, written by the clerk, John McKenzie, was adopted, which is a good missionary document, ending as follows:

"We would now call your attention to the laudable undertaking of this Association, to act in concert with the Ocmulgee and Georgia Associations in establishing a school in the Creek Nation; and, as there are some of our brethren who appear not willing to engage in the work, we believe it is for the want of light. For if the gospel is to be preached in all the world for a witness to all nations; and if the birth of Christ was to be 'glad tidings of great joy to all people;' we ask if they are not a nation? If they are, the gospel is to be preached to them. Are they a people? If they are, then the 'glad tidings of great joy' are to reach them. But they have no written language into which these glad tidings can be translated. They must, therefore, be taught to read them in some language into which they already are, or may be translated. This cannot be done without expense. We entreat you, dear brethren, to open your hearts and hands and come up to the help of the Lord against the mighty. Isaiah saith, 'The wolf shall dwell with the lamb, and the lion shall eat straw like the ox.' From this Scripture we understand that the disposition of the wolf and the lion are to be changed. We have by the sword compelled the Indian to lay down the tomahawk and the scalping-knife, but their disposition is not yet changed, and nothing can effect that but the gospel. Dear brethren, let us call to mind that glorious night on which the Saviour was born. The angels brought the glad tidings to the shepherds, and immediately there was heard a heavenly host singing, 'Glory to God in the highest, on earth peace and good will toward men.' If it was a matter of so much joy to the angels to bring these glad tidings to man, how much more ought we who are the happy participants of this gospel to rejoice in sending it to the poor benighted heathen!"

This is given as a fair illustration of the arguments advanced in that day to incite an interest in Indian mission work. The consequence of this address was a unanimous determination, the next year, 1822, to continue "in that laudable pursuit;" and the report of the Board of Trustees, of that year, for instructing and evangelizing the Creek Indians, was published in the Minutes. It has already been referred to. It tells of two tours made by Mr. Compere, and of the expectation that he would be soon settled in the Nation. The report contains this appeal to the three co-operating Associations: "We entreat you not to suffer yourselves to be too soon shaken in mind, or removed from the 'help of the Lord against the mighty;'" and was signed by Jesse Mercer, Secretary; and yet, in the Minutes of 1823 we find this entry: "Took under consideration the Indian Reform—whether to continue or discontinue; and it was discontinued." The following year, 1824, a motion to reconsider the matter was lost; and so, also, was a motion to reconsider the action of 1823, by which a communication in reference to union with the General Association was "thrown under the table." In all these years we see small evidence of spirituality and growth in the churches. There were no expressions indicating love and harmonious fellowship. Some of the most prominent ministers, such as John McKenzie and John Blackstone, changed their views and became violently anti-missionary in their proclivities, after having manifested a strong missionary spirit; yet the Minutes of the General Association for 1825 assure us that during these years the Ebenezer Missionary Society was in vigorous operation, and had an agent in the field collecting mission money with considerable success.

At that time the churches of the Association were situated in Twiggs, Laurens, Wilkinson, Pulaski, Baldwin, Monroe, Dooly, Washington, and Telfair counties, and its prominent ministers were Eden Taylor, Henry Hand, John Blackstone, Charles Culpepper, James Steeley, John Ross, John McKenzie, Adam Jones, Vincent A. Tharp, and Theophilus Pearce.

Among the ministers of this Association was John Ross, whose name has already been mentioned. He was a Virginian by birth, and born in 1781, emigrating to Georgia with his father in 1798. He was among the earliest of those who settled the long-coveted land between the Oconee and Ocmulgee rivers, and was a man of more than respectable talents as a preacher. He lived in the Ebenezer Association until 1830, and was for several years its Moderator, although differing from the majority of his brethren in that Association in regard to the benevolent enterprises of the day. He was their firm friend and constant supporter, while the Association generally were opposed to them. Their opposition affected his zeal, however. In 1825 he was a messenger of the Ebenezer Missionary Society to the General Association at Eatonton. In 1830 he removed to Upson county, and held church membership within the bounds of the Columbus Association, over which body he presided until his death, in 1837. He was a man of great popularity, of persuasive eloquence and impassioned manner, beloved and confided in by all who knew him. In the last years of his life, he gave freer vent to his zeal in behalf of missions and education, and exerted a commanding influence in the Columbus Association. At the State Convention in Talbotton in 1836, he warmly advocated the establishment of a Baptist college in the State; and attended the noted ministers' meeting in Forsyth in July of the same year, entered deeply into its measures, and was instrumental in accomplishing much good.

Vincent A. Tharp was another leader in the Association. He, too, was a native of Virginia, born in 1760, and a soldier in the Revolutionary war, and was licensed in Georgia about 1800, serving several churches in Burke county. He moved to Twiggs county, and was pastor of the Stone Creek church. He was a man of forecast, benevolence and influence. His ability was great. Among the prominent traits of his character were benevolence and hospitality. Such men as Polhill, Franklin, Ross, Rhodes, Baker, McGinty and Mercer were his frequent guests. He died in 1825, having repeatedly been the Moderator of the Ebenezer Association, Rev. Charnick Tharp was his son, and Rev. B. F. Tharp is his grandson.

Theophilus Pearce was also a Moderator of the Ebenezer Association for several years. He was ordained by Vincent Tharp and Henry Hooten in 1815. He was a useful man, and, though of limited education and indigent circumstances, he was highly respected wherever known. To the sick and dying he was a frequent visitor, and thus made himself greatly useful.

We will now briefly glance at the spirit which seems to have animated the Hephzibah Association during the second and third decades of the century. Its opposition to the General Association has been stated. Its unfriendliness to missions was strongly manifested; and all the mission work accomplished by the Association for years, was through the agency of the Hephzibah Mission Society, which seems to have been quite an efficient organization, owing to the zeal of a few active and benevolent members, notably Charles J. Jenkins. At its third anniversary, held at Providence meeting-house, Jefferson county, this society had $273,40 in the treasury, and reported one missionary in the field. We find its messengers in all the Associations for years, and also several times in the General Association. The Association itself received the messengers of this society and bade it "God speed," but assisted not in its benevolent endeavors. It, however, recommended those friendly to foreign missions to meet and form a foreign mission society, if they felt so inclined, which was done, and the society continued in existence for several years.

In the fall of 1824, it consented "to allow all the brethren that wish to join together and correspond with the General Association, or to join in with mission societies, by correspondence or otherwise, but to be entirely separate and distinct from the Association."

This action, doubtless, was due to the efforts of Rev. J. H. T. Kilpatrick, then a new member of the Association. The next year, 1825, his church, Buckhead, and Isaac Brinson's church, Brushy Creek, by a petition, requested the Association to send messengers to the General Association of the State, to view its order and modes of operation; but Mr. Kilpatrick was absent from the session of 1825 and, to forestall any further efforts looking to a connection with the General Association, the body ordered the following to be a part of its Decorum: "This Association shall have no right to correspond, by letter or messenger, with any General Association, or Committee, Missionary Society, or Board. Any brother moving either of the above subjects in this body, shall be considered in disorder and, therefore, reproved by the Moderator. But we leave any brother or brethren free to correspond or contribute or not—just as their feelings may be in the case." But, at the request of the churches, the act was cancelled the following year, 1826, and the old Decorum was restored.

To account for this unhappy condition of affairs, it is necessary to state that Rev. George Franklin, a ruling spirit, and who had been strongly missionary in sentiment, died in 1815 or 1816. Rev. Charles Culpepper, another strong man, and a ruling spirit, had become connected with the Ebenezer Association. Charles J. Jenkins had moved into the bounds of the Sarepta Association. The Rosses, R. E. McGinty, Edmund Talbot, F. Flournoy, had become members

STATE OF RELIGION.

of the Ocmulgee Association. Henry Hand, also, had moved to a distance, and Winder Hillsman was dead.

All the strong missionary men had thus been removed from the Association, while J. H. T. Kilpatrick, having but recently become a member of the Association, had not, as yet, acquired sufficient influence to counteract the anti-missionary element which, assisted by Joshua Key and Jonathan Huff, he finally succeeded in overcoming. A turn of the tide occurred in 1828, as will be seen hereafter, but it was not until 1830 that the body officially recognized the General Association, when M. N. McCall, Jonathan Huff, Beasley, Polhill, Dye, Hudson, Sinquefield and Allen were appointed a committee to visit the Convention as spectators, witness its order, ascertain who composed it, and learn its methods of procedure.

A few data will exhibit its growth and spiritual prosperity. In 1813, it numbered 36 churches and 922 members; in 1817, there were 33 churches, 2,197 members and 125 baptisms; in 1820, there were 34 churches, 2,107 members and 110 baptisms; in 1821, 35 churches, 1,806 members, 155 baptisms; in 1824, 36 churches, 1,447 members, 77 baptisms; in 1825, 35 churches, 1,085 members.

During these last five years there had been a decided decrease, which was recovered in the years following, which included the grand revival times from 1827 to 1831.

In the Sarepta Association there seems to have been a much better benevolent tone. It commended missions, praised its mission society, encouraged tract societies, corresponded with the Foreign Mission Board, sent its ministers on domestic mission tours and appointed messengers to the General Association, but declined to become a constituent member; nor did it consent to do so, until 1835. It should be borne in mind, that Charles J. Jenkins, Sr., who resided so many years of his life within the bounds of the Hephzibah Association, resided in the limits of the Sarepta Association, from 1818 to 1822, when he moved to Apalachicola, Florida.

Two new Associations were formed in 1824, two years after the constitution of the General Association. These were, *The Yellow River*, and *The Flint River* Associations. The former was constituted September 18th, by a committee, the members of which had been appointed by the Sarepta and Ocmulgee Associations at Harris' Springs, Newton County. The presbytery was composed of Isham Goss, Reuben Thornton, Edmund Talbot, James Brooks, Iverson L. Brooks, Richard Pace and Cyrus White. The latter was organized by brethren appointed by the Ocmulgee and Ebenezer Associations, namely, Edmund Talbot, J. Nichols, D. Montgomery, J. Callaway, J. Milner, V. A. Tharpe, T. Pearce. To form these Associations twenty-one churches were dismissed from the Ocmulgee Association, but six newly constituted churches also united with the Flint River, making twenty in all; while the same thing happened in the case of the Yellow River, six newly constituted churches uniting with seven dismissed from the Ocmulgee, making thirteen which at first composed the Association.

At its first session the Yellow River appointed five messengers to the General Association, one only of whom attended—Joel Colley, who was Moderator of this Association for many years.

The Flint River, at first, flatly refused to correspond with the General Association.

Both shared richly in the glorious benefits of the great revival of 1827 and 1828, and both enjoyed the valuable evangelical preaching of such men as A. Sherwood, John E. Dawson, Jonathan Davis, E. Shackelford, J. H. Campbell, J. S. Callaway and V. R. Thornton. Yet the Yellow River departed from the old Baptist faith of missions, Bible societies, etc., refused a seat in its body to Rev. A. Sherwood, as a representative of the State Convention, in 1833, and to this day has never connected itself with the Georgia Baptist Convention; while the Flint River, which for nearly twenty years declined co-operation with the Convention and with missionary Associations, came into full accord with them, and has heartily and most liberally engaged in mission, Sunday-school and educational enterprises to the present day.

We have thus given a glance at the general state of religion, in our denomination in Georgia, in the first half of the third decade of the century, and have touched lightly upon the history of the Associations formed in the State at that period. After a study of the records, we present the following as an approximately correct table of the statistics of our denomination in Georgia, for the year 1824. The figures were taken from the printed Minutes of the various Associations:

ASSOCIATIONS.	CHURCHES.	ORD. MIN.	LICENTIATES.	TOTAL.
1. Georgia,	37	23	5	3,194
2. Ocmulgee,	42	16	2	2,973
3. Sunbury,	18	10	0	5,257
4. Yellow River,	20	11	1	662
5. Sarepta,	32	5	5	1,366
6. Hephzibah,	36	13	4	1,447
7. Ebenezer,	29	14	2	969
8. Flint River,	20	5	2	523
9. Tugalo,	15	10	4	1,017
10. Piedmont,	15	8	0	700
	264	115	25	18,108

While as correct as statistics usually are in our Associational Minutes, yet the following considerations will show that the aggregate was larger than these figures represent. In the first place, the statistics of some churches for 1823 are given in the Minutes; in the second place, some churches were dismissed from one Association to aid in forming another, and had not yet made application for admission, and, therefore, are not estimated here; and, in the third place, there were new churches constantly forming which had become attached to no Association, and whose statistics do not appear in this table. Still, these figures are somewhat below those given by Dr. Sherwood, in the General Association Minutes of 1825, and quoted by Dr. Campbell, on page 15 of his book, as applying to 1825, by a slip of the pen, perhaps. The discrepancy is due to the fact that Dr. Sherwood counts the membership of six South Carolina churches, belonging to the Tugalo Association, which, of course, should be omitted from the Georgia statistics. He gives, also, the statistics of 1821, for the Hephzibah and Ebenezer Associations, while, in the mean time, various churches had been dismissed from these to form other Associations, thereby reducing the total membership of the Ebenezer and Hephzibah Associations, in 1824.

XII.
EDUCATIONAL.
1825-1829.

XII.

EDUCATIONAL.

"INDIAN REFORM" ONCE MORE—CONCLUSION OF THAT MISSION—CAUSE OF ITS ABANDONMENT—SKETCH OF E. L. COMPERE—CONTRIBUTIONS OF THE GEORGIA BAPTISTS—INTEREST IN EDUCATION—FEW EDUCATED MEN—THE STATE CONVENTION AND EDUCATION—ADDRESS OF 1826—COLUMBIAN COLLEGE—A FUND FOR THEOLOGICAL EDUCATION—OPPONENTS OF EDUCATION, SOME OF THEIR NOTIONS—ANECDOTES ILLUSTRATIVE OF IGNORANCE—"GO .PREACH MY GOSPEL"—WHAT MERCER SAID ABOUT "INSPIRED SERMONS"—DR. A. SHERWOOD.

We now turn our attention to those matters which occupied the attention of the denomination subsequent to 1824. One of these was the matter of "Indian Reform," which consisted in the support of an Indian Mission and school among the Creek Indians in Alabama, at Withington Station, thirty miles south of Montgomery.

Though sustained largely by the Georgia Baptists, this mission was under the control of the General Board, at Philadelphia, which had been formed in 1814. That board appointed Rev. Francis Flournoy superintendent, but he declined the appointment, and Rev. Lee Compere, of South Carolina, was appointed in 1822. The mission was actually commenced in 1823, much to the gratification of many Georgia Baptists.

It has not been deemed necessary to dwell very minutely upon this Indian Mission, for the reason that no very special results ensued, and because the Baptists of Georgia soon lost their interest in it. Indeed, the last contribution for it was sent up to the Convention in 1828, and the amount was thirty dollars only. The reasons for this are put on record in the report of the Mission Board of the Georgia Association for 1825. After stating, among other items, that three hundred dollars had been appropriated to the Withington Station, the Board continues as follows:

"The indisposition of some Associations, and many churches and individuals, towards missionary effort and friendly co-operation, are sources of our regret. This is attributable, in a considerable degree, to a circumstance which your Board would willingly have passed by in silence. A general expression of disapprobation against the part which the superintendent of Withington Station has acted, has come up from the churches and many individuals, which calls for his removal. But very few churches have contributed at all to replenish our funds this year, and where any sum has been sent up, it was prohibited by most of them from being appropriated to said Station. Hence your Board think that they are called upon to act immediately on this subject; for, as individuals, they are not able to support said Station, and are unwilling any longer to be responsible for the monied transactions of said superintendent. They are not wholly unaware of the responsibility of their situation, nor of the delicacy with which they should handle the feelings of their brethren, They intend to make an expression of their opinion, not on the private or moral character of Mr. Compere, but upon those parts of his conduct which have rendered him odious in the eyes of this community, and which have dried up the stream of munificence which flowed to his support. They have not formed their opinion concerning him from public rumor, nor from paragraphs of party papers, but upon his own public and private letters. They feel confident that his acts have a bearing so unpropitious on the whole course of missions, that very little, if anything, will be done in their behalf until he is removed. As we stand connected in his support with the General Convention of our denomination, we do not feel fully authorized to depose him; but we think we cannot do less than to disclaim any connection with a man whose acts have brought said cause into such disrepute. Therefore, the Board recommend the adoption of the following resolution:

"'*Resolved unanimously*, That we withhold further support from the Withington Station.'

"The reasons which have induced us to recommend the adoption of the resolution are: That the Rev. Mr. Compere has meddled with concerns foreign to his mission; he has, unasked, charged the United States Commissioners with corruption in making the treaty; he has taken sides with those who are endeavoring to render it (though an act of the general government) null and void, and he has vindicated the murderers of McIntosh. He has violated his agreement with this Board, and disobeyed the instructions given him; he has treated these instructions with indifference and contempt; when written to and cautioned by the President of this body, 'that the course he was pursuing would bring the mission to ruin,' instead of returning a respectful answer, he has endeavored to vindicate his conduct; and has since continued to act so opposite to the spirit of his instructions, and that of a cautious missionary of the Cross, that they are compelled, though reluctantly, to take the present course.

"*And be it further resolved*, That a copy of these proceedings be forthwith transmitted to the General Convention of our denomination in the United States.

"JESSE MERCER, *President*.

"J. P. MARSHALL, *Secretary*."

The Mission Board, which suggested such summary and decided measures, was composed of Jesse Mercer, Adiel Sherwood, Malachi Reeves, J. Roberts, J. H. Walker and E. Battle.

Of course we are obliged to accept the statements of the report made by such men as correct. Mr. Compere, however, felt it to be his duty to act as he did, in justice to the Indians, among whom he resided, and he claimed to the day of his death, that his course met the emphatic approval of John C. Calhoun, Secretary of War during Mr. Monroe's administration. Nevertheless, his conduct must have been decidedly injudicious, for a Christian missionary acting under instructions to which he had consented to yield compliance.

He was born in England, November 3d, 1789, and died in Navarro County, Texas, at the residence of his son, T. H. Compere, June 15th, 1871, in his 81st year. He was educated at Bristol, England, under Dr. Ryland, and was raised to business in London. By the Baptists of England, he was sent out as a missionary to Jamaica, but the sickliness of the climate compelled him to remove to South Carolina. In 1822, he was appointed missionary to the Creek Indians, among whom he remained six years, with his wife and family, faithfully and zealously performing his official duties. When he was at the head of the Creek Mission-school it contained about two hundred Indian children as pupils. These he taught, assisted by his wife and Mr. Simons, afterwards a missionary of the Boston Board to Burmah. His wife's maiden name was Susannah Voysey, who was born, reared and educated in London, and an extraordinary woman of great worth and strength of character. The prayer-meetings in the mission house were largely attended by the Indians and their children. The colored slaves of the Indians were also fond of attending, which was offensive to some of the more wicked ruling chiefs. On one occasion, in the absence of Mr. Compere, when his wife was conducting the meeting, about twenty of the negroes who were in attendance were forcibly ejected from the meeting and whipped. The next day, Mr. Compere rode to the Indian Court or Council, dismounted, walked boldly up to the scowling chief and took a seat by his side. Perceiving the ill-temper of the Indians and a desire to intimidate him, he turned and looked the chief fully in the face, and said mildly but firmly, "I am not afraid of you," and gazed fixedly into the chief's eyes. Presently the stern features of the chief relaxed and a smile appeared on his countenance. He then proceeded with the business of the meeting. At the proper time, Mr. Compere took his stand in front of the chief and remonstrated against the cruel treatment of their slaves by the Indians in a set speech, during which a prominent chief fiercely raised his club to strike. As he was behind the speaker, his act was unknown by Mr. Compere until he had finished his address, when the Indian himself approached and apologized for raising his club to kill him, saying he could not and would not kill so good a man. Afterwards Mr. Compere had no further troubles with the Indians. The removal of the Indians to the Territory, broke up the mission and Mr. Compere bought and lived upon a farm twelve miles east of Montgomery. He afterwards resided in Tennessee, Mississippi, Arkansas and Texas, always preaching when his physical ability enabled him to do so. He met heavy pecuniary reverses before the war, and lost all the rest through the vandalism of armed ruffians in Arkansas, during that struggle; everything was destroyed, even his library, memoranda, papers and relics of his past life and history.

Mr. Compere is described by one who knew him well, as a man of quiet unassuming dignity, urbane and deferring to others, yet conscious of his own abilities. Untrammelled by hobbies and independent in thought, he was decided in his convictions and opinions, and very pronounced in favor of everything generally acknowledged to be morally or religiously right He was decidedly a Regular Baptist, and an emphatic preacher of what is called "doctrine," but never preached often on exciting topics of dispute among denominations. Always endeavoring to have a conscience void of offence towards God and man, he made himself at home in every company, With the lowly and unlettered he was unpretending, and, yet, without straining he showed himself the peer of the most pretentious, without seeming effort commanding the respect of the highest and most distinguished. In sentiment and practice he was a whole-souled "Missionary." His style as a preacher was lively, pointed, earnest, solemn and solid. In holy things he never indulged in lightness, yet he was a most pleasant and affectionate fireside companion, and possessed a smiling, pleasant countenance, with eyes whose expression was full of kind feeling. He was twice married, left several children, some of whom have proved very useful. One of them Rev. E. L. Compere, resides at Witcherville, Arkansas, Rev. Thomas Hechijah Compere, lives in McLainsborough, Texas, and Mrs. Susannah Muscogee Lyon, a daughter, lives at Moulton, Alabama. The last two were born while Mr. Compere was a missionary at Withington Station, and were named by the chiefs.

No more money was sent up by the churches of the Georgia Association for the Creek Mission; but, for three years longer, the Auxiliary Societies of the Ocmulgee and Ebenezer Associations send up gradually-diminishing sums; and then the Withington Station Mission disappears from Georgia Baptist history. It was a fair and honest endeavor, nevertheless, on the part of men burning with a desire to benefit their fellow man, and the flame kindled then has never expired since, for no State in the South, perhaps, has felt a deeper interest in Indian Missions than Georgia, or contributed more to maintain them. The Mission actually concluded with the removal of that portion of the Creek Indians west of the Mississippi, in 1829, and, until their departure, Mr. Compere remained with them as Superintendent of the Withington Mission Station.

In the Minutes of the General Association for 1826, we find this entry: "According to the wish of the Ocmulgee and Georgia Associations, as expressed in their Minutes, their funds were transferred to this body, to be appropriated in such manner—for missionary purposes—as it shall deem best," and one hundred dollars were appropriated to insure to the delegates appointed by the Ocmulgee Association a seat in the General Convention.

The General Association thus, in 1826, became the recognized common medium through which the Georgia Baptists made their contributions for benevolent purposes of all kinds. Two years before, in 1816, the Georgia Association had established its Mission Board, and during that time this Board received, from individuals and churches, about $5,000. It donated about $1,900 to the Creek Indian Mission, about $1,000 to Columbian College, and over $1,100 to general missionary purposes, through the General Convention, besides turning over more than $1,000 to the Treasurer of the General Association of Georgia.

During these years the mission societies of the Sunbury, Hephzibah, Ocmulgee, Ebenezer and Sarepta Associations have all been collecting and disbursing funds for State itinerant work, for Indian Missions, for Foreign Missions, and for Columbian College. The Sunbury Association, through its Mission Board, continuously maintained several missionaries on the seaboard, who labored mostly among the colored people, and performed a work which redounds to the credit of that body, and which the historian could not fail to chronicle without being recreant to duty.

Among the items reported, at the Convention, of 1825, by Rev. C. White, was the collection of $17.50, for educating ministers; $10.00 for Indian Reform, and $5.00 for Burman Mission. It is but appropriate to record again that, at the same session, a collection of $218.00 was taken up after the missionary sermon was preached by Jesse Mercer on Sabbath morning. In the following year, 1826, he preached on missions, Sunday night, and $67.25 were collected. In the morning Dr. William B. Johnson, of South Carolina, had preached on the education of pious young men, and $108.00 were collected for the purpose. Luther Rice and Basil Manly, Sr., were present and, it is presumed, lent their influence to the cause of education; for the body engaged to support Jonathan Toole, in classical and theological studies, as a beneficiary, and instructed its Executive Committee, M. Reeves, B. M. Sanders, J. H. Walker and J. P. Marshall, to prepare some plan by which a fund for bestowing a theological education upon beneficiaries might be provided. This was the first definite action, looking to education, that was taken by the State Convention.

Faithfulness to history requires the statement that, with few exceptions, the ministers of our denomination, during the third decade of the century, were unlearned men, and most of them were ignorant men. As bright exceptions among ministers, the names of William T. Brantly, Jesse Mercer, Adiel Sherwood, Henry J. Ripley, Iverson L. Brooks, James Shannon, Henry O. Wyer, Jabez P. Marshall, B. M. Sanders, and J. H. T. Kilpatrick, may be mentioned. Most of these were men of fine classical education, and all of them desired the establishment of a denominational college of high order. This desire was, of course, participated in by many others, including numbers of very intelligent laymen, of whom our denomination could claim a large host; but, strange to say, there was much opposition to education by not a few in the denomination.

From its organization, our State Convention unhesitatingly sustained the cause of education. In the years 1824 and 1825, Mercer, Brantly and Sherwood were appointed a committee to consult with a similar committee of the South Carolina Convention with reference to co-operation in the establishment of an institution of learning in the latter State; and in 1820 we find our State Convention, then called the General Association, expressing a deep and lively interest in the design of the Convention of South Carolina to establish a seminary of learning in the neighborhood of Edgefield Court-house; and, cordially concurring in the design, it promised contributions to its advancement to the best of the means at its disposal. Jesse Mercer and William T. Brantly were appointed a committee to meet the committee of the South Carolina Convention, at Edgefield, in March of that year.

The Executive Committee was also authorized to employ itinerants to travel and preach, and explain the designs of the General Association. This was set forth so plainly in the "Address to Associations and Individuals," adopted by the Convention, that, as part of the history of the times, it is quoted in full. It is not difficult to discern in its composition the hand of Adiel Sherwood, Secretary of the body.

After an introduction which refers to the opposition, *open* and *secret*, which the Convention had encountered, the Address proceeds :

"The feature in the Constitution of this body, which is odious to some is, that which proposes to afford the means of education to pious young men, fitting for the gospel ministry. It is designed to establish a seminary, where, not only candidates for the ministry, but every child of the denomination, may be educated. Opposers think they discover something in this clause which will, by and by, seek to 'lord it over God's heritage,' undermine the independence and liberty of the churches and introduce a host of imposters to corrupt the pure principles of Christianity. Let us examine the tendency of the principles held by this Association.

"We think, and we believe every liberal minded man will coincide with us, that the encouragement we offer to learning would exert a most powerful influence against such a state of things as is here apprehended. If the friends of the General Association were desirous of effecting that with which they stand charged; if they wished to engross all the authority in the churches; and induce all the members to act in accordance with a wicked design, they would *cry down* learning. They would oppose it in every shape and in every degree; because in proportion as the community is enlightened, it will be the better qualified to resist attempts upon liberties and privileges. How do you think the Pope has acquired such an ascendancy over millions that they suppose him 'infallible' and able to forgive sin? Not by educating them, but by keeping them in ignorance and shutting up the sources of information. This is his policy; for he well knows if access to the Bible were easy; if it was read from childhood, and as much pains taken to explain it as by Protestant ministers, the people would learn that God alone can pardon the sinner—not an imperious priest.

"*Opposers*, and not *patrons* of education as are the friends of the Association, should rather lie under the weight of the censure of attempting to 'lord it over God's heritage.'

"A quack, who has discovered some cure for a disease, never divulges the secret, lest others should be as wise as himself, and then his source of wealth would be dried up; whereas, those physicians who wish well to their country, and commiserate the unfortunate, make public every discovery which tends to cure disease and alleviate sorrow.

"The friends of the Association are, by their opponents, all supposed to be learned. Let it be so! Then, if they had any sinister views to accomplish, they would act the part of the quack and not encourage learning. They would were it in their power, proscribe every school denounce every minister of education who had not joined them, and, like the lawyers of the olden time, keep the key of knowledge in their hands, lest the unlearned should enter in, and become as wise as themselves. But not so! They urge the importance of education, not only to the ministry, but to every individual in the community. * * * *

"Tyrants, who rule with a rod of iron, encourage education among the nobility, and leave the rest of their subjects as ignorant as the Hottentot. More than two hundred students were expelled from a college in Europe, two or three years ago, for expressing *liberal*, or, as we would call them, *republican* sentiments in politics. The ruler well knew that if they became as well versed in the science of government as freemen ought to be, they would discover by how frail a tenure the "*jus divinum regum*" is held. The King of Sardinia has lately decreed that none of his subjects shall enjoy the privilege of education unless they are worth three hundred dollars! Now, we leave it to the candid whether the *friends* or the *opponents* of the General Association ought to be looked upon as dangerous men and ranked with the despots of Europe.

"Having shown, as we trust, that the principles which govern the General Association tend rather to *prevent* than to *bring about* the unhappy state of things in the churches which opposers seem to apprehend, we conclude with a few remarks:

"Friends of the General Association, we have much to encourage us. The late public expressions in favor of education have cheered our hopes and emboldened us to "take courage." It is too late in the day for opposers to object to the utility of learning in the ministry; for the want of it is seen and felt too much to expect to dishearten its friends by crying it down. The illiterate minister himself, who has been useful in his day, and the instrument of winning many souls to Christ, weeps over his need, and the exertions now making for the improvement of his younger brethren causes his heart to leap for joy. The want of such qualifications as sanctified learning furnishes, could not produce opposition, in a liberal-minded man, to its attainment by others.

"In the three Associations fully united with us there are about seventy ordained and licensed preachers and 11,500 members—a majority of the denomination in the State. If these are active at their several posts, much influence in our favor will be exerted, and considerable sums raised, to promote those objects which piety holds dear. Besides, many ministers and very many friends, belonging to other Associations, are our warm patrons and generous supporters. That others may feel the importance of our designs, and be enlisted with us in the cause of God, we will still prefer the petition, which has engaged our hearts for years, to Him who sitteth on the throne. We will not cease to pray for them till every Christian shall bring, with willing heart, his sacrifice to the treasury of the Lord. The spirit of our petition shall not cease till the news of salvation shall have reached every hamlet and every cottage under the whole heaven.

JESSE MERCER, *Moderator.*
ADIEL SHERWOOD, *Clerk.*"

There was, at that time, another educational enterprise to which contributions were largely made by the Baptists of Georgia—Columbian College, at Washington City. The amounts donated by the liberality of Georgia Baptists to that institution, mainly through the advocacy of its agents, Luther Rice and Abner W. Clopton, were about $20,000.

A good deal of money was sent on to Washington City and was acknowledged by the Board of Trustees of Columbian College as received from the "Georgia" and "Ocmulgee" Associations, without its being known who the original contributors were. Mr. Mercer, however, contributed largely to that college, and, at a meeting held June 30th, 1823, its Board of Trustees, in response to a letter received from William Walker, Sr., of Putnam county, announcing his intention to bestow $2,500 on the funds of the college, for the purpose of endowing a scholarship in the theological department, adopted the following:

"*Resolved*, That the thanks of this Board be presented to William Walker, Sr., Esq., of Putnam county, Georgia, for his liberal appropriation of twenty-five hundred dollars to endow a scholarship of the Columbian College, in the District of Columbia, to be paid in two equal instalments of $1,250 each, in October, 1823 and 1824.

"*Resolved*, That the scholarship thus liberally endowed by the aforesaid William Walker, Sr., Esq., be denominated, and the same is, hereby, denominated 'The Walker Scholarship,' in the Columbian College, of the District of Columbia."

The treasurer reported the $2,500 paid in full, July 19th, 1824.

For several years regular contributions for that college were reported in the financial accounts of the Georgia Association; and no doubt Dr. C. D. Mallary, in his Life of Jesse Mercer, states but the simple truth when he says, concerning Mr. Mercer, "From the first he was much interested in the efforts which were made to establish a college in the District of Columbia. His name was enrolled among the trustees of the institution; in the midst of its long and distressing embarrassments, he clung to it with a steadfast affection, and contributed to its support with a bountiful hand. Seldom, if ever, was an appeal to him for assistance made in vain.

"And in no small degree may it be attributed to the example and influence of Mr. Mercer, that such liberal contributions were raised in the State of Georgia, in aid of that college."

This extract appears in the Corresponding Letter of the Georgia Association, for 1827: "We have the pleasure of informing you that the Association was happily united in their efforts to aid in the relief of Columbian College, and other important designs, calculated to disseminate divine light throughout our world."

Thus, we see that, from 1825 to 1830, many of the Georgia Baptists were rendering very material assistance towards maintaining the existence of Columbian College; the General Association was seriously consulting with the brethren of the South Carolina Baptist Convention in regard to co-operation in the establishment of a literary and theological institution; and the State Convention was seeking to devise a plan for the education of pious young men with the ministry in view.

With reference to the scheme of establishing an institution of learning in conjunction with the South Carolina brethren, it may be briefly stated that it was soon abandoned; for insurmountable difficulties arose, owing to State local partialities, which prevented the co-operation necessary to its consummation.

At the session of the General Association which met at Washington, Wilkes county, in 1827, the Executive Committee, which had been requested to prepare a plan for providing a fund for theological education, submitted the following: "They recommend that each member of this body, and the several ministering brethren within our bounds, be requested to use their exertions to advance this object by removing prejudices and showing the value of education to a pious ministry. There are in the State more than 20,000 members. Is there one of these who would be *deprived of the privilege* of giving fifty cents for so desirable an object?" This report was accepted, as was also a very animated and hopeful address to the constituents of the General Association and to the other bodies of Baptists in the State.

The address was read before the Georgia Association, at its session for 1827, and it was

"*Resolved*, That we congratulate the members of the General Association at their pleasing prospects expressed in their address, and we recommend that body to go forward in its benevolent designs, trusting in the Lord."

In addition, the Georgia Association recommended each of its members, and the several ministers within its bounds, to use their exertions to advance the objects of the General Association by removing prejudices and showing the value of education to a pious ministry.

That noble Association was never backward nor remiss in lifting the banner of progress in the work of missions, education and religion; and, what can be said of no other Baptist Association in Georgia, may be said of this—not a single one of its churches became anti-missionary in sentiment, or an opponent of the benevolent schemes of the day for the advancement of religion, temperance, Sunday-schools, education and missions.

The necessity of education among many of the early Baptist ministers of Georgia was most apparent, and this partly explains the persistency of our fathers in their determination to establish institutions of learning. They argued that it was impossible for our denomination, as such, to be elevated and become even respectable, so as to compare favorably with other denominations and maintain itself before the world, without education of a high character. Facilities and conveniences for acquiring such an education they considered an absolute necessity; but, strange to say, the opponents of education were more numerous than its supporters. One of their strange arguments was, "If learning is to help the preacher, why not pray to learning instead of to the Lord?" Some of them claimed to be inspired to preach, averring as they rose in the pulpit that they had given their text no consideration until that moment, when they opened the Bible, and that they intended to preach just as the Lord "handed out" the message to them. Hence, the sermon by Sherwood, preached before the State Convention in 1830, which repudiated the prevalent theory of inspiration, was made the butt of ridicule in many a sermon, and was condemned as false teaching. It was contended that the Convention itself, as tending to cultivation and education, would corrupt the simplicity of the truth; wherefore many opposed the Convention.

A few anecdotes may be given illustrative of the ignorance of some of the ministers of that day. Humphrey Posey, being invited to preach for Joel Colley, who was for twenty years Moderator of the Yellow River Association, took for his text St. Paul's assertion, "I am not ashamed of the Gospel of Christ," etc.; and observed: "If Paul, a learned man, brought up at the feet of Gamaliel, was not ashamed of the Gospel, I ought not to be." In closing the services, Joel

Colley corrected a supposed error of Mr. Posey's, asserting that *his* Bible was not like Posey's Bible, for his Bible, instead of "brought up at the feet of Gamaliel," read "brought up at the foot of Gammel hill"—a hill so poor it wouldn't sprout a pea; and, therefore, Paul was a poor man, unable to get an education, and had to learn tent-making to gain a living.

Another minister, preaching from the parable of the "Pounds," in Luke 19th, claimed that "an austere man," in verse 21, proved John to be an oyster-man, who employed his time fishing for oysters. As Dr. Sherwood says, "If such ignorance was ever called to preach, it brings to mind the importunity of a good Methodist brother in Milledgeville by the name of Pierson, who averred that the Lord called to him, almost every night, 'Pierson! Pierson! go preach my gospel!'" But his brethren refused to license him because of his destitution of qualifications. He importuned, and they finally informed him that he *mistook the name*, and that it was *Pierce* whom he heard the Lord call—alluding to Dr. Lovick Pierce.

Among this class of our preachers *spiritualizing* was exceedingly common, and many fanciful interpretations were given to Scripture. They represented Saul's armor, which was put on the stripling David, as *education;* while the pebbles, which he slung at Goliath, were *inspiration*—the one a hindrance, the other achieving success. Had there been no such man as Jesse Mercer to stem this tide of ignorance and fanciful interpretation, the Bible might have been regarded as a book of enigmas, and the *inspired sermons* of the day better than the words of the apostles themselves. The files of THE CHRISTIAN INDEX show the continuous and sturdy blows Mercer dealt against the views of those who opposed missions and education, and the inspiration theory. In 1834 he said, in THE INDEX: "The argument drawn from the gifts and promises of God to *inspired men* in favor of the advantages of ministers now is, in our judgment, a very deceptive one, because the analogy is not true. Will any man pretend that ministers are *now inspired*, so that their sermons may, with equal propriety, be styled *inspired sermons?* If so, then the Scriptures are not the only rule of faith and practice, but these sermons have equal claim." It is not a matter of surprise that Mercer was so strongly in favor of education.

Another strong friend of education, in our denomination in Georgia, was Dr. Adiel Sherwood, who resided at Eatonton, but was pastor of the Baptist churches at Eatonton, Greenesboro and Milledgeville. He was also principal of the academy at Eatonton, and taught a class in theology, which was supported by the generosity of the Eatonton church. Among his pupils were J. H. Campbell, J. R. Hand and others. This was in 1828, 1829 and 1830.

XIII.
MERCER INSTITUTE.
1829-1839.

XIII.

MERCER INSTITUTE.

THE PENFIELD LEGACY—WHO HELPED TO SECURE IT—SHERWOOD'S RESOLUTION—$1,500 RAISED—INSTRUCTIONS TO THE EXECUTIVE COMMITTEE—DR. SHERWOOD'S MANUAL LABOR SCHOOL NEAR EATONTON—MERCER INSTITUTE OPENED JANUARY, 1833—PLAN OF MERCER INSTITUTE—B. M. SANDERS PLACED AT ITS HEAD—A BAPTIST COLLEGE AT WASHINGTON PROPOSED AND ABANDONED—MERCER UNIVERSITY—REPORT OF TRUSTEES FOR 1838—ACTS OF INCORPORATION, OF CONVENTION, AND COLLEGE—THE FIRST BOARD OF TRUSTEES—THEIR FIRST REPORT, SHOWING THE ORGANIZATION OF THE COLLEGE AND ITS FINANCIAL CONDITION—CLASSES ORGANIZED IN JANUARY, 1839—B. M. SANDERS THE FIRST PRESIDENT OF MERCER UNIVERSITY—HIS FAREWELL ADDRESS—THE BLACKS NOT FORGOTTEN.

We will now narrate the principal events that led to the establishment of Mercer Institute at Penfield, in 1833.

In the year 1829, the Georgia Baptist Convention met at Milledgeville, and it was announced to the body that Josiah Penfield, of Savannah, having died, had bequeathed to the Convention the sum of $2,500, as a fund for education, on condition that an equal sum was raised by the body for the same purpose. Thomas Stocks, Thomas Cooper, H. O. Wyer and J. H. T. Kilpatrick were appointed a committee to consider the matter and report the following Monday. In their report they suggested that the amount be subscribed immediately. This was promptly done and the notes were given to Dr. Sherwood, the clerk and treasurer, it being understood that these notes would begin to draw interest whenever the legacy became available, and the principal should be payable when called for by the Convention. To obtain these subscriptions was the work of fifteen minutes, and as a matter of historical interest, a list is given of the persons who contributed to secure the sum required, together with the amount contributed by each, for which his note was given: Jesse Mercer, $250; Cullen Battle, $200; James Shannon, $100; Armstead Richardson, $75; James Davis, $50; H. O. Wyer, $150; I. L. Brooks, $100; James Boykin, $125; Barnabas Strickland, $30; William Walker, $100; B. M. Sanders, $150; Adiel Sherwood, $125; Thomas Cooper, $110; Wm. Flournoy, $100; James Armstrong, $50; J. H. T. Kilpatrick, $100; Joshua Key, $100; Andrew Battle, $50; R. C. Shorter, $50; Jonathan Davis, $50; Thomas Stocks, $50; Jabez P. Marshall, $100; Edmund Shackelford, $150; Robert C. Brown, $50; Peter Walton, $25; J. Whitefield (cash) $10. Total, $2,500.

These were the men who secured the Penfield legacy for the denomination, thus fairly originating what, in the end, indirectly, attained to the dignity of an endowment for Mercer University; for securing the Penfield legacy resulted in the purchase of the Redd property and in the establishment of Mercer Institute, which was subsequently made a University and for which an endowment was raised.

Dr. Sherwood tells us, in his manuscripts, that he had the resolution proposing the establishment of a manual labor school drawn, and ready to be offered at the Convention in 1829, but that he withheld it in deference to the wishes of some of his brethren of the Executive Committee. For two years he had been residing at Eatonton, where he was principal of the academy and pastor of the church, at the same time serving the churches at Greenesborough, and Milledgeville also. One of the very few Baptist ministers in the State, who had enjoyed the privilege of a thorough collegiate education, and, also, a theological course at Andover, Massachusetts, he not only taught in the academy at Eatonton, but instructed a class of eight or ten theological students during the years 1828, 1829 and 1830. Among these students who were sustained by the members of the Eatonton Baptist church, were J. H. Campbell and J. R. Hand. In 1831, at Buckhead, Burke county, Dr. Sherwood offered the following resolution at the State Convention :

"*Resolved*, That, as soon as the funds will justify it, this Convention will establish in some central part of the State, a classical and theological school, which shall unite agricultural labor with study, and be opened for those only preparing for the ministry."

The Executive Committee was requested to devise a plan for raising $1,500.00 before the first day of the following December, and if they succeeded, a school was to be opened as soon as possible. It is rather a singular fact that when B. M. Sanders was asked if he would be one of thirty to raise the $1,500.00, he replied that he would be the thirtieth, implying a want of faith in its procurement.

At the Convention which met at Powelton in 1832, this resolution was altered so as to read thus :

"*Resolved*, That, as soon as the funds will justify it, this Convention will establish in some central part of the State, a literary and theological school, which shall unite manual labor with study; admitting others besides students in divinity, under the direction of the Executive Committee."

At the same session it was reported that the $1,500.00 had been subscribed and half of it paid. It was reported also, that several eligible sites in different counties for the proposed manual-labor school had been offered on favorable terms. The Executive Committee was directed by the Convention to purchase the one seven miles north of Greenesborough, offered by James Redd, and to adopt the necessary measures for putting the school in operation by the first of January, 1833. Thus was adopted the site of what proved to be the Mecca of Georgia Baptists for nearly half a century.

The Executive Committee that year was composed of the following brethren: Thomas Stocks, Jesse Mercer, Adiel Sherwood, B. M. Sanders, James Armstrong, J. Davis and John Lumpkin. Even as late as August of 1832, these brethren were not altogether convinced of the feasibility of such an educational enterprise; for in that month they visited the manual-labor school, which Adiel Sherwood had opened on a small farm he had purchased for the purpose near Eatonton, and where he was then instructing ten or twelve pupils. This enterprise he had ventured upon for the express purpose of testing the manual-labor school theory, and it was only after a careful examination of his school, in August, 1832, that the Executive Committee became thoroughly convinced of the practicability of the scheme, and thenceforth unhesitatingly proceeded in the establishment of Mercer Institute, and even going so far as to request Dr. Sherwood to discontinue his school, lest it should appear as an opposition to the institution of the Convention. To this that amiable person assented, of course, and discontinued his school, sending his pupils to Mercer Institute; but it soon became evident that the precaution was unneccessary, for the Institute was not able to accommodate half the applicants who sought admission as pupils.

Shortly after the session of the Convention, iu April, 1832, the Executive Committee purchased of Mr. Redd, 450 acres of land seven miles north of Greenesboro,' for $1,450.00, engaged Rev. B. M. Sanders, as principal and steward, made all other necessary arrangements, and opened the school, with thirty students, on the second Monday in January, 1833. Many circumstances recommended the site of the institution to the favorable consideration of the Convention.

Among others were the following: Its beauty and healthfulness; the soil was free and productive, and the timber abundant: it was in a neighborhood noted for its high moral character, and for the liberality of its residents in their subscriptions for the support of the Institute; and the situation was a central one to the most active friends of the contemplated institution.

The plan adopted by the Executive Committee, and upon which the institution was organized, is worthy of being put on record as a matter of historical interest; it was as follows:

"The ultimate and conclusive direction of all the interests and operations of the institution, shall be in the Executive Committee, as agent for the Convention.

There shall be five trustees near the institution, who shall be Baptists in full fellowship, not under twenty-five years of age, who shall make by-laws for its detailed operations, supervise its interests, and decide on all differences between the teachers and steward. With their consent, the principal teacher may expel from the institution any student guilty of immoral conduct or disobedience to the by-laws; but in all cases an appeal may lie from them to the Executive Committee. They shall be appointed by the committee, and shall report the state of the institution to it, quarterly. No debts shall be contracted by the committee, or trustees, on the credit of the institution, without funds in hand to pay, otherwise, in every such case, it shall be on their own individual responsibility.

"There shall be a steward appointed by the committee, who shall be a Baptist in full fellowship, of industrious habits and fair reputation, who shall take charge of the farm-tools, provisions, stock and other appendages, and be accountable for the faithful use or return of all that is put into his charge. He shall direct the pupils in their labor, shall labor himself, and devote his whole time to the interest of the institution, being subject, in all his operations, to the direction of the trustees.

"There shall be a principal teacher appointed by the committee, who shall be a Baptist minister of sound principles, according to the generally received views of the Baptists in Georgia—a good classical scholar and of energetic character—who shall have charge of the literary and theological departments of the institution. Assistant teachers shall be appointed as the committee may deem advisable. All applicants, of good moral character shall be admitted as students, till the school shall be full. At the opening of each term, should there be conflicting claims for admission, preference shall be given to those who live upon the premises. All shall be required to labor three hours each day; the time of labor to be arranged between the teacher and the steward, the teacher having preference."

The Executive Committee resolved on the following additional regulations for the contemplated institution:

"The scholastic year shall be divided into two terms, the *first*, of six months, from the second Monday in January to the second Monday in July; and the *second*, of five months, from the third Monday in July to the third Monday in December. The rates of tuition shall be $1.50 per month, for all students in English grammar, geography, history and common arithmetic; $2.50 per month for all in the learned languages, criticism, philosophy, mathematics and other higher English branches of science. All over sixteen years of age shall have board, room-rent and firewood for $4 per month, exclusive of their labor; and those under sixteen shall pay $6 per month, and have the value of their labor deducted, as may be estimated by the steward and trustees; washing shall be furnished for $8 per year. All of which shall be required each term in advance. Each student shall furnish his own bedding and candles.

"No student shall be received for less than a year; but abatement may be made by the trustees, for the board and washing of a pupil, for any absence that is rendered unavoidable by an act of Divine Providence."

As the institution had been designed principally for the benefit of young men engaging in the ministry, all such, that were of good moral character, and members of some orderly Baptist church, having a license from their church to preach, and who could furnish satisfactory testimonials of their want of means to procure for themselves a suitable education, were invited to participate in the benefits of the Institute, and were, for several years, supplied with common clothing, by benevolent societies of females. In 1834, there were seven young men in the institution, preparing for the ministry.

The institution was named *Mercer Institute*, after Jesse Mercer, the most influential and distinguished minister of our denomination in the State, and the most liberal friend of the enterprise. The village which sprang up on the site of the Institute was named *Penfield*, in honor of deacon Penfield, of Savannah, whose legacy of $2,500 was the immediate cause of the establishment of the institution.

At the head of the Mercer Institute was placed Rev. B. M. Sanders, one of the few educated Baptists of the time, who brought to his work great energy, indefatigable industry, and sincere devotion to duty. Young men flocked from all parts of the State, and the faithful educational work done in the halls of the institution contributed greatly to popularize education in the minds of the people. But this school was not intended to impart a collegiate education. Its elevation to the character and dignity of a college was an after-thought resulting from an effort made by the Presbyterian denomination, in 1835, to establish a Presbyterian college at Washington, Georgia, where Rev. Jesse Mercer resided. This college, called Oglethorpe University, was finally located at Midway, near Milledgeville, but the discussions had greatly impressed the mind of Mr. Mercer, and he immediately began measures to secure funds for founding a Baptist college, at Washington, Wilkes county. As he himself expressed it, "the notion took like wild fire." Agents were put in the field, and in 1837, at the end of two years, $100,000 were reported as subscribed to "The Southern Baptist College," as it was expressed by the charter. At that time, however, a great financial crisis occurred, and this, coupled with some dissatisfaction with the location, led to the surrender of the charter and to the abandonment of the Washington educational enterprise. This event caused doubt, confusion and discouragement in the Baptist mind.

But the Baptists of Georgia had become thoroughly aroused on the subject of a denominational college. The Central Association, a body of liberal and intelligent brethren, who had subscribed $20,000 to endow the Central Professorship of Languages and Sacred Literature, suggested the elevation of Mercer Institute into a college.

This solved the problem. The Executive Committee of the Convention took the matter in hand, changed the name of *Mercer Institute* to *Mercer University*, procured the transfer of most of the subscriptions which had been made to "The Southern Baptist College" and, in December, 1837, obtained a charter for the new University.

These events will all be comprehended better by extracts made from the proceedings of the Georgia Baptist Convention for the year 1838. In its report to the Convention, in April of that year, the committee make the following statements:

"On the 25th of last August, the following resolution, adopted by the late Board of Trustees of the Southern Baptist College, was laid before the committee:

"*Resolved*, That the important business of rearing and organizing a Southern Baptist College in Georgia, entrusted to the care of this board, has been maturely examined and inquired into. They have duly considered the means and resources required therefor, and are of opinion that it is inexpedient to undertake the building of a college under present circumstances. The reasons that have brought the board to this conclusion are, in part, the following: First, the embarrassment of the times; secondly, the different views of brethren in regard to the plan proposed; lastly, the inadequacy of the means in hand. Be it, therefore,

"*Resolved, further*, That the whole subject be referred to the Executive Committee of the Baptist Convention of the State of Georgia, with the recommendation of this board that they surrender the present charter and abandon the enterprise, or seek to set on foot a plan that will command the resources demanded for the accomplishment of the great undertaking."

"In regard to the particular plan referred to in the preceding resolution, and which the trustees, who have been clothed with power for its execution, had abandoned, the committee felt that they had nothing to do but to surrender up the charter and the project to the Convention. This they have done, by express resolution. But still an important question urged itself on our minds: Can no plan be devised to secure, in some form or other, the great object which had so deeply enlisted the feelings of our brethren, and which, in its general bearing, was just as important and desirable as ever?

"After mature and, we trust, prayerful reflection, the committee resolved upon a measure which they deemed the only hopeful alternative, viz.: the connecting a collegiate department with the Mercer Institute. This they believed they had the power to do, inasmuch as 'the ultimate and conclusive direction of all the interests and operations of the institution' had been vested 'in the Executive Committee, as agents for the Convention;' and they had been 'left at liberty to alter or amend as expediency might seem to require.' They were well assured, from the most authentic information, that no other location would, to any considerable extent, harmonize the efforts of the denomination in the State. The consideration that some of the early patrons of the school had in view its ultimate advancement to a more elevated character, was not without its weight, and it was evident to all that the investments which we had already made, in lands and buildings, would enable us to commence collegiate operations at much less expense than at any other location. If anything was to be done, prompt action seemed to be necessary. The establishment of an elevated seminary of learning had for some time engaged the attention of our brethren; delay, we had reason to fear, would produce an unfavorable reaction in their feelings, abate their zeal, increase discouragement, and result in failure. Besides, there was a reasonable prospect of being able to secure a considerable portion of the old subscription, should we act with promptness.

"Since the adoption of the above named plan for the advancement of the institution, the committee have been cheered by many decided expressions of approbation from their brethren in different parts of the State. The Georgia, Central and Washington Associations have passed resolutions approving of the arrangement, and urging the denomination to vigorous and liberal co-operation in its support. Between fifty and sixty thousand dollars in new subscriptions have been obtained, with a reasonable prospect of a large increase, should suitable exertions be made. About fifty thousand dollars of the subscription have been taken up in notes. Nothing is necessary (with God's blessing) but energy and perseverance to secure an ample endowment for the institution. This being secured, we shall have the means of sustaining an able faculty, and of providing all other means that may be important to render our seminary an ornament to our country and a blessing to the world.

"Early measures were taken by the committee to secure such an amendment of the act incorporating the Convention as would authorize the establishment of a collegiate institution. By this amendment it will be seen that the Convention is empowered to appoint a Board of Trustees for the management of the college; this Board, we trust, will be appointed at the present meeting of the body, that the committee may at once transfer the interests of the institution to their hands. Preparatory arrangements are in such a state of forwardness that, with suitable exertions, the exercises of the entire collegiate department might be commenced early next year.

"The committee have determined to adopt a seven years' course of study, commencing with the common English branches, and closing with the highest branches taught in our best colleges. The preparatory department is to embrace three years, and the collegiate four: the whole course to be under the direction of the same faculty. The plan of study for the first five years has been arranged, subject, of course, to such modification hereafter as further reflection and experience may recommend. The manual labor system will be continued in connection with both departments of the seminary. The institution is to be known by the name of MERCER UNIVERSITY.

"Considerable exertion has been made by the committee to secure the services of suitable persons as professors in the institution. Brother Adiel Sherwood has been appointed to the professorship of Sacred Literature, and brother Otis Smith has also been invited to accept a professorship; they have not yet signified their acceptance, but there is ground to hope that they will yield to our wishes, and to what we have every reason to believe are the wishes of the friends of the institution generally. Brother Albert Williams and brother Palemon L. Janes, graduates of the Franklin College, have been appointed teachers, with a view to their permanent connection with the institution. Brother Williams had been previously appointed principal classical teacher in place of brother Cowdry, whose feeble health compelled him to resign. Brother Janes is now at the North prosecuting his studies with a view to his more thorough improvement in the higher branches of mathematics and civil engineering. It is expected he will enter the institution as mathematical teacher early in next year. Brother B. M. Sanders has been appointed college treasurer, whose report is herewith presented. During the last year there has been a decided improvement in the school, both as to its general order and discipline and the advancement of the young men in their literary pursuits. Both teachers and pupils, in their respective spheres, have exhibited a degree of industry, punctuality and zeal highly commendable. We would record with grateful emotions the goodness of God in again reviving His work in the institution. Towards the close of last year the Lord was pleased to pour out His spirit and gather into His fold a goodly number of precious youths. This we regarded as a special token of His favor, and were greatly animated thereby in the prosecution of our labors for the improvement of the school. The number of students the last year has varied from seventy-five to ninety. Several of our present number are in the Freshman class. The brick building has been completed, and is now in the occupancy of the students. There are now upon our premises seven good buildings, five belonging to the institution, viz: two large school buildings, a dining hall, two comfortable dwelling houses and two other buildings belonging to the Ciceronian and Phi Delta Societies, a part of which has generally been occupied by some of the students of the school. Brethren Conner and Mallary, the former college agents, were appointed to collect funds for our institution, and as their previous labors would be mostly converted to the benefit of the Mercer University, we agreed to assume the payment of their salaries under their first appointment. Brother Jonathan Davis has also been appointed as one of our agents, to labor mainly in the western and southwestern sections of the State.

"One of the most important measures adopted by the committee, with the concurrence of the trustees, with whom they held a consultation, has been the laying off of town lots contiguous to the school for the accommodation of such families as might wish to remove to the institution to superintend the education of their children. Lots to the amount of nearly ten thousand dollars have been sold already, under salutary restrictions, and several families have already removed to the place and commenced their improvements. The town is to be known by the name of PENFIELD—a tribute of respect to the memory of the late Mr. Josiah Penfield, of Savannah, who was known as one of the most liberal and efficient patrons of the benevolent plans of the Convention.

"The committee, with the concurrence of the trustees, in the exercise of the authority granted them by the last Convention, have resolved upon the establishment of a respectable female seminary at Penfield. A lot has been reserved for the institution, and three thousand dollars of money accruing from the sale of lots, have been voted to this object. Under the direction of the trustees and principal teacher, it is expected that the building will be completed by the first of January next, and that the institution will then be open for the reception of pupils.

"A school for small children was opened on the premises early in the present year, under the direction of brother Smith, formerly a student in the institution. This school is in quite a prosperous condition.

"JESSE MERCER, *Chairman.*

"C. D. MALLARY, *Assistant Secretary.*"

MERCER INSTITUTE.

The female school, established as here indicated, flourished at Penfield for about a dozen years, and then became extinct, the chief cause of its demise being, perhaps, the existence of the Georgia Female College, at Madison, which attracted the patronage of the Baptists.

The two legislative acts, alluded to in the Report of 1838, are possessed of value in the eyes of Georgia Baptists, and are here given as a part of our denominational history. The first is the Act incorporating the Convention, passed in December, 1830, and the second is an amendment of that Act, incorporating Mercer University, and passed in December, 1837.

AN ACT

To incorporate the Baptist Convention of the State of Georgia.

SECTION 1. *Be it enacted by the Senate and House of Representatives of the State of Georgia, in General Assembly met, and it is hereby enacted by the authority of the same,* That, from and after the passing of this Act, Jesse Mercer, Moderator, Adiel Sherwood, Clerk, J. P. Marshall, Assistant Clerk, James Armstrong, B. M. Sanders, Jonathan Davis and Thomas Stocks, who compose the present Executive Committee of said Convention, and their successors in office, shall be, and they are hereby declared to be, a body corporate, by the name and style of the Executive Committee of the Baptist Convention of the State of Georgia, and, by the said name and style, shall have perpetual succession and power to use a common Seal to alter and amend the By-Laws of the same, provided such By-Laws be not repugnant to the laws and Constitution of the State, or of the United States.

SEC. 2. *And be it further enacted by the authority aforesaid,* That the Executive Committee aforesaid, and their successors in office, elected agreeably to the Constitution of said Convention, shall have full power and authority, under the name and style of the Executive Committee of the Baptist Convention of the State of Georgia, by which name they shall sue and be sued in any court of law or equity in this State, and to take, hold and enjoy any real or personal property: to sue for and recover any sum or sums of money now due, or that may hereafter be due to said Convention, at any court of law or equity in this State, or at any tribunal having jurisdiction thereof, and the rights and privileges of said Convention to defend in any tribunal whatever; also to receive any bequests or donations whatever, made to said Convention; and they shall be vested with all powers, privileges and advantages of a society incorporated; any law, usage or custom to the contrary notwithstanding.

ASBURY HULL, *Speaker of the House of Representatives.*
THOMAS STOCKS, *President of the Senate.*
Assented to December 22d, 1830.
GEORGE R. GILMER, *Governor.*

AN ACT

To amend an Act entitled an Act to Incorporate the Baptist Convention of the State of Georgia.

SECTION 1. *Be it enacted by the Senate and House of Representatives of the State of Georgia, in General Assembly met, and it is hereby enacted by the authority of the same,* That if by the Act entitled an Act to incorporate the Baptist Convention of the State of Georgia, said Convention, or their Executive Committee, are invested with taxing power, all such power is hereby annulled and made void.

SEC. 2. *And be it further enacted by the authority aforesaid,* That the Executive Committee of the Baptist Convention of the State of Georgia shall have power to establish and endow a collegiate institution, to be known by the name of the MERCER UNIVERSITY, on the premises owned by said Convention, in Greene county; and said committee are hereby authorized to make all necessary by-laws and regulations for the government of said University, provided they be not repugnant to the Constitution or laws of this State or the United States, until a Board of Trustees shall be appointed by the aforesaid Baptist Convention.

SEC. 3. *And be it further enacted*, That the Baptist Convention of the State of Georgia, may, at its next meeting, or at any subsequent meeting, elect a Board of Trustees for the said Mercer University, consisting of not less than fifteen, nor more than thirty-one, in number, who shall, or their successors in office, be a body politic and corporate by the name of the Trustees of Mercer University, and as such, they shall be capable of and liable in law, to sue and be sued, plead and be impleaded, and shall be authorized to use a common seal, to hold all manner of property, both real and personal, for the purpose of making a permanent endowment of said institution, and to raise funds for the support of the same, and for the erection of buildings, or to confer literary degrees, and to exercise such other power not inconsistent with the laws of this State or of the United States, as the aforesaid Convention may see fit to vest in their hands.

SEC. 4. *And be it further enacted*, That the aforesaid Convention shall be authorized to determine the manner in which said Board of Trustees shall be perpetuated, and the character of the individuals from whom they may be chosen.

SEC. 5. *And be it further enacted*, That upon the premises now owned by the Baptist Convention of the State of Georgia, in Greene county, or that may hereafter come into their possession, no person shall by himself, servant or agent, keep, have, use or maintain a gaming house or room of any description, or permit with his knowledge any house or room occupied or owned by him, to be used by any person whatever as a gaming place; nor shall any person, upon the premises aforesaid by himself, servant or agent, keep, employ or allow, with his knowledge, to be kept or employed on the premises he may occupy, any Faro Table, Billiard Table, E. O. Table, A, B. C. Table, or any other table of like character; nor shall any person, by himself, servant or agent, upon the premises now owned by the aforesaid Convention in Greene county, or that may, hereafter come into their possession, be allowed to sell ardent spirits, wine, cordials, porter, or any other intoxicating drinks whatever, nor permit the same to be done with his or her knowledge or approbation, on the premises which he or she may occupy, provided, however, that the Trustees of the Mercer University, may have power to authorize any individuals to sell ardent spirits, wine, etc., upon their premises for medical and sacramental purposes. Any person violating the prohibitions contained in this section, shall be liable to be indicted for a misdemeanor before the Supreme Court, and on conviction, shall be fined in a sum not less than one thousand dollars for each and every offence.

SEC. 6. *And be it further enacted*, That the Executive Committee of the aforesaid Convention, in executing titles for lots, which they may sell from time time, shall have power to insert such conditions, as may tend further to defend the premises aforesaid from the nuisances specified in the foregoing section of this Act.   JOSEPH DAY, *Speaker of the House of Representatives*.
ROBERT M. ECHOLS, *President of the Senate*.

Assented to 22d December, 1837.
GEORGE R. GILMER, *Governor*.

The Convention approved of the course adopted by the Executive Committee in surrendering the charter of the Southern Baptist College, and in taking the steps requisite for elevating Mercer Institute to the dignity of a college, with the name of Mercer University. A Board of Trustees, consisting of the following brethren, was elected, to whom was entrusted the management of the college: Jesse Mercer, C. D. Mallary, V. R. Thornton, Jonathan Davis, John E. Dawson, Malcolm Johnston, W. D. Cowdry, J. H. T. Kilpatrick, J. H. Campbell, S. G. Hillyer, Absalom Janes, R. Q. Dickerson, William Richards, Thomas Stocks, T. G. Janes, J. M. Porter, Lemuel Greene, James Davant, F. W. Cheney, E. H. Macon, William Lumpkin, John G. Polhill, L. H. Warren, Mark A. Cooper, John B. Walker, I. T. Irwin and W. H. Pope. And the Executive Committee was instructed to petition the next Legislature to amend the charter, or act of incorporation of Mercer University, so as to authorize the Convention to elect the

Board of Trustees once in three years, and to require them to make an annual report to the Convention.

The petition was made and the desired Act of amendment was passed by the Legislature; and, at its session in 1839, held at Richland, Twiggs county, the Convention elected, as a Board of Trustees, for three years, Jesse Mercer, C. D. Mallary, V. R. Thornton, Jonathan Davis, J. E. Dawson, W. D. Cowdry, J. H. T. Kilpatrick, J. H. Campbell, S. G. Hillyer, Absalom Janes, R. Q. Dickinson, Thomas Stocks, T. G. Janes, J. M. Porter, L. Greene, J. Davant, F. W. Cheeney, E. H. Macon, W. Lumpkin, L. Warren, M. A. Cooper, J. B. Walker, W. H. Pope, B. M. Sanders, A. Sherwood, A. T. Holmes, James Perryman, J. S. Law, W. B. Stephens.

The report of the Board of Trustees for the year 1838, made at the Convention of 1839, is appended as presenting an interesting statement of the organization of the college, and its financial condition at the time:

"At an early period, after the last session of your body, the trustees elect met at Penfield, and, after organizing, proceeded to discharge the important duties committed to their charge. The board were not unmindful of the responsibilities of their station, and of the vast importance of a good beginning, in an enterprise of such interest. They, therefore, opened their session, by imploring divine direction, in everything pertaining to the interests of the University. It was a deeply solemn and interesting occasion.

"Immediately after the organization of the board, the Executive Committee, turned over to us all the funds belonging to the University; and the board, to carry out the views of the Convention, proceeded to the organization of a faculty, at least so far as they thought expedient under the circumstances. Rev. B. M. Sanders was elected President, which he accepted temporarily, and upon condition that the office might be vacated whenever an opportunity presented of filling it permanently. Rev. A. Sherwood was appointed professor of Ancient Literature and Moral Philosophy, which he accepted. Brother P. L. Janes was elected prospectively, professor of Mathematics; but, by an unexpected dispensation of Providence, he was removed to his final reward. We had promised ourselves much from the talents and attainments of brother Janes; but God, who worketh all things after the counsel of His will, saw fit to take him from our midst, and to His will it becomes us to be resigned. Brother S. P. Sanford and A. W. Ataway, were appointed assistant professors. But, in consequence of the imperfect organization of the faculty, the various duties were divided for the present, among all the members of the faculty, so that all are actually employed. The collegiate department was more fully organized at the beginning of the present term, and there are now, in the Sophomore class, seven young gentlemen prosecuting their studies with vigor and success. There is, also, a Freshman class, consisting of seven, to whom we look with great interest. There are in all—in both departments—about ninety-five students; and we entertain no doubts of the success of the enterprise, if the friends will only come up liberally to the work.

"The Board have had in their employ, as agents, brethren C. D. Mallary and Jonathan Davis, at a salary of $1,000 per annum. Brother Connor has, also, been employed at $400 per annum. Brother Sherwood has also performed some service in this way.

"In reference to the finances, the Board have only to say that they have under their control, in subscriptions and notes running to maturity, notes on demand and cash, about $100,000; of this amount there is about $50,000 on interest, invested in good stock.

"The board have adhered rigidly to the settled policy of the Convention, in avoiding all responsibilities for the meeting of which they have not the means in hand. And they have the satisfaction to state that the University is entirely free from debt; so that, if we have moved slowly, we have gone surely. We feel that it is also due to say that all the donations have been appropriated as directed by the donors. Your board felt that it was important, inasmuch as the great design of the institution was the promotion of God's glory, at a suitable time to dedicate the University to Him to whom we are indebted for our past prosperity, and on whom we depend for all future success. They consequently appointed a meeting early in February last, which continued several days, for this purpose. Many of the brethren attended, several sermons were preached, and all the religious services had reference to the prosperity of the University. It was a deeply solemn season. The Spirit of the Lord seemed to be poured out, and many prayers were offered up to God in its behalf, which we hope will be answered in time to come.

"Your board feel justified in saying that with patience, diligence and prudence the institution will not only meet the expectation of its friends, but prove a lasting blessing to the world." JESSE MERCER, *Chairman.*
JOHN E. DAWSON, *Secretary.*

This board held its first meeting at Penfield in July, 1838, and then assumed the management of the institution; and this date may, therefore, be regarded as the official beginning of Mercer University. The college classes were not organized, however, until January, 1839, since, at that time, the collegiate year corresponded with the civil year in most American colleges. The members of this Board of Trustees, all of whom were re-elected for three years, were fair representatives of the denomination in Georgia in piety, wealth, intelligence and in social and political influence. They gave the University its shape and character, and to their wise counsels, in its formative period, is due much of its past success. Thomas Stocks, a layman of Greene county, who labored in building up the Institute, was the first president of the Board of Trustees, and was re-elected for about twenty-five years, until failing health unfitted him for the duties of the office. He also presided over the Senate of Georgia for eight years, and was, nine years in succession, president of the Georgia Baptist Convention.

Thus we have seen that Mercer Institute was proposed in 1831, and set in operation January, 1833. It had no endowment, but was sustained by tuition and voluntary contributions. Fellenburg had conducted a manual labor school successfully in Europe, and the system found many admirers and imitators in America, and when Mercer Institute was established, the manual labor system was incorporated as a part of it, and was conducted for some years without loss; but, when the Institute was elevated, the system became unpopular, onerous and expensive. The Board of Trustees accordingly submitted the question of its suspension to the contributors of the University fund, as far as they could; and, with the concurrence of the contributors, as far as could be ascertained, manual labor was suspended indefinitely in December, 1844.

The Institute, as such, really existed six years, as the college classes were not organized until January, 1839. During those six years, and during 1839, the first year of its collegiate existence, Rev. B. M. Sanders presided over the institution with great ability, and made it the success it was, with the aid of his advisers and co-adjutors. Appropriately, here, may be given extracts from his valedictory address, delivered before the trustees, faculty, students and friends of the University December 12th, 1839, when he resigned the presidency of the institution, and retired from active official labor. These extracts present a concise history of the institution from its inception, and a vivid statement of the principles on which it was conducted:

VALEDICTORY ADDRESS, BY B. M. SANDERS.

"In retiring from the charge of this institution, to which I was called in the commencement of its operations, and over which I have presided, through its various gradations, now seven years, I am constrained to contemplate with gratitude the indications it has experienced of the favor of both God and man. Its founders, being deeply impressed with the advantages to be derived from the connection of manual labor with literary instruction, and especially by candidates for the gospel ministry, and the system not having been fully tested in the Southern States, and not very successfully in the Northern, determined on making the experiment, and solicited the aid of my services in carrying it into effect. Although the system was opposed in the beginning by numberless predictions that it could not be sustained, it has not only been well sustained for seven years, but the institution, from a feeble grammar school, has been elevated, by the divine blessing upon the exertions of its friends, to a state of high respectability. Notwithstanding the objections some feel to labor, it has this year numbered its hundred students, and applications for the next are already swelling to such an amount as to excite well-grounded apprehension that all the accommodations that can be provided will not be sufficient to supply the demand. These indications of public favor cannot but gratify the friends of the institution, while they afford satisfactory evidence that it will only require suitable arrangements with a moderate share of industry and perseverance on the part of the officers, to ensure the success of the system, and to secure to the institution its undoubted advantages.

"The origin, the design and the progress of our institution to its present state, may be proper subjects of reflection on this occasion. At a meeting of the Baptist Convention of this State in 1829, it was reported that a brother, Josiah Penfield, of Savannah, having died, had left a bequest of $2,500 to aid in the education of poor young men preparing for the ministry, and to be under the direction of that body upon the condition of their raising an equivalent sum for the same object, the interest only of which should be used. The equivalent was at once subscribed by the brethren and friends present, although it was not until the beginning of the year 1833 that the legacy was paid over to the Convention, and the equivalent made collectable.

"In prospect, however, of realizing this amount in a short time, and already in the possession of small sums received from Associations and benevolent societies for the same object, it was thought expedient by the Convention, in 1831, to establish a school, theological and literary, connected with manual labor, at as early a period as practicable, in some convenient and central part of the State. To effect this without delay, the Executive Committee of the Convention, whose province it is to transact all its business during its recess, was directed to procure subscriptions, to examine locations, to receive propositions and to report to their next annual meeting.

"At the meeting of the Convention in 1832, a subscription of $1,500 was reported, and the respective advantages of a variety of locations that had been examined. The one we now occupy was selected, the purchase ordered to be made, and the school to be gotten into operation, if practicable, by the beginning of a new year. The committees, with whom it was a maxim 'not to go in debt,' speedily made the best arrangements *the means in hand* would admit. These arrangements consisted of two double-cabins, with a garret to each, for dwelling, for dining and for study, for both teachers and students. With these limited accommodations and with one assistant. I opened the institution in January, 1833, with thirty-nine students, having thirty-six of them to board in my own family. Among those were seven young men preparing for the ministry.

"I shall ever remember with lively emotions of pleasure the patience and cheerfulness with which the students of this year sustained the privations and trials to which they were subjected by their cramped circumstances. They may be truly said to have borne hardness like good soldiers. While living as in a camp in their midst, and burdened with the charge and responsibility of the literary, theological, laboring and boarding departments, I found no little support in all my cares and labors from witnessing that, while they lived upon the cheapest fare, had no place for study but the common school-room, no place to retire to for rest but a garret without fire in the coldest weather, and labored diligently three hours every day, no complaint was heard, but that the most entire cheerfulness ran through all their words and actions.

"In a word, those favorable indications of the success of the enterprise soon began to inspire its friends with confidence, and to animate their efforts for the extension of its advantages. An amount was soon raised to erect another large wooden building with eight comfortable rooms for dormitories, and a brick basement for chapel and school-rooms.

"The second year's operations were commenced with increased accommodations, with an additional teacher and eighty students, seventy of whom boarded in commons. During the second and third years, the building of a larger and more comfortable dwelling, a commodious dining-room and two society halls, abundantly increased both the comforts and conveniences of the institution.

"Thus did its interests advance, from year to year, by the multiplication of its friends, and the increase of their bounty, under the superintendence of a committee whose watch-word was, 'Owe no man anything,' until 1837, the fifth year of its operations. During this year two circumstances occurred to give a strong impulse to the advancement of its prosperity. Just at this period a project that had been gotten up for a Baptist college to be located at Washington, Wilkes county, was relinquished, after nearly one hundred thousand dollars had been subscribed for its accomplishment. This event was promptly improved by the Executive Committee of the Baptist Convention, charged with the interests of this institution, and a resolution was at once passed by them to elevate it by the addition of a collegiate department. An agent was appointed to obtain, if possible, a transfer to it of the sums that had been subscribed to the contemplated college at Washington. In the execution of this labor, he was peculiarly successful, and to the Convention of 1838, he made a report of the transfer of between fifty and sixty thousand dollars.

"During this year, also, a town was laid out around the institution, and named after the donor of the first contribution, which had laid the foundation for its existence. Several thousand dollars' worth of lots were at once sold, with a condition prohibiting the admission on them of gambling-houses or tippling-shops, on pain of forfeiture of title. The number of lots sold, as well as the prices, were abundantly increased by a judicious arrangement of the committee appropriating $3,000 of the avails to build a female academy in the town.

"Arrangements were now also made to have the male institution transferred to a separate board of trustees, to be appointed by the Convention once in three years, and required to make annual reports of the state of the institution. By the Convention of 1838, that board was appointed, and shortly after met and organized, and made the necessary arrangements for the commencement of the operations of the institution in its elevated character, under the title of the *Mercer University*, in the beginning of the present year. That board I now have the pleasure to address. It is well known to many of you, my brethren, with what doubtful apprehensions of duty, and with what consequent reluctance, I gave up the more general and active labors of the ministry, to take upon me the charge of this institution in its infancy. Yielding, however, to the strong impressions of my brethren that, as its more immediate and especial design was for the improvement of the ministry, it would afford one of the best opportunities of promoting ministerial usefulness; and encouraged, moreover, by my own convictions of the importance of early attention to the religious sentiments and ideas of duty to be entertained by young men entering into the labors of the ministry, I eventually consented to take the charge of it until a suitable opportunity might be presented of having the office supplied by another.

"After laboring six years in the complicated, oppressive and responsible duties of principal of all the departments of the institution, and after it had, in the dispensation of Divine Providence, been so promoted as to justify the division of its several departments, and the appointment of a separate officer to the charge of each, I supposed the occasion had occurred that would justify my retirement. I consequently availed myself of it, and obtained your acceptance of my resignation. But, being unable to procure the services of the officer of your choice to preside over the literary department, I was again induced to consent to your wishes in assuming that charge till the office could be otherwise satisfactorily filled.

"The desired arrangements have now been made. You have been able, in all departments, to obtain the services of officers of proven abilities to fill their respective appointments, and I now, with pleasure, again resign my charge into your hands. In retiring from your service as an officer of the institution, permit me to assure you that the testimonies, which I have received from time to time, of the satisfaction which my services have given, have constituted no small share of the reward of my labors.

"Permit me here to recount some of the principles upon which your institution was first organized, and on which it has since been conducted by its founders; principles which have no doubt contributed eminently to its past success, and in favor of which evident indications of divine approbation have been manifested. In the first place, it was a principle with them to deliberate maturely on every subject of investigation, and to examine well the ground about to be occupied before they took their position. So far from being hasty in their conclusions or rash and precipitate in their acts, they took care to satisfy themselves fully with regard to the merits of every subject, that presented its claims to their attention, before they put forth their labors in its behalf.

"Although since the origin of this institution, there have been but few among us entering the ministry, yet it has, no doubt, been the means of abundantly enlarging the sphere of usefulness of a portion of that few, not only from our own State, but also from neighboring States. It has aided about twenty young brethren in their preparation for their labors, and fifteen of them gratuitously. Several of these are now engaged acceptably and successfully in the field of labor. Their efforts have already been abundantly blessed, in promoting revivals of religion in the different sections of country to which they have been called, as well as in advancing the benign objects of Christian benevolence.

"Your institution has also been built upon the faith of that divine principle of truth, 'that except the Lord build the house, they labor in vain that build it.' Its founders have not stopped in making sure of a good object and then laboring diligently for its accomplishment. In all their efforts they have acknowledged God, and sought his blessing in earnest prayer. How often and how fervently have they, in the language of the pious Psalmist, prayed, 'Establish thou the work of our hands upon us, yea, the work of our hands establish thou it.' And the Lord hath graciously heard their prayers, and wonderfully granted their desires, and exalted their institution to an elevation of character and usefulness, transcending in so short a time, the most sanguine anticipations of its warmest friends. In retrospecting its history we are called upon to recognize the hand of God, not only in building up the interests of the institution, and giving it favor in the eye of the people, but more particularly in the frequent revivals of religion, with which he has been pleased to visit it; and these mostly through the instrumentality of the young brethren here preparing for future labors in the ministry.

"It is a heart-cheering subject of contemplation that, but one year out of seven has passed away without more or less religious revival among the students; and that nearly one hundred of them have, here, hopefully been translated from the kingdom of darkness to that of light; some of whom are already actively engaged in the labors of the ministry. Who can tell the influence these may have on the destinies of the world, through the instrumentality of their labors and their prayers?

"Another principle, early laid down, and firmly adhered to by the founders of your institution, was, 'to keep out of debt.' The Convention of 1832 passed a resolution, 'that no debt, shall be contracted by the committee or trustees on the credit of the institution, without funds in hand to pay, otherwise, in every such case, it shall be on their own individual responsibility.' The wisdom of this policy cannot be too highly appreciated.

"Mt. Enon in our own State, and the Columbian College in Washington City, were beacons of warning for our denomination; and well have they improved the melancholy lessons of instruction, that had *here* been taught them. Instead of embarrassment, and perplexity and loan, and abatement of funds by usury, you have now before you the free and unfettered use of all the property and funds of your institution.

"My brethren of the Board of Trustees of the Mercer University, permit me in taking my leave of you on the present occasion, pressingly to recommend to your consideration, the wisdom of the policy and the sacredness of the obligation of the holy injunction of the apostle '*Owe no man anything*.' Let me entreat you, never to forget the happy results of the example of your worthy predecessors, in their rigid adherence to it. It is a principle commended by the counsel of Heaven, and well reported of by all who have experimented on it.

' You will no doubt be told that your library and apparatus are not complete, that your college buildings need enlarging and improving, and that you lack separate professors of several important branches of science. All these things are readily to be admitted, and should stimulate the friends of mental and moral improvement to bring in their offerings to aid in the accomplishment of those objects; but none of these, nor all combined, can be a justification for running into that error which has embarrassed the operations of so many other institutions of our own day; and that has been the ruin of so many in days gone by.

"Another important principle with the founders of your institution, was, 'to *go more for substance than for show, and more for sense than sound.*' In digesting systems, in erecting buildings, in arranging studies, in selecting teachers, in a word, in every operation of the institution, this principle has had its influence. It was the high consideration in which this principle was held, that recommended so strongly to them the manual labor system of education. They could readily see that if thoroughly carried out, it was well calculated to make effective practical men; men, not only able to understand, but also able to perform whatever service might be necessary to promote the interest of their country or their own prosperity. It is on this principle, that the instructions of the teachers have been addressed to the understanding of the pupils, and not merely to the memory, and that public examinations have been required to be thorough and undeceptive; and on this principle it is that more attention has been paid to the solid branches of mental and moral improvement than to any of the forms of fashionable etiquette.

"The result has proved that honesty is the best policy; that, however the world may labor to deceive, it is not willing to be deceived; and that its imitators in hollow show are not the objects of its confidence and respect. While on this subject, I would remark that if I have understood the views of this board, they are in entire harmony with this principle; that they consider it a matter of more importance to have good instructors than fine buildings; that the elevation of the character and usefulness of a college depends more upon the talent and learning and moral principle of its faculty than on the number and splendor of its edifices. That you may be enabled to improve upon the best examples of your predecessors in honor of this benign principle, permit me to suggest for your consideration the propriety of giving the study of the Bible a more conspicuous place in this institution than it has ever heretofore had. It is true that it is read every morning and evening, and a portion of every Sabbath is devoted to Bible-class exercises; but, as it is the only divinely-inspired book we have, and must embrace that course of instruction that will eventually be found most essential to the interest and happiness of man, is it reasonable that in an institution, designed by a religious people for the instruction of youth, so *much* respect should be paid to the authorities of men, and so *little* to that of God? What will human science avail without morality? and where can we find a system of morals to be compared with that taught us in the Bible? How sublime its doctrines! how pure its precepts! how solemn and imposing their sanctions! They take hold not only of the external conduct, but control the secret workings of the heart. But with you, my brethren, the Bible needs no eulogium."

The University entered upon its career with a liberal endowment for the times. Four agents, Posey, Connor, Davis and Mallary, were employed in obtaining the subscriptions, the last of whom was engaged in the work three years, 1837, 1838, 1839. Rev. Jesse Mercer was, by far, the largest contributor; for, during his life and by will, he donated to the institution about $40,000. Among those who contributed amounts varying from $1,000 to $5,000, were Cullen Battle, R. Q. Dickinson, W. H. Pope, James Boykin, T. G. Janes, Absalom Janes, W. Peek, Solomon Graves and John B. Walker. Subscriptions came from seventy counties, and a few from adjacent States, all amounting, in 1840, to $120,000.

While seeking to build up its own educational institutions, the Georgia Baptist Convention manifested a lively interest in the success and prosperity of Furman Theological Institution, in South Carolina; by resolution promised such aid as was in our power to bestow, and invited the agents of that institution to visit the State and obtain subscriptions.

And, while manifesting so much zeal in the education of the whites, the Convention, also, exhibited a strong interest in the religious instruction of the colored people. In 1835 the following was adopted by the body:

"*Resolved*, That we recommend to all our brethren a due consideration of the best method of affording religious instruction to the black population among us; and that such facilities be afforded for this instruction as in their best judgment may be deemed most expedient."

At its session in 1839, the Convention went further, and "*Resolved.*, That the Executive Committee be instructed to make inquiry respecting the practicability of affording oral religious instruction to the colored people in our State, and to make such arrangements as their means and information will permit."

We have thus glanced at the steps taken by the friends of education in our denomination within the State, during the fourth decade of the century, and the second of the Convention's existence. We must now consider the opposition, bitter and persistent, which was exhibited towards benevolent institutions, and which led to the sad rupture in our denomination in Georgia, in the year 1837.

XIV.
ANTI-EFFORT SECESSION.
1817-1837.

XIV.

ANTI-EFFORT SECESSION.

THE SPIRIT OF OPPOSITION—ITS CAUSES—FIRST MANIFESTATION IN THE HEPHZIBAH—THE MISSION SPIRIT IN THAT ASSOCIATION IN 1817, 1818—CHARLES J. JENKINS—SKETCH OF HIS LIFE—THE ASSOCIATION GIVES THE COLD SHOULDER TO MISSIONS AND EDUCATION—JORDAN SMITH LEADS OFF A FACTION IN 1828—WHICH FORMS THE CANOOCHEE ASSOCIATION—RESOLUTION OF THE PIEDMONT ASSOCIATION IN 1819—ISHAM PEACOCK—THE EBENEZER ASSOCIATION, SESSION OF 1816—ENTERS UPON INDIAN REFORM MISSION IN 1820—ABANDONS IT IN 1823—IN 1836 DECIDES IN FAVOR OF MISSIONS, ETC.—A DIVISION OCCURS—ITS CIRCULAR LETTER OF 1836—THE ANTI-MISSION SPIRIT IN THE OCMULGEE—IT DECLARES NON-FELLOWSHIP WITH THOSE FAVORING BENEVOLENT SCHEMES—TROUBLES BEGIN—FORMATION OF THE CENTRAL ASSOCIATION—THE SAREPTA JOINS THE CONVENTION—A DIVISION OF THE ASSOCIATION ENSUES—"PROTEST" AND "ANSWER"—THE ITCHECONNAH DIVIDES—THE YELLOW RIVER FOLLOWS SUIT—THE FLINT RIVER KEEPS THE BALL ROLLING—WHILE THE COLUMBUS AND WESTERN FEEL THE DOLEFUL EFFECTS OF THE ANTI-MISSION SPIRIT—DIVISION IS CONSUMMATED—THE GENERAL FEELING OF THE TIMES, 1833-1837, ILLUSTRATED BY INCIDENTS.

A general view of the denomination at the time which we are considering, from 1820 to 1830, would not be complete without a more special reference to that spirit of opposition to missions and education which finally, in 1837, resulted in a division of the denomination in Georgia.

At this day, it is hardly possible for us to appreciate the bitterness of feeling, and rancor of speech which prevailed, for years, among many of the churches, and in most of the early Associations. There is no doubt that ignorance and prejudice were the true causes of these denominational troubles ; and, at this time to say so can justly wound no one's feelings, since all the active participants have ceased their earthly labors and gone to their long home. A very few only can remember the later stages of the dissension.

While there was considerable opposition to missions, and an opposition which gradually augmented, there seems to have been a more bitter opposition to education, and to the establishment of Baptist colleges. The real ground of this opposition to benevolent enterprises, as they were designated, was a conviction that they were mere human inventions and schemes, and contrary to the simplicity of the instructions enunciated in the New Testament for the spread of the gospel. With some, influences of a much lower nature had potency, however. Against missions it was argued that preachers would fail to obtain a support, if mission collections were pressed. John Blackstone used to say that once he could go out on a preaching tour among the churches, and collect for his services from fifty to sixty dollars ; but that, since missions had grown into favor he could get nothing.

Against education it was argued that the Holy Spirit, by inspiration, instructed the preacher at the moment of delivery, and that, hence, education was unnecessary, if not indeed a violation of divine injunction. Others said, "These larn'd preachers will git all the pay, and we must work or starve !"

The long-continued opposition to the General Association was not genuine merely, but even violent, and excites surprise. In the Ocmulgee Association several churches agitated the question of *withdrawal* for years, and, in 1830, a majority carried the measure. It was urged that the Convention would succeed best through the co-operation of mere auxiliary mission societies, and would, thus, be enabled to obtain more money. Even James Henderson, a violent opponent, promised his assistance to the Convention if the Association would withdraw and let the Convention be carried on through the co-operation of mission societies. But, while this opposition on the part of many arose mostly from a disinclination to co-operate in missionary, educational and other benevolent enterprises, yet, in a great measure, it was due to a sturdy spirit of independence, inherent in Baptists, which feared the formation of a body that might seek to exercise legislative or judicial prerogatives unwarranted by Scripture, and incompatible with the genius of Baptist churches.

It should be recollected that the General Committee of 1804, sought to promote union among all denominations; then followed the attempt to procure the adoption of a common confession of faith by the Associations; and this was succeeded by an endeavor to establish uniformity in church discipline. The sturdy independence of spirit which seems ever to have characterized the Georgia Baptists, rendered all these attempts futile; and we now clearly perceive their impracticability.

But, perhaps, one of the most potent causes of opposition to missions and education, and, therefore, one of the most effective causes which led to the disruption of the denomination, was the influence of such anti-mission papers as "The Signs of the Times," and the "Primitive Baptist," published in other States. In fact it is hardly too much to say that it was the violent state of feeling wrought immediately by these papers in 1835 and 1836, which resulted in the anti-missionaries disfellowshipping the churches and Associations which engaged in the benevolent schemes of the day, in the years 1836 and 1837. This effected a rupture. In fact, this was itself disruption; although the missionary churches and Associations never declared non-fellowship with the anti-missionaries.

We will now devote a chapter to those "anti-effort" proceedings, and to that anti-mission spirit and excitement, which with such a bold front, resisted the endeavors of the Convention men to promote missions, education and temperance, and which, finally, resulted in that division in our denomination, which took place in 1837. It will be seen that these sentiments, though gradual in their manifestation, made very rapid progress.

Among the first acts on record, which may be considered hostile to benevolent institutions, is that of the Hephzibah Association in 1817, when the Circular Letter for the year, written by Charles J. Jenkins, appointed at the preceding session, was rejected because of its strong missionary sentiments. This action was taken by an Association which, in 1815, had appointed a missionary meeting at Bark Camp, to be held in February, 1816, for the purpose of organizing a missionary society; and which, in 1816, returned the following answer to the letter sent by the society formed, soliciting the approbation and advice of the Association: "We received your friendly communication, soliciting our advice and concurrence, in what we think to be your laudable designs. All we can say, at present, is, dear brethren, go on in the prosecution of your designs—in that way you think may be most conducive to the glory of God, and the prosperity of Zion; and may the God of Israel grant you success in the same, is our hearty prayer," etc.

At the same session in which it rejected a missionary Circular Letter, written by Charles J. Jenkins, that gentleman, who was clerk of the body, was appointed corresponding secretary, to communicate with the Baptist Board of Foreighn Missions, at Philadelphia, with witch the Association resolved to correspond; but the body decided in the negative, when a vote was taken whether or not the Association should contribute to the funds of the Board of Foreign Missions. All those who were friendly to Foreign Missions were recommended, however, to meet, the following January, at the Bethel meeting-house, near Louisville,

Jefferson county, for the purpose of forming a Foreign Mission Society, distinct from the Association.

At that time this body was, in conjunction with the Hephzibah Missionary Society, supporting an Associational Missionary, Rev. C. Bateman; and, at its session of 1818, the churches of the Association were earnestly counselled to promote the dissemination of the gospel throughout the bounds of the Association and the adjacent destitute parts, by sending up their contributions for the purpose the following year. A letter was received from the Baptist Board of Foreign Missions, and it was agreed "that we express our warm acknowledgments to the Board for their very interesting communication, and our favorable disposition towards *the great and good work* in which they are engaged; and that we wish them 'God-speed,' remaining hopeful that at a future day (not far distant, perhaps), we shall add to our prayers such contributions as may aid their laudable designs."

A letter was also received from the Kentucky Missionary Society, in response to which the clerk was instructed to express the thanks of the Association, and its earnest desires for the prosperity and success of the Kentucky Missionary Society. "But contemplating to engage, ourselves, in domestic missions, as far as our ability will enable us, and feeeling a desire, if practicable, to contribute our mite towards the foreign missions, we cannot honestly flatter our brethren with any hopes of pecuniary aid." These events occurred in 1816, 1817, and 1818. At that time Charles J. Jenkins was the clerk and treasurer of the Association, and, as such, held $226.68 of Associational funds. In the two resolutions quoted his hand is plainly visible, for his influence in the body was great, but he moved into the bounds of the Sarepta Association in 1819, and acted no longer as a constituent member of the Hephzibah. Henceforth, for years, we find this next to the oldest of our Associations in opposition to missions. The following is Dr. A. Sherwood's estimate of Charles J. Jenkins, in his own handwriting: "He was a Carolinian by birth, a man of acquirements and usefulness. Clerk many years of the Hephzibah Association, he took hold of religious and educational measures with a strong hand. He died comparatively a young man, but his memory is precious in all that region." This is, perhaps, the proper place to present a few facts in the life of this notable member of our denomination.

CHARLES J. JENKINS was a quiet and unostentatious man, but very energetic in all that he undertook. Kind and benevolent in disposition, he was a very useful man, and, in every neighborhood where he lived, became a sort of adviser-general to the less intelligent; but he was of that temperament which never lets the left hand know what the right hand does. During his minority his parents resided partly in South Carolina and partly in Georgia, but he was born in Georgia, in the year 1780—a fact for which his own son, ex-Governor Jenkins, is our authority. About 1804 he married Miss Susan Emily Kenny, of Beaufort district, South Carolina, in which district he resided until his wife's death, which occurred in the spring of 1815. Three years previous to that event he and his wife both became deeply interested in the subject of religion, and both had united with the Euhaw Baptist church, being baptized by Rev. James Sweat. For many years Mr. Jenkins was successively the ordinary of Beaufort district and the clerk of the Court of Common Pleas, and it was his acquaintance with law, and with legal forms, which, together with some medical knowledge, enabled him to become useful, especially to the poor, as an adviser, a lawyer and a physician, wherever he resided. About the beginning of the year 1816 he moved to Jefferson county, Georgia, and united with the Providence church, twelve miles west of Louisville, and at once took an active part in the affairs of the Hephzibah Association. For a short time he resided within less than a half mile from Providence church, Jefferson county, and not more than three or four miles from Fenn's bridge, on the Ogeechee, the further end of which rested on Washington county soil. But in the early part of 1819 he removed to Madison county, in the Sarepta Association, of which he was elected clerk, and as such, in 1820, read Dr. A. Sherwood's resolution which led to the formation of our State Convention. While in Madison county, he built a Baptist meeting-house near his residence, and was instrumental in the organization of a church. In 1822 he was appointed United States Port Surveyor and Revenue Collector of Apalachicola, Florida, but owing chiefly to the deprivation of church privileges he resigned, after holding the appointment three years, and returned to Georgia, and re-purchased his old farm in Jefferson county, where he died in July of the year 1828.

Mr. Jenkins had enjoyed fair educational advantages, possessed excellent business capacities, and by his zeal, energy and sterling integrity, gained a controlling influence in whatever vicinity he lived. He was deeply interested in all denominational matters, and, outside of domestic life and private business, all his efforts were devoted to extending the borders of our Baptist Zion and widening Baptist influence and usefulness. In associational matters he took a very decided and active part, especially in advancing Foreign Missions; and when, in 1817, a Circular Letter written by him was objected to and its adoption declined, because of its strong advocacy of the Mission cause, he at once secured the adoption of a resolution recommending the formation of a Foreign Mission Society near Louisville, which existed for several years.

He was, also, for years, an active member in the Hephzibah Baptist Society for itinerant and missionary exertions, conducting its correspondence and promoting its usefulness. Plain and unostentatious in his manners, his piety was constant and unaffected, and to every trust imposed upon him, whether as a deacon or church clerk, associational clerk or treasurer, or an officer of public trust, he was ever faithful; and in every community in which he lived, he became a leading and influential man, enjoying the confidence of all. Of his two wives, the first was the mother of his only living child, Hon. Charles J. Jenkins, ex-Governor of Georgia.

The following is extracted from a letter from him to Dr. Sherwood, dated Apalachicola January 2th, 1823: "My situation is a lamentable one, and claims largely the commiseration and prayers of my brethren. I am in a land of darkness and cruelty, excluded from the privileges of the sanctuary, and from the society of Christians; and, indeed, I am destitute of any society at all. But, hitherto, the Lord hath helped me to be resigned to His will. I sometimes have a refreshing from His presence, and then my soul doth magnify His name; but, when I am in darkness, it is distressing indeed. I beg you to remember me at a throne of grace. Pray the Lord that I may possess my vessel in patience; and that I may not be permitted to do anything which may cause a reproach on the name of the Saviour whom I have espoused."

It is plainly observable that just after Mr. Jenkins left the Hephzibah Association, anti-missionary influences began to prevail. At the very next session, that of 1819, a vote was taken to ascertain, as the Minutes express it, "whether this body will take any part in the missionary;" and it was negatived. By this was meant, not the missionary cause, in general, but the various benevolent enterprises, and especially the missionary effort for Indian Reform, co-operation being invited by the other Associations, which were becoming interested on that subject. On motion, it was agreed "not to correspond with the (Baptist) Foreign Mission Society," of Philadelphia; and, two years later, in 1821, at the Darien meeting-house, Washington county, Rev. Elisha Perryman presented, and requested permission to read a letter to the Association from the Foreign Mission Board; but a majority of the brethren refused to have it read.

This opposition to benevolence extended to the State General Association, correspondence with which was rejected, and, in 1825, (as we have stated elsewhere) a resolution was adopted declaring that the Association had *no right* to correspond, by letter or messenger, with any General Association or Committee, Missionary Society or Board; and any brother who even made a motion on the subject of such a correspondence, was to be considered in *disorder* therefor, and to be reproved by the Moderator.

The most violent anti-missionaries in the Association, at that time, were John Blackstone, James Gray, Jordan Smith, James Granade, and Claborn Bateman, who, for several years, had been employed as an Association missionary.

About 1825 the anti-missionary spirit culminated in the Hephzibah Association, and a reaction gradually took place, although the leading men opposed to missions, Bible societies and benevolent enterprises continued to use active and violent measures to nullify the spirit of missions. About 1827 Jordan Smith, for several years Moderator of the Association, re-published some resolutions of the Kehukee Association, called the "Reformed Association," of North Carolina, which declared non-fellowship with Bible societies, missions, etc., thus putting in the entering wedge to division. This was answered, soon after, by a writer named *Nehemiah* in a pamphlet, which had three of four editions, and put a quietus on the misrepresentations of the North Carolina mission-haters. Nehemiah, we have strong reason to believe, was Adiel Sherwood. Under the disguise of "*grievances*," Jordan Smith,* James Granade, James Gray, and others, at a Convention which they called, inveighed against evangelical enterprises, and they sought boldly to antagonize their spirit and nullify their effect upon the popular mind in the Association.

This anti-Convention assembled at Limestone meeting-house, Washington county, September 27th, 1828, and "a letter of grievance," with some of the articles adopted by the brethren in Convention, were read in the session of the Hephzibah Association for 1828, under a suspension of the order of business; but it was decided, by vote, not even to take up and consider the letter. Thus proved abortive the efforts of the violent anti-mission clique to accomplish their endeavor to render the Association completely anti-missionary. In consequence, the churches under their control seceded from the Hephzibah, formed a body which they called the Canoochee Association, lying mostly in Bullock, Washington and Emanuel counties, which was anti-missionary in spirit.

This body formed by these seceders was not at first called an *Association*, but a *Conference*. The name *Canoochee Baptist Association* was given to it in 1838; but it called itself "an advisory council." The 6th article of the Constitution ran thus: "As the love of money is the root of all evil, and has produced so much distress among Christians, and we wishing to live in peace; therefore, this Association shall not engage in, nor in any wise encourage, any religious speculation, called the missionary, or by any other name, under pretense of supporting the gospel of Christ." After the death of Jordan Smith the body languished, and some of the churches did not represent themselves, and others rejoined the Hephzibah Association. In 1832 it had sixteen churches, ten ministers and 365 members; in 1838 four churches were received—Lower Black Creek, Jones' Meeting-house, Wade's, and Luke—some, perhaps all, from the Hephzibah. It then had twenty churches and 804 members, of whom 247 were reported as baptized that year. This body has never held correspondence with any other Association.

The only action of the Association, at the time, with reference to the churches so withdrawing, is contained in this extract from the Minutes of 1830:

"Relative to those churches which once constituted a part of this Association, we think it our duty to state to the Christian community at large, that said churches went off from us without having so much as asked for a dismission; and we, therefore, leave it with the churches of Christ, generally, to say whether this was orderly conduct or not; and also to say in what point of light we are to view those churches who have thus acted!"

Two years afterwards, in 1832, a letter, brought by three messengers, from the Canoochee Association, was presented. It stated that the Canoochee Association was not only sensible of its disorderly standing, but desired the friendly interposition of the Hephzibah Association to restore it, if possible, to good order; and it was

"*Resolved*, That the only course which this Association can pursue, in justice to herself, and according to good order, is to recommend to all those

---

*Jordan Smith resided in Washington county, and was an uneducated man of large wealth. He was kind, genial and liberal of his means, when he could understand properly the circumstances of the case. He possessed the confidence of his brethren and of the men of the world as a man of sincere piety. He was specially noted for his hospitality, usually carrying from church on Sabbath from thirty to fifty of the poorer class to dine with him. Had he been properly instructed, his position on the subject of missions would have been different. When the secession occurred in the Hephzibah Association, he said to the seceders, "Come, brethren, let us go! Come and go to my house, all of you!"

churches which wrested themselves from this body in a disorderly manner, as we conceive, to come back to us at our next Association, by letter and messengers, and make the proper and necessary acknowledgements; and that, upon their doing so, this Association stands pledged, not only to receive them, but also to grant them letters of regular and orderly dismission."

A committee was appointed to visit the Canoochee Association, confer with it and report in 1834. But no conference occurred, no report was made, nor was any further communication ever held between the dissevered bodies.

It seems that the Canoochee brethren denied that they gave their correspondent, D. Coleman, any authority to state, in the letter to the Hephzibah, that they made any "acknowledgements," but that they merely instructed him to "ask for letters of dismission." Therefore, when the messengers of the Hephzibah visited the Canoochee Association, they were not even invited to seats! Consequently, no official communication took place. As usual, in his quaint but expressive way, Dr. Sherwood says in regard to this, "Ask letters of dismission from a body whose messengers were unworthy of a seat! No doubt the Canoochee churches felt that they had done wrong in breaking off so abruptly, and desired to cover up their error as much as possible Marriage after a misstep does not sanctify or atone for guilty acts committed before honorable wedlock."

It may be well to state that about the period of 1819 or 1820 there was not a minister in the Hephzibah Association who possessed an education extending beyond the merest rudiments of learning; and of course where such ignorance prevailed, prejudice and bigotry also presided, and we need not, therefore, be much surprised at the course taken by the Association.

In the same year, 1819, that the Hephzibah voted "to take no part in the missionary," the Piedmont Association voted to have nothing to do with missionaries—meaning the missionary Baptists. Dr. Sherwood says, in his manuscript history:

"It is to be presumed that this little body was organized to keep away from the light of missions and other benevolent associations! What a converse to the directions of the Saviour: 'Ye are the light of the world.'"

Rev. Isham Peacock, of whom mention has already been made, was the father of this body, and he was not only anti-missionary, but anti-temperance. He would argue strongly against temperance societies, though he was not in the habit of inebriation. Dr. Sherwood, on the authority of Rev. Wilson Conner, states that Mr. Peacock carried whiskey in his cane, and would drink before his congregation, to illustrate his position that he *could* drink and not become intoxicated. "It looks strange," says Mr. Sherwood, "to see a minister nearly one hundred years old using such *strong* but *dangerous* arguments to carry his point!"

To such an extent did Peacock carry his anti-temperance principles, that in 1833 he would not attend the meeting of the Piedmont Association because Mr. Westbury, another minister of the Association, had joined a temperance society.

In November, 1816, Luther Rice was an attendant on the session of the Ebenezer Association, at Mount Horeb, Pulaski county. He appeared on Sabbath morning, on which day Winder Hillman, of the Hephzibah, Dozier Thornton, of the Sarepta, and Jesse Mercer, of the Georgia, were appointed to preach. It was thought proper that Mr. Rice should have an opportunity to preach, and Winder Hillman politely gave way, that the opportunity might be afforded. It is reported that brethren Rice, Mercer and Thornton "delivered interesting sermons to a numerous concourse." As the messenger of the Baptist Board of Foreign Missions, Luther Rice presented a letter requesting correspondence with the Board. The request was acceded to, and Ezekiel Taylor was appointed corresponding secretary, and yet the correspondence was closed the following year. The surplus money on hand was, nevertheless, voted to support itinerant preaching in the lower counties of the State. Correspondence with the Foreign Mission Board was resumed in 1819, and Indian reform missionary work was formally entered upon by the appointment of a co-operating committee. The next year, 1820, the Ocmulgee plan for Indian Reform was acquiesced in, and the collection of funds was recommended. The following is the action of the Association: "Agreed to concur with the Ocmulgee Association relative to a plan for Indian Reform, and appointed the following brethren trustees, to act in concert with those appointed by that Association and any sister Associations that may come into the measures, to-wit: Fulgham, Love, Ross, Steighley and Tharpe. It is, therefore, recommended that the ministering brethren explain to the churches the object of the Association, and that such plans be laid as shall be thought most advisable to raise funds to carry this laudable scheme into effect."

For two years the scheme received favor and assistance, but suddenly, in 1823, interest in the Indian Reform Mission was abruptly discontinued, although correspondence with the Mission Board in Philadelphia was continued. For the thirteen years following there was no special manifestation of hostility to missions or education in the Association; yet it had not connected itself with the State Convention. At the session of 1836, held at Beersheba, Twiggs county, the following appears in the Minutes:

"WHEREAS, it is inferred from the reading of some of the letters from the churches that the members of this body which hold to the benevolent institutions of the day have departed from the Articles of Faith and the Constitution of this Association, it was therefore ordered, that the said articles be read, which was unanimously assented to, and the following query was received, to be discussed to the satisfaction of the body : 'Are the institutions of this day, such as missions, temperance, etc., consistent with the Articles of Faith of this Association?'"

After special prayer by C. D. Mallary, the whole of Tuesday, September 27th, was spent in discussing this subject, and on the vote being taken, the question was decided in the affirmative. The delegates of seven churches—Myrtle Spring, Mount Nebo, Ramah, Cool Spring, Pleasant Plains, Camp Creek and Bulah—being dissatisfied with the result of the discussion, and being also opposed to the benevolent institutions of the day, left the house.

Upon which the Association adopted the following :

"*Resolved*, That differences of opinion in regard to the benevolent institutions of the day should not be the ground of non-fellowship among brethren."

Three churches—by name, Camp Creek, Ramah and Bulah—having sent up a declaration of non-fellowship with all the benevolent institutions of the day, and the persons engaged in them, it was—

"*Resolved*, That we regret, very much, this hasty act of those churches ; and, hoping that upon a reconsideration of the matter by them, they will come to a different conclusion, we, therefore, most earnestly recommend to those churches to reconsider that matter and report to us upon the subject, at our next session,"

The Corresponding Letter to the churches, for that year, 1836, contained a plain statement of these facts : " It was decided by our body, after a lengthy discussion, that the benevolent institutions of the day are not inconsistent with the articles of faith upon which the Association was constituted. In consequence of this decision, the delegates from seven churches, being a small minority in the body, withdrew, claiming to be the true Ebenezer Association. It did not appear to the body that, in this proceeding, these delegates acted upon the authority of the churches they represent, consequently no act of censure was passed upon these churches; and the charitable hope was indulged that, when the matter should be properly considered by them, the difficulty would be removed. It was decided by our body that differences of opinion in relation to the benevolent institutions of the day should not constitute a ground of non-fellowship among brethren."

As an actual part of the history of the times of which we write, and bearing intimately upon the "everlasting altercation about the institutions of the day," as Dr. Benedict expresses it, a copious extract from the Circular Letter of the Ebenezer Association for the year 1836 is here given :

"Great divisions have an existence in our denomination, and, so far as we are able to discover, without substantial cause. Those divisions have for their *ostensible* cause the friendship for, and support of, missionary and temperance societies by some of our brethren. Though to many it seems that this affords no sufficient cause for division, to others it appears to be abundant ground for the declaration of non-fellowship for churches and members favoring these societies, and the rending asunder of associations of long standing, composed of brethren who have for a long time seen eye to eye and face to face, and have communed at the same table in commemoration of the death and sufferings of our Lord.

"These being the known consequences of the difference of opinion on the subject of these societies, let us inquire what are the opinions of each party. First, if we are not mistaken, it is the opinion of those who oppose missionary and temperance societies, that God will cause the gospel to be preached to all the nations of the earth; that He will accomplish this in the fulness of His own time and by the use of His own means; that, to do this, human plans are not necessary; and that the present operations have not the sanction of the Word of eternal truth.

"Those favoring these societies believe that God will send the gospel to all nations of the earth, and this in the fullness of His own time and by the use of His own means; and, further, that *now* is the time, and that the redeemed of the Lord, and all that they can do and that they have, being the immediate gift of God, are *His means*; and they trust that the Spirit of the Lord has made them willing to be used for this purpose. They have no doubt that the Scriptures of eternal truth sanction the plans now in operation for the spread of the gospel of Christ. They call upon the opposers of these *human plans*, as they are called, to say what *other* course can be pursued for the accomplishment of this purpose. They speak of the blessing of God in favoring brother Judson with life, health, and ability to translate the whole of the Scriptures into the Burman language; and they consider the blessings of God on the labors of the missionaries sent to various stations as *proof* that God's own time is *now*; and that His *own* means are employed in doing His *own* work—the spread of the gospel of Christ. And these things are spoken of by our missionary brethren as encouraging them to go on in discharge of what they believe to be their duty. To our anti-missionary brethren we repeat the words of our Redeemer, 'forbid them not;' they are not against our Lord; for they cause the Scriptures to be translated and published in languages in which they have not heretofore been known. They cause the gospel to be preached to the heathen and God blesses the sermons to the conviction and conversion of heathen sinners. These missionary brethren are not 'against' Jesus, and, therefore, by the authority of His own word we say, 'forbid them not.' Can this be the cause of non-fellowship for these brethren? O, Spirit of the Lord forbid it!"

Then follows an exhortation to "let charity prevail," and the conclusion is: "Without taking part in these divisions, or expressing an opinion in favor of either party, we conclude this epistle by using the exhortation of the apostle to the Corinthian church: 'Be perfect, be of good comfort, be of one mind, live in peace, and the God of love and peace shall be with you.'

"C. A. THARP, *Moderator*.
"JAMES H. LOFTON, *Clerk*."

The anti-mission spirit, when it began to burn in the Ocmulgee Association, blazed forth more determinedly than in any other body, culminating in withdrawal from the Convention in 1830, and in a declaration of non-fellowship in 1837.

At the remarkable session of that Association, held with the Antioch church, in 1827 when the great revival commenced, several churches petitioned to withdraw from the General Association; but the matter was postponed until the succeeding session, when it was discussed and again laid over. Nor was it until 1830 that the anti-missionary leaders in the Association were able to induce a majority of the churches to send up petitionary letters to withdraw from the General Convention; of course, such being the case, the withdrawal was effected. This took place at Harmony church, eight or nine miles northeast of Eatonton. That this was the result of opposition to benevolent enterprises, rather than mere opposition to the Convention, is shown by the fact that in

1836, the Association, by resolution, concurred in the action of the Mt. Gilead church, Putnam county, declaring non-fellowship with all benevolent societies. The following year, 1837, the Ocmulgee Association itself, as a body, declares the benevolent institutions of the day "unscriptural and non-fellowship," and, furthermore, appoints a committee to help constitute a small minority of the churches of the Sarepta Association, which had seceded in 1836, into another body which was called the Oconee Association.

These high-handed measures of the Ocmulgee immediately brought their legitimate fruits—division and disintegration, Liberty church, in Newton county, withdrew from the Association, thus repudiating the right of the Association to prescribe what a church shall or shall not consider unscriptural. It declared by resolution adopted in conference, that it regarded all the benevolent institutions of the day as *human institutions*, designed professedly to do good in elevating the morals of the community and the standard of piety in the churches, as well as to disseminate useful and religious knowledge, spread the glorious gospel and circulate the Bible in the world. It declared, also, that to unite with or contribute to such benevolent societies was right, discretionary with individuals, and should not be a barrier to fellowship or communion; and it resolved neither to censure nor use harsh or compulsory measures, to influence one another to act contrary to freedom of will, in relation to missionary purposes or benevolent institutions. (See INDEX of March 29th, 1838.)

This, however, was, by no means the first withdrawal from the Ocmulgee; but has been referred to merely that the reasons on record might be given. In 1834 seven churches which had seceded from the Ocmulgee and Flint River Associations, impelled thereto by associational usurpations and fierce opposition to benevolent institutions, united and formed the Central Association, at Indian Creek, February 1st. Such men as Adiel Sherwood, John E. Dawson, Thomas Cooper, J. H. Campbell, Jeremiah Clark, James Fears, J. Swanson, and Jesse Travis assisted in organizing this Association, which was constituted on a basis which recognizes and approves of Sabbath-schools, missions, the education of ministers, Bible, temperance and tract societies, and giving them all a hearty co-operation; but averring that fellowship will not be disturbed, if a member does not feel it his duty to contribute to these various benevolent causes. This Association united with the State Convention in 1835.

In that same year the Sarepta Association, at its session held with Falling Creek church, Elbert county, decided by a "large majority" to become a constituent member of the State Convention, and appointed delegates by whom she was represented the following year. One result of this action shows plainly its result upon the churches of the Association—in 1836, $782.86 were sent up by them. Previously, about $200.00 was the largest amount sent up, Another result was a *schism* in the Association. At the session for 1836, the propriety of becoming a constituent of the Convention was discussed very fully, and the action of 1835 was confirmed by a large majority. Rev. George Lumpkin and others, representing Beaver Dam, Big Spring, Big Creek, Skull Shoals and Bethlehem churches, protested, and requested permission to enter their protest against this action upon the Minutes of the Association. Their request was granted and their protest was entered; but brethren A. Chandler, J. Matthews and J. F. Hillyer were appointed a committee to bring in an answer, also to be entered upon the Minutes. The following is a copy of the *Protest:*

"We, the delegates from the churches at Beaver Dam, Big Spring, Skull Shoals, and Bethlehem, representing, as we believe, the feelings of the above churches, do enter this our protest against the act of a majority of this Association, for the following reasons:

"1st. Because we think the Association transcended her delegated powers, in constraining the opposing churches to become in part constituent members of the Baptist State Convention by said resolution, and thereby infringed upon the liberty and internal rights of the opposing churches.

"2d. Because we are unwilling to be governed by the Baptist State Convention, believing it to be founded upon anti-republican principles, and may, some day, be the overthrow of our denomination.

"3d. We consider the lawful protection, or powers conferred by legal sanction, in the act of incorporation, one great step towards the subversion of civil and religious liberty in the constituents of said Convention.

"4th. That by said resolution we are brought into union and Christian correspondence with the Central Association, with which we have no fellowship, as we are among those who have no confidence in the flesh.

"5th, and lastly. Because we are constrained to correspond with bodies of professors against our will, and [are] prohibited from correspondence with such as we have fellowship [for.]

"Therefore, the above and foregoing reasons constrain us to say to the Sarepta Association that we are no longer members of your body.

"GEORGE LUMPKIN, JAMES O. KELLY, *Beaver Dam;* MARK JACKSON, MATTHEW VARNER, *Skull Shoals;* JOHN LACY, THOMAS ARMS, *Big Creek;* HARRIS THURMAN, VINES SMITH, *Big Spring;* WILLIAM PATMAN, DAVID PATMAN, *Bethlehem,*"

NOTE.—Mark Jackson and Harris Thurman, seeing the spirit and tendency of the Protest, had their names stricken off.

The *Answer* to the Protest reads:

"On the *first* article, we observe, That we do not conceive that constraint is laid on any one, as the Association is but an advisory council, and her resolutions [but] advice; and, therefore, no one is constrained to give only as he chooses. The internal rights of the churches are not affected.

"On the *second*, we remark, That we cannot conceive that the Convention is anti-republican; nor how it can exercise any control over the churches. Its Constitution does not allow any such construction.

"On the *third*, we observe, That the act of incorporation of the Convention confers upon it no power to oppress the churches. The act of incorporation is, merely, that it may hold property. Many churches in the State are also incorporated for the same purpose; therefore, the apprehensions of oppression are wholly groundless.

"On the *fourth*, we remark, We correspond with the Central Association, as they are of the same faith and order with us.

"On the *fifth*, we observe, That we do not think the act complained of involves such consequences as are represented."

We have here a fair presentation of the flimsy reasons presented in those days for entertaining objections to the Convention; although they may have had weight with some minds.

We now gather that it was simply to avoid disturbing fellowship which made the Sarepta delay its union with the Convention. At length the majority determined that they would no longer yield complaisance to the feelings of the minority; and so they cut the knot of difficulty and retardation by firmly carrying out the purpose to unite with the Convention. The consequence was the formation, in 1837, of the Oconee Association out of the seceding churches. This Association has never united with the State Convention.

Another schism took place in 1837, on account of a difference of opinion touching the benevolent operations of the day, which resulted in the formation of the Rehoboth Association. Most of the ten churches at first composing this Association seceded from the Itcheconnah (or Ichaconna) Association, because, on account of their missionary views, a non-fellowship resolution passed against them by that Association, in 1837, beginning as follows:

"*Resolved*, That the systems of the day—benevolent, so-called—such as Bible, missionary, temperance, tract societies, etc., are unscriptural, unsupported by divine revelation, and, therefore, anti-Christian, etc., etc.," and fellowship is withdrawn from those churches favorable to such societies, or, rather, they are declared to be in disorder, and are cut off.

The Rehoboth Association has proved itself to be one of the most efficient and zealous of the Baptist Associations of Georgia. Acting, for a great many years, independently, of the Boards of the Southern Baptist Convention, it has sustained as missionaries Rev. Cæsar Frazer, in Africa, a native African; Rev.

J. S. Dennard and wife, in Africa, also, both of whom died at their post; Rev. T. A. Reid and Rev. J. H. Clark, in Central Africa, both of whom returned after years of useful service; Rev. J. S. Murrow, among the Indians of the West, who still remains at the post of duty, laboring most faithfully; and Rev. E. B. Barret and Rev. B. F. Tharp, among the soldiers of the army, during the war. This Association has, also, assisted in educating several young men for the ministry. Its moving spirits have been B. F. Tharp, Jacob King, J. M. Wood, H. C. Hornady, T. E. Langley, J. S. Shannon, A. J. Holmes, Wm. C. Wilkes, E. W. Warren, C. D. Mallary, S. Landrum, B. L. Ross and J. R. Kendrick.

The formation of the Rock Mountain Association is another case of division on account of a difference of missionary sentiments.

At her regular session in 1838, the Yellow River Association adopted this very remarkable non-fellowshipping resolution:

"*Resolved*, That the institutions of the day, called benevolent, to-wit: the Convention, Bible Society, Tract Society, Temperance Society, Abolition Society, Sunday-school Union, Theological Seminary, and all other institutions tributary to the missionary plan, now existing in the United States, are unscriptural, and that we, as an Association, will not correspond with any Association that has united with them; nor will we hold in our communion or fellowship any church that is connected with them."

This resolution, so similar to that adopted by the Itcheconnah, cut off and caused the withdrawal of six churches—Rock Bridge, Bay Creek, Long Shoals, Cool Spring, Macedonia and New Hope. The record from which these facts are drawn asserts that the words, "Abolition Society," were artfully incorporated in the resolution with the benevolent and religious institutions specified for the purpose of casting odium upon them, as it was well known that there was not a single Abolition Society in the State of Georgia. One of the reasons given by the Towaliga Association why fellowship with Missionary Baptists should not be continued was, that in the Northern section of the United States, there was a connection between the Society of *System Baptists* and the *Abolitionists*, a statement which Benedict characterizes as a "gross misrepresentation." In the discussion which followed the introduction of this resolution at the Yellow River Association, several of a respectable minority took part in a firm and resolute opposition to its adoption, but Rev. Luke Robinson was especially distinguished by his able and eloquent advocacy of education, temperance and missions. When the leader of the anti-missionary party, a venerable old man with hoary locks, raised the rallying cry, "Down with education! down with theology! down with temperance societies! down with the Convention!" the vote was taken, and the resolution was adopted. The minority immediately left the house. They agreed to meet on the 19th of July, 1839, and form a new Association, at Mount Zion, Newton county. At the appointed time delegates from ten churches assembled, among whom were Luke Robinson, George Daniel, A. R. Almond, Lewis Towers, and J. R. George, assisted by J. S. Calloway, C. D. Mallary, and T. Phillips. G. Daniel was elected Moderator, and E. Henderson, Clerk; and thus the Stone Mountain Association was formed.

At its session in 1837 the Flint River Association had a discussion which produced a division of the body. This was a result of a consideration of the question which, the year previous, had been referred to the churches—whether or not non-fellowship should be declared towards those churches in favor of "benevolence," as the benevolent institutions of the day were designated. The result was that, by a vote of twenty-three to fifteen, the Association decided against non-fellowshipping the benevolent churches. This meeting took place at the Holly Grove church, Monroe county, Rev. Joshua Calloway being Moderator, and R. M. Still, Clerk.

The following was passed:

"*Resolved*, That we are unwilling to go into any new declaration of fellowship or non-fellowship, but feel disposed to continue in the same old Baptist path of faith and practice which this Association has heretofore pursued."

As soon as the result was known, Rev. William Moseley arose and said:

"I am in the minority, where I expected to be, and it is unnecessary for me to remain here any longer. Therefore I bid you farewell. We will meet no more as brethren, but as men!"

He then requested all who coincided with him in sentiment to meet him out in the woods. The delegates from fifteen churches left the building, held a consultation in the woods, and agreed to meet in convention with the County Line church, in Pike county, in July, 1838. They did so, and constituted the Towaliga Association. Its total membership at that time was 1,022, only twelve baptisms being reported.

It is worthy of note that the Flint, at its session in 1837, received messengers from the Itcheconnah Association by a two-thirds vote, after that Association had passed its non-fellowship resolution.

Mention has been made, also, of the discussion lasting a whole day, which took place in September, 1836, at Beersheba, Twiggs county, and which resulted in an affirmative answer to the question, "Are the institutions of this day, such as missions, temperance, etc., consistent with the Articles of Faith of this Association?" The result was that the messengers of seven churches left the house, viz: Myrtle Spring, Mount Nebo, Ramah, Cool Spring, Pleasant Plains, Camp Creek and Bulah, "being dissatisfied with the institutions of the day and with the course pursued by the Association." These churches held a meeting in the following November, and published their Minutes, in which they call themselves the *True Ebenezer* Association, and affirm that they had demanded the records of the body as belonging to them by right. And this reminds us that William Moseley was deeply chagrined because the Towaliga Association was not called the *Flint River*, as he desired. When asking aid of the Ocmulgee to constitute the Towaliga Association, he intimated that the name of the new Association would be "Flint River." This was so violently opposed by James Henderson that Mr. Mosely declined to preach the next day, which was Sunday, although appointed to do so by the Association.

In 1837 three churches, the Horeb and the Upatoi, in Talbot, and the Bethel, in Meriwether county, seceded from the Columbus Association by not sending messengers, foreseeing the strong missionary spirit which was becoming prevalent in that body, and being themselves of an opposite disposition. They sent messengers to the Flint River Association in that year, but instead of presenting themselves as correspondents to the Association, they offered their letters to the Moseley faction at its meeting in the woods, and were received. Subsequently uniting with a few other small churches, these seceders from the Columbus Association formed the Apostolic Baptist Association.

In the same year, 1837, ten churches left the Western Association and formed a new union of the same name. The reasons assigned by them were that the Association corresponded with those who approved of missions and education, and refused to non-fellowship them.

Enough has been written to show when *division* took place in the Baptist denomination in Georgia, and what the causes of it were.

The causes of it were the deep-seated opposition in the minds and hearts of many Baptists to missions, education, temperance, and to the societies, or schemes, originated for their support and propagation, and for the dissemination of tracts and the Bible. That this opposition was the result of a want of enlightenment—that is to say, of ignorance and prejudice—is but too painfully apparent. It began to manifest itself openly in the Ocmulgee Association in 1830, and, in 1837, culminated in a general declaration of non-fellowship with Missionary Baptists, on the part of all opposed to the benevolent schemes of this day. *This was division*, or "schism," as Dr. Sherwood calls it. He says: "Prior to 1835, the notion that missions, etc., were *new schemes* was not entertained, except by a few only; but *then*, it was proclaimed that all institutions of the day were unscriptural."

That was the period when a violent anti-missionary paper, "*The Signs of the Times*," began to be circulated in Georgia; and, perhaps, it was the influence of this paper, and the "*Primitive Baptist*," started in North Carolina, in 1836, which caused the violence and bitterness of feeling in Georgia, and thus really led to the disruption of the denomination. For it was an article in the former of these papers that instigated the non-fellowship resolution passed by the Ocmulgee Association.

In the summer of 1835 Jason Greer and Rowell Reese published letters in the *Signs of the Times,* suggesting the propriety of declaring non-fellowship with those who favored all the new schemes of the day. In their wake soon followed Joel Colley, who, for twenty years, was the Moderator of the Yellow River Association. To the members of most of the Associations, even of those which opposed the mission cause, this was, at first, astounding.

The *Primitive Baptist* came near beginning its existence in Georgia. It seems that William Moseley, James Henderson, and others, held a Convention in 1835, to consult concerning the origination of a paper in Georgia to counteract the influence of THE INDEX. Rev. Joshua Lawrence, of North Carolina, was invited to remove to Georgia and become its editor, as it would be "a money-making business.,' Lieutenant Doct. Biddle was, also, expected to become its editor; but he decamped very suddenly. On consultation, it was agreed that the *Primitive Baptist* should be issued at Tarboro, North Carolina. For all these statements Dr. Sherwood is our authority.

It is almost impossible to state fairly the exceeding bitterness of feeling and expression excited by the controversy on these matters. Rev. A. T. Holmes, in a letter to THE INDEX, dated October 21st, 1837, writes: "The Flint River Association adjourned on Tuesday last, after the most stormy and unpleasant session I ever witnessed. On Monday, the body presented the most disgraceful aspect that I ever witnessed in a religious meeting. It did more harm, and I have no doubt had a worse effect on the community, than it will ever do good. Other denominations looked on with wonder and astonishment, and even regret, to see the Baptists so much divided; and even the world were pointing the finger of scorn and saying, 'See how these professors hate, and are trying to devour, each other.'"

The whole denomination was torn up and disorganized by the dissensions, ruptures and acrimonious criminations and recriminations, which continued between 1830 and 1840. Associations were torn asunder: churches were divided; friendships were broken, and Christian fellowship terribly interrupted. Indeed, it was one of the greatest afflictions of Jesse Mercer's life, that these differences of opinions and violent dissensions alienated some of those brethren with whom he had co-operated on terms of Christian affection and confidence, and caused them to go so far, even, as to accuse him of departure from the gospel faith.

This state of feeling may be illustrated by an authentic anecdote in the life of that good and useful man, Rev. Jacob King, who lived near Thomaston, in Upson county. Soon after the "Hard-shells," as the anti-missionaries were called, had withdrawn from the Missionary Baptists, old brother Nichols, a staunch Primitive, came to one of Jacob King's meetings. As he entered the house, Mr. King met him and saluted him with: "How do you do, brother Nichols?" at the same time extending his hand. The extended hand was refused, and the only answer deigned was: "No brother of your'n!" Nevertheless, the sermon proceeded, and Mr. King could not but perceive that Nichols was pleased with the discourse. This was verified by the early appearance of Nichols in attendance upon another of Jacob King's services, taking a seat near the pulpit. Mr. King preached on *Christian Experience* for some time, and then observed in his own quiet and quaint way: "I don't know whether I have any brethren present that approve of this kind of preaching," when, much to his gratification and the amusement of the audience, old brother Nichols lifted his head up and exclaimed, "Yes, you is!"

In 1833, Adiel Sherwood, a messenger from the Georgia Association was, by the Yellow Association denied a seat, as a messenger from the State Convention. Two or three years later, in the same Association, Rev. Reuben Thornton, Moderator of the Sarepta Association, was prohibited from preaching in a meeting-house, on account of his missionary sentiments, About 1833, Sardis church, in Pike county, refused the use of its meeting-house to a Domestic Mission Society, for the purpose of holding its anniversary, although several of the church members and the pastor himself were connected with the society. And a year later, New Hope church, (in Pike or Upson county,) of which John Hambrick was pastor, decided that it was not "orthodox to receive into their pulpit, preachers who are members of benevolent societies."

In the Tugalo Association, Jesse Mercer, though invited to a seat as a messenger from the Georgia Association, was refused a seat as a messenger from the General Association or State Convention, which he represented.

In the Western Association, several churches divided because of difference of opinion on the subject of missions; and, in one, the Antioch, both parties used the same meeting house. All over the State, except in the eastern part, there was trouble and division and disruption of fellowship, because of difference of sentiment, laxness of discipline and disregard of proper church order.

A notable difficulty occurred between the Eatonton and New Salem churches, owing to the disorderly reception by the latter of a member of the former. The trouble augmented and resulted in the formation of the Central Association, and for several years disturbed the harmony of various Associations in the State.

Sharon church, in Henry county, asked the Flint River Association to appoint and send a committee to her to act as pacificators or arbitrators in a difficulty among the members. The committee appeared at the appointed time, and authoritatively demanded the moderatorship, as a right. This claim the church denied and withheld. The committee then withdrew from the church to a grove and sent word for such of the members as recognized their authority to appear before them. Seven or eight did so, and were recognized by the committee as the church, and were so reported to the Association. At its next session, thinking to smooth over the matter, the Association voted to receive both factions of the church. The result was the secession of several churches from the Association.

Almost any number of instances might be adduced, exhibiting the exceedingly deplorable and disagreeable results, in the denomination, of that state of strife and dissension, which existed prior to 1837, and which culminated in a denominational separation in that year, which has been well marked ever since. It was not uncommon for anti-mission churches to excommunicate members who entertained missionary sentiments, and for Associations to withdraw from or attempt to discipline churches that retained such members. James Henderson, Moderator of the Ocmulgee Association, contended "that Associations have the same power over churches, that churches have over their members." This gave rise to a dissertation by Jesse Mercer, published in the Minutes of the State Convention for 1833, on "The Resemblances and Differences between Association and Church Authority."

But about 1836 a brighter day dawned. Another chapter, however, must be devoted to a still further exposition of the state of religious feeling in this dark period of our denominational history.

XV.
RELIGIOUS HISTORY.
1826-1836.

XV.

RELIGIOUS HISTORY.

THE GREAT REVIVAL OF 1827—ACCESSIONS TO THE DIFFERENT ASSOCIATIONS—REPORTS FOR 1829—THE ANTI-INTEMPERATE SOCIETY—GEORGIA ASSOCIATION OF 1828 AND 1829—THE SUNBURY ASSOCIATION—RELIGIOUS CONDITION IN 1830—DENOMINATIONAL STATISTICS—RELIGIOUS CONDITION FROM 1830 TO 1836—DESCRIBED BY JESSE MERCER—DR. C. D. MALLARY'S STATEMENT—WHAT A WRITER IN "THE INDEX" SAID—THE CONVENTION STILL PRESSES FORWARD—REVIVAL INCIDENTS—THE CONVENTION RESOLUTION OF 1835—CAMPBELL'S CALL FOR THE FORSYTH MEETING—THE FORSYTH MEETING—ITS PROCEEDINGS—COMMUNICATIONS FROM DR. HILLYER, DR. CAMPBELL AND REV. T. B. SLADE—PEACE DAWNS ONCE MORE—THE MEETING AT COVINGTON.

There seems to have been no special religious interest manifested in the Baptist churches of our State during the year 1826. In 1827 a remarkable revival commenced in July, at Eatonton, then in the Ocmulgee Association, under the ministry of Adiel Sherwood. While serving three churches—Milledgeville, Greenesboro and Eatonton—he dwelt at the last named place and taught the academy there. In September he preached on Sabbath in the open air, at Antioch church, Morgan county, during the session of the Ocmulgee Association for that year. The Holy Spirit descended with mighty power, and at the conclusion of the sermon four thousand people sought the benefits of prayer in their behalf. Among the first to spring forward towards the stand was John E. Dawson, then twenty-two years of age, and exceedingly handsome; he had been, even then, married three years. He was one of the many whose conversion resulted from the descent of the Spirit that day; and for the fifteen following years there were converts joining Baptist churches in the neighboring region who dated their first serious impressions from the day they heard that wonderfully blessed sermon at Antioch church. Brethren Colley and James Shannon also preached on Sabbath, and much excitement was produced, and thousands were convicted. In the words of Dr. Sherwood himself, "The oldest of God's ministers were constrained to say they never saw such a wonderful appearance of the outpouring of God's Spirit before." The work spread throughout the State, resulting in the baptism, within two years, of about sixteen thousand persons.

Ministers all over the State, aroused by the Holy Spirit to a pitch of lofty enthusiasm, went from church to church, and from neighborhood to neighborhood, preaching with a most unusual and heaven-blessed fervor. Dr. A. Sherwood, in his private memoranda, records that, in thirty counties, he "tried to preach" three hundred and thirty-three times during the year 1828.

The Minutes of the Georgia Association, in the Letter of Correspondence, bear witness to the increase in itineracy among the ministers. William Moseley, James Reeves and others, of the Flint River Association, who had attended the Ocmulgee in that year, caught a glorious impulse for preaching Jesus, and soon communicated their enthusiasm to others, and ere long the whole Flint River Association was ablaze with religious fervor, and a most powerful work was the result in all its bounds. Nineteen hundred baptisms were reported at the session of the Flint River Association for 1828.

With but one or two exceptions all the Associations of the State felt the influence of this remarkable revival in a marked degree. The number of baptisms reported at the Ocmulgee in the year 1828, for the previous twelve months, was 1,772, and in 1829 the number of baptisms reported was 810. In the Georgia Association 1,761 baptisms were reported in 1828, and 708 in 1829. To the Ebenezer Association 200 baptisms were reported in 1828, and 270 in 1829. At the Convention held in May, 1828, in Monticello, the Committee on the State of Religion reported that it was "more flattering in Georgia than it ever was before. On the Ocmulgee, Flint River, Yellow River and Georgia Associations the Lord has poured out His Spirit in rich profusion, and many have been added to the churches. From the Ebenezer and Tugalo Associations we have nothing very encouraging. The spirit of opposition to missionary efforts in the Hephzibah Association seems to be giving way. From the Sunbury Association, a member of this Convention, we have some encouraging prospects. Nothing special is heard either from the Piedmont, Sarepta or Chattahoochee Association. We have great reason to bless God that the glorious light of Zion is spreading far and wide, and will soon cover the earth."

The following year, 1829, the Convention met at Milledgeville, and the report on the State of Religion gives us a little further insight into the spiritual condition of the churches and Associations: "In the bounds of those Associations hitherto unfriendly to the views and objects of this Convention, there is a considerable change. Some partial revivals have taken place, family altars have been erected, weekly prayer-meetings constantly kept up in many churches, some tract, Bible and Sabbath-school societies formed, and the missionary spirit considerably increased. In the bounds of those Associations which have united with this Convention, there have been many Bible, tract and Sunday-school societies formed, and a very great accession of members by experience and baptism. Nearly eight thousand (8,000) were baptized during the last associational year; but it is agreed that the revival is on the decline. Family prayer is generally attended to, prayer-meetings kept up in churches, and many spend every Sabbath in the public exercises of religion. A spirit of religious improvement seems to prevail."

The following, on the subject of Temperance, from the same report, is interesting:

"The Anti-intemperate Society for this State is increasing, and it is worthy of remark, that in public assemblies hitherto accustomed to use ardent spirits to great excess, not half the quantity formerly made use of is now consumed. Very few families use it habitually; and it is not now considered a breach of common politeness to neglect placing the dram-bottle on the board. Public labors, such as reaping the harvest fields, etc., are performed, frequently, without the use of the inebriating bowl; and even at weddings, in respectable families, there have been many instance of entire abstinence from this liquid."

This extract gives us a hint of the exceeding great evil intemperance had become in the State prior to this time. The records of the best Baptist Associations of the State evince the strenuous and persistent efforts made by those Associations to abate the evil and dethrone King Alcohol. Year after year the churches and church members are besought urgently to combat intemperance, and its evils are deplored in the most feeling manner. Many church members deemed it no inconsistency to drink; and the anti-missionary Baptists were as bitterly opposed to temperance societies as they were to mission, tract and Bible societies.

The first temperance society in the State of Georgia was organized at Eatonton, in the last part of July, 1827, at a union meeting of the Baptist church; and the great revival of that year broke out before the meeting was closed. In the following spring, that of 1828, the State Temperance Society was formed, at Monticello, at the close of the session for that year of the Georgia Baptist Convention. The constitution, at the request of A. Sherwood, was written by Rev. Abner W. Clopton, of Virginia. General Shorter was elected President, and Rev. Edmund Shackelford was chosen Secretary. Dr. Sherwood soon succeeded E. Shackelford as Secretary, and served for five or six years, until he went to

Washington, District of Columbia, to become a professor in Columbian University. This State Temperance Society continued to flourish until 1834, holding its meetings at Milledgeville during the sessions of the Legislature. It had between fifty and one hundred auxiliaries. The society gradually became extinct after the removal of the Secretary to Washington City; but the cause was not abandoned by the Baptists. On the contrary, the publication of a temperance paper, called the *Temperance Banner*, was begun at Washington in 1834, by Mercer & Stokes, and it was the means of doing much good All these exertions resulted in a great temperance reformation in the State, in effecting which the Baptists took a most honorable part.

At its session, in October, 1828, the Georgia Association, in its Corresponding Letter to the sister Associations affirmed: "We are constrained to believe that the God of Abraham has poured out, in these latter days, the most holy influence of His Spirit of truth, and through its effectual teaching, the old and the young, the rich and the poor, the bond and the free, have flocked together to the feet of our Lord Jesus Christ," and "many of our sons and daughters and servants have rallied to the gospel trumpet's joyful sound and waving banner, and have become the willing subjects of the Cross of Christ." And, in the regular proceedings for 1828, we read that "As the Lord is abundantly blessing the churches, and calling into them many young men:

"*Resolved*, That we urge upon the churches the importance of fostering prominent gifts, and of encouraging those who possess them to exercise them frequently:

"And, as the Lord has been pleased to favor us with a large increase of precious souls the past year, who have been converted by mighty grace, and that He may abide with us, and revive those churches unvisited by the showers of mercy, that the residue of children, neighbors and servants perish not, and that our poor efforts to send the gospel to those who are perishing for lack of knowledge, may be more united and successful,

"*Resolved*, That we observe the 13th day of November, 1829, as a day of thanksgiving and prayer, and release to our domestics, at our respective places of worship." It was, also,

"*Resolved unanimously*, That we encourage the formation of Sabbath-schools, at all our houses of worship." And, at the same session, B. M. Sanders preached the missionary sermon, after which a collection, of $75.31¼, was taken up.

In 1829, the same Association resolved, "That we consider it a matter of gratitude to God, that He disposes the churches in our bounds to sustain the cause of missions and education with increased energy," and it was agreed that "The members and friends of this body, for themselves and friends, become obligated to raise three thousand dollars, (including one share of $250.00 which has been subscribed by a benevolent lady in Augusta,) in favor of the Columbian College."

To the Sarepta Association five hundred and nine baptisms were reported in 1828, and, by it, the fourth of July was appointed as a day of thanksgiving. In 1829, the same day was again appointed as a day of thanksgiving; all heads of families, in Baptist churches, were recommended to have daily family worship; and several brethren were appointed, as missionaries, to visit destitute neighborhoods, during the ensuing year and preach the gospel. The churches were recommended to make the sale of ardent spirits and the frequenting of tippling shops a "matter of dealing," and, for the first time, the churches were recommended to send up contributions in aid of missions. It was resolved to take up a collection, at each annual meeting, for the same purpose; and the first public collection for missions the ensuing year amounted to $50.46. At this session the Sarepta Association for the first time committed itself decidedly as favorable to the cause of foreign missions, several contributions being for the Burman mission.

During the years 1827, 1828 and 1829, the Sunbury Association continued its associational missions, strongly encouraged the cause of missions and Sunday-schools, and greatly deplored the evils of intemperance, recording it as the "standing vote" of the body, that, considering the demoralizing effects arising from the intemperate use of ardent spirits: "*Resolved*, That we feel it a duty to use our exertions, by every means, to suppress this great and growing evil." In its Corresponding Letter for 1829, this Association affirms that "the exhibitions of Divine Mercy towards our churches have not been as remarkable as are experienced in some favored sections of our country." Its Letter for 1830, laments "additional and deplorable evidence that the churches are in a state of spiritual declension."

But a brief summary of the general religious condition of the denomination for the year 1830, is found in the Minutes of the State Convention for that year:

"In the Georgia Association 708 were baptized during the last associational year, and there is cause of gratitude that there is so much attention to family religion and other Christian duties, and so few departures from the standard of our Saviour. In this Association are twenty-eight Sabbath schools, containing more than 1,000 pupils; ten tract and nine temperance societies, besides other benevolent institutions. The churches are redoubling their exertions in the cause of missions and ministerial education. Seven hundred dollars were contributed for these objects, at the last annual meeting, and nearly $3,000 were subscribed for Columbian College. Here we see works and faith consistently operating together; the churches evince by their conduct that they are in earnest when they pray for more laborers to be sent into the harvest, and for a wider extension of the Redeemer's kingdom.

"With regard to the Sarepta, Tugalo and Chattahoochee Associations, the accounts are somewhat favorable, especially as respects the first named. In that Association 394 were baptized during the last year, and in its bounds are seven temperance societies, eight tract societies and nine Sabbath schools. Many of the ministers have caught the spirit of domestic missions; and that of foreign missions is also gaining ground. In the Tugalo Association 255 were baptized, and in the Chattahoochee 124. There are no benevolent societies in either of these two last-named Associations; but the cause of missions is advancing. In the Ebenezer Association there has been considerable attention to religion, especially in the church at Rocky Creek. The views of many of the ministers in this body have been turned favorably towards the Convention. Opposition among lay members is giving way. Several Sabbath schools and temperance societies are in existence.

"We regret to learn that in the Ocmulgee and Flint River Associations there are divisions and contentions; and religion, of course, is at a low ebb."

The Executive Committee, at the session of April, 1830, reported four State missionaries employed, who had performed much useful labor. Several churches were reported as sustaining beneficiaries with a view to the ministry; and the Convention itself, through its Executive Committee, had sustained three, among them J. H. Campbell, who, the Executive Committe says, "has been, under the direction of the Clerk (Adiel Sherwood), pursuing his studies, conducting a Sabbath school and Bible class, and preaching statedly in Eatonton and Greenesboro. The people of the former place have strongly solicited his residence among them, and promise his support. The Committee recommend that he remain, and still be directed in his studies by the Clerk. Brother Thomas Cooper, who had boarded him last year, made no charge. The Committee voted him forty dollars."

It is pleasant to record that after more than half a century of ardent ministerial labor this beloved brother still lingers on the confines of Time, and still as ardently continues to do faithful and useful work as a minister of Jesus; while the "Clerk," too, lingered on earth for a half century, beholding with joy and gratitude the wonderful growth of the denomination he aided so much in years long gone by.

In the year 1829 there were sixteen Associations, three hundred and fifty-six churches, about two hundred ministers and twenty-eight thousand two hundred and sixty-eight members.

In the year 1831, there were seventeen Baptist Associations in Georgia, namely, the Columbus, Ebenezer, Flint River, Georgia, Hephzibah, Houston, Piedmont,

Sarepta, Tugalo, Washington, Western, Chattahoochee, Canoochee, Echaconee, Oclochonee, Ocmulgee and Yellow River. In these Associations, there were five hundred and six churches, two hundred and seventy-one ministers, and thirty-seven thousand four hundred and ninety members. In that year the number of baptisms reported to these Associations was three thousand one hundred and forty-seven. These figures are taken from THE CHRISTIAN INDEX of March 17th, 1832, and the editor extracts them from the Baptist Tract Magazine, and says they were prepared by Rev. I. M. Allen, agent, with great labor and care. The table appears to quote the upper and lower Canoochee as one Association.

In 1835 we find four more Associations formed, namely, the Appalachee, the Arbacoochee, the Chastatee and Lawrenceville, thus making a total of twenty-one Associations, with five hundred and eighty-three churches, two hundred and ninety-eight ministers, forty-one thousand eight hundred and ten members. The growth of the denomination, therefore, from 1824 to 1835 may be thus discerned:

	CHURCHES.	MEMBERS.	MINISTERS.	ASSOCIAT'S.
1824	264	18,108	145	10
1829	356	28,268	200	16
1831	506	37,490	271	17
1835	583	41,810	298	21

The remarkable fact becomes apparent, here, that from 1827 to 1831, inclusive, the additions to the churches averaged, at least five thousand annually; while the annual average of the additions for the four years succeeding 1831, was but little over one thousand. This gives us a hint of the spirit of strife and dissension that was raging during those years.

In 1830 the Ocmulgee, while holding its session at Harmony church near Eatonton, withdrew from the State Convention, and, although the Sunbury Association never severed its connection with the body, yet so seldom did its delegates attend that, for half a dozen years, delegates appeared from the Georgia Association only, as a constituent. The Convention was composed of delegates from the Georgia Association and about fifteen auxiliary societies. Messengers appeared, however, occasionally from a few of the Associations, not connected with the body. In 1835 the Georgia Association contained forty-eight churches and six thousand communicants, about one-third of whom were colored.

In 1835 the Central became connected with the Convention, and in 1836 the Sarepta united. For a year or two more auxiliary societies continued to unite with the Convention; but when, in 1838, the Appalachee and Hephzibah joined, followed by the Columbus and Rehoboth in 1839, and the Washington in 1840, the auxiliaries ceased to send delegates, for in rapid succession the Flint River, Western, Bethel and other Associations joined the Convention and the auxiliary societies became extinct.

The state of religion in the Baptist churches of the State from 1830 to 1836, was deplorable. It was a time of chaos and confusion; of bitter animosity and dissension, and of course religion was at a very low ebb in most parts of the State. In the Circular Letter of the Convention, written in 1831, Jesse Mercer himself says: ' That the standard of Christian morality is deplorably low among the ministry and churches of our denomination, is too obvious to be concealed.

"Are there not many professors among us whose spirit, life and conversation illy become the gospel of Christ—worldly in their views and mercenary in all they do, so that if they were not seen in the church meeting, or at the Lord's table, they could not be told from mere worldlings? And yet do they not go unreproved?

"Are there not many who, to the entire neglect of all family religion, seldom attend church meeting, and habitually live irreverently, if not immorally? And are they not suffered to go undisciplined?

"And others there are, who, in the plainest sense, are drunkards, and though no drunkard hath any place in the Kingdom of God and Christ, yet do they not, by some means—by feigned repentance or empty and vain resolves—continue from youth to old age in the church, frequently, if not habitually, drunk? And are there not many such cases?

"And more: is it not common that *mere* negative goodness is all that is requisite to constitute a member *in good standing*, and to recommend him, *as such*, to a sister church?

"And, moreover, is there not evidently a want of union and concert among both ministers and churches of our denomination?

"Have not instances occurred in which some churches have disciplined their members for what others have winked at, or even commended, in theirs? And have not censured, and even excluded members of some, been received and nurtured by other churches? And have not ministers gotten into heated and hurtful controversies with one another, breathing towards each other the most crude asperities and cruel animosities? And is it not true that one has preached what another, in and to the same congregation, has contradicted and exposed as unsound and dangerous, by which questions which engender strife have abounded? And has not all this passed off, too, without any effort to correct the evil or reconcile these inconsiderate brethren?"

Mr. Mercer then proceeds to inquire into the causes of these afflictions, and he comprehends their causes mostly, if not altogether, in the three following particulars:

1. A want of carefulness in the admission of members.
2. The want of a close and godly discipline.
3. An inefficient ministry.

Dr. C. D. Mallary, in his life of Jesse Mercer, presents the following sombre view of the state of affairs which prevailed in our churches during the fourth decade of the century:

"A disposition on the part of some of the Associations to interfere, in what was considered an arbitrary and unscriptural manner, with the affairs of the churches, was one of the most fruitful sources of the many distressing evils which so long afflicted the Baptists of Georgia. The encroachments of Associations were met with prompt resistance on the part of many of the churches, mingled oftentimes, no doubt, with a spirit not the most lovely and conciliating. This, in some instances, was followed by attempts on the part of the Associations to justify their previous course, and by further acts, which the churches deemed an unwarrantable interference with their rights. The result of these proceedings was, that some of the churches withdrew from the Associations, and some were withdrawn from, whilst others were sadly divided among themselves and rent into fragments. In many cases associational correspondence was laid aside, ministerial friendship and intercourse were entirely suspended, and the communion and fellowship of the churches broken. Bitter jealousies, evil surmisings and uncharitable accusations were multiplied, whilst the occasional attempts which were made to bring about a more desirable state of things seemed for a time only to aggravate the disorders they were intended to cure.

"In the meantime the anti-missionary spirit, which it is supposed had been secretly operating for years, burst forth in great violence, and by its rending, non-fellowship policy, increased still further the work of strife and confusion."

There seems to be little doubt that the violent and long continued opposition to the General Association and State Convention engendered a bad state of feeling, especially in the central and western portions of the State, and more particularly in the Ocmulgee, Flint and Yellow River Associations; and this state of feeling manifested itself unpleasantly in various ways. The assumption of undue powers by some of the Associations caused a great deal of trouble and dissension. The opposition to education and missions, resulting in opposition to the Convention, was exceedingly strong and bitter. The opposition to Bible societies, tract societies and temperance societies, was bold and outspoken. Various questions pertaining to church order and doctrine were unsettled, and excited the greatest violence of speech and manner. Church discipline was lax, and ignorance and prejudice prevailed to a lamentable extent. Criminations and recriminations, which resulted in much personal ill will and bad feeling, were but too prevalent. Churches were split; Associations were divided; harsh, and sometimes unjust discipline was exercised; non-fellowship was frequently declared, and the greater part of the denomination was for years in a state of embroilment and dissension excited by feelings unbecoming true Christians.

It does indeed appear as if the great Adversary of Christianity, jealous of the prosperity of religion and of the churches during the extraordinary revival period of 1827, 1828 and 1829, sowed the tares of strife and discord among the churches, effecting a great reaction in the zeal and piety of many of the ministers and members. Practical godliness became neglected, *for the means to multiply and perpetuate the happy results of the revival were neglected;* and thus the efforts of the great Adversary were, as Dr. Mallary expresses it, "so sadly and extensively successful."

A writer to THE CHRISTIAN INDEX, then published at Philadelphia, under date of March 6th, 1832, states the case plainly and without any over-wrought coloring, and his testimony may well be admitted, as he evidently was an adherent of the anti-Convention party. He writes:

"For several years past a controversy has been carried on between us and the advocates of the Convention about the objects and exertions of that body. Upon this subject there have been criminations and recriminations. That brethren holding the same faith, and generally the same discipline, should be thus unhappily arrayed against each other, is a fact to be deplored most sincerely. It would seem that matters ought not to remain in their present situation, if it could possibly be avoided. Many efforts have been made already to remedy this evil; but hitherto they have been unavailing. And shall we be contented that matters remain in this situation? Shall our contentions drive us farther and farther asunder? Shall we stand still and behold our beloved Zion lacerated and torn by our contentions, and make no exertion to bring about a better state of things? No."

He then proceeds to state the grounds taken by both parties in the controversy, and, briefly summed up, it consists, on the part of the Convention brethren, in "a deep interest manifested in foreign and domestic missions, for the support of which they contribute and call upon the whole denomination for efficient aid. For the attainment of these ends they are pressing forward; but to succeed, they well know that an efficient ministry is indispensable. Hence they are desirous to afford to all their young brethren, not otherwise provided for, who are coming into the ministry, an opportunity to store their minds with useful information in view of the arduous work before them. The work, in their view, is great, requiring the united counsels and energies of the whole denomination."

This is a truthful and plain statement of the case: The Convention brethren favored foreign and domestic missions and ministerial education, and sought to unite the denomination in their support. Now hear the other side:

"In regard to ourselves, brethren, you know we have uniformly contended that there was no need of such an institution as the State Convention. Therefore, we have opposed it at every step of its progress. We know that many good brethren are engaged for its promotion; but we have hitherto regarded them as led on to this more from the novelty of the thing than from any positive proof of its utility. But, brethren, *we may have been all this time in the wrong;* and *some recent developments seem to favor this idea.* It is a fact which cannot be dissembled, that during the last year, whilst the Lord was pouring out His Spirit and reviving His work gloriously in many parts of His earthly vineyard, the Convention brethren were signally blessed. Look, for instance, at the Georgia Association! To many of her churches hundreds have been added, whilst the additions to our own have been very few. And, what is still more humiliating, our churches are rent asunder by party broils and dissensions. These facts ought to have their influence in settling the question as to the propriety of a Convention. *The question between Elijah and Baal's prophets was decided by fire from heaven upon Elijah's sacrifice!*"

The writer then goes on to suggest prayer for a knowledge of the truth, adding, "Perhaps in our debates on this subject we have indulged too much angry feeling. Perhaps, whilst with frowns on our countenances, we have charged upon our brethren visionary projects, *we have fought against our best interests!*"

But the clouds of discord and dissension still hung loweringly over the denomination for years.

In pursuance of its objects, the Convention went forward steadily in its missionary and educational projects. Its Minutes show liberal contributions for foreign and domestic missions, and for the establishment of Mercer Institute. In 1833 and 1834 its missionary, J. Reeves, travelled 1,600 miles in the Cherokee country; preached 162 sermons, and constituted five churches. The best ministers of the Convention persistently maintained their evangelistic efforts, and sought faithfully, travelling two and two, to counteract the prevailing lethargy, and infuse more spiritual life into the churches. It was in 1833, while a leaden lethargy was settled on the churches, that Mercer and Sherwood, in a preaching tour, came to Walnut Creek church, in Jones county, of which the venerable Edmund Talbot was then pastor. There was a large week-day congregation, and it was Sherwood's lot to preach first. Mercer followed, but was not warm in his discourse, yet there was some feeling manifested among the older members, and especially by the pastor himself. When Mercer sat down he rose to say a few words, but his feelings overpowered his utterance, and he was about to take his seat when Mr. Mercer caught hold of him by the breast of his coat, near the collar, and held him in his position, saying. "If you can't *talk*, stand and *cry!* That is the loudest kind of preaching you *can* do!" The aged man tried again, but in vain. Utterance was choked. And he did stand and weep over his congregation, but not alone, for nearly all in the house were affected to tears, and were weeping in sympathy. The preachers descended from the pulpit, when most of the church members came forward, and with tears in their eyes, asked for prayer in their behalf, in which service Mr. Mercer led, deeply affected. Those only who have heard him pray under such circumstances know how deeply his heart was stirred and how humble and impassioned were his petitions; he was the importunate beggar at the footstool of mercy; and there were few present who did not partake of his spirit. "If I were about to die," said a worldly man, "my first and last request would be for Jesse Mercer to pray for me."

In 1833 there was a revival in progress in Milledgeville. At one of the meetings a brother King, who lived in the neighborhood, was called on to pray. He was a most excellent man and a great admirer of Jesse Mercer, and when he knelt in tears, perceiving the deep feeling that pervaded the assembly, he began thus: "Lord, we don't want to make a big Jesse Mercer prayer, but a little cornfield prayer," etc., alluding to the prayers negroes sometimes make, while at work in the cornfield.

The men who now walked the stage of action and controlled the destinies of our denomination in Georgia were not the men to put their hands to the plough and then look back. They were men who knew the duties incumbent upon Christians and who appreciated the advantages of education; the necessity and duty of missions and temperance; and they were determined to "go forward." They were Jesse Mercer, A. Sherwood, C. D. Mallary, Thomas Stocks, B. M. Sanders, J. H. T. Kilpatrick, John E. Dawson, S. G. Hillyer, J. H. Campbell, H. Posey, V. R. Thornton, A. T. Holmes, James Carter, J. Reeves, Jacob King, Isaiah Langley, Francis Callaway, Reuben Thornton, George Granberry, W. H. Stokes, James Davis, Thomas Cooper, James Perryman, J. Lumpkin, Asa Chandler, W. Conner, W. R. Wellborn.

At the same time they were men to do what was right and to act justly. In compliance with the desires of some—desires, excited either by apprehensions or prejudices—they, by the following action amended the Constitution of the Convention, in 1835, so that in articles 5, 10 and 11, there might appear no semblance of control over the churches, nor any right or power to infringe upon their sovereignty and independence:

"WHEREAS, It has been argued that this Convention, by a construction of her Constitution, may assume an absolute control over the churches and, thereby, infringe on, or even destroy, their rights, independence and sovereignty; therefore,

"*Resolved*, That this Convention disclaims all power by which she can exercise any dominion over the Faith, or control the Discipline of the churches, or in anywise coerce them to do, or contribute, anything whatsoever, contrary to their own sense of propriety and duty."

Still, feelings of estrangement and disagreement prevailed to a lamentable extent in the denomination, and the hearts of many good brethren were pained by this sad state of affairs. At length, on the 28th of April, 1836, the following appeared in THE CHRISTIAN INDEX, then published in Washington, Georgia, and edited by Rev. Jesse Mercer and Wm. H. Stokes:

To the Baptist Ministers in the State of Georgia:

DEAR BRETHREN—The divided condition of our denomination, in various parts of the State, is a matter of deep lamentation to all who delight in the prosperity of Zion. There are many neighborhoods where ministers and churches have no fellowship, and no pleasant Christian intercourse No Christian, certainly no Christian minister, can contemplate these divisions with any other feelings than those of anxiety and grief. It is an object for which all should fervently pray, that the breaches which have been made should be effectually healed, and that those who are agreed in the observance of one important and distinctive ordinance of religion, should be united together in faith and labors of love.

Several propositions for this purpose, have been submitted to our consideration, but no serious and united effort has been made to carry them into effect. Many have expressed a wish that there might be a meeting of the Baptist ministers, from all the Associations in the State, for the purpose of praying and consulting together, with reference to the divided state of our denomination. Such a meeting, conducted with prudence and in the spirit of Christian affection, would, no doubt, lead to the most happy results. With God's blessing it might be the means of binding together in lasting fellowship the hearts of many of God's dear children, who have been too long estranged from each other, and of ushering in a brighter day upon the churches in Georgia. Deeply impressed with the importance of the subject, and anxious to be instrumental in promoting, in some humble measure, the cause of righteousness and *peace*, we, whose names are hereunto affixed, have agreed to unite in earnestly requesting our ministering brethren to attend such a meeting. The meeting will be held at Forsyth, Monroe county, commencing on Thursday before the second Lord's day in July next. The brethren in that place are desirous that we should assemble there and share their hospitalities. You are, therefore, dear brethren, affectionately invited to attend the meeting at the time and place above specified.

What particular points will be proposed for discussion, or what shape will be given to the meeting, we cannot tell; but *union—union on Christian principles*, is what we need, for which we trust all who assemble will be willing to labor in the spirit of the gospel. We hope you will accept of this invitation, and appear on the day named, and that you will request your churches to pray now and during the continuance of the meeting, that we may be guided by the Holy Spirit; that our interview may be pleasant and profitable; and that it may be the occasion of producing fraternal feeling for one another and union amongst the churches, of reviving religion in all our Zion and of bringing glory to God. Should these be the blessed results, you will not regret the time and trouble of your journey, nor the inconvenience which may attend the absence from your families. May the Lord incline you to enlist as peace-makers in the momentous matter and give you the peace-maker's blessing as your reward.

N. B. As it would seem probable that a considerable portion of the first day of the meeting would be spent in special prayer for the direction of the Holy Spirit, we would venture to request that all the Baptist churches in the State would assemble on that day (namely, Thursday before the second Lord's day in July), and unite in prayer for a blessing upon the meeting, and for a general and powerful revival of religion. It would also be desirable that they should connect fasting with prayer, on that day.

Signed: JESSE MERCER, *Georgia Association;* REUBEN THORNTON, *Sarepta Association;* RICHARD PACE, *Ocmulgee Association;* C. A. THARP, *Ebenezer Association;* ISAIAH LANGLEY, *Flint River Association;* EDWIN DYER, *Yellow River Association;* HUMPHREY POSEY, *Tugalo Association;* J. P. LEVERITT, *Washington Association;* JACOB KING, *Itcheconnaugh Association;* C. D. MALLARY, *Central Association;* OBADIAH ECHOLS, *Monticello church.*

On the appointed day a large number of ministers appeared as the advocates of peace, and more than fifty associated themselves together, in alliance, for its promotion. Matters of great moment were under consideration, and questions were discussed which were well calculated to produce fearful distraction, had not the Spirit of the Lord been present. Brethren met upon ground heretofore considered almost forbidden, and found, to their mutual joy, that they were heirs to the same promise, subjects of the same faith, and children of the same heavenly Father; and they became willing to bury all animosities.

From THE INDEX of July 28th, 1836, the proceedings of the meeting are copied as a matter of denominational history:

"1. Pursuant to public notice, a large number of Baptist ministers met at Forsyth, Monroe county, Georgia, on the 7th of July, 1836, for the purpose of endeavoring to heal the unhappy difficulties which have existed for some years in the denomination. The morning was spent in prayer by those brethren who arrived in season, and at half past eleven o'clock, at the request of those assembled, brother Jesse Mercer preached from Canticles ii, 15.

"2. At 2 o'clock P.M., the meeting was organized by calling brother Mercer to the chair, and appointing brother I. Langly, clerk, *pro tempore.* The names of the following ministers were enrolled: Jesse Mercer, Wilson Conner, Jonathan Nichols, Humphrey Posey, James Steely, John Ross, Benjamin Bussey, John Milner, Joseph R. Hand, Jonathan Davis, Isaiah Langly, C. D. Mallary, Green B. Waldrop, Davis Smith, Joseph Chipman, Richard Pace, Henry Collins, Francis Callaway, A. T. Holmes, William A. Callaway, J. H. Campbell, George Granberry, Benjamin Roberts, John R. Humphrey, Isaac E. Deavers, Andrew Cumbie, V. R. Thornton, Reuben Thornton, Gideon Leverett, William Henderson, James Reeves, Jacob King, Allison Culpepper, Zed. R. Gordon, James Perryman, Obadiah Echols, James Carter, William R. Wellborn, John W. Cooper, William Maund, George B. Davis, James Davis, Charnick A. Tharp, Ephraim Strickland, Adiel Sherwood, S. G. Hillyer, John Reeves, Jeremiah Reeves, William Byars, Albert G. Beckham, Allen Morris, Jesse H. Davis, Robert Burt.

"*Licentiates*—Thomas Wilkes, Isaac Asteen, John Hughes, William Ross, Edward Parks, Abisha Horn, T. B. Slade, Charles Stillwell, William Tryon.

"Jesse Mercer was chosen Moderator, and Adiel Sherwood, Clerk.

"A letter was handed in from Little River, Morgan county, by brother Parnell, expressive of the approbation of that church in the design of our meeting, and bespeaking for it the blessing of God.

"4. On motion, all the lay brethren present were invited to take part in the deliberations of the body. Ministers of all orders, and those not residing in the state, were also invited. Brother Richards, of Baltimore, and Rev. Mr. Patterson took a seat. Voting to be confined to the ministers.

"Brother J. Davis moved that a committee of seven be appointed to arrange the business suitable to come before the meeting, and brethren J. Davis, Mallary, R. Thornton, Ross, Posey and Pace, were appointed.

"6. Committee on Preaching: Brethren Langly, Stevens, Sandford, Beall and Edward Callaway.

"7. Agreed to hold our deliberations in the Presbyterian meeting-house, which is kindly offered, so that preaching may go on in the Baptist.

"8. On motion of brother James Ross, brother James Carter and E. Beall were added to the Committee on Business; afterwards the Moderator was added.

Agreed to adjourn *business* and spend the remainder of the afternoon in devotional exercises. Adjourned to 9 o'clock Friday morning.

"9. Friday morning, brother John Milner was excused in order to attend a general meeting in his own neighborhood.

"10. Agreed to observe the ordinary rules of decorum, for government in our deliberations.

"11. Brother J. Davis, from the Committee on Business, read their report in part, and asked farther time to complete it; on its reception, brother Nichols objected to some parts, and begged to withdraw his name as one of the meeting. Provision had been made for such cases at the commencement of the meeting.

"*Report on Business.*—The Committee on the Arrangement of Business beg leave to report in part, and ask permission of the body to sit again for the consideration of other matters not embraced in this report, which they deem important to bring to the view of this meeting.

"The Committee recommend to the meeting the adoption of the following agreement:

"Agreed, that we, as a convention of ministers, utterly disclaim any intention to dictate to one another, or to the Associations and churches, but that we aim at nothing more than, by friendly intercourse, and consultation, to encourage fellowship and union.

"The Committee recommend to the meeting the consideration of the following queries:

"1. Do we, as a body, on doctrinal points, hold those sentiments which have characterized orthodox Baptist churches from time immemorial, and particularly as embodied and set forth in the Articles of Faith adopted by the Georgia, Flint River, Ocmulgee and Yellow River Associations?

"2. Is not a church, constituted on gospel principles, an independent body in regard to its government, and not subject to any authority but that of Christ the Great Head of the Church?

"3. Have Associations executive or disciplinary power?

"4. Or are they merely advisory councils, without authority to enforce their advice?

"5. Does the mere secession of a church from an Association affect its character as an orderly body?

"6. What are the circumstances connected with the secession of a church from an Association which impair the standing of that church?

"7. What circumstances connected with the withdrawment of an Association from a church impair the standing of that church?

"8. Under what circumstances may a minority of a church be justified in withdrawing or separating from the majority?

"9. Is it the sense of this meeting that differences of opinion in the missionary and such like operations should affect the fellowship of brethren or churches?

"10. When a church or churches have seceded from an Association, and produced by such secession a division of the church or churches, in what manner consistent with good order and discipline can a union be had?

"11. Is it, in the opinion of this meeting, right to re-baptize any person who has been baptized on a profession of faith, by a Baptist minister who is held orderly in the estimation of the church to which he belongs?

"12. Is it the sense of this meeting that the correspondence of Associations should cease on account of difference of opinion between them until all proper means have been exhausted to remove it?

"13. Is it the opinion of this meeting, that Baptist churches should close their doors against ministers without evidence of their unsoundness in faith or immorality in practice?

"14. Will this meeting appoint a committee to whom they will confide the business of drawing up a Circular Address of a conciliatory character to the denomination in the State, to be reported to this body for its approval?

"*Propositions.*—1. Whereas, it frequently happens that rumors unfavorable to the character and standing of ministers, churches and private Christians, are circulated, and a disposition to believe and encourage these reports, without sufficient evidence of their truth, is calculated in a very serious degree to originate distance, alienation and strife, and to perpetuate those evils wherever they exist; therefore, we agree, as far as in us lies, to discountenance in ourselves and others, a spirit of evil surmisings, and evil speaking, and to encourage amongst all those with whom we have intercourse, that charity 'which is kind, is not easily provoked, thinketh no evil, hopeth all things.'

"2. Inasmuch as the unhappy divisions which exist amongst us, must be attributed in a great degree to the low state of vital godliness, and believing that one of the most effectual remedies for all our difficulties is to be found in a more elevated standard of piety, we do therefore, agree in humble reliance upon divine aid, to aim at greater attainments in holiness ourselves, and to embrace all favorable opportunities for urging the subject on the minds of our brethren.

"3. Whereas, difficulties of a long standing and of a complicated character, have disturbed the harmony of brethren and churches, and such difficulties as it would be impossible to adjust, by a minute investigation of every particular, it is the sense of this meeting that we and our brethren generally throughout the state, should, as far as possible, endeavor to forget all past afflictions, to make all those sacrifices for the sake of peace which are consistent with gospel principle, and strive by friendly and Christian intercourse, by mutual confession, forbearance and forgiveness to restore harmony to our denomination.

"4. Whereas, in matters of difficulty and difference, Christians are liable to indulge an improper spirit, and to employ harsh and unchristian-like expressions, to the injury of the cause of Christ and grief of the brethren; therefore, if in time past. we have in conversation, writing, or preaching, evinced an improper spirit, or employed unchristian expressions, we do most sincerely regret it, and ask forgiveness of one another and of God, and do most sincerely pray that we may be enabled by God's grace, in all our future discussions, to exercise the utmost prudence and caution, and exhibit to none any just cause of offence.

"12. The first article was adopted unanimously without discussion. On the first query, after reading one of the Articles named, a general expression of approbation was given by almost every member present, except some few belonging to the United Association, who dissented. Then each name was called separately, whether the doctrines of the Confession were heartily believed, and all answered *Yes*. The members of the United Association handed in their answer afterwards.

"The second query was answered unanimously in the affirmative.

"The third unanimously, No; that is, Associations have no disciplinary power.

"The fourth unanimously, that Associations are mere advisory councils.

"The fifth, No, unanimously.

"The sixth answer: Those circumstances which clearly prove unsoundness in faith, or immorality in practice, the sister churches being judge.

"The seventh: When the withdrawal is for unsoundness in faith or immorality in practice, the churches being judges.

"13. The eighth and ninth queries, after some discussion, were laid over till morning.

"14. Saturday morning. The Committee presented the balance of their report on business. Accepted.

"15. The eighth query was taken up and postponed indefinitely.

"The ninth was answered unanimously, No.

"16. The members from the United Association handed in their answer in writing, touching the Articles of Faith: 'Nothing in the Articles of Faith alluded to, presents any difficulty, except a part of the fourth Article, and some connexion with it in the sixth,' signed E. Strickland, John Reeves, Andrew Cumbie, William Byars.

"From this it is seen clearly that they do not agree with us in faith. The fourth and sixth Articles alluded to, are those in our Articles touching election and effectual calling.

"17. The eighth query was, by vote, dropped from our list of queries, because there was considerable difference of opinion, and time would not allow longer discussion.

"18. The tenth query was thus answered; By humble confession of faults of all parties; by fervent prayer, a forbearing spirit, friendly intercourse and abhorrence of *big self.*

"19. The eleventh was dropped for want of time to discuss the subject fully; most who spoke, however, were for answering it No.

"20. The twelfth was answered No, by all except two.

"The thirteenth, unanimously, No.

"The fourteenth, Yes; and brethren Mallary, Sherwood, J. Davis, V. R. Thornton, and Holmes, the committee.

"The Address was read afterwards and adopted.

"21. The *Propositions* were all adopted unanimously. After the adoption of the fourth and last, most of the ministers present made acknowledgement of faults, and begged of each other forgiveness, which was mutually granted. It was a sight on which angels could not but look with peculiar delight, to see those who, for years, had been cold and distant, who had thought and spoken hard things against their brethren, and even cast out their names as evil, acknowledging their errors with tears, and begging pardon, The readiness with which it was granted melted all in the house. Every eye was wet and every heart *full.* The feelings of that hour more than compensated for all the toils and difficulties of attending the meeting. All seemed to feel, 'I'm glad I came.'

"22. Voted that 4,000 copies of the proceedings be printed under the superintendence of the Moderator; and that the editors of THE INDEX, *Primitive Baptist,* and *Signs of the Times,* be requested to give them an insertion in their respective papers.

"The hymn, 'Blest be the tie that binds,' was sung 'with the spirit and the understanding,' while all gave the parting hand, and brother Posey closed with prayer.

"Preaching was kept up during the meeting, though the interest in our deliberations was so strong that the congregations at the Baptist meeting-house were small except at night—all desired to hear the discussions. Scarcely an unkind word escaped any lip; the solicitude for *peace* absorbed every mind.

"24. On Sabbath morning assembled, heard and adopted the Address.

"25. Agreed to recommend a similar meeting of ministers to commence on Saturday before the fifth Sabbath in October next.

"26. Agreed that said meeting convene either in Morgan, Walton, Henry or Newton county, to be determined by a committee consisting of brethren Mercer, V. R. Thornton and J. Davis. The churches in those counties which desire it will please apply to brother Mercer, Washington, Georgia.

"After a hymn and address by the Moderator, the meeting was dissolved.

"JESSE MERCER, *Moderator.*
"ADIEL SHERWOOD, *Clerk.*

"Brethren Sherwood, Mercer, Mallary and Posey preached on the Sabbath in the Baptist meeting-house, and brethren J. Davis and Conner in the Presbyterian. Saints were evidently comforted, and many sinners alarmed."

The following communications, from some of the few survivors of this meeting, and written at the request of the author, will be read with deep interest;

From Dr. S. G. Hillyer:

This meeting was called by an article in THE CHRISTIAN INDEX, at that time edited by Dr. Mercer, at Washington, Georgia. The call was made, I think, by brother J. H. Campbell. The design of the meeting was, if possible, to bring about a better understanding between the discordant sections of the Baptist denomination. There were then three parties among us. First, those who were in favor of what were called the "benevolent institutions of the day," viz: Missions, Sabbath-schools and temperance societies; secondly, those who were opposed to these institutions, and thirdly, a party of Baptists calling themselves "United Brethren." These last, as far as I now remember, occupied rather neutral ground as to the benevolent institutions aforesaid, but signalized themselves as opposed to what they considered extreme views on the subject of Calvinism.

Out of these dissensions had risen much controversy, accompanied with much bitterness of spirit. The evil was wide-spread, and great injury to our denomination was the result. It was hoped that, by getting the representative men of all parties together in one fraternal conclave, and by kindly talking over their differences in a spirit of candor and courtesy, much good might be done.

Well, the meeting was held. I do not know how many ministers were present, but it was an imposing assembly. I recall the names of brethren Mercer, Mallary, Sherwood, Echols, Bussey, Jonathan and James Davis, Tharp (father of our brother B. F. Tharp), Holmes and J. H. Campbell.

The meeting was organized by electing brother Mercer Moderator, and, I think, brother Sherwood, Clerk. After some of the older brethren had indulged in a sort of informal discussion of the design of the meeting, and of the best method to secure that design, a committee was appointed to draw up a Confession of Faith, in order that we might test the views of the brethren present upon our denominational differences, hoping thereby to develop the harmony of our faith, and thus to remove the charge of alleged departures from the faith which had been, more or less, urged against the Missionary Baptists by their opponents.

Either the same committee or another, I do not remember which, was instructed to draft resolutions which should give the views of the body as to the proper course to be pursued by all our people towards one another, in order to allay animosity and to restore good will and fraternal feeling. I do not remember which report was taken up first, but both were, in due time, presented.

The confession of faith reported was, substantially, the confession of the Georgia Association. It underwent considerable discussion. The design was to allow a free and full expression of views. The discussion was very interesting. After many brethren had spoken, a motion was made asking the Moderator to favor the Convention with his views, especially upon that portion of the confession which refers to the doctrines of election and predestination. Having called upon some brother to occupy the chair, he took his stand in the aisle, about midway the house, and delivered an elaborate and characteristic address. I wish I could report it. I was young then, knew nothing about theology, and was eager to hear that great man on these profound subjects. I confess my own mind had not been clear in regard to them. Indeed, I had been greatly perplexed. But as Dr. Mercer proceeded to unfold God's sovereignty, man's depravity and utter helplessness, his need of divine assistance to exercise repentance and faith, I was enabled to see the subject in a *new light*. While I cannot remember all his topics, or the order in which he presented them, yet the impression made on my mind was abiding. One sentence I distinctly recall. It was at the conclusion of one of his most powerful paragraphs. If I remember right, he had been speaking of God's *electing love.* Just as he reached his conclusion, pausing for a moment, he suddenly exclaimed, "*This is the ground of all my hope!*"

As he spoke, tears rolled down his venerable cheeks. The effect upon the audience was subduing. Evidently his meaning was just this: Jesse Mercer would not have been saved if God had not called him with a holy calling, according to his eternal purpose and grace, given him in Christ Jesus before the world was. I could not fail to see that if this was true of Jesse Mercer, *a fortiori* it was true of me and of everybody else. I have had no trouble about the doctrine of election since that day.

But the brother's argument afforded me relief upon another point. I had been grievously perplexed with the fascinations and subtleties of Campbellism. I had read extensively the pages of the *Millenial Harbinger*, and in my inexperience I was bewildered with its reasonings. But to my mind brother Mercer's argument broke down completely the fundamental doctrine of Campbellism, *viz*: that the Holy Spirit is not needed to bring a sinner to Christ. I saw, I think, very clearly, that the condition of the sinner, in his depravity, is utterly helpless; if he is ever saved, it must be by a power other than his own—*i. e.* by the Holy Spirit. Thus, on this point also, my mind was greatly relieved. That noble exposition of our doctrines convinced me that the denomination had not overestimated the ability of the great and good man who delivered it.

It is hardly nenessary to add, that the Confession of Faith which had called forth the discussion was adopted.

The other report to which I alluded was very interesting. I cannot recall much of it at this distant day, but its design was eminently conciliatory. It deplored, if I remember right, the hard feelings and harsh words which had marred the peace of our Zion. It recommended a more Christian spirit towards opponents. One of its items, especially, recommended that brethren should be willing, if conscious of having indulged towards any one improper words or feelings, to make, as far as they had the opportunity, the *amende honorable*. When this item was adopted, I remember brother Sherwood rose in his place and said :

"Brother Moderator, I feel like acting at once on this suggestion. I have before me a brother of whom I have had harsh thoughts. I wish to acknowledge my fault. Brother Echols! I have sometimes thought hard of you, and perhaps I have said about you more than was right. I now ask your forgiveness, and offer you my hand as a token of Christian fellowship and love!"

Brother Echols was taken by surprise. But he promptly rose, and accepted in suitable terms the proffered overture; and, as the brethren shook hands across the Secretary's table, deep emotion pervaded the house. Old brother Tharp gave vent to his feelings by exclaiming, in audible words, "I am glad I came!" Other brethren followed Sherwood's example, and, I trust, many unkind feelings were then and there buried.

It was at that meeting that I first saw brother C. D. Mallary. He impressed me most favorably. He was then in the vigor of his early but fully matured manhood. Thr closing service of the occasion was a sermon from this gifted and beloved brother. His text was: "Ye seek Jesus which was crucified. He is not here; for he is risen, as he said. Come, see the place where the Lord lay." (Matthew, 28: 5, 6.) The design of the discourse was to show how fundamental is the resurrection of Christ in the Christian system. And ably did he show it.

Thus closed the ministers' meeting at Forsyth. Nearly forty-five years have passed away. So far as I know, two only of the ministers who were then present are now living—brother J. H. Campbell and myself—and we are on the banks of the Jordan. We will soon go over; but, thank God, we shall leave the glorious cause in the hands of the Master.

From Dr. J. H. Campbell:

For several years, there had been much controversy and strife among the Baptists on missions, ministerial education, Sunday Schools, temperance and kindred subjects. Churches had been split asunder, associations divided, and a general want of confidence prevailed. Many worthy brethren were perplexed, and knew not where to go nor what to do. The Missionary Baptists were suspected and accused of heresy, a departure from the faith, Arminianism and of designing to destroy the independence of the churches. Such was the state of things at the commencement of the year 1836. The writer was convinced that the best and only way to remedy these evils was for the ministers of the denomination to hold a meeting, and endeavor to come to a better understanding. Having fully matured the matter in his own mind, he submitted it in writing to several of his brethren—Sherwood, Mallary and others. An extra session of the Central Association was to be held at Antioch church, Morgan county, in March, 1836. It would afford a good opportunity to submit the question to the brethren. But the condition of his family seemed to forbid his leaving home. The night preceding the meeting, he was anxious and restless for fear his plan for calling a ministers' meeting, which he had sent to the brethren at the Association, would neither be understood nor adopted. His wife, having inquired into the cause of his anxiety, insisted he should go. Mounting his horse, at daylight, he rode forty miles by two o'clock p. m., got a number of brethren together at Lot Hearn's—Sherwood, Mallary, Dawson, Thomas Cooper, Mark A. Cooper, etc., laid the matter before them, and had the satisfaction to see his views fully endorsed and adopted. A committee was appointed, with Mallary as chairman, to correspond with brethren, especially with the Moderators of Associations, on the subject of the divisions and strifes prevailing among us, and to get them (or a sufficient number of them), to unite in an invitation to the ministers in the State to hold a meeting with a view to the restoration of harmony and peace. (It was insisted that the writer, as the originator of the project, should be one of that committee. But he declined, and insisted that his name should not be known in the movement, feeling assured that his very name would excite prejudice against it. Though young, circumstances had brought him into frequent and fierce conflicts with the anti-missionaries, for which they had not forgiven him). Jesse Mercer, then owner and editor of THE CHRISTIAN INDEX, entered heartily into the movement, an invitation, numerously signed, was soon published in THE INDEX, and was circulated otherwise, and Forsyth was fixed upon as the place.

"When the time arrived, Mallary came to my house, at Clinton, Jones county, and spent a night with me, and we went on to Forsyth together. His object was to refresh his mind as to *the plan* which I thought ought to be adopted in the conduct of the meeting. What number of ministers was present I do not now remember, but I think there were fifty or sixty. The most prominent among the Hardshells—Henderson, Moseley, Colley and others—were not there; but the number and standing of those who composed the meeting were such as to give their deliberations great weight. Of course Jesse Mercer was elected Moderator. I think Sherwood was clerk. Mallary was chairman of the committee on business, and reported substantially *the plan* I had submitted to him: 1. To agree on a Confession of Faith. 2. To declare that difference of opinion about missions, Sunday-schools, Bible societies and other 'benevolent institutions,' should not be a ground of non-fellowship; and 3. That the independence of the churches should never be infringed. The report recommended that as the Georgia Association was the oldest in the State, her Articles of Faith should be used on the occasion, and that the members of the meeting should, each for himself, subscribe to the same. Every minister present had his name attached to the Confession above named accordingly. Resolutions were adopted in accordance with the recommendation of the committee on business, and mutual confidence and brotherly love prevailed in the meeting. The effect throughout the State was magical, and from that day until now the great mass of the denomination have striven together as one man for the faith of the gospel, thus securing for Baptist principles a greater triumph in Georgia than in any other country on earth."

From Rev. T. B. Slade:

"It gives me pleasure to respond to your request concerning the Forsyth meeting of 1836. But I do not think anything can be added by my recollections of which you are not already in possession.

"I think the meeting was held in the Methodist church, near the railroad. Though there were a great number of ministers present, I have a distinct recollection only of Jesse Mercer, Vincent Thornton, Jonathan Davis and Granby Hillyer.

"I remember that Mr. Mercer was Moderator; and that he, Mr. Davis and Mr. Thornton, figured as speakers, and that the meeting was occasioned by an unhappy feeling among some of our denomination. Arminian sentiments were gaining ground, contrary to our Calvinistic opinions. No doubt this assemblage of ministers was productive of good, as it led to a better understanding among the brethren."

The second Ministers' Conference was held at Covington, Newton county, October 29th, 30th and 31st, of the same year. It was attended by many very prominent brethren, and was a very important and useful gathering, as may be discovered from the proceedings, taken from THE CHRISTIAN INDEX of that date:

"1. Agreeably to a recommendation of the first Ministers' Meeting, held at Forsyth, Monroe county, in July last, the following ministers named met at Covington, and organized a second meeting:

"Jesse Mercer, Humphrey Posey, Henry Hardin, Adiel Sherwood, C. D.

Mallary, B. M. Sanders, Jeremiah Reeves, James Reeves, Richard Philips, Allen Morris, Joel Colley, Jonathan Davis, A. T. Holmes, John E. Dawson, George Daniel, Asa Chandler, John Almand, William R. Wellborn, William Byars, D. G. Daniel, James Mathews, Hartwell Jackson, James Wilson, John Harris, Thomas U. Wilkes, William Richards, Edwin Dyer, John W. Wilson, V. R. Thornton, J. R. Humphries, Nathan Johnson.

"A. B. Cook, William M. Tryon, licentiates.

"Brother H. Posey preached an introductory sermon from Romans 6: 23: 'The wages of sin is death.'

" 2. Brother J. Mercer was elected Moderator, and brother A. Sherwood, clerk.

" 3. The following committees were appointed :

"*On Preaching.*—E. Dyer, Johnson, T. Cooper, E. Henderson and George Daniel.

" *On Business.*—J. Mercer, Posey, Wellborn, D. G. Daniel, Holmes, Mallary, George Daniel, Almand, Dawson, Byars, James Reeves, Philips and Harris.

"The Committee on Business consisted of one minister from each of the Associations, any of whose ministers attended and had their names recorded.

" 4. All ministers of the several denominations, and lay members of our denomination, present, were invited to seats.

" 5. Agreed to spend the remainder of the day in devotional exercises. Several brethren spoke and prayed; others acknowledged their hard spirit, and asked forgiveness for unkind feelings and harsh expressions which may have been indulged. Adjourned to nine o'clock Monday morning.

"6. *Lord's day.*—According to arrangement of the committee, brother Posey preached at the Methodist meeting-house in the morning, followed by brother Sanders in exhortation; brother Thornton in the Baptist meeting-house, followed by brother Jeremiah Reeves in exhortation. In the afternoon brother Mercer preached in the Methodist meeting-house, followed by brother Harris in exhortation, and brother Mallary in the Baptist meeting-house, followed by brother James Reeves in exhortation.

"The day was rainy and the weather unpleasant, but the congregations were attentive, and saints were evidently comforted, and we trust edified.

"7. *Monday morning.*—Met according to adjournment. Prayer by brother Almand.

" 8. Called for the report of the Committee on Business, which was received and made the order of the meeting.

" 9. Brethren composing the meeting, who were not present at Forsyth, expressed their hearty concurrence in the faith which was assented to at that meeting. Brother James Wilson remarked that he could not go so far on election as the others.

" 10. Agreed (as at the meeting held at Forsyth,) that we, as a Convention of ministers, utterly disclaim any intention to dictate to one another, or the Associations and churches; but that we aim at nothing more than, by friendly intercourse and consultation, to encourage fellowship and union.

" 11. The following queries and propositions were discussed in a spirit of Christian candor and affection, and answered and adopted as stated below:

" I. Recommended, that each important subject for discussion be introduced by prayer. Adopted.

" II. Is it proper to declare nonfellowship with individuals, churches or Associations, without making all possible efforts, according to the spirit of the gospel, to reclaim them?"

"*Answer.*—No, unanimously.

" III. Is it proper to rebaptize persons who have been baptized by a Baptist minister, who holds regeneration and faith as prerequisites, and who is in regular standing in his own church? This query, after some discussion, was postponed until to-morrow morning.

" IV. Is the Central Association, considered as to its constitution, and the circumstances under which it was formed, such a body as should be admitted into the general union? The discussion of this query being protracted until a late hour without coming to a decision, adjourned till candle-light, to meet at the Female Academy. Prayer by brother George Daniel. Met according to adjournment, when the discussion was resumed, after prayer by brother Choice, a Methodist minister, and decided by the adoption of the following:

"*Answer.*—Inasmuch as the churches of the Central Association have come together upon a sound faith, and appear to be laboring for the advancement of the Redeemer's cause, in an orderly manner, it is the opinion of this body that those early difficulties, in which some of our brethren conceive a few of the churches to have been involved, should be overlooked in a spirit of love and forbearance, and that the Association may be, consistently, recognized as an orderly body. Brethren Colley, George Daniel and Almand dissenting."

"12. Adjourned to meet at the Baptist church to-morrow morning nine o'clock. Prayer by brother Moderator.

"13. *Tuesday morning.*—Met at nine o'clock. Prayer by brother Richards. Brother Sherwood being compelled to leave, brother Holmes was appointed to act as clerk during the remainder of the meeting.

"14. The following queries and propositions were discussed in the same spirit which prevailed yesterday, and answered and adopted according to the subjoined statement:

"I. Is it expedient that the Baptist State Convention should continue in its present form of operations, under existing circumstances? After much discussion, the following answer was adopted, brother Colley dissenting:

"*Answer.*—We see no good reason why the Convention may not continue in its present form. Still, this body would not presume to say that the Convention in its organization is perfect. And we would recommend to the brethren throughout the State who think it susceptible of improvement, to submit their views to the next meeting of the Convention; and should this be done, we would respectfully recommend to that body to take these suggestions into prayerful consideration.

"II. Is it proper to rebaptize, etc.? The discussion of this query being resumed according to postponement, it was answered No—two dissenting.

"III. Would it not be calculated to promote the cause of peace, if all the ministers in the State were, on some particular day, to address their churches on the subject of harmony and brotherly love?

"*Answer.*—Yes, unanimously, and ministers are recommended to preach on this subject in their respective churches, commencing on the first Sunday in April next.

"IV. Would it not be desirable for all those Associations, churches and individuals who have been more immediately concerned in our unhappy divisions, without further delay, to discuss seriously and prayerfully this question: What efforts and sacrifices can we consistently make for the sake of peace and unity?

"*Answer.*—Yes, without exception.

"V. Whereas, we have heard with extreme regret that many of our brethren have declared non-fellowship with the plans which are in operation for the advancement of the cause of Christ, and with those who are friendly to them, we do most earnestly and affectionately recommend to our brethren to reconsider their course, and prayerfully inquire whether they have acted consistently with the charity of the gospel. Adopted without exception.

"VI. Is not the low state of religion that generally exists in the churches a just cause of sorrow and lamentation?

"*Answer.*—Yes.

"VII. What means can be adopted to encourage a general revival of practical godliness? Answered by the adoption of the following:

"We recommend that the first Lord's day in January be observed by all the churches in the State as a day of fasting, humiliation and prayer, with reference to the languishing state of religion and the unhappy divisions which exist among us.

"We suggest that it would be, probably, attended with good, if on the above mentioned Lord's day all our ministering brethren would preach a discourse on the causes of spiritual declension, and the means which, with God's blessing, might be calculated to promote a general revival of religion.

"We recommend that each minister and lay brother throughout the State endeavor, as far as possible, at least, during the ensuing year, to spend a portion of each day in special prayer for a general outpouring of God's Spirit upon the churches.

"We suggest the importance of a more strict and conscientious observance of the Lord's day.

"We recommend to ministers and private Christians the more careful and diligent perusal and study of the Holy Scriptures. Cannot each brother and sister read the Scriptures through once a year?

"We recommend more family religion as being of great importance.

"We recommend to our ministering brethren to preach more on the subject of holiness, and to urge the importance of seeking high attainments in piety.

"We deem it highly needful that all our brethren cultivate a meek, childlike and forgiving spirit, and that they ever hold themselves ready to make all Christian efforts to remove stumbling blocks and heal those unhappy divisions which exist.

"VIII. Are the reception, dismission, exclusion and restoration of members and the choice of pastors among the internal rights of churches?

"*Answer*.—Yes, unanimously.

"IX. Can a church consistently receive or dismiss without unanimity?

"*Answer*.—No, unanimously.

"Should unreasonable objections be raised, what should be done with persons raising such objections?

"*Answer*.—All reasonable efforts should be made to remove those objections; but if the persons persist in them to the grief of the church, we recommend that they should be dealt with as any other offender.

"XI. Does a church, in joining an Association, part with any of its internal rights?

"*Answer*.—No, unanimously.

"XII. Is it the sense of this meeting that associational correspondence should, in all cases, necessarily involve fellowship with churches and individuals?

"*Answer*.—No, one exception.

"XIII. Recommended that a committee be appointed to prepare a circular address on the nature and importance of Christian unity, and the best means of promoting it; (to be appended to the Minutes of this meeting,) and that the brethren of different Associations be requested to have said address read before their respective bodies at their next meeting.

"*Adopted*, and that brethren J. Mercer, C. D. Mallary and A. T. Holmes appoint the committee to prepare the address.

"*N. B.* The queries respecting the Central Association, and the Baptist State Convention, were submitted by brother George Daniel, on Monday morning. Brother Daniel had been prevented from attending the meetings of the committee by the inclemency of the weather.

"15. Recommended that another meeting be held on Thursday before the second Sunday in July next.

"16. Appointed brethren Mercer, V. R. Thornton and B. M. Sanders a committee to determine as to the place of holding said meeting.

"17. *Resolved*, That the editors of THE CHRISTIAN INDEX be requested to publish the proceedings of this meeting in that paper, and to print them in pamphlet form according to the amount of money given in for that purpose.

"18. *Resolved*, That the members of this meeting are gratefully sensible of the kind hospitality extended to them by the citizens of Covington, and that they duly appreciate the politeness of the brethren of the Methodist Episcopal Church, and of the Reformed Church, in offering their houses of worship for their use during the meeting.

"19. After singing and prayer, the meeting was dissolved.

"A. T. HOLMES, *Clerk.*   JESSE MERCER, *Moderator.*"

That the reader may see the doctrines that were discussed, and which met the general approval of these meetings, the Articles of Faith then held by the Georgia Association are given:

" 1. We believe in one only true and living God; and that there is a trinity of persons in the God-head—the Father, the Son, and the Holy Ghost; and yet there are not three Gods, but one God.

" 2. We believe that the Scriptures of the Old and New Testament are the word of God, and the only rule of faith and practice.

" 3. We believe in the fall of Adam, and the imputation of his sin to his posterity. In the corruption of human nature, and the impotency of man to recover himself by his own free will—ability.

" 4. We believe in the everlasting love of God to His people, and the eternal election of a definite number of the human race, to grace and glory: And that there was a covenant of grace or redemption made between the Father and the Son, before the world began, in which their salvation is secure, and that they in particular are redeemed.

" 5. We believe that sinners are justified in the sight of God only by the righteousness of Christ imputed to them.

" 6. We believe that all those who were chosen in Christ will be effectually called, regenerated, converted, sanctified, and supported by the Spirit and power of God, so that they shall presevere in grace, and not one of them be finally lost.

" 7. We believe that good works are the fruits of faith, and follow after justification, and that they only justify us in the sight of men and angels, and are evidences of our gracious state.

" 8. We believe that there will be a resurrection of the dead, and a general judgment; and the happiness of the righteousness, and the punishment of the wicked will be eternal.

" And as for Gospel order:

" 1. We believe that the visible Church of Christ is a congregation of faithful persons, who have gained Christian fellowship with each other, and have given themselves up to the Lord, and to one another, and have agreed to keep up a godly discipline, agreeably to the rules of the Gospel.

" 2. We believe that Jesus Christ is the great Head of His Church, and only Law-giver, and that the government is with the body, and is the privilege of each individual; and that the discipline of the church is intended for the reclaiming of those Christians who may be disorderly, either in principle or practice; and must be faithfully kept up, for God's glory, and the peace and unity of the churches.

" 3. We believe that water baptism and the Lord's supper are ordinances of the Lord, and are to be continued till His second coming.

" 4. We believe that true believers in Jesus Christ are the only subjects of baptism, and that dipping is the mode.

" 5. We believe that none but regular baptized church members have a right to communion at the Lord's table.

" 6. We believe that it is the duty of every heaven-born soul to become a member of the visible church, to make a public profession of his faith, to be legally baptized, so as to have a right to, and to partake of, the Lord's supper at every legal opportunity, through the whole course of his life."

XVI.
GENERAL STATE OF DENOMINATION.
1840-1846.

XVI.

GENERAL STATE OF THE DENOMINATION.

THE CONVENTION OF 1840—THE CHRISTIAN INDEX REMOVED TO GEORGIA—INFLUENCE OF THE PAPER—MERCER UNIVERSITY IN 1840—STATE OF RELIGIOUS FEELING—REPORT ON STATE MISSIONS FOR 1842—DEATH OF JESSE MERCER—REPORT ON HIS DEATH, BY C. D. MALLARY—HIS INFLUENCE—GEORGIA BAPTIST STATISTICS—REPORT ON STATE MISSIONS FOR 1845—REPORT OF BRETHREN APPOINTED TO ATTEND THE ORGANIZATION OF THE SOUTHERN BAPTIST CONVENTION—ACCOUNT OF THE ORGANIZATION OF THAT CONVENTION—CAUSES WHICH LED TO IT—GEORGIANS PRESENT—PREVIOUS COURSE OF THE ABOLITIONISTS—EFFECT OF THE DIVISION ON SOUTHERN CONTRIBUTIONS—SKETCH OF DR. JOHNSON, ITS FIRST PRESIDENT—MESSENGERS TO THE OLD TRIENNIAL CONVENTION.

We have, thus far, brought our sketch rapidly down to 1840; have seen Mercer University begin a long and successful career, as an educational institution, in 1839; and find the denomination gradually rallying around the State Convention. In 1840 the Convention met at Penfield, and, besides various missionary societies, eight Associations were constituents of the body; namely: the Georgia, the Central, the Sarepta, the Columbus, the Appalachee, the Rehoboth, the Hephzibah and the Washington. The Convention was composed that year of a remarkably able body of Georgia Baptists, as much so, perhaps, as ever assembled together at any of our conventional meetings. Jesse Mercer was elected president for the nineteenth time; John E. Dawson was chosen clerk, and C. D. Mallary, assistant clerk. The members of that Convention have all become historical characters in our denomination, and are men of whom we may well be proud. To them we are mainly indebted for the lofty position attained by our denomination in the State. It was at that session that THE CHRISTIAN INDEX was accepted as a donation from Jesse Mercer. That paper was originally established at Washington City, in 1822 and called the *Columbian Star*, It had been published and edited in Philadelphia, to which place it was removed by Dr. William T. Brantly, the elder, and had been transferred by him to Jesse Mercer in July, 1833. More than two years previously the matter had been broached to Mr. Mercer by Dr. Brantly. In May, 1831, he wrote, "I have, of late, thought much of the state of things in South Carolina and Georgia, in reference to THE INDEX. The time has come when a southern paper of the kind that I am editing, will be required for Carolina, Georgia and Alabama. As mine is already (taken) there, and the difficulties of mail transmission are many, I have thought it probable that it would be acceptable to the brethren in that region to encourage the idea of an entire removal of THE INDEX to some central point in one or the other of the two states." In the latter half of 1833 the removal was effected, and Mr. Mercer became the editor. He soon, however, called to his assistance Rev. William H. Stokes, who was made assistant editor, and the paper was published at Washington, Ga., until removed to Penfield, in December, 1840.

Through the instrumentality of this paper Mr. Mercer exerted a great and very beneficial influence upon the denomination in Georgia. Coming to Georgia, as it did, in the "troublous times," THE INDEX became a vehicle of much bitter controversy, but, fortunately, was the means by which Mr. Mercer cast much light on many subjects, but imperfectly understood by the generality of church members, and he was enabled to settle the churches in a stable manner upon Scripture principles. It is, perhaps, impossible to overrate the good influence THE CHRISTIAN INDEX has exerted in the State, and for this it has ever been, and still is, revered.

There were fifty thousand Baptists in Georgia in 1840. In February of that year Mercer University was opened with one hundred and thirty-two students in the collegiate and academic departments. The Faculty were Rev. Otis Smith, President and Professor of Mathematics; Rev. Adiel Sherwood, Professor of Sacred Literature and Moral Philosophy; Rev. Robert Tolifree, Professor of Chemistry and Natural Philosophy; Rev. Albert Williams, Professor of Ancient Languages; S. P. Sanford and J. W. Attaway, Assistant Professors. The Convention supported five beneficiaries in the institution; sustained three domestic missionaries, and one missionary among the Cherokee Indians.

A much better condition of affairs now began to exist among the churches, and a stronger missionary spirit and a more benevolent disposition began to prevail in the Associations. The report made to the Convention in 1842, on State Missions will enable us to obtain a fair apprehension of the prevalent state of feeling among many of the Associations with reference to benevolent operations:

"*Flint River Association.* At the request of several of the churches, this Association has appointed an Executive Committee to devise and carry into effect some plan by which some of her ministers may be employed to travel among the churches and labor in destitute neighborhoods, and give themselves wholly to prayer and the ministry of the Word. Arrangements have been made to have two in the field, laboring gratuitously, in the bounds of the Association through the year.

" *The Hephzibah Association* appointed last year, a missionary to ride in her bounds, and report at the next Association.

" *The Western Association* has an Executive Committee for missions. It paid $115.00 for domestic missions last year; had $183.00 sent up by the churches to the last Association for domestic missions; and has appointed the preaching of a mission sermon at their next Association, and the taking of a collection for the same object.

" *The Ebenezer Association* has an Executive Committee for missions, who report one hundred and twenty days of mission service, one hundred and one sermons preached, at an expense of $120.00. After the mission sermon preached on the Lord's day $23.62 were collected.

" *The Appalachee Association* has an Executive Committee for missionary operations. It reported for last year one hundred and eighteen days of domestic mission service, for which they paid $147.50. There were sent up to the Association by the churches, and collected, after the mission sermon on the Lord's day, $188.31 for domestic missions, and five dollars for Texas missions. They report one Sabbath-school library containing one hundred and fifty volumes. Their circular to the churches is on the subject of the religious instruction of children.

" *The Coosa Association* had received, at its last meeting, $71.12 for domestic missions, and appointed an Executive Committee to disburse it, allowing their missionaries $20.00 per month for their services. The subject of the circular of this Association is: 'The Importance of Sunday-schools.'

" *The Sarepta Association* has an Executive Committee to direct their missionary operations, who report two hundred and seven days' labor, and two hundred and eight sermons preached, for which they paid $197.68. They recommend ministers to devote more of their time and labor for the edification of the churches, and that the deacons see that their pastors are supported.

" *The Bethel Association* has an Executive Committee to search out the destitute places in the bounds of the body and contiguous regions, and to employ missionaries to labor therein. To sustain these missionaries the churches make to the body their annual contributions at the annual meetings of the body. A collection is also taken up from the congregation. There is also a committee to procure tracts and other valuable publications to circulate among the churches, for the purpose of encouraging a taste for reading, and to advance the intelligence of the brethren. Two depositories of these books have been established, one at Palmyra and one at Lumpkin.

"*The Chattahoochee Association* earnestly recommends to the churches to assemble every Sabbath for divine worship, but, as yet, are not engaged in domestic missions.

"*The Ocmulgee Association*, in its circular to the churches, urges the duty of ministers to devote the whole of their time to the gospel ministry, and, on the other hand, the churches ought to provide for their support.

"*Rock Mountain Association.*—In this Association a commmittee reports that, as far as the views of the churches have been expressed, they are in favor of the spread and support of the gospel; and the Association gives it as her advice, that all who feel inclined to do so, should form themselves into a society, and make such arrangements as will soonest and best carry out their views, in relation to missions, both foreign and domestic. It, also, recommends the churches to examine the Scriptures minutely in respect to their obligations to hold religious meetings every Sabbath.

"*The Central Association*, at its last meeting, reported $5.86 paid by its Executive Committee for domestic missions during the past year. It recommends, in most pressing terms, Sabbath-schools in every congregation, and has appointed a special agent, in every county in its bounds, to superintend Sabbath-school operations in its churches. It has, for several years, urged the churches, to meet every Sabbath for religious worship.

"*The Georgia Association.*—This body annually turns over all its funds, for domestic as well as foreign missions, into the hands of the Exective Committee of the Convention; but gratuitous mission labor, in its own bounds, is urged upon its ministers, almost at every meeting of it. Considerable labor is done within its borders in this way. A new impulse has, lately, been experienced among its churches in relation to Sabbath-schools and weekly Sabbath meetings."

This report, prepared and offered by B. M. Sanders, manifests a great advance in missionary sentiment in the State, since the division. While the anti-missionaries have separated themselves and have performed no missionary labor, we see that the other Associations have organized for that work and are proceeding to collect money systematically for the purpose.

The session of 1841, held at Thomaston, was made memorable by the absence, for the first time, of Jesse Mercer who was detained at home by family afflictions. On the 6th of September following, he expired at the residence of Rev. James Carter, near Indian Spring; and the Convention of 1842, held at LaGrange, was called upon to take action concerning his demise. As the report adopted, written by Rev. C. D. Mallary, has, with the characteristic modesty of its author, been omitted in his Life of Jesse Mercer, it is given here:

"Your Committee deem it a matter of special gratitude to God that death has made so few inroads upon the ranks of our ministering brethren, since our last session. Yet He has aimed at one lofty and shining mark, and brought our venerated and beloved Mercer low. We deem it proper that some memorial of our sorrow; some brief tribute of our respect, should be entered upon the records of our body. In speaking of brother Mercer as an eminently wise, pious and useful man, we do not use the language of exaggeration. For half a century did he occupy a high and influential position among the Baptists of Georgia; and few men could be named, on the entire lists of the denomination in our country, more wise in counsel, more profound in the knowledge of divine things, more unwearied in pious labors, more constant in appropriations to the cause of benevolence. The influence which he exerted was extensive and powerful; and, yet, with how little alloy was it mingled! It was as salutary as it was extensive, and as pure as it was powerful. The gospel which he unfolded with so much skill, clearness and heavenly unction, had exerted much of its transforming power upon his heart, and rendered him, in his character and life, an eminent illustration of the truth and purity of the doctrines which he proclaimed.

"Long will his useful counsels and labors in this Convention be remembered! Long shall we remember his patriarchal form, his meek, simple and condescending deportment! Yes, thou man of God, long will we remember thee with filial reverence and affection!

"We feel that we are a bereaved family. Yet, whilst we mourn our loss, we would express our gratitude to God that he was spared so long to bless the Church, and that he has bequeathed an example to us so well calculated to rebuke our follies and stimulate us to every good word and work. We are reminded, by his death, that our lives and labors are hastening to a close, and that whatever our hand findeth to do, we should do it with our might."

It is not too much to say that no one has ever exerted upon the Baptist denomination in Georgia a more beneficial, healthy and powerful influence than Jesse Mercer; no one did more to give a sound scriptural tone to its doctrine and practice; no one more zealously and persistently promoted all those benevolent institutions sanctioned by the gospel, and in accordance with Scripture principles; nor has any one in our State been so liberal in donations to denominational enterprises. In the pulpit, at associational and conventional meetings, by circular addresses, in ministerial conferences, and through THE CHRISTIAN INDEX, not to speak of continuous and multitudinous personal labors, he did more to elevate our denomination in the State, and give shape to its destiny, than any one man who ever lived. Without the brilliancy, eloquence and intellectual power of Dr. Holcombe; or the cultivation and scholarship of the elder Brantly; or the mental training and collegiate lore of Dr. Sherwood, he nevertheless possessed such characteristics of pious zeal, such rugged, intellectual ability, such far-seeing and practical wisdom, all united to a life of unflagging exertion and continual study of Bible truth, and to a liberality bounded by his means only, that he wielded a more powerful influence, and accomplished results more beneficial, than any other man. He began his religious life when there were not twenty Baptist churches in the State of Georgia, and hardly fifteen hundred members. He lived to see the time—over half a century later—when thirty-seven Associations were formed, and when there were nearly eight hundred churches, over three hundred ordained ministers, eighty licentiates, and about fifty thousand church members.

Dr. J. H. Campbell, in his "Georgia Baptists," gives the Georgia statistics for 1835 at 21 Associations, 583 churches, 298 ministers, and 41,810 members. An editorial in THE INDEX, for January, 1841, says that there were 50,000 Baptists in the State.

In THE INDEX of September 29th, 1843, Dr. Joseph S. Baker published a Baptist statistical table of Georgia, giving the statistics of thirty-six Associations. But in a private letter to Dr. D. Benedict, dated, Penfield, Georgia, September 13th, 1843, which is now before us, he gives the names of nine Associations not in his table, and of which he had no Minutes, nor any statistics, and adds: "The probable number of Baptists in Georgia, in 1842, was 55,000; the probable number baptized that year, 6,000." This accords very well with Campbell's statement in his "Georgia Baptists," taken from the Convention Minutes of 1846, that in 1845 there were 46 Associations, 464 ministers, 971 churches, and 58,388 communicants (page 15).

For nine years Rev. W. H. Stokes, as assistant editor of THE CHRISTIAN INDEX, was indefatigable in his labors, and to him much of the good done by the paper should be credited. He resigned in 1842, and in January, 1843, Dr. J. S. Baker, being elected by the Executive Committee of the Convention, assumed editorial control of THE INDEX, which influential position he occupied, with great credit to himself and usefulness of the denomination, for half a dozen years. He was a very clear and forcible writer, and, by his piety and ability, wielded a strong influence for many years.

There was reason for the growth in the denomination which we have chronicled, for the Minutes of all the Associations, nearly, indicate the performance of much State mission work; and the summary, published each year in the Convention proceedings, is very gratifying to the student of denominational history. For the information of those desirous of knowing something of our

GENERAL STATE OF THE DENOMINATION. 203

denominational activity in the fifth decade of the century, we make another extract from the Convention Report on State Missions, made in 1845, by Joseph Polhill. Twelve Associations were then constituents of the body, and the report is a condensed summary of associational work :

" *The Hephzibah Association* has twenty-two churches, eleven ordained ministers, and an Executive Committee. They employed a missionary who rendered one hundred and twenty-one days' service. There are some temperance societies, Sabbath-schools and regular monthly prayer meetings in some of the churches, and special conferences for the blacks.

" *The Appalachee Association* has a missionary who travelled one hundred and fifty days, preached one hundred and seventy-six sermons, aided in the ordination of one minister and the constitution of one church, baptized a number of persons, and visited many families. The missionary cause is on the advance.

" *The Central Association* contains nineteen churches, ten ordained ministers, and eight licentiates. She has three missionaries at present in her employ, who, together, rendered about fifteen months' service. Her ministers preach once a month to the colored people. Sabbath-schools are most cordially approved, and many are in successful operation. The temperance cause is encouraged by ministers and the people generally.

" *The Rehoboth Association* has twenty churches and eight ordained ministers, keeps a missionary in the field (for which purpose she has a fund of about $600), and has a book depository in the city of Macon. Sabbath-schools are supported in her bounds. The religious instruction of the blacks is carefully attended to in some of the churches, and particular attention is paid to the colored church in Macon.

" *The Columbus Association* employs two missionaries, one engaged in preaching to the destitute in her bounds, the other in visiting churches and families, and forming Sabbath-schools. Both have been very successful in their labors. Most of the churches have Sabbath-schools. Eight hundred dollars were collected for the above objects. Some of the churches give oral instruction to the colored people.

" *The Coosa Association* employs one missionary, and has fifteen or twenty Sabbath-schools, though she finds great difficulty in procuring Sunday-school books. The temperance cause has been retrograding, but is now advancing.

" *The Flint River Association* reports a domestic missionary constantly in her employment. A Sunday-school Convention was held with much interest, and many of the churches are zealously engaged in their support. The temperance cause is on the advance. In some instances oral instruction is given to the colored people. There is a flourishing Bible Society in Butts county.

" *The Georgia Association* has thirty ordained ministers, fifteen or twenty licentiates, and twenty-seven churches. Efforts have been made for several years to induce the churches to have regular worship every Sabbath. A few have adopted the measure, more have preaching thrice a month and some are in the old order of monthly worship. Sunday-school instruction is becoming more common, and some efforts are made for the oral instruction of the blacks in Sabbath-schools, which promise well.

" *The Sunbury Association* has been and still is engaged in the support of foreign missions and in giving the gospel to the colored people within its bounds. During the last year it contributed $417.57 to the former. For the colored mission it employs two misssionaries—one for the Savannah River, and one for the Altamaha. They received $635.00 for their services. Most of the churches have Sabbath-schools and impart oral instruction to the blacks.

" *The Western Association* has an Executive Committee to whom is entrusted the management of domestic missions. They keep a missionary in the field. Sabbath-schools have been established successfully in some churches and neighborhoods; but there is a want of Sunday-school books. No regular system for the instruction of the colored people has been practiced by this body.

" *The Sarepta Association* has three missionaries employed, who rendered about one hundred and thirty days service, preached about one hundred and forty sermons, and rode upwards of a thousand miles. They now have two brethren who devote a portion of their time to domestic missions. Sabbath-schools are at a very low ebb, and no special instruction is given to the colored people.

"In the *Tugalo Association* nothing is now doing in the department of domestic missions. It is a very destitute section.

"*The Bethel Association* is engaged in most of the enterprises of the denomination. She has an Executive Committee; keeps, generally, a domestic missionary employed; encourages Sunday-schools and general benevolence in her churches; and, in some churches, regular religious instruction is afforded the blacks."

During the years of this decade the Convention takes very strong ground in favor of temperance, in its reports; encourages education and Sabbath-schools in the highest degree; and vigilantly guards the interests of Mercer University. A theological department with a three years' course, was established in 1844 and Dr. J. L. Dagg was made Professor of Theology.

Several missionaries were maintained in different parts of the State, by the Executive Committee, who, also, sustained six beneficiaries in Mercer University, three of them in the theological department, besides one at Cave Spring.

Fourteen Associations are now connected with the Convention, and sixteen were represented at the session of 1845.

That year forms an important era in our State denominational history, because, in 1845, the Southern Baptists severed their organic connection with their Northern brethren, and formed Boards of their own, through which to carry on their benevolent operations; and this was the result of events which occurred in our own State.

The particular and originating cause of this separation was an application made by the Executive Committee of the Georgia Baptist Convention, John L. Dagg, V. R. Thornton, J. B. Walker, Thomas Stocks and B. M. Sanders, to the American Baptist Home Mission Society, of Boston, for the appointment of Rev. James E. Reeves, as a missionary within the bounds of the Talapoosa Association. As Mr. Reeves was a slaveholder, the American Baptist Home Mission Board declined even to entertain the application, lest they should appear to sanction slavery. The Executive Committee immediately instructed the treasurer of the Convention, Absalom Janes, not to pay over any funds he might have in his hands for that Board, until further instructions, and at the same time issued an address to the Baptists of the United States, reciting the conduct of the Board. The State Convention, which met at Forsyth, in 1845, adopted the following resolutions, which were brought in by a special committee, consisting of Joshua S. Calloway, James Granberry, Jacob King, C. S. Gaulding, and W. P. Burks:

"*Resolved*, 1st. That this body disapproves of the course pursued by the Board of the Baptist Home Mission Society, in refusing to appoint, as a missionary, the brother recommended to their notice by the Executive Committee.

"*Resolved* 2d, That we highly approve of the act of the Executive Committee, in withholding said mission funds until the present meeting of this body; and that they be instructed to pay over the same to the Southern Baptist Domestic Mission Board at Marion, Alabama."

At the same Convention a special committee, composed of Albert Williams, Henry O. Wyer, C. D. Mallary, A. T. Holmes and James Perryman, appointed to consider the report of the Executive Committee, who attended the formation of the Southern Baptist Convention, in Augusta, as representatives of the State Convention, made the following report, which was adopted:

"While this body deeply regret the necessity of separating from our Northern brethren, we highly approve the action of the late meeting in Augusta, and earnestly recommend our churches throughout the State to support this Southern organization with liberal, benevolent contributions. Therefore,

"*Resolved*, That this Convention become auxiliary to the Southern Baptist Convention, and proceed to elect five delegates to represent us in the meeting of that body, to be held Thursday before the second Lord's day in June, 1846" (in Richmond, Va.)

It is an interesting fact that this same Convention appropriated one hundred dollars to aid the American Indian Mission Association of Kentucky, which was an Association formed by a convention of Western Baptists, at Cincinnati, in 1843, and whose Board was located at Louisville, Ky. The formation of this Association, somewhat like that of the Southern Baptist Convention, grew out of a backwardness in sustaining Missions, among the Indians of the West, by the Northern Board. It continued until 1855, when, almost overwhelmed with debt, it was merged into the Domestic Board of the Southern Baptist Convention, at Montgomery, which thenceforth became known as the "Domestic and Indian Mission Board."

The mention of these facts, in Georgia Baptist history, exhibiting, as some of them do, the immediate causes of the formation of the Southern Baptist Convention, renders it pertinent and appropriate to dwell somewhat in detail on the organization of that Convention, and on those relevant events which preceded and led to its formation.

At Augusta, Georgia, on Thursday May 8th, 1845, three hundred and ten delegates, from Maryland, Virginia, North Carolina, South Carolina, Georgia, Alabama, Louisiana, Kentucky and the District of Columbia, met in the Baptist house of worship and organized by the election of Dr. William B. Johnson, of South Carolina, as President, and Hon. Wilson Lumpkin, of Georgia, and Rev. J. B. Taylor, of Virginia, as Vice-Presidents, and Jesse Hartwell and James C. Crane, as Secretaries. The next morning the following was adopted:

"*Resolved*, That for peace and harmony, and in order to accomplish the greatest amount of good, and for the maintenance of those scriptural principles on which the General Missionary Convention of the Baptist denomination of the United States was originally formed, it is proper that this Convention at once proceed to organize a society for the propagation of the Gospel."

The reasons given for this was a declaration of the Board of the General Convention, at Boston, that if "any one should offer himself as a Missionary, having slaves, and should insist on retaining them as his property, we could not appoint him."

This innovation and departure from the course previously pursued by the Triennial Convention was an infraction of a resolution passed at the last session of that Convention. The rule of the Convention, defining who might be appointed missionaries, was this: "Such persons only as are in full communion with some church in our denomination, and who furnish satisfactory evidence of genuine piety, good talents and fervent zeal for the Redeemer's cause;" and the resolution, of which the declaration of the acting Board was an infraction, was as follows:

"*Resolved*, That in co-operating together, as members of this Convention, in the work of foreign missions, we disclaim all sanction, either expressed or implied, whether of slavery or anti-slavery; but, as individuals, we are free to express and to promote, elsewhere, our views on these subjects, in a Christian manner and spirit." In less than six months the Board of the General Convention declared that it could not appoint a slaveholder to be a missionary, and "could never be a party to any arrangement which implies approbation of slavery."

As many Southerners were, at that time, slaveholders, self-respect forced the Southern Baptists to withdraw from the General Convention.

The Board of Managers of the Virginia Foreign Baptist Mission Society, issued a call to the Baptists of the South to send delegates to a convention to meet at Augusta, Georgia, and it was in pursuance of this call that a large number of delegates met and formed the Southern Baptist Convention. Two Boards were appointed, one for Foreign Missions, at Richmond, Virginia, and one for Home Missions, at Marion, Alabama, which have now been in useful existence for thirty-six years, and have done much to foster and develop the missionary spirit in the South. It should be a matter of congratulation to Georgia Baptists that this organization had its birth in their State, and was incorporated by their State Legislature, the charter being granted on the 27th of December, 1845.

Many prominent Georgia Baptists took part in the formation of the Southern Baptist Convention, among whom were J. F. Hillyer, J. H. Campbell, H. Bunn, J. Hendricks, D. G. Daniell, C. M. Irwin, P. H. Mell, I. L. Brooks, T. J. Burney, P. W. Walton, B. M. Sanders, J. L. Dagg, A. Janes, V. R. Thornton, Thomas Stocks, W. H. Stokes, J. S. Baker, L. Steed, N. Polhill, Wilson Lumpkin, W. Richards, A. M. Walker, T. U. Wilkes, S. G. Hillyer, J. Polhill, G. W. Evans, James Carter, W. J. Harley, J. Davis, M. N. McCall, E. Perryman, H. H. Lumpkin, E. Calloway, Asa Chandler, J. B. Slack, J. H. T. Kilpatrick, C. H. Stilwell, C. D. Mallary, B. Thornton, M. Brinson, T. C. Armstrong, J. S. Law, W. O. Cheeney, Wm. H. McIntosh, E. H. Bacon, V. Sanford, William T. Brantly, Jr., W. R. Gignilliat, N. M. Crawford, W. H. Pope, W. F. Baker, D. E. Butler, J. F. Dagg, J. W. Stapleton, P. Robinson, E. R. Carswell, J. S. Calloway, H. Posey, John E. Dawson, Benjamin Brantly, T. A. Gibbs, R. Tolefree, W. P. Steed, George Walker, J. Huff, besides various others.

At the North this separation was desired by many, regretted by few, and expected by all. In fact, the separation was inevitable, as a Free Mission Society had been already organized, in 1843, at Boston, in opposition to the Board of the Triennial Convention, and upon the expressed basis of non-cooperation with Southern churches. This Society gained favor rapidly, and, consequently, hastened the complete rupture between the North and South, as a measure which effectually prevented a division of the Baptist churches at the North. In reality, in April 1845, before the Convention met in Augusta, the Home Mission Society, at its meeting in Providence, R. I., adopted the following Preamble and Resolutions:

"WHEREAS, The American Baptist Home Mission Society is composed of contributors, residing in slave-holding and non-slave-holding States; and, whereas, the Constitution recognizes no distinction among the members of the Society as to eligibility to all the offices and appointments in the gift of the Society and of the Board; and, whereas, it has been found that the basis on which the Society was organized is one upon which all the members and friends of the Society are not now willing to act; therefore,

"*Resolved*, That in our opinion it is expedient that the members now forming the Society, should hereafter act in separate organizations at the South and at the North, in promoting the objects which were originally contemplated by the Society.

"*Resolved*, That a committee be appointed to report a plan by which the object contemplated in the preceding resolution may be accomplished in the best way, and at the earliest period of time, consistently with the preservation of the constitutional rights of all the members, and with the least possible interruption of the missionary work of the Society."

This led to further steps, one of which was a recommendation "that the existing organization be retained by the Northern and other churches, which may be willing to act together upon the basis of restriction against the appointment of slave holders."

The adoption of this, by a unanimous vote, left the Southern churches no alternative but to withdraw and form a Southern Baptist Convention. The effect of this separation upon the Southern Baptist churches was to heighten their sense of responsibility and develop their resources and energies, as was evidenced by their contributions. During the time they had been connected with the Home Mission Board—from 1832 to 1845—their contributions amounted to $38,656. In the same number of years, after the separation—from 1864 to 1859—their contributions to the Domestic Board at Marion amounted to $204,614, besides $61,614 for Indian Missions, making a total of $266,356 against $38,656. Certainly the separation was providential.

The following is a brief sketch of the first president of the Southern Baptist Convention: "Rev. William Bullein Johnson, D.D., first president of the Southern Baptist Convention, and for four years—from 1811 to 1815—pastor of the Savannah church, was born on John's Island, near Charleston, South Carolina, June 13th, 1782. His parents were both Baptists. In his boyhood he enjoyed the companionship of Edmund

Bottsford, and was, in Georgetown, South Carolina, instructed by Dr. William Staughton, afterwards president of Columbian College. While pursuing the study of law, in Beaufort, South Carolina, he was converted at the close of a remarkable revival of religion, in October, 1804, being baptized by Joseph B. Cook and uniting with the Beaufort church. He ascribed his conversion to the labors of a pious lady, Miss Lydia Turner, of London, who, together with her household, had been baptized in Savannah, by Dr. Henry Holcombe. Licensed in January, 1805, he was ordained in January, 1806. Besides serving as a pastor of the Euhaw church, St. Luke's parish, South Carolina, he acted in the same capacity for the Savannah, Columbia, Greenville and Edgefield chuiches. For five years he gave a general supervision of the Johnson Female Seminary, Anderson, South Carolina, which was thus named in compliment to him, by its founders, taking no part in the labors of instruction, although many years of his life were employed both as a minister and a teacher of young ladies. He died October 2d, 1862. A man of high and unquestioned Christian integrity, he was frequently honored by his brethren with positions of official dignity. For many years he was moderator of the Savannah River Association; for thirty years he presided over the South Carolina Convention; he was president of the Triennnial Convention when it met in Baltimore; and at the first meeting of the Southern Baptist Convention, in 1845, at Augusta, his venerable form was, by the suffrage of his brethren, placed in the chair. For such a post he was eminently qualified by his dignity, urbanity and impartiality. To a clear intellect he united eminent pietv, learning, fixedness of purpose, promptness and punctuality; and to the most transparent honesty, he added independence of thought and a large public spiritedness. As the sun was going down, in the close of a glorious autumn day, he sank to his final rest, with the softness of an infant's sleep, presenting a death scene of perfect tranquillity and peace."

We will close this chapter with a list of Georgia delegates to the old Triennial Convention, from its organization at Philadelphia, in 1814, to the rupture, in 1845. It will be seen that long before our General Association was formed, Georgia was represented in that Convention, by delegates sent from her associational mission boards and societies. Indeed, frequent mention is made in the denominational annals of money appropriated to secure seats in that Convention.

In 1814, W. B. Johnson, then pastor at Savannah, went from a society in the Savannah River Association. In 1817, Jesse Mercer attended as messenger from the "Powelton Missionary Society," and as proxy from the "Ocmulgee Missionary Society." In 1820, Jesse Mercer attended as messenger of the "Mission Board of the Georgia Association," and Elijah Mosely, as messenger of the "Ocmulgee Mission Society." In 1823, Adiel Sherwood represented the "Mission Board of the Georgia Association," and Major Abner Davis represented the "Ocmulgee Mission Board." In 1826, Jesse Mercer attended as messenger of the "Mission Board of the Georgia Association;" Abner Davis, of the "Mission Board of the Ocmulgee Association;" William T. Brantly, as appointee of the "General Association" or State Convention. A. Sherwood was appointed but did not attend. In 1829, A. Sherwood attended as messenger of the Georgia Baptist Convention. In 1832, A. Sherwood and Thomas Stocks represented the Georgia Baptist Convention. In 1835, Jesse Mercer and A. Sherwood were delegates of the State Convention. In 1838, A. Sherwood and John E. Dawson were delegates of the Georgia Baptist Convention. In 1841, B. M. Sanders, Jonathan Davis and Thomas Stocks were the State Convention delegates. In 1844, the State Convention was represented for the last time in the old Triennial Convention, by Thomas Stocks, B. M. Sanders, V. R. Thornton, John L. Dagg and Jesse H. Campbell.

XVII.
DENOMINATIONAL HISTORY.
1845-1861.

XVII.

DENOMINATIONAL HISTORY.

ACTION OF THE STATE CONVENTION IN REGARD TO SEPARATION—EFFECTS OF THE RUPTURE ON SOUTHERN BENEVOLENCE—WASHINGTON ASSOCIATION—WESTERN ASSOCIATION—REHOBOTH ASSOCIATION—BETHEL AND COLUMBUS ASSOCIATIONS—COOSA AND TALLAPOOSA ASSOCIATIONS—THE UNITED BAPTISTS—STATE OF RELIGION IN 1850—THE HEARN MANUAL LABOR SCHOOL—NOBLE MEN OF THAT PERIOD AND WHAT THEY DID—THE CHEROKEE BAPTIST CONVENTION—WHY CONSTITUTED—ITS FORMATION AND PROGRESS—CHEROKEE BAPTIST COLLEGE AND WOODLAWN COLLEGE—MISSION AMONG THE CHEROKEES—DAVID FOREMAN AND E. L. COMPERE—"THE LANDMARK BANNER AND CHEROKEE BAPTIST"—THE NORTH GEORGIA MISSIONARY ASSOCIATION—THE TEN YEARS PRECEDING THE WAR—THE BIBLE BOARD AND COLPORTER SOCIETY—EXCITING QUESTIONS—ASSOCIATIONS IN THE GEORGIA BAPTIST CONVENTION, AND CHEROKEE BAPTIST CONVENTION, BEFORE THE WAR, AND THEIR BENEVOLENT CONTRIBUTIONS.

The year 1845 was an era in our State denominational history, made so, mainly by the events narrated in our last chapter. Heretofore the benevolent funds of the State had been disbursed chiefly through the Mission Boards at the North, for both Foreign and Domestic Missions; but anti-slavery fanaticism among the Northern Baptists rendered a separation necessary, as well as expedient. In consequence our benevolence took another channel, in 1845, and our operations were brought under the immediate control of Southern Baptists. They have continued so to the present day, doubtless in accordance with a wise ordering of Providence. History informs us that it was the firm and decided stand taken by Georgia Baptists, which was the immediate cause of that rupture. The condition of public sentiment in our denomination, at that time, may be gathered from the action of the State Convention, in 1846, when the following was adopted:

"*Resolved*, That, in the opinion of this Convention, it is expedient for the Southern Baptist Convention to adopt such a course at their meeting, in Richmond, as will, unequivocally, separate the South from the North in all the general organizations for Christian benevolence."

It may also be gathered from the action of the Executive Committee, in September, 1845, which was ratified by the State Convention, in 1846. In that month the committee had before it for consideration a circular addressed to their chairman, B. M. Sanders, from the agent of the American Baptist Publication Society, inquiring into the expediency of sending an agent to Georgia. The Executive Committee passed the following resolutions:

"*Resolved*, 1. That it is the opinion of this committee that it would not be expedient for the American Baptist Publication Society to send an agent among us.

"*Resolved* 2, That, in our opinion, public sentiment requires the formation of Southern Boards for Bible and publication operations." In fact a Southern Baptist Publication Society was organized at Savannah, in 1847, located at Charleston, South Carolina, and continued in existence until the war of secession.

We may, by a few facts, not only discover the manner in which the denominational rupture was received by the Georgia Baptists, but we can learn the effects of that rupture upon the benevolence of the churches and Associations.

At its session, in 1845, the Georgia Association adopted the report of its Executive Committee, in which the churches were informed of the Convention held in Augusta, "to devise ways and means whereby all the benevolent objects contemplated by us, as a people, might be more efficiently promoted," and the churches were respectfully urged to adopt vigorous measures to enable the several Boards appointed by the Southern Baptist Convention "to prosecute their praiseworthy designs." In that year $1,444.90 were collected for mission purposes, of which $1,163.32 were paid over to the Treasurer of the Georgia Baptist Convention, for various mission purposes, and $281.58 were sent to the American Indian Mission Association, at Louisville. The following year, 1846, $2,647.21 were reported as contributed to missions, during the year, of which $1,554.51 were sent up to the Association. Thus we see, that in one Association alone, mission contributions more than doubled.

By an examination of the records, we find that the amount sent up to the Convention from the Associations, for benevolent purposes, in May, 1845, was $1,148.41; in 1846, the amount was $5,946.77; in 1847, it was $9,885.73; in 1848, it was $8,714.24; in 1849, it was $7,392.49, and in 1850, it was $10,181.86. In those six years the number of Associations, in connection with the Convention, had increased from fourteen to twenty-two. Besides these, there were in the State, not connected with the Convention, in 1846, thirty-one Associations; and in 1850, thirty-five Associations. The total number of Associations, in 1846, was forty-six, with a membership of 60,000; and, in 1850, it was fifty-seven, with a membership of at least 70,000—a gain of 2,000 a year.

In the same time the number of ordained ministers, in connection with the Convention, increased from 240 to 365, and the total number of ordained ministers increased from 464 to 628. But these figures are confessedly incomplete, especially in regard to the pecuniary contributions, for they represent the contributions only which were sent up to the Convention annually, which, as a matter of fact, were about one-half of the usual yearly benevolent contributions of the various Associations for all purposes. And, furthermore, these figures represent the contributions of those churches and Associations only, which were in connection with the State Convention.

The names of the Associations in connection with the Convention in 1846 are as follows: Appalachee, Bethel, Central, Columbus, Coosa, Ebenezer, Flint River, Georgia, Hephzibah, Rehoboth, Sarepta, Sunbury, Washington, Western, Florida. This last one had been admitted in 1845, and twenty-nine of its thirty-two churches were in the State of Florida. It became necessary to alter the Constitution of the Convention, that its application for union with the Convention might be granted.

The Washington Association was formed in December, 1828, at Sisters' Meeting House, in Washington county. On Friday, December the 12th, William R. Stansell, Job Thigpen, and Jonathan Huff, a presbytery appointed by the Hephzibah Association the preceding October, met and constituted five churches into an Association, which was called the Washington. These churches were, Darien, Beulah, Bethlehem, Sisters' and Jackson's, and they had all been dismissed from the Hephzibah Association. Brother Thigpen was Moderator, and gave the charge; Jonathan Huff offered the benediction prayer, while William R. Stansell preached the sermon and pronounced the Association constituted. He was elected the first Moderator, and Lee Reaves, Clerk. The total membership of the churches was 318, as follows: Darien, 119; Beulah, 51; Bethlehem, 81; Sisters, 37; Jackson's 30. In 1830, the Association had nine churches and 533 members; in 1835 it had twenty churches with 1,239 members; in 1841 there were seventeen churches with 1,227 members; and in 1846 there were eighteen churches, containing 1,278 members There seems to have been no special interest taken in missions until 1837, although it had been customary to have a missionary sermon preached on Sabbath morning, and a collection taken up. D. G. Daniel preached the introductory sermon at the session of 1837. On

Sabbath morning Rev. P. Roberts preached the missionary sermon, after which a collection was taken for domestic missions, and "in the evening brother Mallary delivered a soul-animating sermon, in which he ably defended the cause of missions, and we believe that many hearts received the truth in love, and thanked God and took courage." So say the Minutes. In that year the objects of the Convention were commended, and the elevation of Mercer Institute to a University was approved. The following year, 1838, the Association agreed to unite with the Convention, formally.

The Western Association was formed at LaGrange, by the union of sixteen churches, on the 7th of November, 1829. The constituting presbytery was composed of two committees, appointed by the Yellow River and Flint River Associations, and consisting of J. Colley, R. Gunn, G. Daniel, J. Milner, William Moseley, William Henderson, J Carter and J. Nichols. Joel Colley was elected Moderator, and J. Milner, Clerk. J. Nichols, William Moseley and A. Sherwood were appointed to preach on Sabbath. The first Moderator was James Reeves, and the first Clerk, John Wood.

It is a singular fact that the sixteen churches composing this Association, and which, in 1830, refused to correspond with the Georgia Baptist Convention, were gathered through the instrumentality of James Reeves and John Wood, both of whom were missionaries of the Convention. The Association, however, by a vote of forty-two to twenty-six, determined, in 1836, that the *non-fellowship resolution*, with all benevolent institutions, adopted by four churches, should not affect fellowship, thus refusing to follow the example of those four churches, as they had requested and desired.

For years this body was harrassed by some churches which bitterly opposed all benevolent institutions, and broke up correspondence with various Associations. At length, in 1837, some churches withdrew, and formed an anti-missionary Association, which they denominated "Western Association," assigning as their reason for acting thus, that the Association "had become connected with a variety of institutions not known in the Scriptures, which caused a general confusion in the churches, by attempting to unite them with the world in the spread of the gospel. *Come out from among them, be ye separate, touch not,* etc.," was the language these seceders used to their brethren in an address. A better state of things began to exist immediately. In 1839, correspondence was opened with the Rehoboth and Rock Mountain Associations, and was *resumed* with the Columbus, Sarepta, Georgia and Tallapoosa. At the same time a resolution was adopted, declaring that this was designed merely as a reciprocation of Christian regard and courtesy, and did not, in anywise, express an opinion with regard to the benevolent institutions of the day.

This Association applied for union with the State Convention in 1842, and was cordially received.

The Rehoboth Association was formed in 1838, by the union of ten churches, principally from the Itchaconnah Association, against which that Association had passed a non-fellowship resolution, thus virtually exscinding them. These churches were strongly missionary in their views and designs, which they had no sufficient opportunity, or room to expand in their *old* connection; hence, in the *new*, they took the name of *Rehoboth—room, space*. Genesis 26:22. This Association united with the Convention in 1839, and has continued, to the present day, one of the strongest missionary bodies in the State. Both in Africa and the Indian Territory, it has maintained missionaries without the intervention of our general Boards; and this, no doubt, has served to stimulate the churches to a performance of duty to an extent exceeding that of most Associations.

The Bethel Association united with the Convention in 1843. This Association had been organized just ten years, and, from the first, was one of the strongest in the State. In 1839, it took hold of Domestic Missions in earnest, and soon entered upon a career of most zealous and liberal missionary effort, not only at home, but in Africa and among the Indians. For years it supported William H. Clarke, in Africa and R. J. Hogue, in the Indian Territory. Its missionary spirit has never flagged to the present day; and some of the noblest and most liberal and devout men of our denomination in the State, have been in its connection and shaped its counsels.

The Hephzibah and Appalachee Associations were admitted as constituents of the Georgia Baptist Convention in 1837. The latter Association was organized in 1835, with three churches only and two ministers—John Hendrirks and A. Hadway; but it grew rapidly, and was a Missionary Association from the first. Its controlling spririt for years was Rev. John Hendricks, of whom Dr. Sherwood says in his manuscripts : " John Hendricks, of Greenesboro', was baptized by the author, about 1827–28. He had been a Methodist preacher, but *baptism* troubled him, and he would not remain in uncertainty on a subject of so much importance. He became very useful in the Baptist churches, and removed to the Cherokee country. I think a son of his wears the mantle of his departed **father."**

The Columbus Association, which became a constituent of the Convention in 1839, was organized in November 1829, by two committees, one from the Itchaconnah and one from the Flint River, and was, at first, disinclined to side with the Missionary Baptists ; but, gradually, under the influence of better counsels, it came out boldly in favor of benevolent schemes and united with the Convention. It has long been a staunch supporter of missions, education and Sabbath schools.

The Coosa united with the Convention in 1842. It has shown itself to be one of the noblest Associations in the State. Formed in 1836, it spread over the northwest corner of the State, in the counties of Floyd, Chattooga, Walker, Murray, Cass and Paulding, and was very extensive in territory. It performed a great work in evangelizing the northern part of our State and sustained missionaries within its own bounds and among the Cherokee Indians of North Georgia, without the intervention of our General Boards, until near the close of the war. This was the first Association in Georgia to adopt the "Independent plan" of conducting missions, which it did by employing David Foreman, a native Indian, as Missionary to the Cherokees. The example was followed by the Flint River, Rehoboth and Western Associations, together with a long train of exciting circumstances, all of which grew out of delay on the part of a General Board to appropriate $100.00, sent on by the Coosa Association. It has proved itself to be a great friend of education, by its support of colleges, for both males and for females.

In 1842, the Flint, which had been formed eighteen years before, made application for admittance to the Georgia Baptist Convention, and was admitted. At first, and for a number of years after its organization, anti-missionary sentiments prevailed in this Association, but, one after another the Primitive churches withdrew, uniting with sympathetic Associations, and, at length this noble Association came out boldly on the side of benevolence, united with the Convention and has, down to the present, maintained a consistent and faithful record. Although it has not seen proper to work through our Convention Boards, it has nevertheless performed a full share in spreading and maintaining the Gospel at home and abroad.

In 1850 the Middle and Middle Cherokee Associations were admitted to the Convention. The former was organized in 1841 and the latter in 1845. The Piedmont applied for admission, and was received in 1848, but no delegates appeared until 1855. It was the Association, formed in 1817, as we have stated, which voted "to have nothing to do with the missionaries."

The Tallapoosa, formed in 1838, was received into the Convention in 1848; and the Hightower was constituted, at Silver Spring, Forsyth county, November 20th, 1835, of ten churches, most of which had been connected with the Chattahoochee Association. The presbytery was composed of Wayne, Philips, Hudson and Mears. At its session in 1836, held at Mount Zion, Cherokee county, a mission committee on Domestic Missions was appointed, consisting of Compton, Haynes, Foster, Hembree and A. Philips ; and approval was expressed of Richard Philips, missionary of the State Convention, who was preaching in their bounds. It will, therefore, be seen that this Association was missionary in sentiment, from its origin. The organization of Rock Mountain Association (now called Stone Mountain) in 1839, has been given; it united with the Convention in 1848, as did the Houston, also.

Dr. Sherwood says that, in September, 1830, Big Creek, Shalom and Mount Horeb, of Pulaski county, Camp Creek, of Dooly, and Poplar Spring, of Washington, petitioned for letters from the Ebenezer Association, for the purpose of forming this Association. Some of the churches forming it came from the Itcheconnah Association, and the constitution took place at Beulah church, in Houston county. It prospered moderately until about 1837, when it split. Its eighteen churches became equally divided on the subject of missions, and much heart-burning and confusion arose which gradually passed away, and in 1848, when it joined the Convention, it had two missionaries employed within its bounds.

Slight reference has thus been made to all the Associations which joined the Convention prior to 1850, at which period there were, in the State twenty-three anti-missionary Associations, with a membership of 12,507 in 416 churches, and ten Associations, not professedly anti-missionary, with a membership of 5,225, in 123 churchees; besides two United Baptist Associations, with twenty-four churches and 816 members.

The United Baptists, several Associations of whom still exist in the State, were originally "Whiteites," or the followers of Cyrus White, whose preaching was tinctured with Arminianism, and who secured quite a large following. They were an active, zealous people, not anti-missionary, and strongly "strict-constructionists" in their Bible views. Entirely different from the Primitive, or "old school" Baptists, they were full of effort and enterprise for the spread of the gospel and the propagation of their sentiments. They composed the third party alluded to by Dr. Hillyer, in his communication to the author, and were, by their opponents, deemed heterodox in sentiment.

Of Cyrus White Dr. Adiel Sherwood writes, in his invaluable historical repertory:

"Cyrus White, a laborious minister, became somewhat erratic about 1830, and formed a small party around him, of a few churches and pastors of churches. His views on the atonement were regarded as rather Arminian. Mr. Mercer wrote ten letters to him, in pamphlet form; others wrote criticisms on his views; but he did not live long." The doctor here, doubtless, refers modestly to himself.

Between the years 1845 and 1850, the Baptists of Georgia interested themselves exceedingly in all the great schemes of Christian benevolence—domestic and foreign missions, education for males and females, Sabbath-schools, temperance, Bible and tract societies, and assisting the Southern Baptist Publication Society.

With reference to the state of religion, the Convention adopted, in 1850, a report, of which a portion was: "Religion, generally, is in rather a low condition, but with an upward tendency, while a number of our churches have enjoyed refreshing showers of divine grace. The churches are steadfast in the faith of the gospel, and in peace and harmony among themselves, being disturbed by but very few cases of disorder requiring the exercise of church discipline. They are, doubtless, increasing in liberality of sentiment and feeling upon the long neglected subject of pastoral support, while there is a great increase of the true missionary, or apostolic spirit becoming so settled, firm and abiding as to promise (under God's blessing) great results in the future; in short, there is a firmness and union in the churches, an 'abounding in the work of the Lord,' in all the diversified aspects of Christian benevolence, which constitute a firm ground of hope for the future, and should urge us forward in the greater diligence and zeal in the prosecution of the great objects of our high vocation."

One of the objects frequently alluded to is the "Hearn Manual Labor School." This was an institution begun by the Baptists of North Georgia, in 1839, at Cave Spring, where a Baptist church had been constituted, September 20th, 1836. In 1839 Humphrey Posey became the agent for this school, obtained for it an act of incorporation, and succeeded in having it turned over to the State Convention, in 1844, and a board of trustees was appointed to take charge of it. Its title, *Hearn School*, was given to it in honor of Lott Hearn, of Putnam county, who pledged himself to endow the school with $12,500 at his death. The following account of this school is taken from "Campbell's Georgia Baptists:"

"In 1846, it is mentioned, in the Minutes of the Convention, that Mr. Lott Hearn had died, and the treasurer had commenced suit against his executor for a portion of his bequest to the institution, then due. It was under the instruction of Mr. Alfred J. King and Mr. Oliver P. Fannin. It had opened a department for the indigent deaf and dumb, under State patronage, and six or eight of this unfortunate class had been removed thither from Hartford, Connecticut.* Mr. O. P. Fannin, for many years principal of the State Asylum for the Deaf and Dumb established at this place, was their first teacher.

"The school was in a highly prosperous condition in 1848, with sixty students in attendance; $5,412.00, in part of the Hearn legacy of *twelve thousand five hundred dollars*, had been paid. The year following, the school was still in a flourishing condition, though the principal teacher, owing to some unhappy difficulties in the community, had resigned. About *seven thousand dollars*, besides its landed interests, etc., were in hand.

"In 1850, some of the members of the Executive Committee of the Convention visited Cave Spring 'to aid in healing the dissensions that had, for so long a time, existed amongst brethren' there. What success, if any, attended their errand of love, does not appear. Mr. J. S. Ingraham had been secured as the principal, and the school was in a 'highly prosperous state.'

"For a series of years the institution continued in a prosperous condition under Mr. Ingraham, generally varying from fifty to sixty pupils, notwithstanding the persistent opposition arrayed against it by the 'restless spirits' already alluded to. Its income more than met all its expenses, and its trustees were enabled to take an interest, for the accommodation of its pupils, in a brick meeting-house, built by the Baptist church, and also to provide a comfortable residence, lot, etc., for the use of its excellent principal and his family.

"In 1855 the school was under Mr. Ingraham, and was doing well in all respects. Sixty-six pupils had been received during the year, among whom were two young preachers, beneficiaries of the Convention. It was clear of debt, and its income exceeded its expenses, enabling its managers to add, by purchase, another lot of ground, so that, in all, the school owned about forty-five acres. The buildings and premises were in good repair. The report of the following year is but a repetition of this.

"Mr. Ingraham continued at the head of the school until the close of 1857, when Mr. A. J. King, its former principal, was again called to the charge of it, under whom prosperity still attended it, both in its patronage and finances. The number of pupils admitted was *eighty-four*, its endowment had increased, and 'various additions and improvements in apparatus and school furniture had been made.'

"Mr. King resigned again at the close of his second year, and Mr. James Courtney Browne, a young man of unusual ability, and a graduate of Mercer University, was called to the charge of the institution in the beginning of 1860. His administration gave entire satisfaction; but, in the spring of 1862, he and most of his older pupils having joined the army of the Confederate States, the exercises of the school were suspended, and the remaining pupils turned over to the Cave Spring Female School.

"In 1863 the Hearn School and the female school at Cave Spring were united temporarily under Rev. S. G. Hillyer, D. D. There were thirty-five pupils in the male department, and the smiles of Providence, as heretofore, seemed to rest upon the enterprise. That fall, however, it became necessary again to suspend the exercises, in consequence of the proximity of the contending armies. This suspension is supposed to have lasted until the close of the war. The buildings were much injured and the library and apparatus destroyed by

---

*This Asylum for the Deaf and Dumb was originated by the author, then State Agent for this class.

the enemy. The funds of the school, in the hands of the trustees, were invested in Confederate securities, and are thus lost. The amount lost was about *four thousand dollars*. The school, however, still has $12,000 of the Hearn legacy in charge of the Georgia Baptist Convention, and its landed estate, amounting to forty or fifty acres.

"The history of this school should prompt men of wealth to bequeath a portion of their estates, at least, in such manner as may be productive of good after they are gone, and as may perpetuate their memory in the earth."

No nobler men, no men more pious, able and zealous have graced our denominational history than those who guided Baptist affairs in the fifth decade of the century. Among them were Thomas Stocks, B. M. Sanders, J. L. Dagg, C. D. Mallary, John E. Dawson, J. H. Campbell, N. M. Crawford, P. H. Mell, J. Hendricks, Thomas Muse, T. J. Burney, John B. Walker, H. Bunn, J. S. Callaway, V. R. Thornton, Absalom Janes, W. H. Stokes, C. M. Irwin, J. H. T. Kilpatrick, William T. Brantly, Jr., G. W. Evans, William H. Turpin, Eli Warren, Lott Warren, M. A. Cooper, J. M. Wood, B. F. Tharpe, E. G. Cabiniss, A. T. Holmes, S. Landrum, J. S. Law, A. Williams, William H. McIntosh, R. Fleming, J. S. Baker, C. W. Stevens, H. Posey, J. King, J. R. Kendrick, V. Sanford, S. G. Hillyer, T. U. Wilkes, T. B. Slade, W. D. Cowdry, Juriah Harris, Enoch Callaway, D. G. Daniel, J. O. Screven, B. Langford, C. H. Stillwell, T. J. Beck, J. Q. West, Wilson Lumpkin, Z. H. Gordon, Lott Hearn, C. C. Willis, J. Perryman, S. W. Durham, J. Carter, J. Polhill, E. H. Bacon, I. L. Brooks, N. G. Foster, E. W. Warren, and very many others.

All these pressed forward in the march of progress and usefulness, and labored earnestly, not only to build up the Baptist cause in Georgia, but to promote every good word and work in which Christians engage. They established schools and colleges in all parts of the State, notably: at Madison, LaGrange, Perry, Rome, Cuthbert, Columbus, Cave Spring, Cassville, Cedartown, Griffin, and Forsyth, besides maintaining Mercer University and a school for young women, at Penfield. They organized a Bible Board, at LaGrange, in 1852, as auxiliary to the Bible Board of the Southern Baptist Convention. They continued earnestly to support foreign and domestic missions, and missions among the Indians. From $10,181.86, in 1850, the contributions for missions, in 1851, were $15,000. In 1851 the number of Associations in connection with the Convention was twenty-two, with 669 churches, 55,714 members and 341 ordained ministers. The total number of Associations was fifty-seven, with 1,183 churches, about 75,000 members, and over 600 ordained ministers. Ten years afterward, in 1861, at the outbreak of the war, there were sixty-five Associations, 1,435 churches, about 100,000 members, and 757 ordained ministers. In one year 6,678 had been baptized, according to the Convention Minutes of 1861.

We must now sketch the history of that efficient body, the

CHEROKEE BAPTIST CONVENTION.

On the 23d of November, 1854, delegates from the Middle Cherokee and Coosa Associations met at Cassville to form an organization to take charge of the Cherokee Baptist College, at Cassville. John W. Lewis was elected Moderator and C. H. Stillwell, Clerk. There were present from the Middle Cherokee Association: Elders John Crawford, J. W. Lewis, A. W. Buford, A. R. Wright, and Mr. Z. Edwards. The Coosa Association was represented by E. Dyer, W. Newton, J. M. Wood, C. H. Stillwell and S. W. Cochran. G. W. Tumlin, from the Tallapoosa Association, was present, and among the ministers present, who accepted seats, were Dr. N. M. Crawford, J. S. Murray, William Martin, J. D. Collins, T. G. Barron, J. H. Rice, H. S. Crawford, and M. J. Crawford. A committee was appointed to draft a Constitution, which was adopted on the afternoon of Friday, the 24th, and the Cherokee Baptist Convention was constituted by the election of regular officers: Rev. J. W. Lewis, President; Rev. E. Dyer, Vice-President; C. H. Stillwell, Clerk; J. H. Rice, Assistant Clerk; and A. W. Buford, Treasurer. An Executive Committee was also appointed.

The tenth article of the Constitution gives the specific objects of the body:

"1. To unite the friends of education, anc to combine their efforts for the establishment and promotion of institutions of learning, where the young of both sexes may be thoroughly educated on the cheapest practical terms. 2. To foster and cherish the spirit of missions, and to facilitate missionary operations in any, or every, laudable way."

These objects were afterwards enlarged, and were made to include the distribution of the Bible and other good books, and the education of indigent young ministers and orphans. Societies approving and co-operating might send representatives, there being no money basis to the representation.

The main reason for the formation of this Convention was that there was no other feasible plan, apparently, for promoting the Baptist educational and missionary interests in that section of our State. And it was hoped that this formation of a Convention would promote the piety and efficiency of the denomination in North Georgia, by securing union and co-operation.

The body met at Cassville, in 1855, in October, and at Cedar Town, May, 1856. At that session, 1856, the Cherokee Baptist College, which commenced in 1854, and which had hitherto been under the control and direction of trustees appointed by the Middle Cherokee Baptist Association, was received into the care of the Cherokee Baptist Convention, and placed under the direction of trustees chosen by the Convention. This was in accordance with the plan originally contemplated, when the college was established and incorporated, and a transfer of all papers and property was made from one set of trustees to the other. On the night of January 4th, 1856, the main building of the college was destroyed by fire, but was magnificently rebuilt, only to be ruthlessly destroyed by Sherman's army in 1864, with all its valuable apparatus, library and other contents. This obliterated the institution, for it has never been revived.

In May, 1856, the Convention adjourned to meet in July of the same year. C. W. Sparks was chosen President, as Dr. Lewis was absent. A formal tender of the supervision of Woodland College, for young ladies, at Cedar Town, was received from its trustees. The trust was accepted on certain conditions, and the Convention thus became the virtual supervisor and controller of two colleges, one for young men and the other for young women, trustees for both of which had been elected the preceding May.

A resolution adopted May 20th, 1856, shows how much in earnest the brethren of this Convention were in the cause of education; "*Resolved*, That our churches and the brethren in the ministry be earnestly requested to send up, annually, through our Associations, funds for educational purposes, to be equally divided between Woodland Female College and Cherokee Baptist College, or, as the donors may desire; and that these objects be considered paramount in the liberality of our brethren till these colleges be endowed."

While neither of the institutions became endowed, yet they maintained an honorable and useful existence, until the storm of war burst upon the land. Under the Presidency of Dr. T. Rambaut, the Cherokee Baptist College attained a very respectable position and accomplished much good, even under great financial difficulties. The Woodland College, Cedar Town, was so named in honor of Rev. J. M. Wood, its founder. It was originated in 1851, and was, at first, called The Cedar Town High School. A charter for it, as a college, was obtained in 1853, and Rev. J. M. Wood was elected President. The property was bought by the Coosa Association, and placed under the care of the Cherokee Baptist Convention, as already stated. Before its extinction by the exigencies of war, it educated a large number of young ladies.

The Cherokee Baptist Convention met at Petit's Creek, Cass county, in 1857, its constituents then being the Middle Cherokee, Coosa, Arbacoochee, Ellijay and State Line Associations. G. W. Selvidge was elected President, and W. A. Mercer, Secretary. It met in Rome in 1858 and Jesse M. Wood was elected President, G. W. Selvidge, Vice-President, W. A. Mercer, Secretary, and A. B. Ross, Assistant Secretary. J. H. Campbell was received as the agent of the Foreign Mission Board. M. A. Cooper, J. R. Graves, S. G. Hillyer, T. Rambaut, A. S. Worrell, J. McBryde, C. H. Stillwell and John H. Rice were present,

J. R. Graves preached on Sunday to a "crowded house." J. M. Wood preached on education at night; J. H. Campbell, at the Presbyterian, and Dr. Rambaut at the Methodist house of worship, preached on Sabbath. The reports all show great zeal and earnestness in every good cause—especially education, missions and Sunday-schools.

The Convention met at Dalton in 1859, J. M. Wood, President. W. A. Mercer, Secretary. The Noonday Association had joined, and a very large and respectable delegation were present. A. C. Dayton preached Sunday night. There were present as messengers and representatives of various benevolent causes, A. E. Vandivere, of Alabama, T. S. Montgomery and J. M. Bennett, of Kentucky, J. M. Pendleton, of Tennessee, M. T. Sumner, of the Domestic Mission Board, Alabama, D. G. Daniel, Agent of the Foreign Mission Board, F. M. Haygood, General Agent of the Georgia Baptist Bible and Colporter Society, at Macon, and W. W. Odum, Agent and Colporter of the Southwestern Publishing House, Nashville.

Considering the claims represented by all these persons and the special objects of the Convention, likewise, we may form some idea of the important subjects brought forward and discussed by this body; for all agents were permitted to present and press their claims.

It was at this session that the Convention instructed its Executive Committee to procure a missionary to labor among the Cherokee Indians. Among those Indians the Coosa Association already had a missionary at work—David M. Foreman, a half-blood by birth, second Chief of the Nation, the clerk of its Court, a gentleman in manners and a man of tolerably good education. His appointment occurred as a result of the following circumstances: In 1855, the Coosa Association met at Pleasant Grove, Chattooga county, Ed. Dyer was elected Moderator, C. H. Stillwell, Clerk, and C. W. Sparks, Treasurer. In sight of the meeting house were the mounds, formed of loose rocks, which marked the graves of the Cherokee Indians. Evan Powell, a deacon of the Waterville church, Walker county, an humble, pious Christian, and beloved by the whole Association, presented a resolution that a mission be established among the Cherokee Indians. His earnest pleading for the perishing, whose lands the Association was then occupying, among whose very graves, (so much beloved by them,) the Association was then serving God, while the Indians were dying in ignorance of the Saviour, thrilled the whole body and excited an intense missionary enthusiasm. Four hundred dollars were raised, and the Executive Committee was requested to seek for and appoint a proper man to be a missionary of the Association among the Cherokees. The committee was fortunately successful in procuring as their missionary, David Foreman, who accomplished much good among those Indians.

At that time, 1858, the Coosa, Middle Cherokee and Tallapoosa Associations, each had a home missionary at work within their own bounds. Although Rev. J. R. Chambers and Rev. V. A. Bell, were appointed by the Executive Committee of the Cherokee Baptist Convention, as missionaries to the Cherokees, they both declined, and it was not until 1861 that a suitable man was secured, in the person of Rev. E. L. Compere, son of Rev. Lee Compere, whom the Executive Committee was, by formal resolution, instructed to appoint and send to the field. He entered into the service and was so engaged for several years.

It may not be amiss to state the origin of another enterprise of this Convention. At the session of 1859, in Dalton, a mass meeting was held to consider the question of publishing a Baptist weekly paper, and it was not only decided to do so, but Rev. J. M. Wood was elected its editor. The first number of the paper appeared at Rome, in October, 1859, and was designated the "Landmark Banner and Cherokee Baptist." It was afterwards moved to Atlanta and Rev. H. C. Hornady became associate editor. At that time the denomination in Georgia was greatly excited in regard to "the Board Question," "the plan of conducting missions," and other matters, and, in order the more fully to ventilate these and other matters, such as "church independence," "Young Men's Christian Associations," "the rights of minorities," "theological education," "church discipline," "the pulpit and communion issues," this paper was originated, and, was in truth, a lively and spicy sheet, until the devastations of war and the bad management of a business member of the firm blasted the enterprise.

Nearly until the conclusion of the war of secession did the Cherokee Baptist Convention continue in vigorous and useful existence, composed of, and mainly conducted by, earnest and zealous Christians, many of whom still take an active part in the drama of life. The losses, calamities and devastations caused by the war, and resulting in poverty and ruin, ended not only its existence, but that of all its benevolent enterprises.

It is proper to say here that the Cherokee Baptist Convention has had a successor, especially as respects its work in the missionary department. We outline the history of the new body, the North Georgia Baptist General Missionary Association.

The hearts of many brethren in North Georgia have yearned for more concert of action in fulfilling the commission for the evangelization of the world which our Lord on the eve of his ascension gave, not exclusively to the apostles, nor yet to the churches exclusively, but through them to all DISCIPLES. These brethren saw that thousands of Baptists in the Piedmont section of the Commonwealth were doing almost nothing for missions. They realized the difficulty, if not the impossibility of uniting the Associations of Upper Georgia with the Baptist State Convention. The Chattahoochee Association, therefore, at its session in October, 1877, invited any and all Baptist Associations in good standing, to meet with her, by delegates from Associations and churches, at Hopewell church, in Hall county, on Friday before the fourth Sunday in July, 1878, to consider the propriety of organizing for mission work. On the day appointed, between forty and fifty churches from a number of Associations were represented by delegates. By special request, Rev. W. C. Wilkes preached an impromptu introductory sermon, well suited to the occasion, from III John, 8 verse: "That we might be fellow-helpers to the truth." The body was organized by electing Elder J. E. Reeves, Moderator, Elder W. C. Wilkes, Assistant Moderator, Elder D. S. McCurry, Secretary, and Berian H. Brown, Treasurer. The Constitution opened with this preamble: "Whereas, the Lord's people are commanded to 'go into all the world and preach the gospel to every creature,' and to 'work while it is called to-day;' and, whereas, the New Testament clearly teaches that the church is the Lord's instrumentality for evangelizing the world." The objects to be pursued by the Association were thus stated: "To unite the labors of Baptists in preaching the gospel everywhere, to assist weak churches in our bounds, and to aid worthy young men in preparing for the ministry." The meeting was a gracious one, and the three annual sessions since have been marked by harmony of feeling and by brotherly love.

This Association has shown itself to be both a working and a growing body. It has given comfort to two aged, worn-out soldiers of the cross. It is sustaining a native Chinese preacher in a city of 700,000 inhabitants in a province of the empire of "the Anglo-Saxons of the East." It has an Indian preacher, O-las-se Chub-be, laboring successfully among the red men of the West. It assists in the education of young brother Pruitt, a student in the Southern Baptist Theological Seminary. These, we are persuaded, are but the beginnings of its works of faith and labors of love. May the blessing of Heaven and the Spirit of all grace abide on it.

• During the ten years immediately preceding the war, the host of mighty Baptists comprising the Georgia Baptist Convention, were actively engaged in every good word and work, "and there were giants in those days."

In 1857, Thomas Stocks was succeeded as President of the Convention, by P. H. Mell, who, for ten years, had been its clerk, and who inaugurated and established the full and admirable statistical tables which have been so excellently maintained by succeeding clerks down to the present time, especially by its present admirable clerk, Rev. G. R. McCall.

The CHRISTIAN INDEX, donated to the Convention in 1840, was moved to Macon in 1857, and Joseph Walker was elected editor.

In the same year, at the session of the Convention held in Augusta, the Bible Board and Colporter Society was formed on the 25th of April, in the lecture-room of the Baptist house of worship, H. C. Hornady, Chairman, and J. H. Kilpatrick, Secretary. A. C. Dayton, S. Landrum and T. J. Perry were appointed a committee to draft a Constitution, which was submitted and adopted. The officers elected were J. H. DeVotie, President; J. F. Swanson, Corresponding Secretary; S. Landrum, Recording Secretary; and J. DeLoache, Treasurer. A Board of Managers, composed of Macon brethren, were elected, and the society was located in that city. Six hundred dollars in cash and contributions were raised.

On the 30th, at a meeting of the Board of Managers in Macon, W. N. Chaudoin was elected in the place of J. F. Swanson, resigned; but he served one month only, when J. DeLoache was elected Corresponding Secretary and Treasurer. His first report, in April, 1858, showed $2,241.26 collected, and $2,149.09 expended. At its session in Americus, its auxiliary relationship with the Bible Board at Nashville was discontinued, and the society was made to occupy an independent position.

The main object of this society was "to aid in the circulation of the Holy Scriptures and other religious books in our own and other lands." It had a large depository of books in Macon, and with successive depository agents, S. Boykin, James D. Cubbedge and F. M. Haygood, its Board of Managers kept it in useful operation until the end of the war, when it went out of existence with so many other Southern enterprises of a similar character.

The years immediately preceding the war, were years, not only of great activity in our denomination, but of great commotion. Exciting questions were agitating the denomination, and a "split," or division, appeared threateningly imminent, there being, as already chronicled, two Conventions in the State.

"Board" and "Anti-Board," "Landmark" and "Anti-Landmark," "Mission Plan," "Independent Action," "Rights of Minorities," and many other similar expressions became painfully common in the newspapers, and, it is feared, that too much actual bitterness of feeling prevailed, although brethen maintained friendly relations toward each other, personally. One good result of the war was to annihilate those little discussions and unite our denomination in the State more firmly into a large band of loving brothers.

Previous to the war there were sixty-five Associations formed in Georgia, and of these there were in connection with the Georgia Baptist Convention, in 1861, twenty-two, the names of which are, Appalachee, Bethel, Central, Clarkesville, Columbus, Ebenezer, Flint River, Friendship, Georgia, Hephzibah, Houston, Mount Vernon, Piedmont, Rehoboth, Stone Mountain, Sarepta, State Line, Sunbury, Southern, Tugalo, Washington, Western. Their reported contributions for missions, in 1859, amounted to $19,487.02; in 1860, they amounted to $20,329.97; and, in 1861, to $21,180.89.

A very small portion of these amounts was contributed by those Associations which were connected with the Cherokee Baptist Convention, in Northern Georgia, which conducted missions on the independent plan, and, besides, contributing to the home and foreign missions of the Southern Baptist Convention, maintained a Cherokee Indian mission of its own.

There were, in connection with the Cherokee Baptist Convention, in 1861, seven Associations, namely: Coosa, Middle Cherokee, Tallapoosa, Hightower, Ellijay, Noonday and Arbacoochie. At the Convention of 1860, which met at Marietta, May 18th, $720.69 were reported sent up for various benevolent objects, while during the year, ending May 18th, the sum of $881.72 had been contributed for the Cherokee Indian mission alone. The session of 1861 was held at Calhoun, when $545.25 were reported received by the finance committee; while $961 had been contributed for the Cherokee Indian mission during the preceding year.

It is, perhaps, unnecessary to state that it was the Associations connected with these two Conventions, which, previous to the war, made Georgia Baptist history, contributed almost entirely the funds donated by the Georgia Baptists to the great causes of missions, education and the distribution of the Bible, and carried forward the great benevolent and educational plans of the denomination. There were other and good Associations; but to present more in detail their history is not possible in a brief chronicle of Georgia Baptist annals, such as this historical sketch presumes only to be.

XVIII.
DENOMINATIONAL HISTORY.
1861-1881.

XVIII.

DENOMINATIONAL HISTORY.

THE SECESSION OF THE SOUTHERN STATES—ACTION OF THE SOUTHERN BAPTIST CONVENTION, AT SAVANNAH—OF THE GEORGIA BAPTIST CONVENTION, AT ATHENS—OF THE CHEROKEE BAPTIST CONVENTION, AT CALHOUN—THE CHRISTIAN INDEX; ITS HISTORY FROM 1833—THE PROPERTY OF JESSE MERCER UNTIL 1839—OF THE BAPTIST STATE CONVENTION UNTIL 1861—OF S. BOYKIN UNTIL 1865—OF J. J. TOON UNTIL 1873—OF J. P. HARRISON & CO. TO THE PRESENT DATE—EVANGELISTIC LABOR IN THE ARMY—STATE OF RELIGION AFTER THE RETURN OF PEACE—COLORED BAPTISTS; THEIR ASSOCIATIONS AND CONVENTIONS—ATLANTA BAPTIST SEMINARY; DRS. ROBERT AND SHAVER—STATISTICS OF THE DENOMINATION IN THE STATE FOR 1881—FIFTY YEARS AGO AND NOW.

In 1860, by a minority both of the electoral and popular votes, Abraham Lincoln, the Republican candidate, was elected President—a "sectional President," as he was called; and this was deemed the signal for action by those in the South who recognized the right of secession. The union of the States they believed to be merely a voluntary bond, that could be dissolved at will by those States which might choose such a dissolution, whenever a sufficient inciting cause should occur to justify it. The election of Mr. Lincoln, the Abolition candidate was, by the Southern leaders who favored secession and believed it constitutional, considered a sufficient reason for severing the Federal compact. This was regarded as one of the reserved rights of the States, a fair and logical consequence of the doctrine of State sovereignty, then maintained at the South. This doctrine was advocated by nearly all the most prominent politicians in Georgia, even by the Hon. A. H. Stephens himself, who nevertheless opposed secession as an impolitic and unwise measure that would prove disastrous. South Carolina took the lead in secession from the Union, and, in a called State Convention, passed an ordinance of secession, on the 24th of December, 1860. In rapid succession her example was followed by six other States—Mississippi on the 9th of January, Florida and Alabama on the 11th of January, Georgia on the 19th, Louisiana on the 26th, and Texas on the 1st of February. The Secession Convention of Georgia met at Milledgeville, the Capital, and the secession ordinance, written by Hon. Eugenius A. Nisbet, of Macon, was adopted, overwhelmingly. Delegates from the seceded States met at Montgomery, Alabama, on the 4th of February, and on the 8th Jefferson Davis was elected Provisional President, and Alexander H. Stephens, Vice-President.

A new government was thus formed, under the name of THE CONFEDERATE STATES OF AMERICA. It is but right and proper to say that the Southern States firmly believed that they had a right to secede from the Union, and it was a prevalent opinion, and one expressed by President Buchanan himself, that no coercive measures would be employed to keep such States in the Union as, in their sovereign capacity, might decide to go out of it. Of course Southern Baptists held generally to these views, and sustained the political action of their States and section.

In May, 1861, the Southern Baptist Convention met in Savannah, and Dr. Fuller, of Baltimore, was elected President. On motion of William H. McIntosh, of Alabama, a committee, composed of R. Fuller, of Maryland, B. Manly,

Sr., of Alabama; P. H. Mell, of Georgia; R. B. C. Howell, of Tennessee; J. B Taylor, of Virginia; E. T. Winkler, of South Carolina; L. W. Allen, of Kentucky; Wm. C. Crane, of Louisiana; G. H. Martin, of Mississippi; J. E. Broome, of Florida; J. L. Prichard, of North Carolina, was instructed to report on the "State of the Country." The following is the report, which was unanimously adopted, and it should be remembered that about *one-half* of the delegates were Georgians.

Dr. Richard Fuller, of Maryland, made the report:

"We hold this truth to be self-evident, that governments are established for the security, prosperity and happiness of the people. When, therefore, any government is perverted from its proper design, becomes oppressive and abuses its power, the people have a right to change it.

"As to the States once combined upon this continent, it is now manifest that they can no longer live together as one confederacy.

"The Union, constituted by our forefathers, was one of co-equal sovereign States. The fanatical spirit of the North has long been seeking to deprive us of rights and franchises guaranteed by the Constitution; and, after years of persistent aggression, they have, at last, accomplished their purpose.

"In vindication of their sacred rights and honor, in self-defence, and for the protection of all which is dear to man, the Southern States have, practically, asserted a right of seceding from a Union so degenerated from that established by the Constitution; and they have framed for themselves a government based upon the principles of the original compact—adopting a character which secures to each State its sovereign rights and privileges.

"This new government, in thus dissolving former political connections, seeks to cultivate relations of amity and good will with its late confederates, and with all the world; and they have thrice sent special commissioners to Washington, with overtures for peace, and for a fair, amicable adjustment of all difficulties. The government at Washington has insultingly repelled these reasonable proposals, and now insists upon devastating our land with fire and sword; upon letting loose hordes of armed soldiers to pillage and desolate the entire South, for the purpose of forcing the seceded States back into unnatural union, or of subjugating them, and holding them as conquered provinces.

"While the two sections of the land are thus arrayed against each other, it might naturally have been hoped that, at least, the churches of the North would interpose and protest against this appeal to the sword—this invoking of civil war—this deluging the country in fratricidal blood; but, with astonishment and grief, we find churches and pastors of the North breathing out slaughter, and clamoring for sanguinary hostilities with a fierceness which we would have supposed impossible among the disciples of the Prince of Peace. In view of such premises, this Convention cannot keep silence. Recognizing the necessity that the whole moral influence of the people, in whatever capacity or organization, should be enlisted in aid of the rulers, who, by their suffrages, have been called to defend the endangered interests of person and property, of honor and liberty, it is bound to utter its voice distinctly, decidedly, emphatically, and your committee recommend, therefore, the subjoined resolutions:

"*Resolved, 1.* That impartial history cannot charge upon the South the dissolution of the Union. She was foremost in advocating and cementing that Union. To that Union she clung, through long years of calumny, injury and insult. She has never ceased to raise her warning appeals against the fanaticism which has obstinately and incessantly warred against that Union.

"*Resolved, 2.* That we most cordially approve of the formation of the government of the Confederate States of America, and admire and applaud the noble course of that government up to the present time.

"*Resolved, 3.* That we will assiduously invoke the divine direction and favor in behalf of those who bear rule among us, that they may still exercise the same wise, prompt, elevated statesmanship, which has hitherto characterized their measures; that their enterprises may be attended with success; and that they may attain great reward, not only in seeing these Confederate States prosper under their administration, but in contributing to the progress of the transcendent kingdom of our Lord Jesus Christ.

"*Resolved, 4.* That we most cordially tender to the President of the Confederate States, to his Cabinet, and to the members of the Congress now convened at Montgomery, the assurances of our sympathy and entire confidence. With them are our hearts and our hearty co-operation.

"*Resolved, 5.* That the lawless reign of terror at the North, the violence committed upon unoffending citizens, above all, the threats to wage upon the South a warfare of savage barbarity, to devastate our homes and hearths with hosts of ruffians and felons, burning with lust and rapine, ought to excite the horror of all civilized people. God forbid that we should so far forget the spirit of Jesus as to suffer malice and vindictiveness to insinuate themselves into our hearts; but, every principle of religion, of patriotism and of humanity, calls upon us to pledge our fortunes and lives in the good work of repelling an invasion designed to destroy whatever is dear in our heroic traditions—whatever is sweet in domestic hopes and enjoyments—whatever is essential to our institutions and our very manhood—whatever is worth living or dying for.

"*Resolved, 6.* That we do now engage in prayer for our friends, brothers, fathers, sons and citizen-soldiers, who have left their homes to go forth for the defence of their families and friends, and all which is dearest to the human heart; and we commend to the churches represented in this body, that they constantly invoke a holy and merciful God to cover their heads in the day of battle, and give victory to their arms.

"*Resolved, 7.* That we will pray for our enemies in the spirit of the Divine Master, who, "when he was reviled reviled not again," trusting that their pitiless purposes may be frustrated; that God will grant to them a more politic, a more considerate, and a more Christian mind, that the fratricidal strife which they have decided upon, notwithstanding all our commissions and pleas for peace, may be arrested by that Supreme Power who maketh the wrath of man to praise Him; and that thus, through the divine blessing, the prosperity of these sovereign and once allied States may be restored under the two governments to which they now and henceforth, respectively belong.

"*Resolved, 8.* We do recommend the churches of the Baptist denomination in the Southern States, to observe the first and second days of June, as days of humiliation, fasting, and prayer to Almighty God, that He may avert any calamities due to our sins as a people, and may look with mercy and favor upon us.

"*Resolved, 9.* That, whatever calamities may come upon us, our firm trust and hope are in God, through the atonement of His Son, and we earnestly beseech the churches represented in this body (a constituency of six or seven hundred thousand Christians), that they be prompt and importunate in prayer, not only for the country, but for the enterprises of the gospel which have been committed to our care. In the war of 1812, the Baptists bated not a jot of heart or hope for the Redeemer's cause. Their zeal and liberality abounded in their deep afflictions. We beseech the churches to cherish the spirit, and imitate the example of this noble army of saints and heroes; to be followers of them who, through faith and patience, inherit the promises; to be steadfast, unmovable, always abounding in the work of the Lord, forasmuch as they know that their labor is not in vain in the Lord.

"*Resolved, 10.* That these resolutions be communicated to the Congress of the 'Confederate States,' at Montgomery, with the signatures of the President and Secretaries of the Convention.

"P. H. MELL,
"JAMES E. BROOME,
"G. H. MARTIN,
"W. CAREY CRANE,
"R. FULLER,
"JAMES B. TAYLOR,
"R. B. C. HOWELL,
"L. W. ALLEN,
"J. L. PRICHARD,
"E. T. WINKLER,
"B. MANLY, SR."

This report was adopted May 13th, 1861.

On the 27th of April preceding, a committee, composed of N. M. Crawford, chairman, Junius Hillyer, Thomas Stocks, S. Sisk and J. H. Stockton, submitted the following report on the Political Crisis, which was adopted by the Georgia Baptist Convention, assembled at Athens :

"WHEREAS, The State of Georgia, in the legitimate exercise of her sovereignty, has withdrawn from the confederacy known as the United States of America ; and, for the better maintenance of her rights, honor and independence, has united with other States in a new confederacy, under the name of Confederate States of America ; and,

"WHEREAS, Abraham Lincoln, the President of the United States, is attempting by force of arms to subjugate these States, in violation of the fundamental principles of American liberty; therefore,

"*Resolved, 1.* By the members of the Baptist Convention of the State of Georgia, that we consider it to be at once a pleasure and a duty to avow that, both in feeling and in principle, we approve, endorse and support the government of the Confederate States of America.

"*Resolved, 2.* That, while this Convention disclaims all authority, whether ecclesiastical or civil, yet, as citizens, we deem it but a duty to urge the union of all the people of the South in defence of the common cause ; and to express the confident belief that, in whatever conflict the madness of Mr. Lincoln and his government may force upon us, the Baptists of Georgia will not be behind any class of our fellow citizens in maintaining the independence of the South by any sacrifice of treasure or of blood.

"*Resolved, 3.* That we acknowledge, with devout thankfulness to Almighty God, the signal favor with which, up to this time, He has blessed our arms and our policy ; and that the Baptist churches of this State be requested to observe the first and second days of June next, as days of fasting and prayer, that God will deliver us from all the power of our enemies, and restore peace to our country.

"*Resolved 4.* That the Confederate Government be requested to invite the churches of all denominations, within the Confederacy, to unite in observing said days of fasting and prayer.

"*Resolved, 5.* That copies of these resolutions be sent to President Davis, the Confederate Congress, and the Governor of Georgia.

N. M. CRAWFORD, *Chairman.*

On its adoption the President, Dr. Mell, by request, invited the entire congregation to express their opinion on the sentiments of this report, and in testimony of their unanimous approval the entire assembly rose to their feet simultaneously. On motion of J. H. Campbell, the President then called upon Dr. C. D. Mallary to lead in prayer. It was an interesting, solemn and devotional time.

On the 17th of May the Cherokee Baptist Convention met at Calhoun, Georgia, and Mark A. Cooper was elected President, with W. A. Mercer, Secretary, and T. H. Stout, Assistant Secretary. The same day, on motion, the regular order of business was suspended and the following resolution, offered by J. M. Wood, was unanimously adopted :

"*Resolved,* That a special committee be appointed to draft resolutions in reference to the affairs of our beloved country, the Southern Confederate States of America, and that the Moderator act as chairman of said committee." A committee of seven was agreed upon, and that the President appoint the other six. He appointed J. M. Wood, R. M. Young, J. H. B. Shackelford, William Newton, D. B. Hamilton and A. B. Ross.

On Monday, the 20th, the following report was presented by Mark A. Cooper, who addressed the Convention in a clear and forcible manner on the subject of the report. He was followed by J. M. Wood, and afterwards the report was unanimously adopted—the whole congregation voting.

"*Resolved,* That we adopt and sustain the views and opinions of the Southern Baptist Convention, recently held in Savannah, Georgia, as set forth in the report of a special committee, made by Rev. Dr. Richard Fuller, chairman. Also, that we adopt and sustain the opinions expressed by the Georgia Baptist Convention at its late session in Athens, Georgia, as contained in the report of a committee, made by Rev. Dr. N. M. Crawford.

"*Resolved*, That on occasions of great public concern, in which millions of our people find their rights, their liberties and homes invaded, it is proper that the opinions of organized Christian communities should be made known. The condition of the Confederate States of America is such an occasion.

"*Resolved, therefore*, That the Cherokee Baptist Convention of Georgia, do declare, as just and true the following facts and opinions, to-wit:

" 1. The contest waging between the Northern United States and Southern Confederate States, is one of right and wrong, in which the North claims the right (the powers granted by their Federal Constitution being the pretext) to tax the South at pleasure and against its will, to sell us what they make at their own prices, denying us the right to buy elsewhere, at cheaper rates. This takes from us, against our will, the profits of our labor to aid their private enterprises, and enable their capitalists to employ their labor and make good their profits.

" 2. Connected with and incidental to this, is the power claimed and exercised by the North to dictate to the South what kind of labor it shall use, and where it should be employed, restricting us in the use of our property, rendering it unprofitable and valueless, and denying to us equal rights in a common territory for the purpose of destroying the tenure of our property and depriving us of it.

" 3. If the Constitution of the United States of America is what our fathers made it, and true Republicans have ever thought it to be, there is no power granted to do this. Doing it is an assumption of power unjust and oppressive. Northern capital, combined with hired labor, impelled by a spirit of fanaticism, has controlled the majority interest, has perverted the Constitution, and established at Washington a government with practically unlimited power.

" 4. We of the South have resisted in the only peaceable and rightful way known to us. As free and independent States we have formed that Union for purposes expressed in the Constitution, to be carried out by powers defined and limited. For reasons assigned and deemed sufficient, as sovereign and independent States, we have dissolved and withdrawn from it. As such, we have formed a union of Confederate States. We adopted the Constitution of our fathers with all its good features, reforming its defects.

" 5. All this has been done with notice to all the States with whom we were heretofore united. This we had a right to do. Independence as States, freedom and equality as a people, we were entitled to and will have, or will take the alternative not to be.

" 6. We thank the wise Disposer of human events that in this there is but one purpose with our people. We seek peace, and do not desire war. We do not intend to trespass on or invade the rights of others. We do intend that others shall not put hostile feet on our territory. For this we shall meet the invader at the line, and with our lives and fortunes defend our country, every inch of ground, trusting to God and our cause.

" 7. War is forced upon us. The government at Washington city is now a consolidation of arbitrary persons; is a military despotism, ruled by the spirit of a mob, moved by fanaticism, and guided by peculiar, sectional, pecuniary interests.

" 8. It calls us 'rebels' and 'traitors.' To make good this charge it assumes that our union with the States it represents still exists. And yet, so grand and imposing is our movement by our States and government, that, assuming us to be foreign powers at war with the powers at Washington city, it treats us as a belligerent nation!

" 9. It summons, at the will of a man styled President, without the authority of Congress, the army and navy to fight us. Finding this too weak, without form of law, the same man calls on the several States for contributions of troops to subdue us. These being too slow and inefficient, the same man levies troops indefinitely as to number and time of service, without law or authority, to ravage and lay waste our country, destroy our property, and make us subject to a willful and aggressive majority.

"10. They seek to conquer us:

"*First*, By dividing us. To this end they tamper with our people and buy up whom they can, teaching them that one of our counties is to the State what a State was to the Union.

"*Second*, They seek to conquer us by destroying our commerce, having power only to 'regulate' it. To this end they have established, or declared, a regular blockade of all our ports and public avenues of approach, quartering their armies and planting their navy to interrupt our trade. They hope, thereby to starve us out and deprive us of the means and power of self-defence.

"This hope is vain and delusive. If it must be so, let them cherish it. They are as false to themselves as they have been to us. 'They are given up to believe a lie.'

"11. The blockade is doing for us that which we could not do for ourselves. They will remove it or destroy themselves. If it stands it will put them right and open their eyes to truth. It will restore peace to us sooner than the Minnie musket or the Mississippi rifle. It will give us a victory more bloodless than the capture of Sumter.

"12. Brethren, let us abide and sustain it. Their bacon and flour let them keep and consume. Their hardware, plantation tools, house and kitchen furniture, men's and women's clothing, let them take to another market. Let us live without them. As for powder and lead and arms, they will find we have more than Christians should force us to use—enough for the occasion. Whilst we pray that God will rule them and us, and spare us their use, if it is His will let us use them; we will do it with all our might.

"13. Brethren, let their blockade be enforced if it can be, in its rigor. If we can't do without them it is wrong to quit them. If right to quit them, we should now demonstrate virtue enough to cut loose from them, cost what it may. We should hate to look at anything (tempted by a dollar), they would smuggle to us.

"*Resolved*, That we have confidence in our rulers, the President and Cabinet and Congress. With these views and purposes, trusting in the Almighty and the justice of our cause, we have nothing to fear. Let those who would wrong and oppress, move on, until time and events, their own interest, or the will of our Heavenly Father, shall turn their course.

"Mark A. Cooper,
"J. M. Wood,
"R. M. Young,
"A. B. Ross,
"J. H. B. Shackelford,
"W. Newton,
"D. B. Hamilton."

THE CHRISTIAN INDEX.

At the session for 1861, the Georgia Baptist Convention instructed its "Index Committee" to effect a sale of The Index, with as little delay as possible; and it, therefore, seems proper that a brief history of this useful adjunct of Georgia Baptist History should be inserted here.

In December, 1839, Jesse Mercer laid before the Executive Committee of the Convention a proposition to transfer The Christian Index to the Convention, giving, with The Index, the house, presses and type, belonging to his printing establishment. He proposed to furnish the office with $500.00 worth of new type. The Committee recommended the Convention to accept the donation, which it did in May, 1840, and the paper was moved to Penfield, January 1st, 1841, Rev. William H. Stokes having been retained as editor.

The paper had been transferred to Georgia from Philadelphia, in the latter half of 1833, and edited by Jesse Mercer, assisted very ably, most of the time, by William H. Stokes. Mr. Stokes continued to edit the paper, with credit to himself, until January, 1843, when he resigned. Dr. J. S. Baker was then elected editor, a position which he filled with marked ability, until January, 1849. He then tendered his resignation, when B. M. Sanders, chairman of the Executive

Committee conducted the paper until January of the following year, at which time John F. Dagg assumed editorial control. Under his management the paper prospered; and in 1854, it paid into the treasury of the Convention $463.35. The following year it paid into the treasury $276.59.

During all these years the paper had been the organ of the Georgia Baptists, and had exerted a powerful influence for good. Its bane, however, was the credit system, which prevented it from ever becoming a financial success, and gave rise, in a large degree, to those circumstances which finally resulted in its sale. J. F. Dagg was succeeded by T. D. Martin, in December, 1855, and at the next session of the Convention, in 1856, the sale of the paper was strongly recommended by the Executive Committee, but they were instructed to remove it "to some one of the principal cities of the State."

In July, 1856, it was decided to move the paper to Macon, and an INDEX Committee was appointed, consisting of E. G. Cabaniss, B. F. Tharp, H. Bunn, S. Landrum, J. DeLoache, J. Collins, William L. A. Ellis. The Convention of 1857 adopted the following resolutions:

"1. The energy, efficiency and business tact, apparent in everything pertaining to THE INDEX, are worthy of all praise.

"2. The diligence, devotion and ability of the editor are also manifest; and the success with which he is known to have acquitted himself, in various other arduous pursuits, may well have directed the attention of the Committee to that brother."

Rev. Joseph Walker was the new editor, assuming his position in January, 1857. He proved to be a strong and spicy writer and gave great life to the paper, which, under his care, succeeded financially. The editor's salary of $1,500.00, besides a surplus paid into the treasury, were the nett proceeds of the paper. As already intimated, Rev. S. Landrum, chairman of THE INDEX Committee, edited the paper very successfully for two months, when Rev. E. W. Warren being elected to the position, became editor August the 25th, 1859, and so continuing until March, 1860, when he resigned, to become pastor of the Macon church. S. Boykin was then elected editor, and held the position until he purchased the paper in 1861.

The sale of the paper had been agitated for many years. As early as 1849 the Convention recommended its sale, but it could not be effected with propriety. In 1856 the Executive Committee presented an argument in favor of sale, but the Convention declined, lest the paper might cease to be a Baptist paper, and thus be lost to the denomination; and for fear that its sale might injure the circulation of the paper, and impair its usefulness to the denomination. The Executive Committee stated in 1856, "The management of THE CHRISTIAN INDEX from 1840, when it was transferred to the Convention by Rev. Jesse Mercer, has been a source of more perplexity to the Committee than all other matters trusted to their charge."

In 1861 circumstances so favorable to a sale supervened that the measure passed the Convention without much opposition, and the paper continued its career of usefulness, until General Wilson's conquering legions entered the city of Macon. The last issue was mailed when the enemy were in rapid advance upon Macon, having captured Columbus. It had then a larger circulation than it had ever attained previously.

Soon after the war, it was sold by S. Boykin, to J. J. Toon, of Atlanta, for the sum of $2,000 cash, and Mr. Toon, the proprietor, of the Franklin Printing House of Atlanta, in November, 1865, started it upon a widely extended career of usefulness, under the editorship of Dr. H. H. Tucker. At the end of six months Dr. Tucker assumed the Presidency of Mercer University, and after six months more, during which Dr. W. T. Brantly wielded the editorial *baton*, Dr. D. Shaver, of Virginia, was employed, January, 1867, to edit the paper. He retired in September, 1874. Under his able and scholarly care the paper prospered, became a strong Baptist power and exerted a commanding influence.

The Baptist State Convention at its session in Rome, April, 1873, "learning from brother Toon that it was his purpose to sell THE INDEX, pledged its continued and active support in circulating the paper in the hands of any proper purchasers." It also expressed the opinion that "it would be highly gratifying to the Baptists of Georgia, if some satisfactory arrangement could be made, by which Dr. Shaver's services could be retained as editor of the denominational organ." This action was taken by the adoption of a report from a committee, including one from each Association represented in the body, which had been raised to consider the interests of the paper. In pursuance of the policy thus marked out, a sub-committee held a conference in Atlanta with Dr. J. S. Lawton and Mr. J. P. Harrison, (who organized the firm of J. P. Harrison & Co.,) and the wish of the Convention was consummated by the transfer of THE INDEX to this firm in June, 1873. The new proprietors, in the first issue under their management, said:

"The undersigned are conscious of the fact that success can be obtained only by the cordial and active co-operation of the denomination whose tenets it is designed to expound. This co-operation they anticipate, as well from their knowledge of the liberal impulses of the churches as from the pledges of their representative men; and with confidence in this support, they engage most heartily and hopefully in the new duties before them."

On the retirement of Dr. Shaver, Rev. D. E. Butler became managing editor, and held that position until Dr. H. H. Tucker was employed in October, 1878. From 1833 to the present time the paper has remained the staunch supporter of Georgia Baptist affairs, and the regular organ of the denomination in the State, maintaining always a large circulation.

At the last session of the Georgia Baptist Convention, in 1881, in Athens, the following resolutions were adopted, concerning this time-honored paper:

WHEREAS, This Convention at its session in LaGrange in 1878, adopted the following preamble and resolution, to-wit:

"Recognizing THE CHRISTIAN INDEX as the ORGAN of our denomination in this State, and appreciating its importance in every field of denominational labor, whether as the exponent and defender of our doctrines, interests and policy, the medium of communication between the churches, or as an invaluable companion in Baptist homes—we cordially and earnestly resolve:

"1. That THE CHRISTIAN INDEX is worthy of, and should receive, the support of every Baptist in Georgia.

"2. That, as the denominational organ, it has evinced a degree of ability, fidelity and watchfulness over the varied interests of the denomination, which merits recognition by this Convention.

"3. That the enterprise, liberality and zeal which have distinguished the proprietors in their conduct of THE INDEX, commend them to the confidence and support of all Georgia Baptists, and give assurance of unabated efforts, on their part, to increase the usefulness of this denominational auxiliary.

"4. That all Baptist ministers in Georgia—keeping in view the importance of THE INDEX as the ORGAN of our denomination, and as a means of advancing vital Christianity—should regard it as a ministerial duty to urge the members of their respective congregations to give it their support; and we invoke the prompt and conscientious performance of this obligation."

AND WHEREAS, resolutions of the same tone and intent have been repeatedly adopted from time to time by this body for many years past, and were, in substance, reaffirmed by the Convention last year during its session in Savannah, in the following words, to-wit:

"We take pleasure in acknowledging the excellence, ability and soundness of the time-honored INDEX under its present management, and commend it heartily to all Georgia Baptists."

AND WHEREAS, The present managers of THE CHRISTIAN INDEX have increased the editorial force to a larger degree than ever before, at considerable expense to themselves, therefore

Resolved, That we renew all our former indorsements of the "excellence, ability and soundness of the time-honored INDEX," and re-affirm our commendation of it to the hearty support of every Baptist in Georgia.

To quote the words of C. D. Mallary, in a report to the Convention in 1860:
"THE CHRISTIAN INDEX has had an honorable and useful history. For nearly

orty years (now, nearly sixty years), it has been circulating among our churches, mparting valuable instruction to thousands in relation to the doctrines and commands of our exalted Saviour, and advancing, ably and earnestly, wise and udicious plans for the furtherance of the Redeemer's kingdom among men. In the hands of Knowles and Brantly and Mercer, (long since entered into their heavenly rest), it accomplished a noble work; and in the hands of beloved and precious brethren still living, it continued its wholesome and wide-spread ministrations. We pray God that it may live for a long time to come, and that its ife may be one of constantly increasing usefulness."

DURING THE WAR.

The four years of war that ensued very soon, caused a discontinuance of actual participation in Foreign and Indian missions work, by the Southern Baptists, although contributions for those objects continued to be made by the Georgia Baptists, all during the war. Missions among the Indians, in the Indian Territory, were completely broken up, the country ravaged and pillaged, and the tribes scattered, as soon as the dogs of war were fairly let loose. The warlike nature of the Indian tribes was greatly aroused, and the Choctaws, Creeks, and a portion of the Cherokees unhesitatingly dissolved their connection with the United States government, and not only cast in their fortunes with the Southern Confederacy, but took up arms and enlisted in the cause of the young republic. The same was true of the Seminoles and Chickasaws. To all these tribes the sacrifice made, in thus uniting with the South, was tremendous, putting even their national existence in peril. Among these tribes several Georgia Baptist Associations had maintained missionaries—for instance, the Bethel, the Rehoboth, the Ebenezer and the Western—but, of course, their mission work ceased, as the missionaries either joined the army, fled, or became government officers. Invasion destroyed the mission of the Baptists of North Georgia among the Cherokees in that region, also. Gradually, even the scope of Domestic missions became greatly circumscribed, and the benevolent contributions, thus diverted from their usual channels, were appropriated to the sustenance of missionaries in the armies and providing Bibles and religious reading for the soldiers. The war, entered into so hastily and with such a gallant ebullition of spirits, proved to be a far more serious and momentous affair than was expected, and the South, at length, realized that it had taken an awful step in attempting secession. The Mission Report, of 1862, written by William T. Brantly, the younger, for the Georgia Baptist Convention, contained these words: "The Committee on Missions report the satisfaction which they have experienced in finding that the churches continue to make to the mission cause contributions which, under the circumstances, must be regarded as liberal The fact shows the deep hold which this cause possesses on the affections of the churches. We are in the midst of one of the most desolating wars with which it has ever pleased God to visit any nation. Our resources have been taxed well nigh to exhaustion, in making provision for the brave and patriotic men who have taken the field to repel the invader; while the price of living has augmented in an enormous ratio, the ordinary income of the great mass of the people has been greatly abridged; and yet, under all these disadvantages, more than *four thousand dollars* have been paid over during the present session of the Convention, by churches and by individuals, to the different objects of benevolence under the patronage of our denomination. Such contributions, under such circumstances, indicate a noble spirit of self-denial for Jesus. They afford a grateful verdure amid a barren desert—a shining light amid surrounding gloom. * * * * We are happy to learn that our Board at Richmond have been able, under a flag of truce, to send to our missionaries in foreign fields the funds requisite for their support. We are also pleased to know that the recipients of our benefactions, among the Indian tribes, are in cordial and active sympathy with us, in the revolution which is now in progress. Our brethren are also engaged in some systematic effort to preach the gospel to the soldiers in our camps."

At the same session the virtual suspension of Mercer University is recorded, which was followed by the suspension of exercises in our various colleges for young ladies, in the State, the buildings of which institutions were made available for hospital purposes, by the Confederate government.

The report on missions, in 1863, at Griffin, informs us plainly of the course taken by benevolence at that time: "The liberal contributions we have received [at the present session] from various sources, amounting to about seven thousand dollars, shows that our people are in possession of an intelligent appreciation of the position in support of the divine plan for the speedy accomplishment of this great end—[shedding gospel light upon all nations]. For the time being, the Foreign Board is but imperfectly accomplishing its work, through the agency of sympathising friends in Baltimore.

"Our Domestic Mission Board, aided by Bible and colportage societies, is accomplishing a great work throughout the bounds of its legitimate fields. Its attention is chiefly directed to the army. Ministering brethren are sent among the brave and noble defenders of our country, who have gratuitously distributed to them thousands of Testaments, and millions of pages of religious reading matter, in tracts and religious papers."

It is most true that hundreds of our Georgia Baptists ministers attended the armies of the Confederacy, during the war, and labored faithfully as missionaries, evangelists or chaplains, and the beneficial results of their devoted and self-sacrificing labors will be revealed by the light of eternity only. Many of them served as army missionaries, in the employ of our Boards or Associations, but others were voluntary evangelists, declining to receive any compensation whatever. The well-known opposition to State patronage maintained by our denomination, was strongly exhibited by the Georgia Baptist Convention of 1864, held in Atlanta, which also manifested the intensity of the Baptist desire to minister to the spiritual wants of the soldiers in service.

Governor Joseph E. Brown offered the following, which was adopted at that session of the Convention:

"WHEREAS, there is great need of missionaries in the army, and of ministers to supply destitute churches at home; and, whereas, there are many ordained ministers of the gospel now in the Confederate armies, whose services are desired by regiments, battalions and churches; therefore, be it

"*Resolved by the Georgia Baptist Convention*, That a committee of three be appointed by the president of this Convention to correspond with his Excellency, the President of the Confederate States, and request him to pass an order directing the discharge from military service of any ordained minister of the gospel whose services are asked by any regiment or separate battalion in service, or by any church as a pastor.

"*Resolved, further*, That this Convention does not approve of the principle of appointing chaplains for the army, to be paid out of the public treasury, and we pledge ourselves, as a denomination, to do all in our power to support all ministers of our denomination discharged and permitted to attend, as missionaries, upon regiments or battalions, which may petition for their services."

The committee appointed were D. A. Vason, E. Steadman and J. I. Whitaker. And the truth of history requires the record to be made that the Baptists of Georgia poured out their treasures that the soldiers in the armies of the Confederacy, during the civil war of 1861-'65, might be supplied with Testaments, religious literature, and the preached Word. Both ministry and laymen among them bore their full share in the toils, hardships and dangers of the contest, freely venturing life and health on the battle-field and in ministerial service, making sacrifice of personal comfort of pecuniary treasure, and even of life itself, when the exigencies of the service demanded either.

It is a matter of special record that of the $130,000 contributed to the Domestic Board of the Southern Baptist Convention for army missions during the year from April, 1863, to April, 1864, $50,000 were contributed by the Baptists of Georgia. And our denominational records also bear testimony that their faith and devotion never wavered.

The resolutions on the State of the Country for 1862, offered by J. H. Campbell, may testify on that point:

"*Resolved*, That the Convention heartily, solemnly and unanimously re-asserts the sentiments, as far as applicable to the present circumstances, of the resolutions on the State of the Country passed at the last session of this body.

"*Resolved*, That while profoundly feeling that our cause is just, we nevertheless have great reason to humble ourselves before Almighty God, and to acknowledge his chastening hand in our late reverses.

"*Resolved*, That we find in the present circumstances of the country no cause for discouragement; that God, our Heavenly Father, often chastens most promptly those whom he most loves; and that trusting in him with the whole heart, we are more and more determined, by his blessing, to oppose the invader of our soil by every means placed in our power, and to the last extremity."

To this may be added a similar report made by A. T. Holmes, chairman, two years later, in 1864, at Atlanta:

"After three years' experience of the hardships and horrors of the desolating war waged against us by our unnatural foe, we find ourselves unchanged in our feelings and principles, as respects the indorsement and support of the Confederate States of America. While we recognize the hand of God in the reverses of the past year, and acknowledge that the chastisement was justly administered, we take courage from the fact that, to some good extent, these judgments have been sanctified, and that the spirit of prayer and dependence upon the divine assistance is more than ever manifest.

"In the present condition of our country we find occasion for thankfulness to Him who guides the destinies of nations. From every point the indications are cheering, and hope and confidence swell our bosoms as we contemplate the final result. The gracious influence of divine truth upon our army as reported from various sources, is full of encouragement as respects the Divine purpose in regard to our struggling country.

"In view of the past and present, we would call upon our brethren to act with reference to the declaration of the man of God, that it is better to trust in the Lord than to put confidence in princes. England and France may continue to deny us their countenance and help in our great extremity, and the nations of the earth may regard with indifference the tremendous struggle that involves our very existence as a nation; but if the God of Heaven shall recognize us, all will be well."

It cannot be said, either, that the denomination had not fully realized the terrible results of warfare; for in 1863 a committee composed of J. H. Campbell, M. J. Welborn, Thomas Stocks, N. M. Crawford, and B. F. Tharp were appointed a committee to memorialize the State Legislature in favor of the education of soldiers' orphans; and, as their memorial effected no result, the same committee was continued in 1864, and were unanimously requested to renew their memorial to that body; but as no law to effect the desired result was passed, at the suggestion of the Convention, naught was left but the establishment of an Orphan's Home by the Baptists themselves, and it was done; and for fifteen years it proved a necessary and useful institution.

An examination of the Minutes of our various Associations makes it evident that the Baptists of the State were all intensely interested in the war, thoroughly loyal to the Confederate cause, hopeful even unto the end of 1864, all ardently enlisted in the cause of army missions, actively engaged in caring for the orphans of deceased soldiers, and abundant in prayers for the success of the Confederate cause.

In the summer of 1864, July 31st, died, C. D. Mallary, who, by abundant labors and a saintly life, had wielded a most exalted influence over our denomination in Georgia for more than thirty years. The report of the Board of Trustees of Mercer University for 1866, alluded to his decease in the following terms: "Since our last report,* death has created a vacancy in our Board, of no ordinary character. We allude to the decease of our much loved and revered brother, Charles Dutton Mallary, D. D. Whether as pastor in Columbia, S. C., at Augusta, Ga., at Milledgeville, at LaGrange, or elsewhere; as missionary of the Central Association,

---

*The subjugation of Georgia in April, 1865 prevented a session of the Georgia Baptist Convention in that year.

as a member of the Convention or the Board of Trustees, who can ever forget his abundant labors and saintly bearing? The years of 1837-38 and '39 he devoted to the interest of Mercer University, as agent for its endowment. In 1838 his name stands next to Mercer's on the Minutes of the first Board of Trustees, a position which he occupied with untiring fidelity, and pre-eminent usefulness to the day of his death. He was the peace-maker; the man of devout spirit at all times; distinguished for his piety. He was greatly good. His place cannot be filled, either by the Board or the Convention. The fathers are passing away; may their mantles fall upon their younger brethren!"

The report on deceased ministers for that same session of the Convention, written by Dr. S. G. Hillyer, pays the following graceful and just tribute to the memory of one of the best men the host of Georgia Baptists has ever boasted: "As a man, brother Mallary had no enemy. Among all classes he was regarded with profound respect. Even the wicked paid to his worth spontaneous homage; while the virtuous and the good honored and loved him. As a laborer he was indefatigable. He was familiar with almost every neighborhood within the wide bounds of this Convention. Our cities, towns and villages, and our country churches knew him well. He went about, like his Divine Master, doing good. He was the friend of the widow and the orphan. With his kind words he soothed their sorrows, and with his open hand he often relieved their wants. He was a laborer in the cause of temperance. We can never forget his earnest zeal in that cause. To his last hour he was faithful to the principles which he had so faithfully advocated. He was a laborer in the cause of learning. The Convention has already heard how he toiled for our University. Your committee deem it unnecessary to enlarge upon this topic; but his interest in the educational enterprise of our denomination was not limited to Mercer University. While he exhibited such profound solicitude for the proper culture of our sons, he was not unmindful of the wants of our daughters. LaGrange and Cuthbert, in their efforts in behalf of female education, felt and enjoyed the beneficence of his good will, and the effect of his material aid. His labors were abundant and they were useful; but after all, they were only secondary. His great labor—that to which all else was subordinate—was the work of the ministry. While health und strength sustained him, *he lived to preach*. He was the sinner's friend. Who can forget his mellow tones, as he poured forth his stirring appeals to the unconverted! How his soul yearned for their salvation! When he saw the tear of penitence, or heard the sigh of contrition, what sympathy overflowed his loving heart! He delighted to pour into the wounded spirit the consolation of redeeming love, and then to rejoice in the new-born hope of the young convert.

"As a preacher, brother Mallary stood as an equal among our most gifted men. His scholarship was ripe; his theology was sound; his style was perspicuous and forcible, sometimes ornate, rising under the impulse of a chaste but bold imagination, even to the heights of sublimity; while his manner was earnest, impressive and persuasive. Verily, he was a great and a good man! But he is gone. In the summer of 1864 his health rapidly declined. He saw his end approaching. Freely and even pleasantly he talked of his death as the hour of his deliverance. Calm, resigned and happy, he committed himself to the Saviour whom he loved, and patiently waited His summons. Often his countenance seemed to light up with heavenly joy. His last words testified to those about him his perfect peace. Without a struggle, without a groan, and apparently without a pang, he fell asleep in Jesus."

AFTER THE WAR.

It has been said that Georgia was subjugated in April, 1865. Yes, in that month there was a sudden collapse! The Confederate flag went down. Overwhelming force triumphed, Secession proved a failure, and the banner of the stars and bars was furled forever. The greatest confusion and demoralization prevailed, and the whole denomination was virtually paralyzed for awhile. The Georgia Baptist Convention should have convened at Columbus, in 1865, but owing to the occupation of that city by the enemy, as well as to the disastrous termination of the war, no session could be held in the city of Columbus. In fact, that devoted city was plundered and partly burned, wantonly, by the ruthless and unscrupulous invaders ; and, as no measures had been provided previous to that time to secure a Convention in case of failure to meet at the appointed time, there was no session at all of the Georgia Baptist Convention in 1865.

Making Macon his headquarters, the subjugator ruled the State, which cowered before his power. He arrested Governor Joseph E. Brown and sent him to Washington City. His cavalry captured President Davis at night, a few miles south of Macon, on his way to the coast, and brought him to Macon, where he lodged at the Lanier House, until President Johnson ordered him to be sent to Fortress Monroe. On the morning of his departure a large concourse was assembled in front of the hotel, where two lines of soldiers in blue, with muskets, stretched from the ladies' entrance to a carriage in the street. Mrs. Davis appeared and entered the carriage. Shortly afterwards the President stepped down between the two rows of muskets and took his seat beside his wife, an inexpressible sadness resting upon the countenance of each, notwithstanding the dignified bravery with which they bore themselves under the circumstances. The Federal officers politely touched their caps to the departing prisoner, who responded in similar manner. The carriage door was shut amid the melancholy silence of a motionless crowd assembled. Suddenly one man, and one only, had the boldness or thoughtfulness to step within the line of guards to the carriage door and offer his hand to the fallen chief, with the words : "Goodbye, President Davis ! God bless you !" Mr. Davis took the offered hand, with a faint smile, and was then driven to the railroad depot surrounded by an armed guard. The hand which President Davis shook, that April day, is the one which pens these lines.

Afterwards Gen. Wilson was so lacking in generosity as to *taunt* the citizens of Macon with letting their Ex-president depart into a gloomy captivity, without one single line or word of sympathy, comfort or cheer, appearing in the daily paper of the city, to follow him on his way and solace his broken heart ; while it is true, that the same hand which shook his in front of Lanier House, wrote a stirring article expressing love, admiration and sympathy, and sending the good wishes of the Georgia Confederates after the captive, seeking thus to cheer and comfort him. But the editor of the paper refused to let the article appear, professing to fear the commanding general's anger.

Sad and gloomy were the years that followed. An awful pall settled down upon the State. The slaves were all suddenly freed, and many acted in an outrageous manner, though by no means to the extent one would have supposed. The great misfortune, accompanied by loss of so much property, broke many a noble Southern heart, and, here and there, all over the State, aged men were gathered to their fathers, unable to bear up under the impending calamities.

The Minutes of our Associations and of the State Convention, for years, bear evidence to the demoralization caused by the sad results of the war in the churches and among Christians. Without attempting anything like an extensive *expose* we will but lay before the reader a few extracts to show the state of our denomination in Georgia, in the years succeeding the war of Secession.

The following is taken from the Report rendered by the Committee on the State of the Churches for 1868, in the Ebenezer Association, one of our best, most liberal and efficient bodies:

" The war and its results, have largely demoralized many of our church members, and, as such, there is too much intemperance, profanity, neglect of church duties, heresies, dissensions and general unchristian conduct tolerated by the followers of Jesus. Many, perhaps all, of our churches need purifying, and the only way to secure the strength and efficiency of the churches is to keep them pure."

In 1865 the Georgia Association adopted the following :

" It is to be regretted that there is a disposition on the part of many of the members of the churches to engage in, or give their approbation to, practices of doubtful propriety, such as the *innocent* amusements, (as they are called) of parties, the distillation of ardent spirits, directly or indirectly, and other things of like import. Others engage in practices not of doubtful propriety, but plainly condemned in the word of God, namely: the making, selling and drinking of ardent spirits as a beverage; fiddling and dancing; entertaining in our hearts against Christian brethren, envy, malice, or unkind feelings; and other sinful practices, consequent upon yielding to the temptations, by which we are surrounded in the present state of the country;" and the Association appointed a day of fasting, humiliation and prayer.

In the following year, 1866, the same noble old Association in its Report on the State of Religion adopted these sentiments:

"We are painfully impressed with the fact, that there does not exist among our church members, generally, that profound, earnest zeal, in matters of religion, which would fit them for aggressive movements on the world. We have, still, to lament that many are addicted to fashionable amusements of doubtful propriety, to say the least, and that many others are engrossed in schemes of money-making or worldly ambition—the propriety of which is not at all doubtful. We fear that very many whose names are enrolled on our church books, are too little mindful of the solemn vows which they have taken upon themselves."

We can now more readily comprehend why the State Convention adopted the following resolution in 1866:

"*Resolved,* That the Georgia Baptist Convention testifies its entire disapprobation of church members dancing, playing cards, even for amusement, visiting theatres and circuses and drinking spirituous liquors as a beverage."

An extract is now made from the Report on the State of the Churches, made to the New Sunbury Association, in 1869:

"The great body of the membership is not sufficiently active; there is too much worldliness, too little family prayer, too little effort to secure and sustain the ministry. * * * On the other hand, there is a manifest improvement in the condition of our churches. Some most gracious revivals have occurred; general attention is paid to Sunday Schools, and an increasing benevolence is appearing."

The New Sunbury is the successor of the Sunbury Association. On the 24th of November, 1866, in accordance with an invitation issued by Rev. S. Landrum, Moderator of the Sunbury Association, six churches of that body convened at Jones' Creek church, and, after consultation, dissolved the Sunbury Association, which had existed for very nearly fifty years. This was the result of action taken at a regular Conference of the Salem Baptist church, in Liberty county, when it was decided that it would be advantageous to form a new Association by the union of churches from the Sunbury, Piedmont and Union Associations. A Convention of churches lying between the Savannah and Altamaha rivers, within a territory extending seventy-five miles from the coast, was invited to assemble at Salem church, on the 27th and 28th of April, 1866. At the appointed time delegates from Gum Branch, Philadelphia, Tom's Creek, Antioch and Salem, of the Union Association, and Jones' Creek and Elim, of the Piedmont Association, convened and organized by the election of Rev. Lewis Price, Moderator, and J. L. Shaw, Clerk. After due deliberation it was decided to form a new Association, the meeting at Jones' Creek, on the 24th of November, was appointed to be held, for the purpose, and notice was transmitted by a committee to the Sunbury Association.

A sufficient reason for this action was found in the fact that the ravages of war had so reduced the strength of the Sunbury, as to preclude all hope of future efficiency, unless other churches were willing to unite with it in forming a new body.

Delegates from the three Associations met, Rev L. Price presided, and J. L. Shaw acted as Clerk, and as a platform upon which to constitute, the Constitution and By-Laws of the Georgia Association were adopted. It was determined to call the new Association THE NEW SUNBURY. The Convention was then declared closed, the same members convened and were enrolled as delegates to the New Sunbury Association, and organized by the election of Rev. S. Landrum, Moderator, and Lewis Price, Clerk. The ministers present and taking part in the proceedings, were F. R. Sweat, J. Baker, W. F. Willis, J. N. Tatum,

A. Williams, S. Landrum, H. Padgett, William Cooper, T. B. Cooper, S. B. Sweat and W. O. Darsey. There is no use in concealing or disguising the fact that the real cause of the organization of this new Association was the ravages and desolations committed by General Sherman's army, in 1865, which wantonly and maliciously burnt down the houses of worship in much of this territory, the people thus desolated being rendered too destitute to rebuild their meeting houses. In consequence some churches were entirely disbanded, and this singular, yet excusable, action was taken by the Sunbury Association when it dissolved itself.

"*Resolved*, That sister Baptist churches be requested to receive members, who are in good standing, of churches not represented in this body, because of a disorganized condition, which precludes the holding of meetings and proceeding in a regular manner; and that we approve of the action already had in such special cases."

The first corresponding letter of the New Sunbury Association, contains these words: "We are now in a very weakly condition, having, but a little time since, been overrun by the enemy, who laid waste our country, stripped our churches and destroyed some of our houses of worship."

But, perhaps, the best general view of the state of religion and of the religious destitution in the State, will be obtained from the report of Rev. S. Landrum, made to the Georgia Baptist Convention, in 1869, as chairman of the Committee on Religious Destitution and State of Religion:

"In Northeastern Georgia, east and north of Athens, there is not a minister who is supported while preaching the gospel. There are those who hold antimission sentiments, and those who are called *Whiteites*. The benevolence of the churches is low, but improving. Most of the churches have supplies; a few are destitute.

"In what is called Cherokee Georgia, there is a most interesting and promising field for missionary labor. The Cherokee Baptist Convention is dissolved; the Cassville college gone, and the building burned. Could the brethren of this section be persuaded to identify themselves with this Convention and with Mercer University, your committee are of opinion that mutual good would result. In this portion of the State there is a general deficiency in the supply of preaching and Sunday-schools. One minister, for instance, is supplying six churches. There is a low state of spirituality, and a far too general use of intoxicating drinks. Kingston, it is believed, is now destitute.

"In Middle Georgia a district has been brought to our attention, having Knoxville for a centre, with a distance of forty miles around, of most deplorable destitution—churches without preaching and general demoralization.

"From the neighborhood of Newnan, there is a report of a dearth of religious revivals—the letting down of social morals and the existence of intemperance.

"In Southwestern Georgia, Starkville is destitute. In some limited sections, there are not many Sunday-schools; they go into winter-quarters and sometimes fail to come out in spring.

"In the vicinity of Crawfordville all the churches, it is believed, are supplied. It is said that there is more general wickedness than formerly, while there are no general revivals.

"In the Stone Mountain Association there is quite a range of distressing destitution.

"Above Augusta for twenty miles, there is much need of preaching. Belair and Groves' churches are unprovided for. The colored people of Augusta and vicinity are accessible to to the ministry of white men. The Kollock street Baptist church, of Augusta, is in need of a larger building to accommodate the people in its vicinity, and the pastor is seeking means to accomplish the object.

"Burke county, perhaps, possesses the best Baptist meeting houses of any county in the State; but there is much reason to fear that they will soon be deserted, without some better means of supply.

"Most of the city churches have mission stations and Sunday-schools, to reach those who do not attend the regular services. In these larger towns there is much complaint of theatre-going, balls, worldliness, and also want of integrity, in reference to promises and commercial honor.

"On the coast of Southern Georgia, the destitution is well nigh universal. Many church buildings were burned; there is no ability to rebuild; quite a number of churches are dissolved. There are no pastors to gather the poor, scattered flocks. There is no supply from Savannah to Florida but the few points which brother Daniel is able to supply, monthly, as a missionary. At Brunswick we have a house and Sunday-school, but no preaching. At this place, for more than a year, a few brethren have been beseeching the denomination to send them a minister. The town is growing; the Episcopalians and Methodists are doing well. There is no house or preaching at St. Mary's, Darien, or Waynesville; no preaching at several churches in Liberty, Bryan and Chatham counties. There is a very large negro population in this part of the State, and, for some time past, they have manifested much more interest in hearing our preachers, where there has been any one to hear. Here are the heathen at our doors; heathen, too, who have been declared citizens and voters.

"The flourishing town of Thomasville is without a pastor, and the church is able to support a young man.

"We close the report with the following remarks: 1st. That fiddling and dancing, drinking and social irregularities, have characterized our church members, of late—more than at any time within the last twenty years. This, however, is not confined to Baptists, but the like state of things exists with other denominations. 2nd. That the spirituality of our people is low in its manifestations, and there is a sad Laodicean spirit generally prevailing. 3rd. That there is a great want of ministerial consecration and ministerial support. 4th. That there is much destitution among the churches, and many neighborhoods are unprovided with the preached Word. 5th. That there is a Sunday-school revival in the State, and that many new schools have been formed recently. 6th. That the state of religion and religious destitution calls for prayer and self-denial, and for the cessation of putting forward the war and poverty as pleas for the love of the world and the idolatry of covetousness. 7th. That our churches should rely more upon frequent collections of small amounts than upon the annual subscription of large amounts. A church of one hundred members can pay her pastor four hundred and eighty dollars a year, by simply collecting ten cents every Lord's day from each member. How easily done! This is the true system—lay by every Lord's day, as the Lord hath prospered."

Of course such a state of affairs in the churches as this report details, did not continue many years. Gradually a better order of things prevailed, although not even yet is the state of our denomination in Georgia satisfactory.

After the war the Baptists of Georgia did not adopt any series of resolutions expressive of their opinion concerning the result of the war. In truth there was nothing to be said except to acknowledge defeat, and profess resignation to the will of Him who reigns in heaven and over the armies of men.

The most important matter pertaining to affairs outside of Georgia that occurred, at the period just succeeding the war, was the passage, by a unanimous vote, of these resolutions, by the Georgia Association, in 1865:

"*Resolved, 1.* That it is the sense of this Association, and its earnest wish, that the Southern organizations of our denomination remain intact; and we, hereby, pledge ourselves to sustain them by our prayers and substance, according to the ability left us, after four years of desolating war, and as a merciful God shall afford us ability hereafter.

"*Resolved, 2.* That in carrying out the foregoing resolution, we sincerely believe that we shall be using the best means of promoting the true interests and prosperity of our Redeemer's kingdom.

"*Resolved, 3.* That from all we can learn of the light in which Northern and Southern Baptists look upon each other, any attempt on their part or ours, towards united effort, at this time, would be productive of trouble and confusion, and not of good.

"*Resolved, 4.* That it is the duty of all good men to pray that every cause of evil and root of bitterness be taken out of the hearts of all God's people in all our country.

"*Resolved, 5.* That our Domestic Mission Board be invited to occupy our Associational bounds, in its operations amongst the negroes, and that its agents are invited to visit our churches to advocate the claims of the Board."

On the 27th of October, 1871, another of the great men of our denomination departed this life—Dr. N. M. Crawford. The Convention of 1872 honored his memory by the adoption of the following brief memorial tribute, presented by Rev. G. A. Nunnally, chairman of the Committee on Deceased Ministers: "Born of distinguished parentage, graduated with the first honor of the State University, gifted beyond his compeers, he consecrated his life, with child-like simplicity, to the unfaltering service of his Redeemer. Laden then with the highest offices to which the suffrages of his brethren could call him, he still remained the humble, devout servant of God. He was, in early life, a member of the Presbyterian church, until his convictions of duty led him to unite himself with his Baptist brethren. He was long President of Mercer University, and of Georgetown College, Kentucky. Guileless in life, ardent and constant in his affections, and simple and childlike in his habits and tastes, he has left, in the hearts of the living, memories tender, strong, abiding and precious."

In 1877, the Convention, by special resolution, honored the memory of two of its oldest members and most useful servants—T. J. Burney and Thomas Stocks—both of whom had recently deceased. To the former, for many years its faithful and efficient Treasurer, the Convention was indebted for the preservation of much of its funds during the war, by his wise and judicious management, and thus was most of the endowment of Mercer University retained, amid the general wreck that accompanied the subjugation of the Confederacy.

The return of peace beheld the re-establishment of various colleges for young ladies, by the Baptists of Georgia, the more prominent ones being at Madison, LaGrange, Forsyth, Gainesville and Rome. That at Rome, designated The Shorter College, is a monument of the munificent liberality of Colonel Alfred Shorter, a wealthy Baptist residing in Rome, who generously devoted more than $100,000 of his fortune to purchasing the "Cherokee Baptist Female College" and erecting for it magnificent buildings, beautifying the grounds, and providing for it excellent chemical, philosophical and astronomical apparatus.

Another generous deed of a Georgia Baptist deserves record in these annals namely, the donation by Ex-Governor Joseph E. Brown, of Atlanta, of $50,000, in cash and bonds, to the Southern Baptist Theological Seminary, at Louisville, Kentucky.

These noble instances of individual liberality, in the cause of education, deserve to be recorded side by side with the generous deed of Jesse Mercer, in endowing Mercer University; and they secure for the two donors the admiration and gratitude of their fellow-Baptists.

All over the State there was an immense number of colored Baptists, many of whom were organized into churches, in the cities, under the supervision of the whites, while in the country, they were, generally, members of the white churches. It soon became apparent that it was best to separate, and the white brethren advised the colored ones to make a formal application for letters ot dismission, which were willingly granted. The whites invariably assisted their colored brethren in organizing their churches, and also, in building their houses of worship. They even went farther: they advised and aided them in organizing into Associations and in forming a State Convention, after the models furnished by the white organizations. The consequence is that a good state of feeling between the white and colored Baptists of Georgia has continued to exist down to the present day.

The present number of colored Baptists in the State, as far as can be ascertained, is twenty-eight Associations, 9,000 churches, and 110,000 members. About one-half of the colored churches maintain Sunday-schools. Delegates from the colored Associations have formed a State Convention, the main object of which is to establish churches and Sunday-schools throughout the State and promote theological education, as may be seen by the Constitution, which says its objects shall be:

"1. To employ missionaries to travel through the waste places of our State, and gather the people and preach the gospel to them, and aid them in every way possible, and especially in organizing both churches and Sunday-schools.

2. To establish a Theological Institute, for the purpose of educating young men and those who are preaching the gospel and have the ministry in view, or any of our brethren's sons that sustain a good moral character, and to procure, immediately, some central place in Georgia, for the establishment of the same."

Auxiliary to, and a part of this State Convention, is the colored Missionary Baptist Sunday-school Convention, which, though a separate body, is composed of the same members as the State Convention. It is an efficient body and does good work in establishing Sunday-schools; its last Report embracing 200 schools, nearly 1,000 teachers, and 14,000 scholars.

The Northern Home Mission Society established a Seminary for the instruction of colored preachers and teachers, at Augusta, in 1865, which struggled with many difficulties until 1871. At that time an infamous man, by the name of Seigfried, who was at its head, was dismissed; and the Institution was organized in a more effective form by the present Principal, Rev. J. T. Robert, LL.D., a Southern man by birth, but long a resident in Ohio and Iowa, who had been strongly recommended to the Society by white Southern Baptist ministers as a suitable man for the conduct of the enterprise. Eight years of prosperity and progress followed, and, in 1879, it was transferred to the capital of the State, and now bears the name of "Atlanta Baptist Seminary." In the fall of 1878, Rev. D. Shaver, D. D., was associated with Dr. Robert, and still holds a position in the Institution. Since Dr. Robert's connection with the Institution, instruction has been given to 371 students, of whom 142 had teaching and 229 had the ministry in view. Of this latter number, one was a missionary in Africa until his recent death, and another is editor of the *Georgia Baptist*, the organ of the colored Baptists in the State, published at Augusta; while four have been in the employ of our own State Mission Board. At present (1881) it has eighty students, of whom fifty or more are pastors or candidates for the ministry. The Georgia Missionary Baptist Convention of "our brethren in black" cooperates with the American Baptist Home Mission Society in supporting the Seminary.

That body has also evinced a profound interest in female education among its constituency. It feels the force of the maxim, that those who educate the women of a race win and hold the race itself. Anxious to win and hold the race for Christ, and for the truth as Baptists teach it in His name, a movement is in progress as our History goes to press to secure from churches, missionary societies and Sunday-schools, the sum of $5,000 for the erection of suitable buildings. There is a flattering prospect of early success; and, with that amount in hand, the Home Mission Society will at once proceed to consummate this cherished purpose of the leading brethren in the Convention; using for that end the proceeds of the sale of a lot in the city of Atlanta originally purchased by this body as the site of an institution for the education of ministers, and transferred to the Society when the present Seminary was built. This movement, together with the liberal patronage extended to the students of the Seminary as teachers of schools during the annual vacations, shows that our colored brethren are not dupes of the Romish idea that "ignorance is the mother of devotion." "The divine thirst to know" has been awakened in them, and we would fain indulge the hope that they may not seek to slake it, except at the spring of "the knowledge of the truth as it is in Christ Jesus." To assist in the accomplishment of the best possible issue, amid many difficulties, embarrassments and hazards, is a duty not to be disregarded and a privilege not to be undervalued.

We close this chapter by presenting a table of statistics kindly prepared, at the special request of the author, by Rev, G. R. McCall, Clerk, for many years, of the State Convention. It presents as complete and as correct statistics of our denomination in the State as it is possible to obtain, from the year 1845 to 1881.

The table gives the number of Associations, churches, ordained and licensed ministers, and numbers of the Missionary, anti-missionary and colored Baptists in the State of Georgia:

Years.	Churches.	Ordained Ministers.	Licensed Ministers.	Members.	Associations.	Years.	Churches.	Ordained Ministers.	Licensed Ministers.	Members.	Associations.
1845	971	464	142	58,388	46	1862	†				
1846	1,004	505	166	59,467	50	1863	†				
1847	1,060	549	204	63,097	54	1864	‡				
1848	1,105	583	292	67,098	56	1866	1,435	757	229	99,149	65§
1849	1,132	628	177	69,869	57	1867	1,454	800	211	97,345	66
1850	1,183	615	296	71,879	57	1868	1,218	760	194	115,198	69¶
1851	1,213	674	192	75,540	58	1869	‖				
1852	1,242	681	200	77,962	60	1870	1,745	836	259	131,642	72
1853	1,252	709	208	81,043	61	1872	1,973	1,056	210	146,407	86
1854	1,240	706	206	82,307	59	1873	2,001	902	241	164,292	87**
1855	1,333	711	220	86,701	60	1874	2,201	811	216	183,435	107
1856	1,373	710	209	89,989	63	1875	2,307	956	292	193,662	107
1857	1,350	689	177	85,113	63*	1876	2,392	725	236	202,356	107
1858	1,426	769	211	93,447	64	1877	2,532	762	279	209,790	107††
1859	1,429	737	211	95,727	65	1878	2,636	694	217	219,000	107
1860	1,435	757	229	99,149	65	1879	2,636	762	219	210,900	107
1861	1,015	540	141†			1880	2,680	809	278	217,041	110‡‡

* Minutes of several Associations not reported—hence the loss.
† The war made the Minutes hard to get and imperfect.
‡ Reports unsatisfactory.
§ As estimated, but not known.
¶ Colored Associations begin to be formed.
‖ Wanting—not printed, by mistake.
** Only 191 ministers colored. Minutes fail to give names or number.
†† The number of ordained ministers, all white but ten ; licentiates, but five. As many or more colored ministers than whites.
‡‡ There are more Associations, but I have failed to get Minutes.

These figures are taken from the regular Minutes of the Georgia Baptist Convention; but it is, perhaps, no more than proper, in a historical work, to give the figures presented by the Baptist Year Book, for 1881. On some accounts these figures may be more correct than those of Rev. G. R. McCall, who admits that he has not been able to secure the Minutes of all the Associations in the State: Year 1881, 2,755 churches ; 1,630 ordained ministers ; 12,933 additions by baptism ; 235,381 members ; 118 Associations.

This includes, of course, white and colored members, Missionary, Antimissionary and United Baptists, and is, really, the statistics for the year 1880.

The Year Book for 1881 reports, also, the population of Georgia as 1,538,983; number of Baptist Sunday-schools, 1,475 ; officers and teachers in them, 6,630 ; number of Sunday-school scholars, 44,150 ; benevolent contributions for all purposes, in 1880, $32,402.90.

In connection with the striking contrast between these numbers and the statistics of the denomination in the earlier pages of our History, there is something of interest and instruction in other points of difference between half a century ago and the present time, as brought out in the following article contributed by Dr. J. H. Campbell to THE INDEX of July 14th, 1881 :

"Fifty years ago, protracted meetings, as now appointed, were unknown in this State and in this country as well, so far as I am informed. They were not originally appointed, or decided upon, beforehand, but were the result of revivals already existing. Revivals in those days were the result of the ordinary means of grace, and were carried on by those means alone. Happily, there were no professional revivalists, and such meetings were conducted by the pastor, aided by such ministers as he might call to his assistance.

"Fifty years ago, there were not half a dozen Baptist ministers in Georgia, who were college graduates, and the denomination did not exceed thirty thousand members, though there had been an accession of about ten thousand during the great revival of 1827-28, just passed.

"Fifty years ago, instrumental music was practiced in only two Baptist churches in the State that I knew of (Savannah and Augusta), and in very few of other denominations. A majority of our people had no fellowship with the practice, and many are of the same opinion still.

"Fifty years ago, the almost invariable custom, in social and public worship, was to sit during singing, and to kneel during prayer. The irreverent habit of sitting in time of prayer had not then been introduced, and it is to be regretted that it has become so common in our town and city congregations. I trust our country churches will continue steadfastly to adhere to the old and more scriptural way. Who would think of making a practice of sitting in secret and family prayer? Ought not the habit complained of to be corrected?

"Fifty years ago, there was only one college in the State—Franklin College, at Athens, (the A in Athens was pronounced sharp,) then the State College, now the State University. It was controlled almost exclusively by the Presbyterians. There were only two or three female schools, one of the most popular being at 'Cherokee Corner,' on the stage road from Washington to Athens.

"Fifty years ago, there was not a steam-engine, nor a telegraph pole, nor a mile of railroad in the State. The people, male and female, travelled on horseback. If they went on wheels, it was in sulkies or gigs, or in the old-fashioned four-wheeled family carriage. Buggies had not come into use then. In the latter part of his life, Jesse Mercer always travelled in his four-wheeled carriage—not from pride, but because he was an unwieldy person and the subject of many infirmities. The only public conveyance was the lumbering stage-coach, a vehicle admirably fitted for killing horses, and for testing the patience and piety of passengers.

"Fifty years ago, there was not a religious paper published in the State. A small sheet was issued for a short time at Mount Zion, Hancock county, by Rev. Mr. Gildersleeve, a Presbyterian, but it had been transferred to Charleston, South Carolina, and was published in that city as the *Christian Observer*. I doubt if there were ten secular papers in the State at that time.

"Fifty years ago, the question, whether the Baptists of Georgia would be missionary or anti-missionary had not been decided. The Anties were in a decided majority, and the conflict then raging was no child's play. I have lived to see my fellow-soldiers, who stood in the fore-front of the battle, fall one after another until the whole line melted away. But, as the fathers fell, their sons took their places, and the victory is now complete.

"Fifty years ago, the cause of foreign missions was in its incipiency. Its friends were few and feeble, its enemies defiant, formalists indifferent, infidelity sneering, Satan raging. In view of what has been accomplished, may we not exclaim, 'What hath God wrought!' And may we not go further, and hope and expect that in the next fifty years such Scriptures as the following will be fulfilled: 'The earth shall be full of the knowledge of the Lord as the waters cover the sea.' 'The north shall give up, and the south keep not back. He will bring his sons from far, and his daughters from the ends of the earth.' 'The people shall praise thee, O God, all the people shall praise thee.' And that every nation, and kindred, and tongue and people under the whole heaven shall be shouting, 'Alleluia, for the Lord God omnipotent reigneth.'"

XIX.
HISTORY OF MERCER UNIVERSITY.
1813-1881.

XIX.

HISTORY OF MERCER UNIVERSITY.

A BRIEF RETROSPECT—ORIGIN OF THE ANTI-MISSION BAPTISTS, CALLED "OLD SCHOOL BAPTISTS"—SOMETHING OF THEIR CREED AND POLICY—THE REGULAR BAPTISTS SLIGHTLY COMPARED—WAS THE TENDENCY OF THE CONVENTION EVIL?—MERCER'S REPLY—EARLY BENEFICIARIES OF THE CONVENTION—MERCER INSTITUTE, UNDER SANDERS' MANAGEMENT—MANUAL LABOR SUSPENDED IN THE UNIVERSITY IN 1844—FIRST GRADUATES OF MERCER—THEOLOGICAL DEPARTMENT, WHY DISCONTINUED—CLASSICAL DEPARTMENT—LAW SCHOOL—HOW THE WAR AFFECTED MERCER—REMOVAL OF MERCER UNIVERSITY—FUTURE OF THE COLLEGE—PRESIDENTS AND PROFESSORS—THE SEVERAL ADMINISTRATIONS—SOME OF ITS PROFESSORS—MERCER THE RALLYING POINT OF THE DENOMINATION.

We have endeavored briefly to trace the various methods adopted by the Baptists of Georgia for promoting education, missions, temperance and for developing and cultivating the spirit of union and cooperation among the churches of the State. With very few exceptions we have found the ministers of our denomination in the State sadly deficient in education, during nearly the entire first half of this century. On that account there was some difficulty in obtaining thoroughly competent professors for Mercer University, during the earliest years of that institution. We have seen that many in the denomination opposed an institution that afforded learning to ministers, and many also opposed the formation of the State Convention, and, for many years, resisted its progress. We have seen that a still greater number maintained a bitter opposition to missions and to the use of special human effort for the promotion of benevolent objects. These were what are now called the anti-mission, or Primitive Baptists, who are opposed to the academical or theological education of their ministry, and to Bible, Missionary, Publication Societies, and to all other voluntary societies of a like nature. These they regard as of mere human invention, and different from that simplicity of order instituted by Christ, and declared in the New Testament as the law of His kingdom, and by which He would keep His people constantly mindful that, in the building up of His Church, through pastors and teachers who gather in His elect, "the excellency of the power is of God, and not of" men.

When, in 1813, missionary and other kindred institutions were introduced into the Baptist denomination of the United States, chiefly through the conversion to Baptist principles of Judson and Rice, and through the influence exerted by them, a spirit of discontent and opposition arose, in some churches and Associations. This continued to manifest itself more and more decidedly until 1832, when the dissatisfied churches and Associations determined to withdraw and form a separate organization. Therefore, in that year they issued an address to the churches, setting forth that they could no longer fellowship brethren who countenanced the mass of *humanly devised institutions* that had been foisted upon the denomination; the pure doctrines of which they corrupted, the peace of which they disturbed and whose scriptural simplicity they subverted. All, they said, who loved the truth in its integrity and, like themselves, had groaned under the burden of human inventions, were invited to communicate with them. Numbers of churches and Associations promptly responded. A general correspondence was opened, a meeting was held and an organization was formed under the distinguishing appellation of *Old School Baptists*, which name they considered as specially appropriate to themselves, not only as going back to the ancient order of Baptists, but from its having been given to such as adhered to the old doctrines of predestination and particular atonement.

They received the Holy Scriptures alone as their rule of faith and practice—professed to have no confidence in human effort, nor in human schemes for reform. They opposed theological schools and would not tolerate scholastic preachers. For removing abuses of all and every nature; for enlightening the human mind, and for leading men to faith and salvation in Christ, they relied wholly and exclusively upon the sure Word of God and His Holy Spirit. In church polity they did not differ from the regular Missionary Baptists. In Georgia their non-fellowship article, was declared about 1836, and culminated in a general denominational separation, or division, in 1839, after many years of strife and dissension. The Abstract of Principles adopted by them, and which still composes the Articles of Faith held by some of the Primitive Associations in this State, consisted of twelve articles, which were "held by the Baptists in general, agreeable to the Confession of Faith adopted by upwards of one hundred congregations in England, published in Philadelphia in 1742, which is a standard for the Baptists." Such was their general heading, and they were as follows:

"1st. We believe in one only true and living God, and that there are three persons in the God-head, namely: The Father, Son and Holy Ghost.

"2d. We believe the Scriptures of the Old and New Testament are the word of God, and the only rule of faith and practice.

"3d. We believe in the doctrine of eternal and particular election.

"4th. We believe in the doctrine of original sin.

"5th. We believe in the doctrine of man's impotency to recover himself from the fallen state he is in by nature, of his own free will and ability.

"6th. We believe that sinners are justified in the sight of God only by the imputed righteousness of Christ.

"7th. We believe that God's elect shall be called, converted and sanctified by the Holy Spirit,

"8th. We believe that the Saints shall persevere in grace, and shall never finally fall.

"9th. We believe that baptism, the Lord's supper, and washing of the saints' feet are ordinances of Jesus Christ, and that true believers are the only subjects of those ordinances, and that the true mode of baptism is by immersion.

"10th. We believe in the resurrection of the dead, and a general judgment.

"11th. We believe that the punishment of the wicked will be everlasting, and the joys of the righteous will be eternal.

"12th. We believe that no minister has a right to the administration of the ordinances of baptism and the Lord's supper, only such as are regularly called, and come under the imposition of hands by a regularly authorized Presbytery."

That which led immediately to separation was the adoption of the "13th article," as it was called by those bodies in which the anti-mission element prevailed.

The following is the substance of that article, the wording of which varied:

"*Resolved*, That the institutions of the day, called *Benevolent*, to-wit: Convention, Bible Society, Tract Society, Temperance Society, Abolition Society, Sunday-school Union Society, Theological Seminary, and all other institutions tributary to the missionary plan now existing in the United States, are unscriptural; and that we, as an Association, will not correspond with any Association that is connected with them, nor will we hold in our union, or fellowship, any church that is connected with them."

Of course the passage of this resolution separated those who adopted it from their Missionary brethren, and, with regard to an actual schism or division from them, required no action on their part. They have, ever, fairly asserted, therefore, that they did not *non-fellowship* their Anti-Mission brethren, and produce division; but the rupture was effected by those opposed to benevolent schemes, which was indeed true. Undoubtedly the ablest, most pious, most cultivated and influential ministers and members were found in the ranks of the regular Baptists, who strongly favored missions and education, and who founded Mercer Institute, which, in a few years, developed into Mercer University, and has proved beneficial, in an incalculable degree, to the Baptists of Georgia.

They were those who formed and maintained the State Convention, which, perhaps, more than any other human cause, by uniting the Baptists of the State, effectuated their elevation and advancement, as a denomination. Yet the Antimissionaries charged that it was the *State Convention* which caused the destruction of fellowship, resulting in the division of the denomination.

To this, Jesse Mercer replied: "Before any acts can be considered 'fellowship-destroying,' they must be ascertained to be either immoral in themselves, or evil in their tendency. But what immorality or evil tendency was there in the objects of the General Association? For instance, what immorality can there be in an effort to unite the influence and pious intelligence of Georgia Baptists, so as, thereby, to facilitate their union and co-operation? Or, what evil can there be in forming and encouraging plans for the revival of experimental and practical religion? Or, can there be any sin in giving effect to the useful plans of the several Associations? Or, can it be thought a bad thing to furnish the means for the education of young, pious and indigent men, who are approved by their churches, as called of God to the Baptist ministry? Or, can it be regarded by any as an immoral thing to promote pious and useful education in the Baptist denomination? We cannot conclude that any man whose mind has been in any wise imbued by that wisdom which is necessary to direct, will pretend that there is any cause in any of these objects to break the union of the churches."

It is a fact that, before the establishment of Mercer Institute, the Convention sustained several young men, with the ministry in prospect, in different institutions of learning; and in the Minutes for 1826-7-8-9-30-1-2, we peruse regular reports concerning these beneficiaries. In 1832, eight beneficiaries were receiving instruction, sustained by the Convention. At length, in 1833, Mercer Institute was established, and for six years was conducted most successfully and prosperously by B. M. Sanders and his coadjutors, Ira O. McDaniel, J. F. Hillyer, J. W. Attaway, W. D. Cowdry, A. Williams and S. P. Sanford. The attendance on the school was limited only by its capacity to furnish board and lodgings for the students. The number of students the first year was thirty-nine, and the average attendance during the succeeding five years was ninety-one. The young men, members of the most substantial and respectable families in the State, engaged in the manual labor required with cheerfulness and industry, and, at the same time, they pursued their studies with earnestness and perseverance. For several hours each day they performed the usual manual labor of a farm, receiving for pay six cents an hour. They also pursued a course of study that was full and exacting. The discipline of the Institute, under B. M. Sanders, was firm, vigilant and comprehensive, and the school was recognized as one of the very best in the State. Its excellence was due mostly to the capabilities and exertions of B. M. Sanders, who had been educated at Columbia, South Carolina, and who was a man of great energy, strict integrity, good judgment and excellent business tact. He was ordained at Williams Creek church, in Warren county, January 5th, 1825, in the thirty-sixth year of his age, by Jesse Mercer, Malachi Reeves, Joseph Roberts, John H. Walker and Jabez P. Marshall officiating as a presbytery. He was a well educated man, and his practical knowledge acquired in farming adapted him admirably to his position, united as it was to his wonderful energy and administrative abilities. Doubtless the total lack of some of these requisites, on the part of his successors, was one reason of the disgust which soon attached to the manual labor system. The Institute was deservedly very dear to the heart of the denomination, and did much to unite it and concentrate its exertions. In regard to manual labor, it is certain that B. M. Sanders favored it strongly, and so did Ira O. McDaniel, who for six years witnessed its practical exemplification. It seems, however, to have become irksome and burdensome, after the Institute was elevated to a college, and was discontinued after a few years. In December, 1844, the Board of Trustees suspended this department of the Institution by the following action:

"WHEREAS, the Manual Labor Department of Mercer University has been sustained at a heavy expense—an expense which the present state of our fund will not justify, and has, in our judgment, materially retarded the growth of our institution, after as favorable experiment as we have been able to make of the scheme, and, whereas, the contributors of the University fund have, so far as they have been called upon, expressed themselves, with almost entire unanimity, ready to concur in any measure in reference to the system which the Board of Trustees may deem essential to the prosperity of the institution; and, whereas, the Board of Trustees have found themselves, under all circumstances, unable to accomplish, to any desirable extent, the important and benevolent designs for which it was originally organized; be it, therefore,

"*Resolved*, That this department be, and is hereby, indefinitely suspended."

This action was acceded to by the Convention of 1845, which met at Forsyth.

The history of Mercer University and its officers, must be summed up very briefly. As has been stated, the college classes were organized in January, 1839. The first graduating class of three, received the first diplomas of the University in 1841; they were Richard M. Johnston, still living and an eminent instructor in Maryland; Benjamin F. Tharpe, also still living and an eminent divine, with his residence at Perry, Georgia, on whom his *alma mater* has conferred the honorary degree of Doctor of Divinity; and A. R. Wellborn, Doctor of Medicine, still living and residing in Atlanta.

With the exception of seven years, there has been a regular succession of graduating classes since 1841. The denomination had then a small number, only of educated men, from whom to elect professors, and for several years there were frequent changes in the faculty; consequently an efficient faculty was enrolled gradually. But before the close of the first decade, its organization began to attain stability. One of the faculty, Prof. S. P. Sanford, entered the Institute as a teacher, in 1838, and has served continuously through the whole existence of the University to the present time, a period of forty-three years. Another, Prof. J. E. Willet, an alumnus of 1846, who was elected Professor in 1847, has served continuously for thirty-four years. As instructors they have proved themselves unsurpassed in their departments.

The education of young ministers was the primary intention of the founders of Mercer Institute. Theological education in the University was specifically provided for, in some of the legacies and subscriptions. Very appropriately, in 1840, Rev. Adiel Sherwood was elected the first Theological Professor—a man who had received excellent classical and theological training. Since making Georgia his permanent home, in 1818, he had been an active minister, had organized several churches, had preached very extensively, had taught a number of young ministers at his own house, and had been foremost in all measures for the progress of the denomination in the State. The actual originator of the Convention and of Mercer Institute—it was desired that he should develop the Theological Department of the University, which had grown, in a great measure, from his earnest advocacy of liberal education. But he remained a Professor three years only, accepting a call to the Presidency of Shurtliff College, in Illinois, in 1843. In 1845 the Theological Department of Mercer University was more fully organized, and was continued until 1862. In that time seven classes, numbering twelve members, graduated with the degree of B. D. The course was quite extensive and thorough, embracing Greek, Hebrew, Systematic and Practical Theology, Ecclesiastical History and Biblical Literature. Two Professors usually gave most of their time to instruction in this department, and the course of study extended through three years. The exigencies of the civil war caused a suspension of the Theological Department, at that time not much regretted, as the Southern Baptist Convention had organized the Southern Baptist Theological Seminary, at Greenville, South Carolina. A concentration of money and patronage on that enterprise, in order to build up a first class Theological Seminary at the South, was deemed advisable by the Southern Baptists generally, in consequence of which the Theological Department of Mercer University has never been re-opened. Indeed, one of the Theological Professors of Mercer, Dr. William Williams, left in 1859, to join the Faculty at Greenville, being elected to that position.

Within a few years the Southern Baptist Theological Seminary has been removed to Louisville, Kentucky, and in consequence of its distance from Georgia, and by reason of the specific purpose of part of the endowment of Mercer University, the re-opening of the Theological Department at an early day, is canvassed; but, in case of its resurrection, the course of instruction may be more elementary and less regular, than in the Seminary.

Most of the graduates in this department had not received previous training in a literary college, and, therefore, have not impressed themselves on the denomination to the same extent that some students did who graduated in the Collegiate Department, but who did not take a theological course afterwards. This evinces that nothing can take the place of thorough literary training to one who is to move men by writing, speaking and teaching.

The curriculum of the Classical department of Mercer University has been a close one, embracing the studies usually taught in colleges of a respectable grade. The regular course embraces four years, and leads to the degree of A.B.

A scientific course, including all of the regular course, except ancient languages, is completed in three years, and leads to the degree of Bachelor of Science—B.S.; but the great majority of students pursue the regular course. The aim of the trustees and faculty, from the beginning, has been to maintain as elevated a standard of scholarship as the preparatory schools and the condition of the country would justify; and this has made the position which Mercer University has held, among the educational institutions, eminently respectable.

The number of graduates in the Classical department has been (to 1880) 440, in the regular course, and seven in the scientific course. Of these graduates seventy-seven have been ministers of the gospel. Adding to these the twelve theological graduates and seventy-five or eighty who have taken a partial course in the Institute and University, and who have become ministers of the gospel, and we have a total of about one hundred and seventy Baptist ministers, who have received their education in this "classical and theological school," instituted by our Baptist fathers, nearly half a century ago. And, although the Theological department has been maintained through about one-third, only, of the existence of the institution, yet the primary thought of the founders—education of ministers,—has, as we see, been largely realized.

The law school was organized in 1873, with three professors and sixteen students, and its course extends through one year. Twenty-four graduates, with the degree of B.L., have completed the studies of this school.

The civil war affected the interests of Mercer University in more ways than one.

During the spring of 1861 and 1862, the senior classes of those years joined the army almost in a body. The senior class of 1861, the largest ever graduated, lost nine of its thirty-one members in military service. During the continuance of the war, a skeleton, merely, of college organization was preserved, for the reason that the material for classes was almost entirely absorbed by the demands of the service; and, with the close of the war, came temporary confusion and demoralization. The railroads of the State had been torn up, postal facilities were interrupted, civil authority was suspended; investments in stocks, bonds and personal loans became unproductive if not useless; general confusion and derangement in social and political affairs prevailed, and it seemed but the dictate of reason and common sense, to suspend the exercises of the institution. Indeed, in this state of things the University virtually dissolved itself in May, 1865. The Board of Trustees could not have a meeting, and the faculty reluctantly closed the doors of the college. The two senior members of the faculty—Professors Sanford and Willet—however, opened a school in the college buildings, held a *quasi* commencement in July, and, as well as they could, under the circumstances, carried on the mixed studies of preparatory and college classes, until the close of the year. The trustees succeeded in holding a meeting in December of 1865, and began the rehabilitation of the University and the reorganization of the faculty. Three officers were appointed who conducted the school until July, 1866, when two more were elected, one of whom entered on his duties immediately and the other did so at the beginning of 1867. The classes of the period succeeding the war were noted for orderly conduct and great application to study; for they appeared to realize that the issue of the war had wrought a revolution in the fortunes, industries and employments of the Southern people, and that, afterwards, the success of young men was to depend on personal effort, in which education entered as an important factor. Hence, with great earnestness of purpose, they bent all their energies to the acquisition of knowledge.

The war affected the college in another and unexpected manner—in regard to its location; and the result was its removal from Penfield to Macon. In 1850, at the meeting of the Convention at Marietta, a feeble effort was made to move the college to Griffin. In 1857 a more determined effort at removal was made in the Convention which met at Augusta, but it experienced a most decided repulse. But the war, and especially the redundant currency it set afloat, made men and communities more adventurous and speculative, and under this influence the project of moving the University assumed a new phase. Several cities, appreciating the advantages of an endowed college owned by a large denomination, offered valuable pecuniary inducements to the friends of Mercer University, to secure its removal. Consequently the question of removal was reopened and fully discussed in the Convention which assembled at Newnan in April, 1870. By a vote of 71 to 16, it was resolved to move the University from Penfield; and, at a subsequent conference of the Board of Trustees and a Committee of the Convention, the city of Macon was adopted as the location of the college. In consideration of free tuition to a certain number of scholars to be selected by that city, Macon gave the University $125.000 in bonds, and seven acres of land on Tatnall Square. The removal, however, necessitated a change in the charter by the State Legislature, pending which the University was suspended during the spring of 1871, and a collegiate school was conducted by the Faculty, in the city of Macon. The new charter having been perfected, Mercer University was again formally opened in October, 1871, at Macon. The Trustees proceeded to the erection of a large and handsome four-story brick building, containing over thirty rooms, to contain the library and apparatus and rooms for the purposes of recitation. They erected, also, a brick building as a dormitory and dining-hall for students. A chapel and a building to contain the museum and to furnish lecture rooms were in contemplation, but the financial panic of 1873 caused a suspension of further proceedings.

Macon, the new home of the University, is a central, healthy city, which is becoming an educational centre. The site, or campus, of seven acres, looking out upon Tatnall Square, is capable of great ornamentation, and will become as dear to the newer graduates as the beautiful oak-embowered campus of Penfield was to the older classes.

The future of this institution depends upon an exhibition of generous liberality, akin to that put forth by our Baptist fathers, when the denomination in the State numbered not more than 50,000 members. For more than a quarter of a century the endowment contributed by them was managed by T. J. Burney, of Madison, treasurer of the Convention and of the University, of whom Dr. J. H. Campbell, for many years a member of the Board of Trustees, says truthfully, in his "Georgia Baptists:" A more faithful and efficient officer, perhaps, never lived. The Trustees adopted his views on all subjects affecting their finances, and he was authorized to carry them out at his own discretion. And it was, unquestionably, owing to his wisdom and foresight that a large proportion of these funds were saved during the late war, while other institutions became bankrupt.

The presidents and the professors in the various departments have been as follows:

HISTORY OF MERCER UNIVERSITY. 253

PRESIDENTS.

Rev. Billington M. Sanders, 1839; Rev. Otis Smith, 1840–'43; Rev. John L. Dagg, D.D., 1844–'54; Rev. Nathaniel M. Crawford, D.D., 1855–'56, and 1858–'65; Rev. Henry Holcombe Tucker, D.D., 1866–'71; and Rev. Archibald J. Battle, D.D., 1872 to the present date, 1881.

THEOLOGICAL DEPARTMENT—PROFESSORS.

Sacred Literature and Moral Philosophy.—Rev. Adiel Sherwood, D.D., 1840–'41; Rev. William J. Hard, 1841–'42; and Rev. J. L. Reynolds, D.D., 1845–'46.

Systematic and Pastoral Theology.—Rev. John L. Dagg, D.D., 1844–'55; Rev. William Williams, D.D., 1856–'59; and Rev. Shaler G. Hillyer, D.D., 1859–'62.

Ecclesiastical History and Biblical Literature.—Rev. Nathaniel M. Crawford, D.D., 1846–'56; and 1858–'65.

COLLEGIATE DEPARTMENT—PROFESSORS.

Mathematics.—Shelton P. Sanford, LL.D., 1838 to the present time, 1881.

Ancient Languages.—Rev. Albert Williams, 1840–'41; Rev. Patrick H. Mell, D.D., 1841–'55; Uriah W. Wise, 1856–'62; William G. Woodfin, 1856–'62, and 1866–'78; and Rev. Epenetus A. Steed, 1872 to the present time, 1881.

Belles Letters.—Rev. S. G. Hillyer, D.D., 1845–'55; Rev. H. H. Tucker, D.D., LL.D., 1856–'62; Rev. John J. Brantly, D.D., 1867 to the present time, 1881.

Natural Philosophy, Chemistry and Geology.—Robert Tolefree, M.D., 1840–'41; Benjamin Osgood Pierce. 1841–'47, and 1848–'49; and Joseph E. Willet, 1847 to the present time, 1881.

Modern Languages.—William G. Woodfin, 1856–'72, and 1866; and Rev. John J. Brantly, D.D., 1867 to the present time, 1881.

Adjunct Professors and Tutors.—Ira O. McDaniel, 1839; Rev. John W. Attaway, 1839–'41; Rev. William J. Hard, 1841–'42; W. K. Posey, 1841; R. J. Miller, 1842; Rev. Thomas D. Martin, 1843–'55; Thomas A. Seals, 1856; J. Lumpkin Andrews, 1857; John T. McGinty, 1857, and Adrian S. Morgan, 1858.

LAW DEPARTMENT—PROFESSORS.

Equity, Jurisprudence, Pleading and Practice. — Hon. Carlton B. Cole, 1873–'75; and John C. Rutherford, A.M., 1875 to the present time, 1881.

International and Constitutional Law.—Hon. Clifford Anderson, 1873 to the present time, 1881.

Common and Statute Law.—Walter B. Hill, A.M., B.L., 1873 to the present time, 1881.

THE SEVERAL ADMINISTRATIONS.

Rev. B. M. Sanders, who had been the central figure in the Institute, consented to remain one year as President of the University. It was, indeed, fitting that he should launch upon its new career of usefulness, the bark which he had guided so successfully through the six years of its preceding existence.

Rev. Otis Smith, the second President, remained three years, and gave diplomas to the first two graduating classes.

Rev. Dr. Dagg, succeeded in 1844, to a Presidency of ten years. With very superior mental endowments, varied and solid scholarship, venerable presence, affable manners, aptness in teaching and steadiness in discipline, he commanded the love and reverence of the whole institution. He gave dignity and character to the new college, and enabled it deservedly to take high rank among the colleges of the State.

Rev. Dr. Crawford, inherited much of the massive intellect of his father, Hon. William H. Crawford. His mind mastered, with equal ease, almost every department of thought, and in almost every branch of science he was learned. Modest, sincere, sagacious, companionable, independent, and with great clearness and coolness of judgment, he won the respect and admiration of his students, and was beloved as a wise counsellor in the assemblies of his brethren. During his presidency, the rigidity of discipline which American colleges had inherited from the European, was greatly relaxed.

Rev. Dr. Tucker, the next President, was possessed of remarkable acuteness, originality and readiness of intellect: clear, brilliant, magnetic, he excited such enthusiasm as few instructors have the power to do. "You are gentlemen, and the sons of gentlemen," was the key-note of a discipline which banished from college all silly tricks and pranks, and begat true manliness of character. In fact, the fresh vitality of his administration is still felt in the institution.

Rev. Dr. Battle came to the University shortly after its settlement in its new home at Macon. Dr. Cullen Battle, his father, a prominent Baptist of Georgia, had been a liberal donor to the University, but had removed to Alabama, thus carrying his son Archibald to another State, where, on arriving at manhood, he occupied positions of distinction and influence. On his return to his native State, Dr. Battle was received with a warm welcome, and found friends in all. As an educator and a college president, he has proved to be not only a superior scholar, but prudent and firm in administration, and more than equal to the demands of his position. While his career as an educator has been very successful, he has produced some original thought in a work on the Human Will, which has been very highly commended. By his courteous demeanor and high Christian character, he has attached to the College the community which had contributed so liberally to its endowment. Under his administration the College has prospered, and students have sustained a high reputation for good order and studiousness.

Some of the professors of Mercer University have been men of commanding influence and abilities. One of these was Dr. P. H. Mell, who for fourteen years greatly benefitted the College by his services, and acquired a reputation that obtained for him a professorship in the State University, which he retained till two years ago, when he was elevated to the high and honorable position of Chancellor of that institution. As clerk of the Georgia Baptist Convention, he served ten years, the same number of years that Adiel Sherwood served; and as President, he has served nineteen years, the same number of years that Jesse Mercer served, and much of the efficiency of the Convention may be attributed to him. For the last quarter of a century he has been Moderator of the Georgia Association, and in all these situations his influence in regard to Baptist doctrine and usage has been salutary and conservative. He has exerted an influence in the denomination second to that of no other. With, perhaps, no superior as a disciplinarian, he has few, if any, equals as an acute dialectician. From the year 1846, when he first became clerk of the Convention, down to the present time, he has exerted a strong influence for good in the denomination, and the faithful labor of ten years in the institution, places Mercer University deeply in his debt.

Dr. J. J. Brantly is one of the most polished and scholarly professors who has ever been connected with the institution. Professor W. G. Woodfin, for many years Professor of Ancient Languages, was an accomplished and most valuable instructor while connected with the institution. He, too, is now a professor in the State University. Rev. E. A. Steed has been excelled by no instructor in the ancient languages who has ever been connected with the University, nor perhaps by any in any other institution of learning. Dr. S. G. Hillyer, for many years connected with the College, and now pastor at Washington, Georgia, was a sound theologian and eloquent preacher, and exerted a good influence when a professor. Professors Willet and Sanford are unsurpassed in their departments, and, by their long and faithful services, have greatly endeared themselves to the denomination.

The reader now has a fair idea of the inception, the growth and the establishment of Mercer University. It sprung from a desire for an educated ministry, but this intention enlarged into the broader purpose of the higher education of Baptist sons, and in this great work the minds and hearts of those Georgia Baptists who are connected with the Convention have been enlisted. They have brought to it their offerings of time, money and wisdom, and, when necessary, have sacrificed for it their preferences for locations and measures. This fusion of mind and heart has unified and consolidated the regular denomination in the State, and has girded it for the great religious work it has wrought. The University, thus founded in the prayers, sacrifices and best purposes of the

Georgia Baptists, and becoming the centre of its intellectual culture, has ever been the rallying point of the denomination. With the return of stability and prosperity to the country, the institution should enter on a new era of enlightened progress. New buildings, a more numerous faculty and increased appliances of all kinds are required by the larger numbers and greater intelligence of the denomination; and it is hoped and believed that the Baptists of the State are ripe for an enlargement of the aims and works of their beloved University. Upon the Baptists of Georgia Mercer has this undoubted claim, that it was established for grand and useful purposes by the fathers of the denomination, and has been transmitted to us as a sacred trust. It is, therefore, in a peculiar sense, our own heritage, and demands from us unremitting care and devotion; and right worthy is it of all our jealous and watchful solicitude. It has contributed, in a high degree, to the solid growth, the exalted character and the commanding influence of the denomination. It has added largely to the intelligent and influential element of our Baptist brotherhood. It has been a potent factor in the progress of our principles. It has done much to exalt the character of our ministry, and, by its fruitful career and its honorable position, has given a noble prestige to the Christian community which it represents.

In view of what it has accomplished, we cannot afford to dispense with so powerful an agency for good; and to suffer it to languish, would reduce us to inferiority and insignificance.

But, if the University is to go on achieving results in proportion to the advancing intelligence of the age and to the demands of Christian scholarship, and if it is to hold its position abreast of the progressive institutions of the country, it must possess the needful appliances. In order that no material equipment nor any instructional facility may be wanting; in order that buildings, apparatus, library, and the courses and methods of instruction may be such as the times and circumstances require, its endowment must be increased.

Let us hope that the Baptists of Georgia may awake to a deeper solicitude, and a more active zeal, and to an abounding liberality towards this noble legacy of their fathers—Mercer University.

XX.
POSITION ON VARIOUS MATTERS.
1794-1881.

XX.

POSITION ON VARIOUS MATTERS

THE GEORGIA BAPTISTS AND PATRIOTISM—"GOOD WILL TO MAN"—MARITAL RIGHTS OF SLAVES—TEMPERANCE—THE BAPTISTS NEVER LIKELY TO FORM A PARTY—THE ACT OF 1785 TO SUPPORT MINISTERS OUT OF THE PUBLIC TREASURY—REMONSTRANCE OF THE GEORGIA BAPTISTS—THE BAPTISTS AND RELIGIOUS LIBERTY—MERCER WRITES THAT SECTION IN THE STATE CONSTITUTION—A STRONG BAPTIST PROTEST—EDUCATION OF COLORED MINISTERS—PULPIT AFFILIATON IN THE OLDEN TIME—NO OPEN COMMUNION AMONG THE EARLY BAPTISTS OF GEORGIA—PULPIT COURTESIES ALLOWED TO PEDOBAPTISTS, BUT THEIR OFFICIAL ACTS NOT RECOGNIZED—THE CONSTITUTION OF THE RICHLAND CHURCH—THE CASE OF MR. HUTCHINSON—JESSE MERCER ON NOT RECOGNIZING PEDOBAPTIST IMMERSION—EXTRACTS FROM SHERWOOD'S MANUSCRIPTS.

A very interesting chapter might be written concerning the bold stand ever taken by the Georgia Baptists in favor of political and religious liberty. Washington himself praised the Baptists for their patriotism and for the courage they exhibited during the glorious struggle for liberty in the war of Independence. The same spirit was manifested in the war of 1812. As we have seen, the Georgia Baptists exhibited an ardent attachment to country at that crisis; the Associations adopted patriotic resolutions and appointed days of fasting and prayer for the success of our arms; while the ministers incited the community to support the cause of the country.

But underneath the sentiment of patriotism is the feeling of *good will to man*, which takes a higher and broader range than mere patriotism, because it is a higher and nobler sentiment. It was this solicitude for the benefit and rights of others that led our Baptist fathers to proclaim the gospel in all parts of the State, with and without reward, and which induced them to expend their money in the erection of meeting houses, in contributions for schools, colleges, and academies, in missions among their red neighbors, the Creeks and Cherokees, and in sending the good news of salvation to the heathen of the old world. It was this sentiment that led the Georgia Association, in 1794, to memorialize the State Legislature by making a law to prevent the operations of the African slave trade, as far as Georgia was concerned; which memorial Henry Graybill and James Sims were instructed to present to the General Assembly, at its next session.* This same feeling has led the Georgia Baptists, in all their existence, to manifest a lively interest in the mental and moral elevation of the negro race, causing them repeatedly, in their Associations and Conventions, not only to urge the instruction of the colored race, but to contribute its money freely for its evangelization and moral and religious training. The truth of this is evinced by the existence of thousands of colored Baptists, all over Georgia, who formed themselves into churches immediately after the war, and whose good

---

*The following extract from the Minutes of the Georgia Association for 1794, from the only copy known to be in existence, is the action of that body to which reference is made: "A memorial moving to the Legislature that a law be made to prevent the future importation of slaves, was presented, read and approved, and ordered to be signed by the Moderator and Clerk. Also, Henry Graybill and James Sims were appointed to present the same to the next session of the General Assembly."

order, sobriety and religious training was a matter of surprise to Northern visitors, to whom it never occurred that credit should be given to the white Baptists of the State for such a favorable state of affairs.

It may not be amiss to quote here the action of the Georgia Association in 1864, relative to the marital relation among slaves, as exhibiting the sacredness which the Baptists attach to that relation. The following resolution, drawn up and offered by Dr. H. H. Tucker, on the 8th of October, 1864, at the session which met at Pine Grove, Columbia county, was unanimously adopted:

"*Resolved*, That it is the firm belief and conviction of this body that the institution of marriage was ordained by Almighty God for the benefit of the whole human race, without respect to color; that it ought to be maintained in its original purity among all classes of people, in all countries and in all ages, till the end of time; and that, consequently, the law of Georgia, in its failure to recognize and protect this relationship between our slaves, is essentially defective, and ought to be amended."

Mere legal sanction possesses no sacredness in Baptist opinion, when contrary to their prevailing sentiment of good will to man.

The same feeling extended itself towards the young in the establishment of Sunday-schools, and towards all classes and ages in the formation of temperance societies. The Baptists formed and mainly carried on the first temperance society in the State, and were greatly instrumental in the successes achieved by the great temperance crusade in the State between 1825 and 1835, which aided so materially in casting odium upon liquor-drinking, and upon the custom of keeping liquor and offering it to the household guest, and using it on festive occasions.

The first temperance paper ever published in the State was originated and, for some years, published at a pecuniary loss, by a Baptist—Jesse Mercer—and was called *The Temperance Banner*.

RELIGIOUS LIBERTY.

In regard to religious liberty and the rights of conscience, the records show that the Baptists of Georgia have, in no degree, been behind their brethren of Rhode Island and Virginia in fidelity to that great distinguishing trait of our denomination. The most preposterous utterance ever made in the Georgia Legislature, was that which gave for one reason why a charter should not be granted to Mount Enon College that the numbers and influence of the Baptists ought not to be augmented, lest the religious liberties of the State be endangered, because the denomination being then largely in the preponderance in the State, everything would eventually be under Baptist control and direction.

It is a historical fact that, though highly respected by his Baptist brethren, and though extensively known as belonging to the Baptist denomination, yet the Hon. Wilson Lumpkin, when a candidate for Governor, was not generally supported by his denomination. Although elected, he received but a small vote from his Baptist friends. This simply shows that Baptists need never be expected to unite in forming a political party, or to gain political power. This was exemplified in the strongest possible manner in 1785 when the State Legislature enacted the following law, to provide for the establishment and support of the public duties of religion:

"AN ACT *for the Establishment and Support of the Public Duties of Religion.*

"As the knowledge and practice of the principles of the Christian religion tends greatly to make good members of society, as well as good men, and is no less necessary to present than to future happiness, its regular establishment and support is among the most important objects of legislative determination; and that the minds of the citizens of this State may be properly informed and impressed by the great principles of moral obligation, and thus be induced by inclination, furnished with opportunity, and favored by law, to render public religious honors to the Supreme Being:

"Be it enacted by the representatives of the freemen of the State of Georgia in General Assembly met, and it is hereby enacted by the authority of the same, That in each county of this State which contains thirty heads of families, there be duly chosen and appointed a minister of the gospel, who shall on every Sunday publicly explain and inculcate the great doctrines and precepts of the Christian religion, as opportunity shall offer, at such place or places as the heads of families, or a majority of them, shall think best suited to advance the cause of religion and the good of the people within said county.

"And for the encouragement of persons of known and approved piety and learning to devote themselves wholly to so sacred an employment:

"*Be it further enacted by the authority aforesaid*, That of the public tax from time to time paid into the treasury of the State, there be deducted at the rate of four pence on every hundred pounds valuation of property, and in the same proportion for all other taxable property, which shall be appropriated and set apart for the county from which it was received by the treasurer for the support of religion within such county.

"The mode of choosing the minister shall be by subscription of not less than thirty heads of families, which shall be certified by an assistant judge, and two justices of the peace, within the county, on which the Governor shall give an order to the treasurer to pay out of the money appropriated to the support of religion in said county, to the person so chosen as their minister, according to the valuation of the property of such subscribers in the return of the county. A certificate from the justices aforesaid, with an order from the Governor, shall be the mode of obtaining each yearly payment; and, unless it is drawn out of the treasury in manner aforesaid, within one year after it is so received by the treasurer, it shall revert to the common funds of the State for the customary expenditures of government.

"Whenever the number of inhabitants in any county is so much increased as to dispose them to bear a greater expense for their better accommodation, and they are desirous of being made separate and distinct congregations, the same shall be set forth by a petition of not less than twenty heads of families to the General Assembly, and, on their being set off as a separate parish, they shall be entitled to a dividend of the money of the said county, in proportion to the valuation of their property, in the return of such county, such proportion to be drawn out of the treasury in the manner before pointed out.

"*And be it further enacted by the authority aforesaid*, That all the different sects and denominations of the Christian religion shall have free and equal liberty and toleration in the exercise of their religion within this State.

"*Provided always*, That nothing in this Act shall extend or be construed to extend to, effect, or in anywise injure any of the funds, subscriptions or any public moneys which have been or may hereafter be appropriated for the support of any religious societies whatever within this State. And all religious societies heretofore formed are hereby confirmed and established in all usages, rights, immunities and privileges they usually had, held or enjoyed.

"Signed by order of the House of Assembly at Savannah, the twenty-first day of February, 1785. "JOSEPH HABERSHAM, *Speaker*."

It was against this Act that the Georgia Baptist Association remonstrated; which *Remonstrance* was presented in the fall of 1785, by Silas Mercer and Peter Smith, under appointment of the Association. A copy of that remonstrance was procured by Adiel Sherwood, from the Marshall family, though in an incomplete condition, and is here given publicity for the first time:

It was found by the author among Dr. Sherwood's papers, left with the Baptist Historical Society of Philadelphia by Dr. Benedict, and is in Dr. Sherwood's own handwriting, copied by him from the original document:

"*To the Honorable, the Speaker and General Assembly of the State of Georgia, the Remonstrance of the Baptist Association, met at the Kiokee meeting-house, the 16th of May, 1785, sheweth:*

That, according to the observation of Solomon, oppression maketh a wise man mad, and that religious oppression is, of all others, the most intolerable, and, therefore, laws which best secure the liberty of the subjects, and especially those which preserve religious liberty inviolate, will tend most to attach the minds of the citizens to the State, and best promote concord among themselves;

"That your remonstrants conceive the late Act for the regular establishment and support of religion will be so far from subserving the interests of the Church or State, as perhaps, the framers might design that it will, if carried into execution, be injurious to both;

"That civil and religious government ought not to be blended together, as each of them stands on a different basis: *civil* government originates with the people, and every freeman has a right to a share in that to which he is subjected; *religious* government does not belong to the people at large, but the admission and exclusion of the members thereof are to be regulated by the qualifications laid down in the word of God;

"That churches are voluntary societies, who consider Christ as their King and Lawgiver, and who acknowledge no other Master but Him in things pertaining to the conscience. The Holy Scriptures they receive as their statute book, and, as church members, they belong to a kingdom which is not of this world, and, therefore, the sanctions of the laws they are under are spiritual. All the punishments which church rulers have a right to inflict by Christ's authority are excommunication, or an exclusion of an unworthy member from society;

"That religious societies, or churches, are not, as many conceive, to be formed by the Legislature, according to the plan of civil government where Christianity happens to be professed: religion does not need such carnal weapons as acts of assembly and civil sanctions, nor can they be applied to it without destroying it: Christians know they are bound to obey magistrates, to pay them tribute, to pray for them, to fight for them and to defend them, but to give them the honor due to Christ would be the readiest way to ruin them: Christ is the King and Lord of the conscience, and it is an encroachment upon his prerogative for civil rulers to interfere in matters pertaining thereto;

"That when legislators, who were chosen to make laws for the government of the State, presume to make laws for the church, they are acting quite out of their province, and by the same authority [that] they make *one* regulation they [may] make others; your remonstrants, therefore, look on the legislators assuming the headship of the Church and making provision for its support, as a stepping stone to the establishment of a particular denomination in preference and at the expense of the rest;

"That your remonstrants sincerely believe that nothing of this kind was intended by the honorable, the General Assembly, when they passed the late Act, but it is, evidently, a first link which draws after it, a chain of baneful consequences; for, those who are employed by the legislature to act in any post, must expect to have their conduct regulated thereby, and to be accountable thereto, for the discharge of the trust; and it will, probably, by degrees, issue in determining *who* shall preach, *where* they shall preach, *what* they shall preach. When religion is turned into a policy and made subservient to private interest, it will ever bring tyranny along with it and should, therefore, be opposed in its first appearances. The Three Penny Act on tea was a trifle in itself, but a badge of slavery, and a precedent [for] more destructive measures.

"That, whatever rites and ceremonies are established as the religion of any country, some will be found, who, like Eli's posterity, will crouch to the Rulers and say: 'Put me, I pray thee, into the priest's office, that I may eat a piece of bread.' Such time-servers will eye the emolument more than the purity of religion, and be swayed more by *interest* than *principle*. These, while they plead for national churches and the authority of the State in matters of religion, will stand prepared to follow it for the loaves, under whatever form it may assume, and, having prostituted their own consciences to mercenary purposes, they will be the first to insist on the necessity of uniformity, and to urge the State to enforce it, that power and numbers may keep them in countenance.

"That your remonstrants acknowledge that morality is essential to good government, and as rulers should be a terror to evil-doers and a praise to them that do well, laws should be made for the punishment of vice, without regard to any religious denomination, and protection should be offered to each in their just rights, but statesmen derive no authority from God or men, to judge heresy and establish systems of religious opinions or modes of religious worship. Fines, imprisonments, tortures and deaths of various kinds, on a religious account, are the genuine but diabolical offspring of ecclesiastical establishments. It is evident that none of these can take place in a State where all are left free to worship God according to the dictates of their own consciences, unbribed and unmolested. That the general commission given by Christ to his ministers enjoined them to go into all the world and preach the gospel to every creature, that is, as far as they have opportunity; but the Act referred to, by your remonstrants, enacts that the minister shall, on every Sunday, publicly explain the great doctrines of the Christian religion at such place or places as the heads of families, or a majority of them, shall think best suited to the people within said county. Your remonstrants conceive that here are large strides towards taking the " —

Unfortunately the remaining page or pages of the Remonstrance were lost; but the foregoing gives a fair idea of the document, which was written, doubtless, by Silas Mercer. It is a noble production, and was worthy of even such a man. The doctor seems doubtful whether Sanders Walker or Peter Smith was the companion of Mercer in the presentation of the document, but appears to favor the latter. He says the obnoxious act was repealed in the fall of 1785, after the presentation of this Remonstrance.

Surely it was preposterous to assume that the Baptists of that day were in any way likely to be dangerous to the religious liberties of the people.

The presentation of their remonstrance to the Legislature of our State, insisting, as it does, upon full religious liberty, strikingly evinced one great, and it might be added distinguishing, peculiarity of our denomination—its attachment to religious liberty. Theirs was the most numerous denomination in the State, and the Baptists might have formed and supported their churches over the entire State, under the law giving "thirty families the right to choose a minister," who was to be supported from the State treasury ; but, according to their principles, the gospel should be supported by those who hear it, and not by "four pence on every hundred pounds paid into the treasury." They insist upon perfect freedom in worship, and are unwilling that the State shall be taxed to support or maintain religious worship in any way. In other words, they believe in an entire separation of " Church " and " State." So strongly was this feeling manifested during the late war, that many Baptist ministers scrupled to serve as army chaplains in pay of the government, and some served independently as such through a part or the whole of the war without pay, rather than infringe on a principle ingrained in Baptist faith. It is well known that in the first Georgia Constitution, adopted in 1777, the sixty-second article made clergymen ineligible to seats in the Legislature. The State had but few inhabitants then, and there was no Baptist influence in the State worth regarding. But in the Constitutional Convention of 1789, at Augusta, there were at least two Baptists—Abraham Marshall and Jeremiah Walker—and then the article excluding ministers was rescinded. In the Amending Convention of 1795, there were Benjamin Davis, Thomas Polhill and Silas Mercer, Baptist ministers; and in the Convention of 1798, which, while it took for its basis the Constitution of 1789, as amended in 1795, yet formed an independent structure, the following Baptists were members: George Franklin, Benjamin Davis, Thomas Polhill, Benjamin Mosely, Thomas Gilbert, Jesse Mercer, ministers, and Matthew Rabun and others, laymen. Among the "principal actors" in this Convention, Dr. William Bacon Stevens, in his History of Georgia, numbers Jesse Mercer, and says that the section of the Constitution "securing liberty of conscience in matters of religion was written by Rev. Jesse Mercer."

Such Baptists as those named above could not act otherwise than discountenance every measure which might infringe upon inalienable rights—the rights of conscience; for every Baptist church is, in itself, a republic in miniature. "The government is with the body," is a sentiment dear to every member of the Baptist denomination; they rejoice that it is not committed to church wardens, to the preacher in charge, to the bishop, to the ruling elders, to presbyteries, conferences, associations, conventions, nor to any other body or set of officers, but to the church itself. With them "the church is the highest ecclesiastical authority on earth," and they do not admit that the civil courts have any power or right to prescribe regulations regarding worship, or dictate who shall or shall not take part in or conduct divine worship.

This has been exemplified, even in our day, as late as 1863, when a number of Baptists of Georgia sent to the State Legislature a protest against an enactment in the Code of Georgia, which made it unlawful to license a negro to preach, whether free or a slave. This protest, written by Dr. H. H. Tucker, assisted in procuring the repeal of the obnoxious law, and, in a most able and pointed manner, declares the position of the Baptists of Georgia with reference to the principle of religious liberty, and as such it deserves to be put permanently on record in a history of our people.

The following petition was drawn up by Rev. H. H. Tucker, formerly Professor in Mercer University, and was presented to the Legislature just prior to its repeal of the section of the New Code, to which allusion is made. The Legislature, however, left in full force the old law requiring permission to be obtained from the Inferior Court before a slave can be licensed to preach:

" *To the Honorable the Senate and House of Representatives of the State of Georgia :*

"The petition of the undersigned members of Baptist churches, and citizens of Georgia, respectfully sheweth, that whereas, His Excellency the Governor, in his recent message to your Honorable Body, did recommend the repeal of Section 1376 of the New Code which section reads as follows, to-wit:

"It shall be unlawful for any church, society or other body, or any persons, to grant any license or other authority to any slave or free person of color to preach, or exhort, or otherwise officiate in church matters."

"And whereas the objections to said section are of the gravest possible character, to-wit:

"It is objectionable in the first place, because it virtually unites Church and State. Its very phraseology shows that the legislation embodied therein, has reference to '*Church* matters,' and these are matters over which no human tribunal has any jurisdiction. However inexpedient, unwise and improper, it may be for churches to authorize unsuitable persons, whether white or black, to preach, it is still more inexpedient, unwise and improper for civil authorities to take cognizance of matters purely ecclesiastical. As Baptists, we desire to put on record our solemn protest against this encroachment of the kingdom of this world upon the kingdom of Christ. We quote the language of our Baptist ancestors, put on record in the city of London, in the year 1646, when we say that,

"'Concerning the worship of God,' (and the licensing of a preacher being a part of the service of God is equivalent to an act of worship.) 'there is but one lawgiver which is able to save and to destroy, which is Jesus Christ who hath given laws and rules sufficient in his word for his worship; and for any to make more were to charge Christ with want of wisdom or faithfulness, or both, in not making laws enough or not good enough for his house; surely it is our wisdom, duty and privilege to observe Christ's laws only.'

"Section 1376 of the new Code of Georgia is an attempt to improve upon the laws which Christ has given to his people; it is a usurpation of ecclesiastical power by civil authorities; it is a seizure by force of the things that are God's, and a rendering of them unto Cæsar; it is a consolidation under one government, of things which belong to two separate and distinct tribunals. What would be the outcry if a Baptist or any other church were to attempt to prescribe the length of the Governor's term of office, or to say of how many members the Legislature shall consist, or to prescribe the qualifications of Legislators or of voters, or to regulate the taxes, or to make laws for the collection of debts, or for the punishment of crimes; or in any other way to trespass upon the authority of civil government? Yet a church has as much right to dictate to the Legislature on these matters, as the Legislature has to dictate to a church whom it shall authorize to preach. The truth is, the two jurisdictions are worldwide apart, and any attempt to force them into union is as unwise as it is unhallowed. In too many instances already, the Church has committed whoredom with the kings of the earth, and the result has been disastrous.

"The section in question is objectionable, in the second place, because it trespasses upon the rights of conscience, and is a violation of religious liberty. To say nothing of the sacred right of the black, to preach, exhort or pray, if God has called and commanded him to do either, cases might arise, in which we might feel it our duty as Baptists to license a man of color to preach or otherwise officiate in church matters. To grant such license, would then be a part of our religion; but the Code of Georgia forbids our acting according to the dictates of our own consciences, in this particular, and in prescribing what our religion shall *not* be, virtually prescribes what it *shall* be. We protest against this attempt to bind our consciences. Our religion is a matter between us and our God; with which no power on earth has a right to interfere. Soul-liberty is the rightful heritage of all God's moral creatures. Not even over the religion of the slave has civil authority any power, nor yet has it over that of the citizen.

"Involved in this objectionable feature, and forming perhaps a part of it, is another. There are in the State of Georgia, not far from one hundred thousand Baptist communicants, to say nothing of adherents and friends. If the spirit of the section be carried out, the whole of this vast proportion of the population, will be forced to the unhappy alternative, of deciding whether they will obey the law of Georgia or the law of God. If the law were enforced by extreme penalties, we must either violate our consciences or become martyrs. Doubtless some who are among us would forsake their principles in the day of trial; but others, the better part, we hope the great majority, the upright, the conscientious, the pure and the true, would stand by their religion to the last, and say with apostolic boldness: 'Whether it is right in the sight of God to hearken unto you more than unto God, judge ye.' Thus a large proportion of the best part of the population of the State, would be arrayed in hostility to its laws. The rebels would consist, not of the profane and the lawless, but of those whose nature and whose religion prompt them to be peaceable, quiet, loyal and law-abiding. Facts have indeed already transpired which, to some extent, corroborate what has been said. The Baptist church in Columbus, Georgia, with the new Code spread open before their eyes, and with a full knowledge and understanding of the intent and meaning of section 1376, and after a thorough discussion of its provisions, deliberately violated the same, and ordained two negroes to officiate in church matters in the office of Deacon. Should the same intolerant, bigoted and persecuting spirit which prompted the making of the law, be let loose to enforce it, we doubt not, that the Baptists of Columbus would be ready for the gibbet or the stake rather than recede from their principles, and as thousands of Baptists in centuries past, have done, would seal their testimony with their blood.

"It is, however, a remarkable fact, in regard to the law in question, that it has no penalty; and this we regard as another objectionable feature. If we are forbidden to worship God according to the dictates of our own consciences, (for as already said, the licensing of a preacher is an act of worship,) we want to know what penalty we incur. If it be a fine, it will not be the first time that we have been robbed for the testimony of Jesus. If it be imprisonment, we at least have this consolation, that the incarceration of our bodies will be easier to endure than the fetters of despotism on our consciences. If it be death, our history for eighteen centuries has made us familiar with it. As the matter now stands, we are merely liable to be dispersed by a mob without redress. It would seem that the civil authority, either afraid or ashamed to enforce its own laws, turns over the execution of them to the rabble. Virtuous and unoffending citizens quietly worshipping God, are to be made the sport of the profligate and the base. The assembly of the saints of Jesus Christ is liable to be broken up by a mob, just such as that which in Jerusalem cried out 'Crucify him! crucify him!' and the Code of Georgia provides no remedy but encourages the act. We protest against the execution of laws by the lawless. If we must be arrested and arraigned let it be done not by drunkards and ruffians, (for no others would molest us,) but let it be done by the sheriff. Let not the State shrink from the execution of its own enactments; but let the constable come with his tip-staff and arrest the proceedings of the people of God.

"But while the law in question is in the highest degree objectionable at any time, it is especially so at *this* time. Since we have cut loose from our connexion with that peculiar people whose territory lies North of ours, and since we have been from under their pernicious and unhallowed influence, there has been a very general and a very rapid spread of a sentiment among all our people in favor of ameliorating as far as possible the physical, mental, and above all the moral condition of our slaves. Indeed it is well known among us, that this sentiment would long since have accomplished its benevolent plans, had it not been restrained and held in by Northern fanaticism. But now that that horrid incubus is removed, the feeling long pent up, has broken out, and there is a loud and universal demand for reform. Aside from the wicked interference of abolitionists, which while we were united to them, made reform impossible, our minds have heretofore been so absorbed with the defence of our institutions, that we have neglected to cherish and develop them as we desired to do. *Now*, the barrier to progress is broken down; now, we have the leisure, as we have long since had the disposition, to improve the condition of our slaves. Just at this crisis the new Code steps in and commands the voice of reform to be silent; nay it puts back the sun many degrees on the dial; it reverses the wheels of progress, and puts us back to the days of Puritan bigotry and Popish intolerance; it puts us back and puts us down to a point where we have never been; it reduces us to a level with the legislators of early New England. If just at this point of time we do worse instead of doing better, it would seem that Northern influence, instead of restraining us from good as it has done, has actually restrained us from evil. We trust that the speedy correction of the egregious blunder of the Code, will prevent this false impression from going forth to the world.

"But aside from local or temporary objections, and aside from its attempted despotism over the consciences of men, the most objectionable feature of all, in the obnoxious section, is its heaven-daring impiety. It trespasses not only on the rights of men, but on the rights of God. It dictates to the Almighty of what color his preachers shall be.

"The great majority of the human race are of dark complexion. If one of these among us is called by the great Head of the Church to minister in holy things, the Code of Georgia forbids obedience; it stops the preaching of the everlasting gospel on the ground of a police regulation; it says to Omnipotence, 'Thus far shalt thou go, and no farther;' it allows Jehovah to have ministers of a certain complexion and no other, and so exacting and rigid are these regulations imposed on the Almighty, that they not only forbid his having preachers such as he may choose, but also prescribe that none shall even exhort, or in any way *whatever* 'officiate in church matters,' unless they be approved by this self-exalted and heaven-defying tribunal. Nor is there any reason to suppose that the spirit which prompted the act now under protest would stop, if unchecked, at its present point of audacity. Having prescribed color as one qualification for the pulpit to-day, it might prescribe another qualification to-morrow. Quite likely a certain amount of learning might be called for next, and a multitude of Baptist preachers, and of the most useful men who ever lived, would be suspended from their sacred calling. Next, the *dress* of the clergyman might be prescribed; the surplice and gown might be made obligatory, and the uncouth limbs of our rustic brethren be enveloped in silken canonicals. Next, the *ordinances* of the church might come under legislative review, and Baptists be forced to sprinkle candidates for Baptism, which, in their view, is no baptism at all; or they might be forced to perform some ceremony over their children which they believe to be unscriptural in origin and pernicious in influence. Next, the question in dispute between the Calvinist and the Arminian might be the subject of the legislative investigation and decision. Next, we might have fire and faggot.

"In short, all history shows, that when the civil power begins to encroach upon 'church matters," (to use the phraseology of section 1376,) it never ceases until it attains to the triple crown and the keys. Nor does it usually make bold beginnings. Like the little section slipped into the new Code, it begins furtively and claims only one thing at a time. Insidious in its approaches, it is the more important that we should be ever on the alert and crush it at its very inception.

"It is worthy of special mention, and ought, for the credit of the State to be put on permanent and public record, that until the adoption of the new Code, the section under protest never was a part of the law of Georgia. It is indeed a question whether it is a law *now*, violative as it is of constitutional rights, adopted as it was in an unconstitutional manner, and inserted, as it was, into the Code surreptitiously. Three persons were appointed by the Legislature to codify existing laws. Their duties extended thus far and no farther. It was never dreamed that they would *make* laws. Indeed, the Legislature, even if it had the disposition, had not the power thus to delegate its legislative authority. The committee of both Houses, who reported on the Code, affirm that they were the more ready to recommend its adoption because no graft had been made upon the old stock, no new feature had been introduced, and, above all, no new principles brought to bear. Persuaded of this, the joint committee recommended the adoption of the new Code. Believing this, the Legislature *did* adopt it; and now, to our astonishment, we find that a new principle *has* been introduced—a principle which is radical and fundamental, and one, too, which is in direct antagonism to the spirit and genius of all American institutions. How such a thing could have occurred is unknown to us. It may have been an accident. Be that as it may, it is to the credit of the Legislature that this act was never read in the hearing of its members three times, as all laws are; nay they never heard it *once*: nor is it probable that at the time of its adoption, a solitary member of either House was aware of its existence.

"Now, therefore, we, the undersigned, in view of the above objectionable features of section 1376, of the new Code, do most earnestly add to the recommendation of His Excellency, the Governor, our prayer to your honorable body that said section be repealed.

"And whereas, furthermore, before the adoption of the new Code, it was the law of Georgia, enacted —— and to be found, —— that negroes should not be allowed to preach except on a permit, to be granted be the Inferior Court, and, whereas, said law is obnoxious to the very same objections that have been urged against section 1376, of the new Code, and is, in point of fact, just as real, if not as great a usurpation of ecclesiastical power by civil authority, and is just as insidious in its nature, and as unhappy in its natural results; we therefore, do most respectfully but most earnestly petition that said law be also repealed, or so amended as not to infringe upon the rights of the Church of Christ.

"We have heretofore submitted to this law, not because we acquiesced in its spirit, but because the inconvenience to which it puts us was not very great, and because we were not disposed to make an ado about what *seemed* to be a small matter. But we are now convinced that we ought to have protested at the beginning. The first step in violation of our religious liberties, just as we might have expected, has been followed by a second; and the long standing of the first without rebuke, may now be urged as an argument against its repeal. We are now, therefore, the more in haste to enter our protest against both, lest the same argument be urged in favor of both, and the way prepared for still further encroachment upon the rights of conscience. We maintain in this, as in the former case, that the Church of Christ and the Inferior Court are two separate organizations, having each a distinct jurisdiction. The preachers of the gospel are the officers of the church; and the Inferior Court has no more right to say who shall be the officers of the church than the church has to say who shall be the officers of the Inferior Court. We have to confess that we are to blame for not having protested against this law before; but now repenting of this our fault, especially since we have seen the consequences of our negligence, we hereby declare that we cannot conscientiously submit to its provisions : and as we desire, above all things, to be a law-abiding people, we earnestly pray for its repeal, and for the repeal of any other law which may infringe, in the slightest degree, on the religious rights of *any one*.

" In this petition we have spoken of ourselves exclusively as Baptists. We do not, by this, mean to intimate that we are the only people who object to the laws in question. On the contrary, we believe that now that the bearing of these laws has been brought to light which heretofore was not observed, the whole population of the State would unanimously join with us in the petition ; and if there be but few signatures hereunto annexed, it is only because in our haste to get the matter before your honorable body, we have not taken the time to secure a larger number.

" And now respectfully but earnestly urging upon you this, our petition, and praying the blessing of God upon you individually and collectively, upon the State and upon the Confederate States,

" We have the honor to be your fellow-citizens,

D. E. BUTLER,	N. M. CRAWFORD,
THOMAS STOCKS,	T. R. THORNTON,
T. J. BURNEY,	J. L. BLITCH,
J. R. SANDERS,	S. P. SANFORD,
N. HOBBS,	H. C. PEEK,
JOHN E. JACKSON,	JAMES BURK,
THOMAS MOSLEY,	JOHN B. SHIELDS,
J. R. KENDRICK,	W. S. STOKES,
A. B. SHARP,	WILLIAM E. WOODFIN,
J. E. WILLET,	P. ROBINSON,
H. H. TUCKER,	W. B. CRAWFORD,
E. E. JONES,	JOHN B. WALKER,
ISAAC L. CARY,	L. M. WILLSON,
WILLIAM HEARN.	

EDUCATION OF COLORED MINISTERS.

Since the emancipation of the colored race, and the constitution of Baptists among them into churches separate from the whites, the question as to the education of their ministers has assumed momentous proportions. On that question, our people at the South at large, and in this State, have expressed decided views. The Southern Baptist Convention, in its session at Charleston, 1875, said: " In the impoverished condition of the South, and with the need of strengthening the special work which the Southern Baptist Convention is committed to prosecute, there is no probability of an early endowment of schools under our charge for the better education of a colored ministry. The Convention has adopted the policy of sustaining students at the seminaries controlled by the American Baptist Home Mission Society. It is much to be desired that larger contributions for this purpose may be secured from both white and colored Baptists." And with regard to this work as prosecuted in our own State under the auspices of the Home Mission Society, the Georgia Baptist Convention said, in 1875 : " The Institute for colored ministers, under the care and instruction of our esteemed brother, J. T. Robert, is doing a noble work for our colored population. We trust that many will avail themselves of the excellent course of instruction there, and that the school may prove an incalculable blessing in evangelizing and elevating the race." In 1876, it said : " We are pleased to observe that the enterprise of educating colored Baptist ministers, at Augusta, Georgia, is in successful operation," and bespoke " the confidence of the brethren for the enterprise." It said, in 1877 ; " We recommend the school to the patronage of our people." In 1878, it said : " We recommend our brethren to aid in sending pious and promising young men who have the ministry in view " to this school ; a recommendation which was " *urged* in view of the fact, among other facts, that Romanists are making strenuous efforts to control our colored people, by giving them cheap or gratuitous education." It said, in 1879: "The institution deserves our sympathy and most cordial cooperation. It is doing a most important work, and is indispensable as an educator of this most needy class of our population." Some may doubt whether it is not yet too soon to anticipate the verdict of history in this matter; but may we not with reasonable confidence persuade ourselves that posterity will recognize in these views of the two Conventions, 'the sound wisdom which the Lord layeth up for the righteous?' Beyond all question, at least, ignorance is *not* the mother of devotion; and not to educate the ministry of a race would be to doom its churches to extinction, or to a corruption worse than extinction.

PEDOBAPTIST MINISTERS AND IMMERSIONS.

It is rather difficult for us, at the present day, to realize the extent to which, what we are accustomed to designate pulpit "affiliation," was carried by some of the most eminent ministers of our denomination at the close of the last century, and at the beginning of the present one. Of course there existed a corresponding inclination to "Christian union," which the well-defined denominational lines, of the present day, render almost incomprehensible to us. A few extracts from some hitherto unpublished manuscripts of Dr Adiel Sherwood's, bearing on this point, will be given, to enable us to obtain an idea of the sentiment existing at the time of which our record treats. He writes: "Landmarkism was not developed among Missionary Baptists, in Mercer's day. He admitted Pedobaptist ministers into his pulpit, especially agents that were pleading the cause of benevolence. His father before him, Silas Mercer, used frequently to make tours of preaching with the Rev. William Springer, one of Jesse's instructors in the learned languages. He was a learned Presbyterian, and the first minister of that order ordained in the up-country. Ministers of all denominations were invited to seats in both the Georgia Association and State Convention, when Mercer was Moderator." See Minutes of the Georgia Association and State Convention for 1824, 1833, 1834—"ministers of our own and other denominations, not of this body, were cordially invited to sit with us." So, by the Convention in 1826, 1827, 1828, 1829, 1830, 1832, 1833—"ministers of all denominations." Messrs. Davis and Kennedy, in 1826; Webster, in 1828; and Reed, in 1832, took seats. Both Silas and Jesse Mercer frequently preached with Mr. Springer, a Presbyterian. Between 1820 and 1830, Dr. Cummins preached regularly a year, once a month at Shiloh, Greene county, in his trips into Oglethorpe or Clarke. At the close, the church offered him one hundred dollars for his services, which he declined, observing that it was in his route, and hence no trouble.

It was well known that, for two years, Dr. Holcombe was the regular pastor of a congregation composed of different denominations, in Savannah—1800 and 1801; but, if any one supposes him to have been an open-communionist, he has but to read the following from the Analytical Repository of September and October, 1802, in a published letter on mixed-communion:

"I perfectly agree with you that, desirable as *union* among Christians is, it must never be sought at the expense of *integrity*; but an object so important, you will readily admit, ought to be promoted by all means in our power, consistent with the *word of God* and a *good conscience*. Be assured, my brother, that it is only on the ground and principles of eternal truth that I seek *union*. My public expressions, you will find, admit of no other construction. God forbid that I should ever, intentionally, deviate a hair's breadth from *rectitude*, or, which is the same thing—*the rules of the gospel.*

"Among other important object which, as a writer, I have in view, I wish to show to the world that the Baptists hold no illiberal sentiments, and are not only *willing*, but *desirous* to meet their brethren of other persuasions, on any fair grounds, with a view to a scriptural accommodation of existing differences, as far as these may be inimical to peace and our success against the common enemy."

Jesse Mercer's sentiments on this subject may be learned in an extract from a Circular Letter of the Georgia Association, written by him in 1821. He presents briefly the reasons why Baptists "cannot reasonably hold communion at the Lord's table with those who, in Christian profession, differ in faith and practice, to-wit: 1. Because the union is broken and the dependence lost between you and them, so that union would be a shadow without any proper substance—too pretensional for sacred and sincere Christianity. 2. Because there is no discipline instituted among the denominations, the influence of which can preserve such an attempt at communion from the grossest impositions and wildest disorders; and, of consequence, must be absurd, until some regulation be established among the parties and they all agree 'to walk by the same rule,' and 'to speak the same thing.' 3. Because you and they are not, and, in the present state of religious affairs, cannot become members together of the same body; whice is a capital requisition in the gospel to a meet communion. And 4. Because the principles and practices which first produced and still prolong the difference of denominational character among professed Christians, are so heterodox and discordant, that the maintaining of the one is, of necessary consequence, the destruction of the other. To attempt communion in such a state of things, would be to form a religious chaos, and to promote envy and strife as the legitimate tendency. This may be exemplified immediately, by reference to the ordinance of baptism; if the Pedobaptists establish their baptism as true, yours is absurd; but if yours be maintained as the gospel ordinance, then theirs is no baptism at all. It must, then, be improper and disloyal to attempt communion until these discordant principles are done away, and the parties conciliated in Christian love and unison; yet, dear brethren, we exhort and admonish you to carry yourselves towards them as Christian professors; engage with them and invite them to engage with you in exercises of devotion and enterprises of usefulness; go with them freely as far as you can preserve a good conscience and the fellowship of your brethren, and stop where you must, according to the Scriptures."

While courtesies were extended to Pedobaptist ministers as *preachers* by our denomination in the early years of the century, it is certain that their *official acts*, as ministers, were not recognized as valid by the denomination. In 1811, the Ocmulgee Association rejected the application for membership of the Richland Creek church, in Twiggs county, deeming its constitution invalid, because the ordination of Elijah Hammack, one of the two ministers forming the presbytery, was invalid, and because *one minister alone*, Rev. Isaiah Shire, could not form a presbytery. The ordination of Elijah Hammack was invalid, because he "was ordained by William Lord, whose ordination was considered invalid;" and *his* ordination was considered invalid because "he was ordained by a presbytery not of our faith and order"—that is, by Pedobaptist ministers. The defect in the constitution of the Richland Creek church was remedied, for we find it and four others "found sound and orthodox, and cordially received," in 1812.

The denomination had been much agitated about twenty years previous to this strict action of the Ocmulgee Association by a little remissness on the part of the Georgia Association itself, and had gained wisdom by experience. It happened thus: In 1788, at Clark's Station, the Association admitted as a "help" *James Hutchinson*, who had formerly been a Methodist preacher, and who, on a profession of his faith, was "baptized by immersion," (as the Minutes of that year express it,) by Mr. Thomas Humphries, a Methodist minister. Mr. Hutchinson was received into the Clark's Station church on his Pedobaptist immersion, "having declined the Methodist discipline and communion," and having made a public declaration of his experience. Jesse Mercer himself was present at that session of the Georgia Association, and was, with Alexander Scott, Jacob Gibson, Thomas Mercer, Ezekiel Campbell, and others, admitted as a "help." Writing mostly from memory of this matter, Mr. Mercer says, in his history of the Georgia Association, that Mr. Hutchinson appeared at the Association and, after requesting it, was permitted to relate his experience with a view to uniting with the Clark Station church. His relation being satisfactory, he was received into membership. "But although he gave up the Methodist discipline and doctrines and embraced fully those of the Baptist denomination, he did not feel at liberty to give up his baptism, having been immersed upon a profession of his faith by the Rev. Mr. Humphries, a regular minister of the Methodist connection."

This was made a question for the Association to consider, and it decided to admit Mr. Hutchinson on his Pedobaptist immersion, though many were opposed to it. Eloquent and truly fervent in spirit, Mr. Hutchinson conciliated many, and did much good as a minister. He went to Virginia on a visit to his relations, and continued his ministrations there with great success, receiving and baptizing about one hundred persons, as the fruit of his labors, and organizing them into a church, but when the church applied for admission into an Association, it was rejected on account of the invalidity of their baptism.

Thus was practically shown how invalid are the official acts of ministers not of our faith and order—in plain terms, of unbaptized ministers. Mr. Hutchinson afterwards submitted to valid baptism, and all his people, but two or three, followed his example. "Thus," Mr. Mercer says, "terminated a most fierce and distressing controversy."

In the very year, 1811, that the Ocmulgee Association rejected Pedobaptist immersion, the Georgia, having by experience and instruction grown wiser in church order, "*Resolved.* That the subject of the next Circular Letter be our reasons for rejecting Methodist or Pedobaptist baptism by immersion as invalid, and that brother Mercer write the same." The Circular Letter was written and unanimously adopted at the session of 1812, having previously been examined by Abraham Marshall and E. Shackelford, at Mr. Mercer's own request. It is here given in full:

"*The Elders and brethren of the Georgia Association to the brethren they represent—Greeting:*

"Beloved in Christ—From our earliest connection, we have studiously selected for the subjects of our addresses to you, those doctrines and duties which seemed the best suited to confirm and increase your faith in Christ; to edify and comfort your hearts, being knit together in love; and to lead you on to that light and perfection which would honor and commend the cause in which you have embarked, and reflect the highest praise and glory of God who has called you into his marvellous light. But while you have endeavored to keep yourselves unmixed with, and unspotted from, the world *as a chaste virgin to Christ*, you have excited some unpleasantness among the religious denominations around you, because you have not found it consistent to admit *them* and their *administrations* as ORDERLY AND VALID. We therefore propose as the subject of this letter, *the reasons,* briefly, *which lead us to deem Pedobaptist administrations,* though in the proper mode, *invalid.* That this subject may be as clear as our epistolary limits will admit, we propose to lay down a few scriptural propositions, whose legitimate inferences will, we trust, bring into, though a concise, yet sufficiently, clear view, the reasons in question.

"I. *The* APOSTOLIC CHURCH *continued through all ages to the end of the world, is the only* TRUE GOSPEL CHURCH.

"The truth of this proposition is not only frequently intimated, but strongly affirmed by the prophets. They speak of a glorious state of religious affairs to take place on the coming of the Messiah, which they say shall continue or endure, as the sun, or days of heaven—Psalm lxxxix, 29, 36, 37; shall never be cut off—Isaiah lv, 14; and shall stand forever—Daniel ii, 44. Christ affirms nothing shall prevail against His church, no, not the gates of hell—Matthew xiv, 18. But John puts this point beyond all contradiction in his prophetic history of the Church, in which, though he admits of various outward modifications, he maintains an uninterrupted succession from the apostolic age, till the world shall end.

"II. *Of this Church* CHRIST *is the only* HEAD, *and true source of all ecclesiastical authority.*

"Although the Scriptures are illumined by this truth, yet it may not be impertinent to cite a few passages in point. To me, says Christ, is authority given—John v, 22, 27. And knowing the love of power, and the strong propensity to rule, in the human heart, He frequently and emphatically declares Himself, to His apostles, to be their only Lord and Master—Matthew xxiii, 8, 10. The apostles concur in ascribing this honor to Him; and transmit it to all after ages of the Church—Acts ii, 36; Ephesians i, 22, and v, 23; Collossians ii, 10. But the commission of the apostles, the matter, manner, and majesty of which are enough to make a saint triumph, an angel rejoice, and a devil tremble, caps the whole—Matthew xxviii, 18, 19.

"III. *Gospel ministers are servants in the Church, are all equal, and have no power to lord it over the heritage of their Lord.*

"By the examples of a little child in the midst, and the exercise of dominion over the Gentiles by their princes, our Lord teaches humility, and denies to His apostles the exercise of lordship over His Church—Matthew xviii, 2, 6; xx, 25, 26. He calls them *brethren*, and directs that they should not be called *masters*, but servants—Matthew xxii, 8, 11. The Acts and Epistles of the apostles show their observance of their Lord's commands. Here we see them the MESSENGERS AND SERVANTS of the churches, which proves the power to be in the churches and not in them—Acts vi, 5; xv, 4, 22; 2 Corinthians viii, 23; Philippians ii, 25; 2 Corinthians iv, 5. Timothy is instructed how to behave himself in the church, which is the *pillar and ground* of the truth; but if the power had been constituted in him, the advice should have been given the church, that she might have known how to behave herself in the presence of her BISHOP—1 Timothy iii, 15, compared with Matthew xviii, 17.

"IV. *All things are to be done in* FAITH, *according to the gospel pattern.*

"Faith is made capital in the Scriptures, and the want of it equals unbelief. The house of Israel is often complained of for the lack of it; the apostles are admonished to have it, and upbraided for their unbelief—Deuteronomy xxxii, 22; Mark xi, 22; xvi, 14. The apostle Paul declares, without it it is impossible to please God, and that he that doubts of what he does is damned in doing it because he acts without faith—1 Corinthians iv, 13; Hebrews xi, 6; Romans xiv, 23.

"From these propositions, thus established, we draw the following inferences, *as clear and certain truths:*

"I. That all churches and ministers who originated since the apostles, and not successively to them, are not in gospel order; and therefore cannot be acknowledged as such.

"II. That all who have been ordained to the work of the ministry without the knowledge and call of the Church, by popes, councils, etc., are the creatures of those who constituted them, and not the servants of Christ, or His Church, and therefore have no right to administer for them.

"III. That those who have set aside the discipline of the gospel, and have given law to, and exercised dominion over, the Church, are usurpers over the place and office of Christ, are against Him; and therefore may not be accepted in their offices.

"IV. That they who administer contrary to their own, or the faith of the gospel, cannot administer for God; since without the gospel faith He has nothing to minister; and without their own He accepts no service; therefore the administrations of such are unwarrantable impositions in any way.

"Our reasons, therefore, for rejecting baptism by immersion, when administered by Pedobaptist ministers, are:

"I. That they are connected with churches clearly out of the apostolic succession, and therefore clearly out of the apostolic commission.

"II. That they have derived their authority, by ordination, from the bishops of Rome, or from individuals, who have taken it on themselves to give it.

"III. That they hold a higher rank in the churches than the apostles did, are not accountable to, and of consequence not triable by, the Church; but are amenable only to or among themselves.

"IV. That they all, as we think, administer contrary to the pattern of the gospel, and some, when occasion requires, will act contrary to their own professed faith. Now as we know of none implicated in this case, but are in some or all of the above defects, either of which we deem sufficient to disqualify for meet gospel administration, therefore we hold their administrations invalid.

"But if it should be said that the apostolic succession cannot be ascertained, and then it is proper to act without it; we say, that the loss of the succession can never prove it futile, nor justify any one out of it. The Pedobaptists, by their own histories, admit they are not of it; *but we do not*, and shall think ourselves entitled to the claim until the reverse be clearly shown. And should any think authority derived from the MOTHER OF HARLOTS sufficient to qualify to administer a gospel ordinance, they will be so charitable as not to condemn us for preferring that derived from Christ. And should any still more absurdly plead that ordination received from an individual is sufficient; we leave them to show what is the use of ordination, and why it exists. If any think an administration will suffice which has no pattern in the gospel, they will suffer us to act according to the divine order with impunity. And if it should be said that faith in the subject is all that is necessary, we beg leave to require it where the Scriptures do, *that is, everywhere*. But we must close. We beseech you, brethren, while you hold fast the form of your profession, be ready to unite with those from whom you differ, as far as the principles of eternal truth will justify. And while you firmly oppose that shadowy union so often urged, be instant in prayer, and exert yourselves to bring about that which is in heart, and after godliness. *Which the Lord hasten in its season.* Amen, and Amen!

"A. MARSHALL, *Moderator.*

"JESSE MERCER, *Clerk.*"

EXTRACTS FROM DR. SHERWOOD'S MANUSCRIPTS.

For many years Dr. Adiel Sherwood was engaged in collecting materials for his *Gazetteer* and for a history of the Baptists of Georgia. From the material left by him we have made a few extracts on different subjects from his manuscripts, which were written about the year 1840.

"*Sabbath-schools.*—These were encouraged by the resolutions of Associations, and established in every church in some counties, but were neglected in others. The author commenced one at Trail Creek meeting-house, near Athens, in July, 1819. The Anties opposed them, and excluded some persons for attending and allowing their children to attend; but the denomination, generally, have approved them, and have used untiring efforts to circulate knowledge among all classes."

"*Perusal of the Scriptures.*—This has been frequently enjoined from the pulpit and by Associations. In 1834, the Central Association recommended that each church member read the Bible through during the year. This was complied with by several. Other Associations followed in this recommendation, the practice became quite general, and the Bible was perused more than ordinarily. If the religion of Protestants is founded on the Bible, surely they ought to peruse its sacred and enlightening pages!

"It is not to be inferred from these remarks that the Bible was not frequently read through by many persons prior to this recommendation, but only that this increased the amount of reading, and probably swelled greatly the number of readers."

"*Sanctity of the Sabbath.*—On this subject the Associations have expressed themselves freely—that the Sabbath ought to be religiously observed by abstaining from all amusements and all labor, works of mercy and necessity excepted. Yet there are many violations by members of the church, such as visiting, travelling, etc. The following clause is found in the Circular of the Georgia Association, 1832:

"'While we admit that there are some professing Christians who suppose that keeping the Sabbath constitutes the very essence of piety, we maintain that he who makes no difference between it and other days is far from the *true faith.*'"

"*Slavery.*—Similar sentiments to those manifested in the following have been expressed by a large number of Associations:

"'*Resolved*, That we understand the Scriptures fully to recognize the relation of Christian master and Christian servant, without the shadow of censure on the existence of such relation, but that they give full directions how each party should fulfill the duties of such relation.' Minutes of the Georgia Association for 1835."

"*Treatment of Slaves.*—A query on this subject is answered by the Ocmulgee Association in 1819: 'They should treat them with humanity and justice (Eph. 6: 9; Col. 4: 1), and we recommend the members to watch over each other, and if any should treat them otherwise, that they should be dealt with as transgressors.'

"Some churches think that when a slave, a member of the church, disobeys his master, that he should first be cited to the church, and, without satisfaction being given, should be excluded: then the master is at liberty to chastise. But that slaves ought to be cited for disobedience is not avowed by many.

"Slaves generally attend worship every Sabbath, and frequently constitute the larger part of the congregation. The religious ones commune at the same table with their masters. Prior to 1829 there was no law to prevent their being taught to read. In the fall of that year, an inflammatory pamphlet, by Walker, was found in Savannah, by the pastor of the African Church, (an aged and pious African, whose good conduct had purchased his freedom,) and immediately carried to the Mayor; he forwarded it post-haste to the Legislature; and the law referred to was passed.

"The Scriptures are read, however, to their servants, by many families *statedly*, and by most pious families *occasionally*. Missionaries, among the Methodists, especially, go around to preach exclusively to the blacks; much oral instruction is given, in many counties systematically; and many servants know a great deal about the doctrines of the Bible.

"Twenty years ago there were dozens of ordained negroes who used to preach every Sabbath to those of their own color; but the churches have not ordained any lately, though many are licensed, and preach as occasion and convenience may require.

"The African churches in Augusta and Savannah have regularly ordained ministers of their own color—men generally of excellent character, capable of reading the Scriptures and expounding their meaning.

"The owner who treats his slaves cruelly, or feeds and clothes them scantily, is sure to be looked upon with suspicion and contempt; yet there are many, no doubt, who do not act the good master's part."

"*Rough Estimate of Labor Performed.*—The missionaries have performed about fifteen years' labor in destitute parts of the State, *i. e.*: their labors have been equal to the services of one man constantly for that number of years. This is a low estimate: probably twenty-two years would be nearer the truth. They established the first churches in the bounds of the Western Association—in Troup and contiguous counties—out of which the body was formed, in November, 1829. The principal missionaries [in that section] were James Reeves and John Wood.

"The first churches, too, in the Cherokee country were organized by the missionaries of this body—Jeremiah Reeves, Philips and Pearson. Several of those churches which are in Randolph, Lee and other counties, in the Bethel Association, were gathered by the labors of Travis Everett.

"The missionaries of the Convention have circulated, too, Bibles and other good books, besides thousands of tracts on religious subjects designed to amend the heart and life. Volunteer missions, also, have been made by the friends of the institution into various parts of the State, in order to remove prejudice and stir up the churches to practical duties.

"Thousands of volumes of standard books have been given to ministers for their improvement, about twenty of whom have been sustained at schools and academies for a longer or shorter period.

"About $25,000 have been contributed to foreign missions.

"The benefits of the Manual Labor School began in 1833. B. M. Sanders, Principal, will never be fully known till the light of eternity shines upon us. Various revivals have been experienced—one commencing in 1827, one in 1834, another in 1837, others in 1839 and 1840."

APPENDIX.

BOUNDARIES OF GEORGIA.

The boundaries of Georgia, by the charter of the Province, included all the territory "which lies from the most northern part of a stream, or river there, commonly called the Savannah, all along the sea coast to the southward, to the southern stream of a certain other great water or river, called the Altamaha, and westwardly from the heads of the said rivers, respectively, in direct lines to the south seas ; and all that share, circuit and precinct of land, within the said boundaries, with the islands on the sea, lying opposite the eastern coast of the said lands, within twenty leagues of the same, which are not inhabited already, or settled by any authority derived from the crown of Great Britain," etc. By the "south seas" here was meant the Pacific Ocean. Practically, the claim under this charter never extended west of the Mississippi river, as we learn by the fourth article of the treaty between the United States and Spain, dated October 27th, 1795. "It is, likewise agreed that the western boundary of the United States, which separates them from the Spanish Colony of Louisiana, is in the middle of the channel or bed of the river Mississippi, from the northern boundary of the said States to the completion of the thirty-first degree of latitude north of the equator." By the Constitution of the State of Georgia, adopted May 30th, 1798, the boundaries of the State are described as extending from the mouth of the Savannah to the northern boundary line of South Carolina, thence west to the Mississippi; down the middle of that river to the thirty-first degree north latitude; thence to the middle of the Apalachicola, or Chattahoochee, river; thence along the middle thereof to the junction of the Flint river; and thence along the middle of St. Mary's river to the Atlantic coast, and so back to the mouth of the Savannah river. All this, Georgia claimed as eminent domain; but it was the Indian titles to this land which was purchased in Augusta, and it was this purchase, by treaty, from them, which gave Georgia her real title to all that land.

THE BAPTIST STANDARD BEARER, INC.
A non-profit, tax-exempt corporation
committed to the Publication & Preservation
of The Baptist Heritage.

SAMPLE TITLES FOR PUBLICATIONS AVAILABLE IN OUR VARIOUS SERIES:

THE BAPTIST *COMMENTARY* SERIES
Sample of authors/works in or near republication:
John Gill - *Exposition of the Old & New Testaments (9 & 18 Vol. Sets)*
(Volumes from the 18 vol. set can be purchased individually)

THE BAPTIST *FAITH* SERIES:
Sample of authors/works in or near republication:
Abraham Booth - *The Reign of Grace*
John Fawcett - *Christ Precious to Those That Believe*
John Gill - *A Complete Body of Doctrinal & Practical Divinity (2 Vols.)*

THE BAPTIST *HISTORY* SERIES:
Sample of authors/works in or near republication:
Thomas Armitage - *A History of the Baptists (2 Vols.)*
Isaac Backus - *History of the New England Baptists (2 Vols.)*
William Cathcart - *The Baptist Encyclopaedia (3 Vols.)*
J. M. Cramp - *Baptist History*

THE BAPTIST *DISTINCTIVES* SERIES:
Sample of authors/works in or near republication:
Abraham Booth - *Paedobaptism Examined (3 Vols.)*
Alexander Carson - *Ecclesiastical Polity of the New Testament Churches*
E. C. Dargan - *Ecclesiology: A Study of the Churches*
J. M. Frost - *Pedobaptism: Is It From Heaven?*
R. B. C. Howell - *The Evils of Infant Baptism*

THE *DISSENT & NONCONFORMITY* SERIES:
Sample of authors/works in or near republication:
Champlin Burrage - *The Early English Dissenters (2 Vols.)*
Albert H. Newman - *History of Anti-Pedobaptism*
Walter Wilson - *The History & Antiquities of the Dissenting Churches (4 Vols.)*

For a complete list of current authors/titles, visit our internet site at
www.standardbearer.com or write us at:

The Baptist Standard Bearer, Inc.
No. 1 Iron Oaks Drive • Paris, Arkansas 72855

Telephone: (501) 963-3831   Fax: (501) 963-8083
E-mail: baptist@arkansas.net
Internet: http://www.standardbearer.com

Specialists in Baptist Reprints and Rare Books

Thou hast given a *standard* to them that fear thee; that it may be displayed because of the truth. -- *Psalm 60:4*

www.ingramcontent.com/pod-product-compliance
Lightning Source LLC
Chambersburg PA
CBHW031136160426
43193CB00008B/154